PRAISE FOR *THE LOVERS*

"A hopeful tale of youthful romance, of passion and perseverance against the backdrop of a war ravaged Afghanistan. . . . [Nordland's] skills as a journalist are evident in his rendering of this love blossoming against all odds."　　　　—*New York Times Book Review*

"A rich account of Zakia and Ali's romance that doubles as an indictment of the Afghan patriarchy's abuse of women and the failures of all those in power, inside and outside the country, to curtail it."　　　　—*Boston Globe*

"Nordland offers a stark, eye-opening look at the deplorable state of women's rights in Afghanistan through the travails of a brave, determined young couple."　　　　—*Booklist* (starred review)

"From the couple's elopement to their elevation to media prominence . . . Nordland's storytelling remains gripping, with more than a hint of Shakespearean drama."　　　　—*Publishers Weekly*

"An appealing love story of a young couple from neighboring farming families in mountainous northern Afghanistan. . . . A heartfelt, readable account for those interested in the personal impact of a decade of American engagement in Afghanistan."

　　　　—*Library Journal*

"A captivating account of forbidden love in one of the world's most conservative countries. Nordland takes the reader on his personal journey to save a couple from the inevitable doom of secret love in Afghanistan and reveals an unprecedented window into the country's cultural constraints.　　　　—Lynsey Addario, author of
　　It's What I Do: A Photographer's Life of Love and War

"This sensitive and unblinking portrait of love and injustice somehow encompasses Afghanistan's recent tragedy: hope, suffering, disillusionment, resilience. Rod Nordland has come as close as any Western reporter to the human heart beneath the headlines." —George Packer, author of
The Unwinding and *The Assassins' Gate*

"A searing analysis of the endemic gender terrorism in a culture where no woman of any age or class . . . is immune from brutality at the hands of her own kinsmen. You will never use the word 'patriarchy' casually after you read it. And read it you must." —Judith Thurman, critic, biographer,
and winner of the National Book Award

"Rod Nordland has written a riveting, romantic page-turner about two young people fighting to be together against terrible odds. This is a vitally important book that exposes the abominable treatment of women by a society the U.S., in its ignorance, has fought to preserve." —Susan Adams, senior editor, *Forbes*

"With *The Lovers,* Rod Nordland has delivered a true-to-life Romeo and Juliet story that cuts straight to the heart. This saga of Zakia and Ali is raw, poignant, uplifting, and suspenseful, and absolutely compelling throughout." —Jon Lee Anderson,
The New Yorker staff writer and author of *Che Guevara*

"Rod Nordland is a master at bringing war down to the human level." —Jill Abramson, former executive editor, *New York Times*

"A deeply reported and deeply felt book about true love and its political and personal consequences in one of the most dangerous countries in the world, for journalists and lovers, too."
—Ron Javers, former executive editor, *Newsweek International*

"The appalling way Afghanistan denies rights to women, and the indifference of government officials the United States has spent years and billions of dollars supporting there, should make Americans wary of plunging in anywhere else to remake a culture we have no clue about—as this astounding book makes clear."   —Craig Whitney, author of *Living with Guns*

"A gripping read and a compelling exploration of Afghanistan well beyond its headlines. You will be thinking about Ali and Zakia long after you have finished the book."
                    —Gayle Tzemach Lemmon, Senior Fellow,
        Council on Foreign Relations and author of *Ashley's War*

"A lyrical look at a love story that at once inspires and frightens. . . . Nordland introduces the reader to the complexities of Afghanistan's traditions and cultures and the charm of the Afghan people, who cherish hope while struggling against the tragedies that come with decades of destruction."
              —Kathy Gannon, journalist, Associated Press

"The dramatic tale of Zakia and Ali reminds us of the human stakes for women that grow from cultural conventions in so many parts of the world. Nordland's patient tracking of this incredible saga tells us as much about Afghanistan as it does about the contours of the heart."
              —Ann Marie Lipinski, curator at the Nieman
              Foundation for Journalism at Harvard University

"*The Lovers* is a heartbreaking tale of illicit love and religious persecution. Rod Nordland seamlessly weaves the personal and the political in urgent, effortless prose to tell a story that is not only beautifully written but also vitally important for our times."
              —Dr. Amanda Foreman, Man Booker Prize chair

"Rod Nordland develops a captivating and beautifully-written true story of an elopement into an analysis of Afghan misogyny and domestic violence which reveals more about conservative Afghan life and the struggle to change it than most other nonfiction books about the country."
              —Jonathan Steele, *The Guardian* (UK)

THE LOVERS

THE
LOVERS

AFGHANISTAN'S
ROMEO & JULIET

The True Story of
How They Defied Their Families
and Escaped an Honor Killing

ROD NORDLAND

An Imprint of HarperCollinsPublishers

Persian and Dari poetry and song translations by Bruce Wannell and Sahar Dowlashahi.

HarperCollins books may be purchased for educational, business, or sales promotional use. For information please e-mail the Special Markets Department at SPsales@harpercollins.com.

A hardcover edition of this book was published in 2016 by Ecco, an imprint of HarperCollins Publishers.

FIRST ECCO PAPERBACK EDITION PUBLISHED 2016.

Designed by Suet Yee Chong
Photographs by Diego Ibarra Sánchez, Mauricio Lima, Andrew Quilty, Jawad Sukhanyar, and Kiana Hayeri
Map by Studio E Genevieve, designer Sisi Zhu

Library of Congress Cataloging-in-Publication Data has been applied for.

ISBN 978-0-06-237883-5

16 17 18 19 20   OV/RRD   10 9 8 7 6 5 4 3 2 1

In memory of my mother,
Lorine Elizabeth Nordland

With love's light wings did I o'erperch these walls;
For stony limits cannot hold love out,
And what love can do, that dares love attempt;
Therefore thy kinsmen are no stop to me.

ROMEO AND JULIET, ACT 2, SCENE 2

CONTENTS

DRAMATIS PERSONAE

Zakia, Ali's lover, third daughter of Zaman and Sabza;
and
Mohammad **Ali,** Zakia's lover, third son of Anwar and Chaman.

THE AHMADIS

Mohammad **Zaman,** Ahmadi family, Kham-e-Kalak village,
father of Zakia;
Sabza, his wife, mother of Zakia;
Gula Khan, his second son, older brother of Zakia;
Razak, his fourth son, youngest brother of Zakia.

THE SARWARIS

Mohammad **Anwar,** Sarwari family, Surkh Dar village, father of Ali;
Chaman, his wife, mother of Ali;
Bismillah, his eldest son, brother of Ali;
Ismatullah, his second son, brother of Ali;
Shah Hussein, his nephew, cousin of Ali.

OTHERS

Najeeba Ahmadi, director, Bamiyan Women's Shelter;
Fatima Kazimi, Bamiyan Province director,
Ministry of Women's Affairs;
Manizha Naderi, executive director, Women for Afghan Women;
Shukria Khaliqi, lawyer, Women for Afghan Women.

MAP: ON THE RUN IN AFGHANISTAN

Zakia and Ali escaped captivity and eloped, but were hunted by both Afghan police and vengeful family members. They managed to stay one step ahead of their pursuers in the rugged mountains of central Afghanistan, traveling by foot, in cars and buses, and even by air to neighboring Tajikistan. The couple spent their honeymoon in caves and their first anniversary still in hiding.

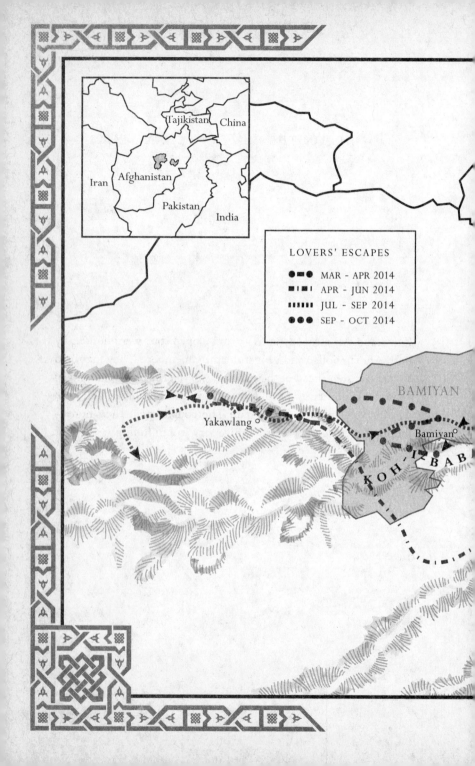

LOVERS' ESCAPES

●━● MAR – APR 2014
▮▮▮ APR – JUN 2014
▪▪▪▪ JUL – SEP 2014
●●● SEP – OCT 2014

Tajikistan
China
Iran
Afghanistan
Pakistan
India

BAMIYAN

Yakawlang

Bamiyan

KOH-I-BAB

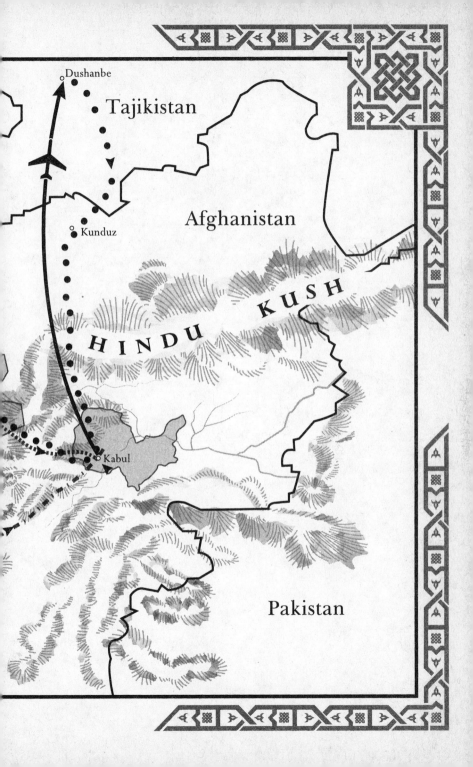

It was a cold clear February day when we finished our first visit to see Afghanistan's most famous young lovers and went out to what passes for an airport in Bamiyan town—a broad cinder runway with a fine view of the cliff niches that once held the Great Buddhas. There was a cyclone fence around a few shipping containers, one of which was the waiting room, another the office of airport management. The United Nations and a private Afghan company, East Horizon Airlines, which had some aging Russian turboprop craft, flew in only a couple of times a week so there wasn't much point in real infrastructure. I remember sitting in the waiting room container next to a *bukhari,* the flimsy, usually rusted stove that burns everything from wood and chips to coal and diesel oil, trying to stay warm as I wrote my first article for the *New York Times* about the lovers. I thought, what a great story, though sad, and with a follow-up that was a death foretold. I expected that the next and final article would be about how the girl's family came one night and dragged her from the shelter or how, out of loneliness and despair or a misguided willingness to believe in her brothers' promises, she would emulate the example of so many other Afghan girls who left shelters to return to their families, believing they'd be safe, and were never seen alive again. We would all be outraged and then turn the page.

That's how such stories usually end, but I was wrong, and theirs was just beginning.

UNDER THE GAZE OF THE BUDDHAS

Her name was Zakia. Shortly before midnight on the freezing-cold eve of the Persian New Year of 1393 she lay fully clothed on her thin mattress on the concrete floor and considered what she was about to do. She had on all her colorful layers—a long dress with leggings under it, a ragged pink sweater, and a long orange-and-purple scarf—but no coat, because she did not own one. The only thing she did not have on were her four-inch open-toed high heels, since no one would wear shoes indoors in Afghanistan; instead the heels were positioned beside her mattress, neatly left shoe on the left, right on the right, next to the little photograph she had of Ali, the boy she loved. It was not the best escape gear for what she was about to do—climb a wall and run off into the mountains—but it would soon be her wedding day, and she wanted to look good.

That night of March 20, 2014, was not the first time Zakia had contemplated escaping from the Bamiyan Women's Shelter, which had been her home, her refuge, and her prison for the past six months, since the day she ran away from home in the hope of marrying Ali. Always before, her nerve had failed her. Two of the other girls who shared her room were awake as well, but they would make no move unless she did first. Though Zakia was still terrified and did not know if she had the courage to leave, she felt she was fast running out of both time and opportunity.

This was no small thing, although Zakia was then eighteen and legally an adult, a voluntary shelter resident rather than a prisoner, and in the eyes of Afghan law she was free to go whenever she pleased. But the law is only what men make it, and nowhere is that more true than in Afghanistan. What Zakia was about to do would change not only her life and that of Ali, who waited for her call on the other side of the Bamiyan Valley. She understood that it would change the lives of nearly everyone they knew. Her father, Zaman, and her mother, Sabza; her many brothers; and her male first cousins—they would all give up their farm and devote their lives to hunting down Zakia and Ali, publicly vowing to kill them for the crime of being in love. Ali's father, Anwar, would be forced into such debt that his eldest son would lose his inheritance, and most of the family's crops would be forfeited for years to come. Others would be touched in unexpected ways. A woman named Fatima Kazimi, who ran the women's ministry in Bamiyan and had recently saved Zakia from being killed by her family, would flee to exile in Africa. Shmuley Boteach, a rabbi from New Jersey who that night scarcely knew how to pronounce Zakia's name, would end up consumed by her case, lobbying at the highest levels of the United States government to intervene on her behalf. In the course of it all, this illiterate and impoverished girl who did not know her numbers up to ten and had never seen a television set would become the most recognizable female face on the Afghan airwaves. She would become a hero to every young Afghan woman who dreams of marrying the one she loves rather than the one chosen for her by her family, sight unseen. To the conservative elders who preside over their country's patriarchy, however, Zakia would become the fallen woman whose actions threatened the established social order, actions that were yet more evidence of the deplorable interference of foreigners in Afghanistan's traditional culture.

That is where I came in, because the articles[1] I wrote about

Zakia and Ali in the *New York Times* in 2014 would bring them that fame and arouse the ire of the conservative Afghan establishment. I didn't know it at the time, but before long I would become their best hope to survive, entangling myself in their lives in ways that threatened my own values and professional ethics. That night, though, on the eve of the spring equinox and the Persian New Year,[2] I had no idea what they were up to and was three days' travel away from them elsewhere in Afghanistan. We were the last people on one another's minds.

I had visited them in Bamiyan only a month earlier, so when I later heard what had happened, it was easy enough to picture the scene. For some reason the words of the Robert Browning poem "Porphyria's Lover" sprung to mind, perhaps because it was about an impatient lover awaiting the arrival of his beloved:

> *The rain set early in to-night,*
> *The sullen wind was soon awake,*
> *It tore the elm-tops down for spite,*
> *And did its worst to vex the lake:*
> *I listened with heart fit to break.*

For elms, substitute the silver birches that are arrayed in proud double rows extending from the southern side of the Bamiyan Valley, where the women's shelter was, along farm lanes cutting down toward the river that runs through it. Tall and slender, the birches are reminiscent of the needle cypresses that flank the lanes of Etruria, except that the silvery backs of their leaves and the mica-like bark all seem to sparkle even in the starlight. Bamiyan town is the capital of the province of the same name, a highland area on the far side of the Hindu Kush mountains, a place of green valleys between barren and forbidding ranges a long way from anywhere. The town is ranged over two broad flatlands on the southern side of the Bamiyan Valley; the lower one holds the ancient town, a collection of mud buildings little different from those there thousands of years ago, interspersed with newer concrete ones, the metal doors on shops in the bazaar painted in primary colors, and, not far below that, the river, still with patches of ice in the middle and snow on its banks.

A few hundred feet higher and farther south, there is the broad plateau that holds the small airport, with its terminal of containers,[3] and a collection of new-build masonry edifices, which were mostly government and aid-group offices. These were constructed by foreign donors along freshly asphalted roads, engineering marvels donated by the Japanese or Korean governments, which are perfectly straight and flat but go nowhere in particular. Among those buildings is the shelter that Zakia was preparing to flee.

Bamiyan town, when it was lucky, would get four hours of electricity a day. There was none at this late hour, so there was no city glare from the darkened town, only the reflected brilliance of the firmament. Earlier in the evening, there was a cold, drizzling rain, but temperatures dropped around midnight and it became a light, windy snow.

The roadside birches promenade from the bottom of the valley up to the elevated plateau, where, even in the dark and at a distance of some two miles from the cliff faces, the niches that once held the Great Buddhas of Bamiyan are impressive. Their huge size and gaping black shapes are at once apparent and on first glance breathtaking, so unlike anything else in the world. The cliffs are just north of the river. The statue of Nelson from Trafalgar Square would be lost within the smaller, eastern niche, where once the Buddha known as Shahmama stood; the larger, western niche that held the Buddha known as Solsal could swallow the Statue of Liberty whole. Ancient craftsmen carved these with hammer, pick, and chisel in a labor of love that lasted lifetimes. Throughout history, Solsal and Shahmama were the two tallest standing Buddhas on the planet.[4] They were fourteen centuries old when they were destroyed over a few days in 2001 by the Taliban, who ranged tanks in front of them and blasted away and then finished them off with high explosive charges.[5] The Taliban rampaged through this valley during their regime, killing the Hazaras who live here by the thousands, motivated by hatred of their race (Asian rather than Caucasian) and their religion (Muslim, but Shiite rather than

Sunni). The Taliban could not, however, destroy the whole vast sandstone cliff, a tawny golden color that reflects well in the darkness and remains an arresting sight. Between and around the niches of the Great Buddhas is a honeycomb of ancient passageways and caves, comprising monks' cells and shrines, some as big inside as the nave of a European basilica, others only a tiny chamber for a long-ago hermit. The cliffs themselves appear to have been flattened by the carvings of ancient hands, to make smooth canvases from which to excavate their shrines, nearly a millennium and a half ago.

All of which is more than just the backdrop to the story of the lovers Zakia and Ali, who as young children fled with their families into the higher mountains when the Taliban came to the valley and who returned after the massacres were over. What happened here long ago, and not so long ago, made these two young people who they are. It shaped not only the destiny that they had defied but also the other one they were on the verge of making on this night when the mountains all around them were struggling to hold on to winter and the Persian New Year was about to begin. In ways odd and thoroughly unexpected, the Taliban had turned Zakia and Ali's entire world on its head and by both their defeat and their bitter resurgence had made the story of these lovers what it would be. Without the Taliban there would have been no Western intervention; without a Western intervention, the story of Zakia and Ali would have been a short tale with a bloody ending.

The warlords who fought the Taliban and later helped form the Afghan government that replaced them were, where women were concerned, as bad as and sometimes worse than the Taliban. Only the insistence of the Western countries on equal rights for women led to a constitution and laws that protected women, at least legally. Culturally was another matter. In recent years, as the Taliban threatened to return to power, Afghan leaders and their Western allies had grown unwilling to expend political capital challenging cultural conservatives on the government side. As a result most gains on behalf of women were made in the early years after the Taliban's fall, with relatively little accomplished once the resurgent

Taliban became a more potent threat after 2012. Western intervention had made it legal for Zakia to choose her own spouse and even to run away with him, but now Western timidity had stranded Afghan women like her in an uncertain limbo of cultural and official hostility.

Zakia was Tajik, and Ali was Hazara; she was Sunni, and he was Shia. Zakia's family was opposed to her marriage on cultural, ethnic, and religious grounds. Now that she had run away, she'd violated another cultural taboo. In Afghan culture a wife is her husband's property; a daughter is her father's property; a sister is her brother's. It is the men in a woman's life who decide whom she will marry, and by running off with someone else Zakia was not just defying their will but stealing what they viewed to be rightfully theirs.

Ali stood outside the earthen wall surrounding the low mud buildings of his family farm compound in the village of Surkh Dar, on the far side of the Bamiyan Valley from the women's shelter that held Zakia. The village was a short way outside Bamiyan town, a few miles past the larger, westernmost of the Buddha niches. Ali was twenty-one then, three years older than Zakia. He stuffed his gloveless hands into the pockets of his faux leather jacket, but it provided little warmth. He, too, was dressed in his finest, getting ready to meet his lover, the woman he hoped soon to make his wife. On his feet were his tan leather shoes with pointy toes, the only pair of footwear he owned besides plastic sandals. If it were not for the holes worn through the sides of their uppers and the caked mud on their soles, these shoes would have seemed more at home on the cobbled lanes of Verona than in the muddy late-winter fields of Bamiyan. Ali stamped the ground, not just to stay warm in the cold and the light freezing rain but because, accustomed as he was to long days of farm labor, any prolonged physical inactivity made him uneasy.

He mulled over how they would greet each other when they finally met for what would be the first time in months, not counting screaming scenes in the Bamiyan provincial courthouse. Would she call his full name, Mohammad Ali, the sound of which had always gladdened and surprised him when she whispered it over the line during the years of clandestine telephone conversations that characterized their early courtship? Zakia was the only woman, besides his sisters and his mother, he had ever heard speak his name. Or would she just say *tu,* the familiar "you" in their language, Dari, a dialect of Farsi or Persian? Three hours earlier she had called and said this would be the night that she made good her escape to elope with him and that she would call when she went over the wall, but it was not the first time she'd said that. As the hour crawled past midnight and his phone didn't ring, he began to lose hope. He kept the cell phone next to his heart, in an inside pocket to protect it from the intermittent freezing drizzle. A battered old knockoff of a Samsung Galaxy, this cheap Chinese smartphone full of love songs and recorded birdcalls bore the story of his life.

One of the songs from their long courtship, which he'd chosen for tonight's ringtone, played on a continuous loop in his head. It was from a song by Bashir Wafa, an Afghan pop singer, covering the story of the Prophet Joseph and Potiphar's wife, who in the Islamic version of that ancient tale are named Zuleikha and Yousef:

> *If Zuleikha repents, sighing from the bottom of her heart,*
> *Yousef will walk free, the fetters fallen from his ankles . . .* [6]

Sometime after midnight of the Persian New Year, he gave up. "I thought she must have been kidding with me and had decided against going through with it," he said. He tried her phone for perhaps the tenth time, but there was no ring, only the impersonal phone-company message: the same nasal female voice both in Dari and in English announcing Zakia's phone to be outside the coverage area. Just in case, he hung his phone on a nail in the wall outside because the signal in their village was too weak within his house. Then he went inside to lie down on his bed, like Zakia's a mattress on the floor, this one of earth. He left the window of his room open despite the cold so he would be able to hear the phone sing; there was only a wooden shutter without glass, simply a pane of plastic sheeting stretched over the opening, which he slit at the bottom and peeled up just in case.

As Ali went dejectedly to bed, Zakia huddled with her two roommates, Abida and Safoora, across the valley.[7] The three of them had planned to creep out of their beds just before midnight and wait inside the front door of the big house until the guard outside was asleep. The Bamiyan Women's Shelter, run by the UN Women organization with an all-Afghan staff, at that time held fifteen girls and young women like themselves, all there because of the threat of beatings or death from family members or forced marriages to people they could not bear or illegal child marriages or because they were raped. Safoora's case was particularly distressing. Brought to court in a dispute between two families over the terms of her engagement at fourteen years of age, she was taken into a back room at the courthouse and gang-raped by court employees. She complained, but the judges blocked any prosecution of the rapists, and so Safoora was in the shelter fleeing their retribution and fearing her own family's wrath against her. It is commonplace for Afghan families to murder a daughter who has had the poor judgment or bad luck to be raped; the rapist is often treated with shocking leniency. They call it "honor killing." Zakia had fled to this shelter to escape an honor killing as well, though for a different reason.

They say that in the heyday of the Bamiyan Buddhas, when this remote mountain valley was a center of pilgrimage and the spiritual capital of the Greco-Buddhist Kushan Empire, the eyes of the great Buddhas Solsal and Shahmama comprised hundreds of precious stones, rubies and sapphires especially but diamonds and emeralds as well. Fires were kept lit at night behind those yard-wide orbs. The gemstone lenses magnified the light and sent multicolored rays across the valley, where they would have been seen sparkling at night from many miles away, particularly on the upper plateau, which lay at nearly eye level opposite the behemoths' gaze.

Tonight on this same plateau, a male guard was on duty in the courtyard of the women's shelter in a small guard shack that was just big enough for him to lie down inside. The girls knew that he was ill and would probably have fallen asleep on duty, which indeed he had done. Zakia had the SIM card for her cell phone, but the phone itself was in the hallway, hidden in a cupboard. Inside the shelter building, there was a woman guard whom they had expected to be asleep, but she wasn't. The guard challenged Zakia when she heard her stepping outside her room. Zakia quickly ducked into the bathroom, making up a story that she wanted to take a late shower. This delayed her another twenty or thirty minutes as the two other girls waited for her and Ali kept trying unsuccessfully to get through on the phone.

Safoora, younger than Zakia, was excited for her but sad to see her go—she was along just to help Zakia and the other older girl, Abida, escape. Zakia had been not only an older sister to her but also the sparkler that lit up their shabby existence: colorful, viva-cious, and, in the privacy of the company of other young women, contemptuous of the social rules that had driven them all to this refuge. Abida, an overweight girl about Zakia's age, married as a child to an abusive husband whose beatings drove her here, had decided the day before that she would flee with Zakia to return to her husband. They agreed to help one another over the wall of the shelter and run together.

It was a shelter from the harm that awaited them outside, but it was also a prison; one of the terms under which all such facilities in Afghanistan operate is that they promise not to allow the girls and women to leave until their cases are settled, if they can be settled. Many of them are in the shelters indefinitely, with few future pros-pects except to return to whatever family hell drove them there in the first place.

Zakia was determined that would not be her fate. The girls hugged and said their good-byes to Safoora and then began drag-ging mattresses out to the wall at the back of the courtyard. The mattresses were stiff, full of cotton tick; doubled over and piled one atop the other, they made a ledge halfway up the eight-foot-tall wall, so Zakia could clamber up. Later on she would insist, as she had agreed with the other girls to say, that no one had helped her escape, that she had simply walked out the unlocked front door when everyone was asleep and hopped the wall on her own. From the top of the wall, she reached down to pull Abida up as well, but the girl was too weak to pull herself up and too much deadweight for Zakia. Abida later claimed that her friend had abandoned her to save herself. Zakia insisted that the girl was too heavy to make the climb, but she also was aware that Abida wanted to return to an abusive husband. Zakia thought it was probably just as well that the girl did not do so. Abida was not driven by love but by desperation and might well have been killed for her efforts.

Looking back from the top of the wall for a brief second, Zakia saw that she had let go of Ali's photo on the way up; it had been clutched in her hand and was crumpled badly. She did not hesitate, though, and at about one in the morning Zakia dropped to the ground outside the wall, in her high heels, carrying a plastic bag full of clothes. She ran lightly down the hill in the direction of the Great Buddhas, pursued by a pack of barking dogs, then stopped under some birch trees on a traffic circle at the edge of the upper plateau and dialed Ali. There was no answer. Digging into her bag, frantic, she pulled out a loaf of bread and began breaking off pieces to throw to the dogs to stop the barking.

Over in his village of Surkh Dar, Ali heard the phone ring on its nail outside and raced from his room, but by the time he reached it, the ringing had stopped. He called her back, and this time Zakia answered. Their situation was perilous. It was just past one in the morning, and she was a woman alone and therefore subject to arrest, not only by police but by any man who passed and wanted to take the law into his own hands—or worse. In a society where rape was often not regarded as a crime if the woman were found alone, worse was likely. Ali woke his father, Anwar, to tell him that the escape was on and then called a village friend, Rahmatullah, who had already agreed to help them elope by driving them to a hiding place higher in the mountains.

Rahmatullah's battered maroon Toyota Corolla wouldn't turn over in the cold at first, but the engine finally caught. Ali stamped his foot impatiently as his friend insisted on warming up the engine for a few minutes. The drive was only fifteen or twenty minutes down the unpaved road, along the front of the Buddha niches, through the old bazaar, and up the hill to the higher plateau, where Zakia waited. The sparse grove of birch trees at that spot was too thin to hide her, so she lay prone in a shallow drainage ditch beside the traffic circle. It seemed to Zakia that it took them nearly an hour to arrive, and by then she could see the alarm being raised at the shelter and hear the commotion there as searchers ran around the walls outside, only a few hundred yards from her hiding place. Hunkered down in the ditch, she did not see Ali in Rahmatullah's car as it first arrived, until he alerted her with another phone call.

When the car stopped near her, it set the pack of dogs to barking again, and Ali jumped out to help her put her bag in the trunk. Each spoke the other's name, and in that small way they were—as they both understood—declaring their rebellion against their society's strictures and customs. There are many husbands in Afghanistan who have never used their wives' names, even when addressing them directly. When they address their own wives, often it will not be with the personal "you"—*tu* in Dari[8]—but with the formal you, *shuma*,[9] the same word one would use to address a stranger or an official. They never mention their wives' names in conversation with others. There are many Afghan men who do not know the first names of their best friends' wives. It is considered offensively intrusive to ask men the names of their daughters, let alone their wives.[10]

Ali led Zakia across the muddy lane, she all aswish in her full-length skirt and *chador namaz,* a long, flowing scarf, and he with a lightweight woolen scarf, a *patu,* pulled around his body against the cold but little else for warmth aside from his thin leather jacket. The snow had stopped and the skies cleared, but the moon was new and the night quite dark. As they got into the car, Zakia took his hand in hers and held it tightly. If she had kissed him it would hardly have been more unexpected and only slightly more subversive.

They had been declaring their love for each other for years now in secret and then publicly for the past six months of her effective incarceration in the shelter. They had never been alone together indoors, let alone in the backseat of an automobile. Mostly they had seen each other only in glimpses and clandestine encounters in the fields of their families' adjoining farms and on one day when they were taken to have their case heard in court. Zakia's death sentence was decreed that day in court: implicitly by her judges and in screamed imprecations by her mother, father, and brothers. For two and a half years before that, they had managed to find glimpses of each other and some stolen minutes together on the farm and along village lanes and footpaths, and they had managed to speak many, many times by telephone. Ever since she entered the shelter six months earlier, however, even telephone calls were difficult; phones were forbidden to the girls. Zakia and Ali had been able to meet, with chaperones, only once during that time. Now here they were holding hands.

It may sound like a small thing, but people who had never heard their parents address each other by name, have certainly never seen them hold hands, even in private, let alone in a public place. Courtship even among engaged couples is usually forbidden. Modernized Afghan families might allow a fiancé and fiancée to meet, but only strictly chaperoned and never alone, and not with any sort of physical contact; more often the couple first meet on their wedding night. Both the wedding ceremony and the accompanying celebration are nearly always segregated by gender. Afghan soldiers often hold hands. Children hold hands. Young Afghans of the opposite sex, married or unmarried, in public, never. Where did Zakia get the idea? Neither Zakia nor Ali had ever been to a movie theater—there wasn't a single one in the entire province— and in their villages there was no electricity, let alone television. Although larger villages would sometimes have one shared TV, usually it would be watched only by men, since women were not allowed to attend public gatherings. What gave Zakia the boldness to take his hand in hers? Is holding hands just an innate human impulse? That, like so much else about their story, was a mystery.

Perhaps it was just as simple as this: Having defied one set of grand conventions, to openly and publicly declare her love for Ali and now to elope with him in defiance of her family, her culture, her tribe, and her sect, Zakia was not now going to be bound by any of her society's petty strictures. If she wanted to hold his hand, she would. When I had an occasion to ask her, much later, why she had done so, Zakia's response was this: "Why not?"

Rahmatullah, in the driver's seat, was stunned to see them sit together so intimately. "He was scared, but he's my friend, so he went along," Ali said. The two lovers in the back, finally together after so many months, didn't know what to say to each other. "We hadn't expected this to happen—we didn't really know *what* would happen," Ali said. The pack of dogs surrounded the car and barked furiously as it pulled away. The couple lay down in the backseat as the car passed the shelter and headed out of town.

The escape had been so unexpected that they still had to arrange the next leg of their flight. Two days later, after the Persian New Year's Day holiday, Zakia's court case was to be moved to Kabul. Bamiyan is a mostly Hazara place, so they felt safer there— the courts were dominated by Tajiks who sympathized with Zakia's family, but the police and the governor, the women's ministry, and the majority of the people were Hazaras and could be expected to sympathize with them. That would not be the case in Kabul, they worried; there were many more Tajiks and Pashtuns than Hazaras there. In Kabul, they feared, Zakia could easily be ordered returned to her family, for what would then become the last few days of her life.

Now they were on their way to the home of a distant relative of Ali's in the Foladi Valley, which cut southwest up into the Koh-i-Baba range, rugged, fifteen-thousand-foot-high mountains running from east to west and framing the southern reaches of the Bamiyan Valley. The relative's name was Salman, and Ali's father and his uncle had only just called him as Ali was driving off to get Zakia; now Ali called him from the car. Salman was reluctant at first, partly because he shared his home with four brothers and he would have to get the fugitives inside without the brothers seeing Zakia.

"Why did you do this?" Salman said.

"It happened, and now that it happened, we can't take it back," Ali said. "This happened, and we're with her, and we're escaping."

They arrived in Foladi at Salman's house around the time of the first call to prayer, the *subh,* when the mullah begins chanting over the loudspeakers in the minarets at the first sign of dawn, which at that time of year was about five in the morning. It was easy enough to hide Zakia; Salman led her into the women's quarters in his part of the house, a compound with several separate mud-walled buildings, one for each of the brothers. Only his wife and young daughters were there, and no male but he could enter. Ali could not go there; staying with his wife-to-be prior to marriage would itself be considered a crime, and hiding Ali elsewhere in the house was much more difficult with so many brothers and their families around. So after a hurried breakfast of bread and tea, Salman and Ali headed out, trudging through a foot and a half of snow, up the flank of the mountain, for the ninety-minute hike to the village of Koh-Sadat.

Elders from Koh-Sadat met them outside the first house in their village; the elders had been watching them climb for the past quarter hour. In so much of this barren, treeless landscape, it was nearly impossible to hide even from watchers miles away. "We have come to buy donkeys," Ali said. Koh-Sadat was locally famous for its donkeys, so it wasn't an implausible excuse. For the rest of the morning, they saw one donkey after another. This one was too small, and that one was too old, and the other was okay but too expensive. By then it was time for lunch, and no one can visit an Afghan community without being invited to lunch. They dragged that out as long as they could, the men sitting cross-legged on the mud floor, picking off small pieces of bread to scoop from the communal plate of pilaf and talking about whatever subject occurred to them.

Finally, in late afternoon, they left with apologies and excuses but no donkey and trudged back down to Foladi and Salman's house. "We drove them crazy with our donkey bargaining," Ali said, sharing a laugh with Salman.

By the time they got back, Ali's father, Anwar, had come and a mullah named Baba Khalili had driven in over the Koh-i-Baba mountains from neighboring Wardak Province to marry them. One of Ali's brothers and his cousin Salman would be the witnesses as they tied the *neka:* the signing of a document agreeing on the terms of the marriage and noting the requisite two male witnesses and the mullah who presided (significantly, the bride need not be present, and often is not). Because all of them, save the mullah, were illiterate, they would dampen their thumbs on an ink pad and press them to the paper in lieu of signatures. The *neka* would specify that Zakia, daughter of Zaman of Kham-e-Kalak village, would receive in the marriage a hundred thousand afghanis (about eighteen hundred U.S. dollars at the time) and a *jreeb* of land (about half an acre), from Ali's family. Normally such a payment would go to her *father* as a bride price, although formally it would be deeded to the woman, since a bride price is officially illegal. Sometimes a small portion would be used to buy jewelry for the woman, but that was at the father's discretion. Zakia's father was not present and in no position to collect the hundred thousand afghanis, which was just as well, because Ali and his father were in no position to pay.

Mullah Baba Khalili demanded thirty thousand afghanis to tie the *neka,* formalizing it with the reading of Koranic verses and his signature and stamp. It was a huge sum for such a service, some five hundred fifty dollars, but the mullah was performing the ceremony without the customary presence of the girl's father—and without asking too many questions. "If I don't tie this *neka,* no one will ever tie it," the mullah told Anwar when he balked at the price. The reputation of mullahs for greed is legendary in Afghanistan, one of the reasons they are the butt of many jokes in an otherwise devout land.[11] "If anyone ever challenges it, I will testify for you," the mullah told him.

The young couple spent their wedding night in the unfinished loft of Salman's home, a low-ceilinged, thirty-foot-long room with no stove; it was far too cold for consummation. "It was a long time before we had a real wedding night," Ali said. "We were so cold all we could do was hold each other for warmth."

The next day they moved on, traveling this time in a taxi that

Anwar had arranged and brought for them from Bamiyan town, a couple thousand feet below. They were heading farther up the Foladi Valley as it climbed toward the highest peak in the Koh-i-Baba range, the Shah Foladi, sixteen thousand feet high. Partway up they were welcomed into the home of a distant relative, Sayed Akhlaqi. This time they could travel together openly because they were now married, but they were still foolishly raising eyebrows, even among those friendly to them, by holding hands.

Their stay was short-lived; the next day Sayed Akhlaqi's son raced up the road from Bamiyan on a mud-splattered dirt bike, breathlessly reporting that the police knew they were in Foladi and were on their way. The son worked as a servant in a government building and had heard the police making the arrangements, urged on by Zakia's enraged family members. The police would arrive by evening, and it was already nearly sunset. The couple and Anwar piled into the taxi and headed farther up the mountain. As they climbed the switchbacks, Ali's phone rang; it was someone from down below alerting them that the police had already left Sayed Akhlaqi's house and would probably catch up to them soon. Looking back, they could see the dust being raised on the lower road by the big, forest green Ford Ranger police pickup truck as it climbed toward them. The bedraggled old taxi had no hope of outrunning it, so they stopped at a glade of small trees and heavy brush, where a creek cut across the road. The newlyweds fled into the brush along the creek on the downstream side of the road while Ali's father, Anwar, went the opposite way, on the upstream side, hoping, if seen, to draw the police's attention from the lovers. The driver carried on, but the police truck soon caught up to him. He refused to give them away and denied having had them along—although there weren't many fares on this lonely road toward the Shah Foladi peak. His story was that he had been on his way to pick someone up but never found the person.

Zakia and Ali hid deep in the bushes, he behind a log and she lying down in the wet streambed nearby. "The driver protected us. He said he was looking for us, too, and hadn't been able to find us." The policemen worked their way back down the hill, stopping and shining their truck's searchlight into the brush. "I don't know how they didn't see us," Zakia said. "It seemed like the light was right on us." At length the police escorted the taxi back down the mountain, holding the driver overnight for questioning before letting him go.

For a while the couple searched for Anwar but had no idea where he was; he searched for them as well, equally fruitlessly. It was inky dark, and no one had flashlights. Ali and Zakia began to walk up the mountain, skirting but staying off the road. They trudged, wet and freezing, through the snow, and then at times through slush brought by a fitful rain, until six hours later they reached one of the lower summits of Shah Foladi. Zakia had to take off her heels after they broke and walk in her bare feet.

Between them, to stay warm, they had only two thin woolen *patus*—Sayed Akhlaqi had given them a second one—which became both blankets and coats for them. The batteries on both their phones were nearly dead, but from the top of the mountain Zakia managed to get off one call to Ali's uncle. "We're lost. Can you tell us where we are?" she said. He wasn't able to help them find their way out, but he did understand from what they said where they were and said he would send help at daybreak.

That night they were too tired even to gather firewood and slept rough on the cold, wet ground, huddled in the *patus*. "We weren't so tired that we weren't happy. We were so happy to be together. We had each other," Ali said.

Zakia was less romantic about it. "I was just cold and scared," she said.

By the next day, they reached another false summit. "We thought we were dead, but we kept climbing. My uncle had said to meet at the top of the mountain, and when we got there, we heard some people, and I shouted 'Sattar!' but no one answered," Ali said. Sattar was his uncle's son, and when he did not reply, they thought the men up there must have been pursuers searching for them, so they hid until the voices receded. Finally they found Azhdar village, a place Ali remembered from going partridge hunting with his brothers and his father; from there a trail went back down to his own village, skirting the Bamiyan Valley. It would be fifteen miles of rugged terrain to cross, but it would take them away from the dangerously cold heights of the Shah Foladi.

The second night they slept outside again but were able to gather firewood to stay warm, and the next day they reached the outskirts of Ali's own village of Surkh Dar. Even then they waited two days, sleeping in monks' caves carved into the soft sandstone of the cliff faces, just a ways up the hill. "They didn't find us, even though the entire police department of one province was looking for us," Ali said.

When they finally made contact with Anwar, early on the fifth night of their marriage, the old man was back in their village; it had taken him two days to find his way off the mountain himself. Anwar arranged for Ali and Zakia to stay with a member of the provincial council who had a home in their village. It was just in time; by then the police had become convinced that the couple could have survived only by coming back to Surkh Dar and hiding there somewhere, so they began searching house by house.

"They even hired women who didn't get along with our women to go into the houses to look for us," Ali said. The couple was safely in the home of that friendly Hazara council member nearby. No one dared ask to enter a councilman's house; it was too much of a stretch to suspect that he would have sheltered these farm kids on their elopement. So for the next week they hid only a few hundred yards from the home of Zakia's own family.

Their two families lived on either side of the highway leading to the west from Bamiyan town and the Great Buddha cliffs, toward Band-e Amir Lakes; her family was in Kham-e-Kalak, the lower village, on the downhill side of the highway toward the Bamiyan River. That village was mostly Tajik families, forty or fifty of them. Zakia was one of eleven children, seven girls and four boys, ranging in age from five to twenty-five. Ali was one of eight, five brothers and three sisters. No one in either of their families had ever been to more than a few years of school, and only a couple of them could read or write at all. They were poor farmers, somewhat better off than subsistence farmers but only barely, with small plots of land on which they raised potatoes as a cash crop and wheat and vegetables to feed themselves. Surkh Dar was the upper village, above the highway, where Hazaras dwelled in much poorer homes, made of mud wattle rather than mud bricks or masonry as in Kham-e-Kalak. Ali's large family shared four mostly windowless rooms facing a barren courtyard. Some of the mud houses were built into ledges and slopes, almost like caves. Among these was a complicated, organic network of narrow lanes, many of them barely wide enough for a mule. The dwellings were close to the highway, while their fields were closer to the river, often some distance from the farmers' homes. So it happened that the fields of Ali's father, Anwar, and those of Zakia's father, Zaman, lay side by side in the bottomland along the river. That is where it all had started, some years before.

2

DEAD FATHER'S DAUGHTER

The past can be your real destiny, and theirs was messy. Both Zakia and Ali were too young to remember when the Taliban came over the Shibar Pass through the Hindu Kush mountains and into the Bamiyan Valley in 1998. By that point, two years into its conquest of Afghanistan, the Taliban were used to winning ground. They held all of central, western, and southern Afghanistan and most of the north, with the exception of areas controlled by the forces of Ahmad Shah Massoud and his alliance, in the far north, and by Hezb-i-Wahdat, the Hazara militia, in the north-central highlands of Bamiyan Province and Hazarajat.[1] There was no love lost between Massoud's Tajiks and Hezb-i-Wahdat's Hazaras, partly because Massoud's forces had carried out a notorious massacre of Hazaras in Kabul during the civil war a few years earlier and partly because the dominant Hazaras had abused the Tajik minority in Bamiyan city. The Hazaras initially beat back the Taliban in 1998. Abandoned by the more numerous and more powerful Tajiks, however, the Hazaras in Bamiyan succumbed when the Taliban returned in force the following year, carrying out massacres in Bamiyan city and in the Yakawlang Valley in which they killed every male they could find older than thirteen.

Both their families fled the valley during that time. First Zakia's Tajik family headed north to Baghlan Province to flee the Hazaras and the Taliban, and then Ali's family fled to the Koh-i-Baba mountain heights and across into Wardak Province to the south, escaping both the Pashtun Taliban and the Tajiks. There had always been religious tensions between Afghanistan's Sunnis, who include Tajiks, Uzbeks, and Pashtun ethnic groupings, and its Shia, who are mostly Hazara. The Taliban's extremist Deobandi version of Islam decreed that all Shia were heretics and justified killing them, a view they shared with Al-Qaeda. There was also a racial aspect to the conflict, since Hazaras are more Asian in appearance while Tajiks and Pashtuns are more Caucasian, although there are many exceptions. Tajiks and Pashtuns have traditionally derided Hazaras as outsiders, seeing them as the descendants of Genghis Khan's invading armies of eight hundred years ago;[2] Hazaras have never forgiven the Pashtuns for enslaving them in the nineteenth century.

After the Taliban conquest of the province, Hazara and Tajik families with young children began to return to their homes, without their men, particularly families whose children were too young to be viewed as fighters, which was the case with the families of Zakia and Ali. Ali is just old enough to remember the last couple years of the Taliban regime and its occupation of the Bamiyan Valley; in 2001, their last year in power, he would have been seven or eight. His older brothers and father were old enough to be considered fighters, so they fled; he stayed with the women at home. "They were treating Shia people badly, even the children," Ali said. "If you were not Shia, you were not treated badly, but even the chicken of a Shia was treated badly."

With the American-led invasion, the Taliban withdrew and the men came back down from the mountains. Ali remembers that as his childhood's happiest time. "My father and brothers came home, and we thought we were reborn then. Even now when my father calls me on the phone sometimes, he remembers that time and cries, 'How can you be away from me for so long?'"

Zakia's family suffered less from the Taliban occupation since they were Sunni Muslims, but her paternal grandfather, Ali Ahmad, had a difficult time during the great Bamiyan drought. Beginning during the latter years of the reign of King Zahir Shah, just before the beginning of the Soviet occupation in 1979, the drought continued through the civil-war years that followed in the eighties and nineties. Bamiyan is a high desert. Agriculture there depends mostly on snowmelt from the mountain ranges that encircle the Bamiyan Valley, and in those days there were no hydraulic works or reservoirs that the farmers could depend upon. Ali Ahmad fell into debt and sold off his fields one by one, until all he had left to pass on to his son Zaman, Zakia's father, was a house and compound in Kham-e-Kalak village—a substantial place by local standards, with doors and glass windows set into the mud-brick walls—and an adjoining small garden patch, half a *jreeb,* about a quarter acre, which went to Zaman's brother. By the time Zakia was growing up, Zaman had been reduced to sharecropping, working fields rented from more prosperous neighbors, and paying his brother to be allowed to use the walled garden patch next to the house.

Ali's father, Anwar, was luckier. Of his modest ten *jreebs* of land (about five acres), six were well watered enough for his crops to survive the drought years, so he never had to sell his land. The Hazara villagers in Surkh Dar generally were worse off than their Tajik neighbors in Kham-e-Kalak down below. Anwar's family was house-poor, and to this day they have little more than mud shacks to live in. But thanks to the vagaries of the region's ancient irrigation system, they survived the drought better than most and were more prosperous than Zakia's family. Anwar was able to spare three of his sons from farmwork so they could go to a few years of school. In Zakia's family only her youngest brother, Razak, who was age nine in 2014, attended any school. Anwar remained in the shabby mud huts, arranged facing a courtyard that did not even have a wall all the way around it as most rural Afghan homes do. But whatever surpluses there were from potato farming he invested in his children's education.[3]

Zakia would see other village girls, especially among the Hazara in Surkh Dar, the upper village, heading off to school in their blue tunics and white head scarves; the Hazara, so long an underclass in Afghanistan, put a great deal of store in education and were early and enthusiastic adopters of girls' schools when they were restarted in Afghanistan after the Western intervention in 2001. When Zakia asked her father if she, too, could go, his answer was, "No, we're too poor." Instead, like her siblings, she was put to work in the fields, bringing in harvests, plucking weeds, gathering hay as fodder for the animals, and tending sheep as they foraged.

When she was a young girl, Zakia's playmates were not her sisters but her brothers; she was the ringleader and the doll maker. Childhood was a happy time, and on the Eid holidays Zakia and the other kids, boys and girls, would go down to the river and try to catch the little fish they saw there in the crystal-clear pools. Gender differences did not matter when they were young. She taught her brothers how to make dolls from rags and straw, string and bits of stick. "We were all close friends then, my brothers and sisters. The happiest times were when there were wedding parties and we could run around having fun on both sides." Unlike adults, children could go to either the male or the female side of the segregated wedding parties, where there was much dancing, although never between the sexes; in their poor community, no one ever had weddings in a hall but used their homes instead, nonetheless strictly separating everyone by gender.

"When we were young, we were all intimate and friendly with one another, but later on, when we grew up, my brothers got so hard with me," she said. That's commonplace in Afghan families; the brothers are often the most enthusiastic enforcers of their sisters' chastity, partly because the family's honor affects their own marriage prospects and possibly sometimes in guilty response to the sexual tension that can exist between siblings of the opposite sex growing up in close quarters. "My brothers had more control over me than my father did. Whenever they saw me, they would ask me to go inside or to hide myself from strangers, ask me to wear a bigger scarf to cover myself. If I went shopping, they would force me to wear the burqa, which I hated."

When I was able to interview her months later while she and Ali were in hiding, Zakia, who usually came across as the properly shy, self-effacing young Afghan woman, would change when recalling those years. "I hated the burqa before, and I hated it then, and I hate it now. It was really something designed to punish women." Made of a rubbery synthetic material, the classic blue Afghan burqa is a heavy garment, deliberately shapeless, with a mesh grille over a small part of the face to allow some air and vision; it is hot and extremely uncomfortable, many times more unpleasant to wear than an Iranian chador or an Arab *abaya*. Some Afghan men insist, in the absence of any theological evidence, that it is a religiously sanctified garment.[4]

Aside from his friendship with the girl from the Tajik village on the other side of the road, childhood was a lonely time for Ali. His older brothers tended to their studies or did serious fieldwork, like digging irrigation channels; he watched the sheep. At one point in the drama that later unfolded over his love affair with Zakia, Ali indicated his father, Anwar, a cheery little man with an elfin white beard and an old black-and-silver silk turban, and said, "I intentionally did this to him. Since he deprived me of studying and education, I did this deliberately. He allowed my other brothers to continue their studies—my brother Sharifullah studied to the eleventh grade. I did this to give him a hard time, so he faces difficulties because he sent me to look after sheep instead of to school." Abashed, Anwar smiled crookedly. It was hard to tell how serious the son's joking tirade really was, but his father did not dispute him.

Ali did get a little education when he turned eleven and enrolled in the first grade at the local school. It was a primary school started by a nongovernmental organization—no one in the family remembers the NGO's name—but it is now a government school. "I have one good memory of my school time. I used to love birds a lot when I was a child. One day I was asked by my teacher to stand up and repeat the lesson in front of the class. When I stood up, my quail suddenly flew out of my shirt. Everyone laughed, but the teacher was angry. He said, 'Did you come to study or to play with birds in my class?' I loved birds in those days." He stayed through the third grade—some of his classmates from back then were just graduating in 2014 from grade twelve. He studied Dari, math, and drawing but retained little of it; he still cannot sign his name, for instance, although he is adept at dialing a telephone and recites the numbers from one through nine, followed by zero, in the order in which they're arranged on a telephone keypad.

Religious education at the local mosque wasn't much better; he attended for one year. While like most Afghans he describes himself as devout, Ali did not get his piety from his mullah's classes. "The mullah was always beating me, a lot, so I could not learn well."

The year before he entered school, Ali attended a wedding party. Someone had set up a big screen outside, and they were playing a movie on it, an Indian movie dubbed in Dari, *Layla and Majnoon*. He had never seen a movie before, on screen or on TV. He was too young, he said, even to know what love was but found himself watching it spellbound, sitting cross-legged on the ground with the other kids. The name Majnoon is variously translated as "the possessed one" and "the madman"—the word means "crazy person" in Arabic, and it is originally an Arabian tale. Majnoon's madness or single-mindedness is at the heart of all the many versions of the story. Knowing Layla from a young age, Majnoon begins reciting poetry in her honor, obsessively and incessantly; in some versions of the story, that madness itself is his downfall as it turns her father against him, but in other versions he was doomed anyway by lower birth or social and economic differences that made him unacceptable to her father. Then, when Majnoon dies, of course Layla dies as well, of a broken heart. "I didn't understand love when I saw it, but something attracted me to that movie," Ali said.

After Ali quit school, he was sent to take his family's sheep to the higher grazing lands on the sides of the mountains. "We used to go into the mountains to collect sticks for firewood, and on the way there or coming back I would recite poems loudly to the other boys," he said. They laughed at him. "They would tell me, 'You're crazy, you've gone mad,' and I would stop, but after a while they would ask me to recite some more, and I would say, 'No, I'm crazy,' and they would beg me, and I would." Around then an older village boy taught him how to play the Afghan flute, a simple bronze tube with six holes, and he played it a lot, "when I was lonely and to get relief from the pain," he said. That is also when he got to know Zakia-*jan,* as he refers to her; the -*jan* suffix is a term of friendship or endearment, used by males and females, perhaps best translated as "-dear."

Watching the sheep, they played together as their animals foraged sometimes miles from their homes. She was attracted to this moody older boy with his flute, but as a child acolyte, nothing more. She was his only audience; he rarely played his flute except when alone or out in the high pastures with Zakia. Zakia's family had ten sheep; Ali's had twenty-five. "As children we would go to the desert and take our animals for foraging, and we used to spend our days in the huts around the animals," he said, but they were small children then, too young to think of love affairs. "At that time we didn't even know of these things," he said.

Then Zakia started to reach puberty, and since Ali was three years older than she, there were propriety issues—she was biologically a woman, and therefore by Afghan custom she had to be separated from all adult males other than her brothers and her father. Her family started keeping her indoors except when there was work to do, and then they made sure she was in the company of her siblings. Ali's own father sold their sheep, so Ali no longer had a reason to find her in the privacy of the high pastures.

Some time went by and, as Ali put it euphemistically, he started thinking of her in that way. He was setting out traps for quail, on the still-unplanted fields one day in early spring, and she was in the next field watching him. He has trouble articulating why that mattered, but perhaps there was something in the possibility that his private passion for birds could be shared with someone else. Or perhaps it was just that he would then have been seventeen, and she had turned fourteen.

Ali himself marks the moment when he decided that he was in love to a day when both of their families were in adjoining fields and, as the two families would often do in those days, helping one another with their work. He and his brother borrowed two donkeys from Zakia's family to haul sacks of rocks off the fields, and they chose to ride them back, somewhat scandalously; in Bamiyan a donkey's back should be reserved for work, not pleasure.

"Death to your fathers!" Zakia declared when she saw them. "You use our donkeys to do your work, and then you think you can ride them, too? Curses on you!" Ali and his brother were so startled by the young girl's invective that they both leaped off the animals, laughing nervously. "I think that's when I knew," he said, though he couldn't really say why. Then a few days later, when he found her alone for a moment, he whispered to her, "I love you." He was just trying the words out and wasn't all that sure of his feelings. She ignored him, but she also didn't curse him for his temerity, and he said, "From that time I was forty percent sure of her."

They began to meet and chat more and more often on the crooked paths through the fields, sometimes even managing to meet twice a day. After a while Ali realized that this was the real thing. "I knew I was in love with her." It wasn't just the birds; it wasn't just their ages; it wasn't all the long hours they had spent alone together as children tending the sheep and growing up, but perhaps it was a little bit of all those things.

From time to time, Ali would spot Zakia crossing the fields, and catch her glancing his way, and notice how she would start when he came into sight and alter her course to pass near him as often as she could. By then, as he put it, he was a hundred percent sure about how she felt. It was rare that he could manage to see her for more than a few moments without arousing suspicion, and then she would often be in the company of her younger siblings. "For one month I was searching for her after I fell in love with her, and I knew she loved me, but I didn't know if she would agree to get married to me."

Finally one day he found her alone with no one else in earshot, and he decided to make his move while he could, "quickly because we couldn't stay there long."

They were both working, weeding in fields that were on either side of a mud wall, three feet high, pretending to be absorbed with what they were doing; several of Zakia's younger siblings were playing or working not far away. "I would have gone down on my knees"—he had heard somewhere that was how romantics did it—"but her brothers and sisters were all around and the wall was between us." Instead he blurted out his intentions. "I love you, and I want to marry you," he said, not looking directly at her for more than a moment.

She did not look at him either, not even a glance. "It's not possible. We're from two different ethnic groups, two different religions. No one would ever allow it," she said. Zakia struck Ali as eminently sensible, beyond her years—she would have been about fifteen then, he eighteen.

"We could run away if our families did not agree," he said.

"Then we would have no families," she replied. "We cannot."

He was crushed. "She rejected me, saying that she was from a different ethnic group and such marriages have not taken place before, so it would not be possible. She swore that the relationship was not going to happen. It was really a no, and I was disillusioned."

Zakia was surprised and realized she ought to be offended by his effrontery. "He was very naughty, Ali, and very clever, trying to turn my head when I was so young," Zakia said. "Proposing was very naughty of him. I said we were too young, but it was also the ethnic and religious differences, not just the age. I told him that." Despite her rejection of him, Zakia started thinking about him in a serious way for the first time. Every day she played his proposal over in her mind, every day for a month until she finally decided to seek him out. As she remembers it, her rejection of him was not as final and definitive as it had appeared to him.

Ali mooned around the village all that month, taking pains to avoid places where he might see her, and then, like many a lovelorn young man before him, he decided to join the army. He had no job prospects and no money, and he hated farmwork; Zakia wouldn't marry him, and the Taliban were an enemy that every Hazara could hate. His friends were all joining, including one of Zakia's brothers.

Others from their village who had already signed up said they were assured that they would be stationed somewhere in the west of the country, where fighting was relatively rare in those days. For doing nothing the pay was pretty good by rural Afghan standards, about two hundred fifty dollars a month, and he ended up in the western province of Farah, remote, quiet, and safe.

The boldness of Ali's proposal and his sincerity had touched Zakia's heart, and she realized that she was falling in love with him, too. By the time she'd decided to tell him this, however, he had enlisted and moved away. "I was upset when I heard that he joined the army, since I thought it was because I gave him a 'no' answer, and I didn't want him to join for that reason," Zakia said. Now she wanted to discuss it more, and he was absent. The longer he was absent, the stronger her feelings became.

Ali's army duty in Farah exposed him to the great Persian love stories to a greater degree than ever, as for the first time he was among young men who had smartphones with movies on them, or little DVD players, so popular among troops. Whenever he could, he immersed himself in these bittersweet stories; he felt he knew a thing or two about tragic love.

"Movies? I had never seen any. TV in the village? In the name of God, no, nothing like that in the village, but in the army I would watch some clips on my phone. My friends, some of them had computers, and they would have clips they would share with me." One of those soldiers knew how to transfer video from a computer onto his cell phone, and in this way Ali watched a long TV serial of the Yousef and Zuleikha story. Mostly, though, he was drawn to music clips, and so many of them were love songs. "Music is like a solace to pain. To people who are in love, it is a balm," he said.

In her adolescence Zakia also learned the Persian love stories, not from movies or music—they had only a small transistor radio at home, and mostly her parents played religious programs—but from other girls. The stories were passed around in secrecy among girls who had learned them from older sisters.

"Girls my age would tell them to one another, never openly. It was a secret we all shared," she said.

"There is a clash that exists in Afghan society about love," says poet Jawed Farhad, who teaches Persian literature at a Kabul university and writes love poems that provoke mullahs, with lines like these:

> *I am not an extremist,*
> *Just a great romantic.*
> *So why try to impose your harsh laws*
> *On my affairs of the heart?*[5]

"According to shariah law and the mullahs, romantic love is forbidden, and falling in love without the consent of the family is wrong," Mr. Farhad says. Despite clerical disapproval, people keep the ancient love stories alive; their great antiquity and their roots in religious literature make them on some level impregnable to serious attack. "The mullahs can try, but they can never really suppress them. All those hindrances to love—class differences, economic differences, family differences, religious and sectarian differences, ethnic differences—love is something that does not understand these things. It can cross all these borders, overcome all those differences."

For all the efforts of the mullahs and the patriarchs, Afghanistan has no shortage of love stories; perhaps the official opposition lends them more force and poignancy.

While talking with Afghan scholars about the persistence of the old Persian stories in a culture that is officially anti-romantic, I kept meeting people who would readily admit they were in love. "I myself, I'm in love," declared Ahmad Naser Sarmast, the head of the Afghan National Institute of Music. "I was in love all my life, and I'm proud of that." Dr. Sarmast's school is one of the few truly liberal institutions in the country, with mixed-sex ensembles among the children, aged eight to eighteen, and a coed playground where head scarves are optional and about half the girls do not wear them. "To express our love, we might use symbols, go back to history to find an equivalent. There are so many love stories in this country—no one is going to stop us. Can I deprive my own daughters of love? Being in love is not a crime in any nation. We should give that freedom to our kids. We should give that freedom to this nation."

One of the most popular programs recently on Afghan radio is called *Night of the Lovers,* which airs weekly on Arman FM Radio 98.1, the country's most popular private station. The format is simple: Young men and women call in anonymously and pour their hearts out about their loves, usually frustrated, imperiled, or forbidden. They record those personal love stories on the station's voicemail system, and the program picks the best ones and airs them. The idea for the show came to the station's manager, Sameem Sadat, when he was stuck in traffic one day and saw young people in all the cars around him happily texting or chatting away, looks of delighted concentration on their faces. Mostly they were texting even if there were adults also in the car. Despite being gridlocked for half an hour or longer, they would keep going without a break. "I realized they were all in love. No one talks to anyone for thirty minutes or an hour unless they're in love. I thought, 'They must have stories.'" The show began on Valentine's Day 2014, at first for an hour once a week, late at night. It was so popular though that in 2015 Arman FM increased the format to a three-hour-long program, from 9:00 P.M. to midnight on Wednesdays. After playing each recorded message, the presenters (a man and a woman) match it with an appropriate love song, broadcasting it all without giving any explicit advice or counseling, to steer clear of the mullahs. After the program the stories are posted on the program's Facebook page,[6] attracting thousands of comments each week. In a typical week, *Night of the Lovers* receives three hundred recorded stories from young people all over Afghanistan, from cities and villages, from educated people and unlettered ones, and it broadcasts about twenty of the most articulate.

The stories are nearly always sad. "I would say in all this time[7] we've had until now ten stories that are happy. Maybe those who succeed in love don't tell their stories, or maybe there just aren't many happy stories, I don't know," Mr. Sadat said. The program's female presenter, Hadiya Hamdard, goes once every few weeks to Badam Bagh prison for women in Kabul, the country's main female prison, and collects stories from the inmates there; when she arrives, she is practically mobbed by women jockeying to tell their stories. Normally, three-fourths[8] of Badam Bagh's inmates are there for so-called social or moral crimes, which are of course crimes of love—sex outside marriage, attempted *zina* (adultery), and so forth. Each episode of *Night of the Lovers* broadcasts one story from a woman who is literally a prisoner of love.

Inevitably, in the messages left with the program, there are sad stories of betrayal and denial, rejection and unrequited yearning. Another leitmotif is how hard it is, in a society that forbids even routine contact between men and women, for lovers to find a way to get together and how easy it is for them to lose each other.

Zakia was in just such a position. With Ali away in the army, she found herself missing him and sorry about turning him down, but there was no way she could communicate her regret to him. She did not have a cell phone, did not know how to use one, and, even if she had, would have had no discreet way to learn his number. Even if she could have found someone to write a letter, there was no mail service in rural Afghanistan. She found herself maneuvering to listen to the men in the family whenever they got calls from brothers and cousins posted in the army, but there was no news about Ali. She felt frustrated and helpless, and as she would come to see it, the powerlessness she felt during those months later drove her to act boldly and take her chances when an opportunity came along again.

Nearly two years of Ali's military service went by, during which he and Zakia had no word of each other. Farah was indeed remote and often without cell-phone service. Once there was a skirmish with the Taliban, and word had trickled back to Kham-e-Kalak. Ali's phone rang, and he was startled to hear Zakia's father's voice; Zaman was calling to find out if his own son, Gula Khan, was okay. Ali was struck dumb for long moments, wanted to ask about Zakia but did not dare, and then assured Zaman that his son was unhurt.

"How is the rest of your family?" he asked Zaman.

"Thanks to God, everyone is fine."

"Everyone?"

"Yes, everyone. What do you mean, boy?"

"That is good. I am glad to hear everyone is fine."

Then one day the Humvee that Ali was in rolled into a ditch, thanks not to the Taliban but to an Afghan National Army driver who, like so many of his comrades, was stoned on hash or opium.[9] The driver had not noticed the small crater in the roadway left by an earlier mine blast. The crash badly fractured Ali's leg. He was shuttled from one hospital to another; it would be nine months before he could walk without pain, and he came home to Surkh Dar to finish his recuperation. That was early in the summer of 2012, a few months into the Persian year 1391.

By then most of the boys who had joined the army from Surkh Dar and Kham-e-Kalak had deserted and returned home as well.[10] Zakia's own brother, Gula Khan, was among the returning deserters, and he related to everyone what had happened to Ali—the only casualty from their neck of the woods. Desperate to see him again, Zakia went to all their usual rendezvous and accidental meeting places, but he was nowhere in the lanes or fields around the village. Ali was lying low, embarrassed about his limp. "I had kind of given up on our love and didn't want to see her then," he said. "Especially with my leg like that."

Finally Zakia saw Ali on the road. She walked up to him boldly and said, "So now it is your turn to avoid me?" There were people around, and she should have been more circumspect, but the words tumbled out; she realized they would have only a couple of minutes to speak without arousing public suspicion, and there was much to say. "You remember what we talked about, what I told you was not possible? Well, now it is possible."

"You see my condition, my broken leg. You wouldn't want me like this. It may never heal correctly," he replied. He does still walk with a slight limp, especially on humid days.

"No, it doesn't matter. It will never matter."

"What are you saying, Zakia-*jan*?"

"I accept your proposal," Zakia told him directly, and then they tried to get away from each other as fast as they could, both appearing as disinterested in the other as possible, as if they had been discussing which well might be best to collect water from. They knew that the moment they aroused any suspicion, their families would intervene to make sure they never found another second alone together.

Ali was so stunned by what had just happened that it wasn't until months after they eloped that he dared to ask her what she had seen in him. When he did, he said to her, "I'm not even that good-looking. What was it that made you love me?"

"You were gentle," she said, "and you spoke to me with kindness."

The next day Ali found a young girl to serve as his messenger and sent a mobile telephone to Zakia, set to silent. All she had to do was answer it, but it soon became clear that she did not know how. He waited impatiently until the moment came when he saw her on the footpaths and could explain to her what to do. "She didn't even know how to drop-call me at first," he said. There was no thought of her dialing his number, because at the time she was innumerate, but he programmed it in for her so it was the only number on her phone. He showed her how to just hit the green button until it dialed and then how to cut it off as soon as it rang on his end, so she did not use up any of the credit on the prepaid SIM card. That would be her signal that it was safe for him to call her back, and all she needed to do when it vibrated was push green again. Never take it off silent, though, he warned her. She had nowhere to plug it in to charge it either; there was no electricity in their house, and if there had been, a phone being charged would be instantly noticed. Many of the little shops and kiosks in such villages would charge a phone's battery for customers for a few afghanis or swap charged batteries for spent ones in popular models. Because a woman would be marked as having a secret affair if she were seen doing that, Ali would charge a spare battery and when they passed in the lanes once every few days, swap it for her old one.

They never fought or quarreled in those days of their secret courtship, until one day when Ali decided to test Zakia's love. Normally Zakia would dial Ali at 8:00 P.M., hang up promptly, and then he would call her back to chat. This time he decided not to, even after she phoned him a second time. On her third effort, he picked up the call and pretended not to know her.

"I found this telephone with this number. Please do not bother me," he told her.

"So you found this telephone and this number?"

"Yes," he said, and she laughed and hung up, expecting him to call back, but he didn't. For several days she did not call him again, and when she finally did, she was angry.

"Why did you do that?" she asked.

"I was trying to see whether you truly love me."

"That was a bad way to do it." Zakia was so angry that she didn't speak to him for another week. When at last she did, he was chastened and promised he'd never play with her affections like that again.

"After that, we never fought or disagreed on anything," Ali said.

Their phone rendezvous were always going to be dangerous, in small homes crowded with many family members. "Once I was on my way up to Qarghanatu in Yakawlang"—a place they would later come to know in their flight—"and it was winter, and snow was everywhere," Ali said. This would have been the winter of 2012–13. "We went to get our family's money from someone who owed us some money. I received a dropped call from Zakia-*jan,* but I did not have credit on my phone to call her back. So I rushed to a shop and put credit on it." That took an hour, by which time Zakia had stopped expecting a return call and had left her phone unattended, forgetting to hide it well. When he called, her brother Gula Khan found the phone and answered it but, suspicious, did not say hello.

"Zakia?" Ali said.

"Who is this?" her brother demanded. Gula Khan had been in the army with Ali, and they knew each other well.

"I'm sorry, I dialed the wrong number," Ali said, hoping Gula Khan wouldn't recognize his voice.

They hung up, but Gula Khan thought he knew the voice, so from his own phone he dialed the number that had just called for Zakia, and when he did, "Mohammad Ali" came up on his screen. Gula Khan could not read and write much, but he could recognize the names stored in his phone.

Gula Khan called Ali back. "Is it Mohammad Ali?"

"Yes."

"Why did you call my sister?"

"By mistake."

Gula Khan did not believe him and yelled at him never to call again. After he hung up, he turned on Zakia, who was three years younger than him. "Gula Khan came and beat me with his hands. He broke my phone, he beat me, he cursed me and warned me not to talk to Ali again," Zakia said. "I didn't mind the beating, but I really hated being cursed."

Before long, Ali had enlisted the same little girl who'd delivered the phone to Zakia, a girl who was not from either of their families, and gave her a few afghanis to carry a small wadded piece of paper to Zakia. On it was written his phone number. Zakia begged some money from her father to buy clothing—it was still a time when he would give her whatever he could, as the prettiest of his daughters. Instead she used the money to buy a cell phone, again through the agency of the girl, who was too young for anyone to suspect that she was doing anything other than carrying out an errand for her parents. The younger girl, who was one of those who went to school, even showed Zakia how to use the phone and how to enter the number Ali had written. Soon they were speaking nearly every evening and managed nearly every day to meet on the footpaths around the village. "Most of the time, it wasn't really an accident that we met," Ali said with a pleased smirk.

One day Zakia had been fiddling with the phone, trying to figure out its mysteries, and had accidentally switched it from "silent" to "normal," without realizing. She drop-called Ali, and he called her back, and to her horror it was really ringing, with her father in the next room. She could not figure out how to quiet it, shook it, tried to pull the battery out, failed, and finally hid it under a cushion. By then Zaman had stormed in and soon found it, still ringing. He threw it against a wall, then took the SIM card out and crushed it. "He just took the phone and cursed me. He didn't beat me. My father never beat me back then. Just my brothers did, mainly Gula Khan."

Her siblings all soon turned on her, she said. "When this matter with Ali happened and they found out about my affair, even my little brothers and sisters tried to distance themselves from me," she

said. "It was very hard. Everyone in my family was against me."
Even nine-year-old Razak, the one she had felt closest to, would
not speak to her.

It took Ali a few days of radio silence to realize what had happened; it was a particularly bitter winter and too cold during that
February and March of 2013 for them to connive to meet in the
lanes and the frozen fields during the day. Instead he resorted to
secretly visiting her home at night. In those days he had taken
a temporary laborer's job at a construction site, working a night
shift that finished at midnight, and he would come over afterward
when the lanes were deserted and the homes all dark. There was
a walled vegetable garden outside the window to Zakia's room,
where Ali would stand and call to her, as quietly as he possibly
could, because she shared the room with the other girls and young
boys of the family. When she heard him, she would steal out of the
house and climb to the flat roof, where she could look down into
the garden and they could talk in whispers. The garden was barren in winter; about a dozen leafless apricot and apple trees lined
the mud-brick walls and surrounded long rows of tilled earth now
frozen hard. In one corner was a pair of ragged bamboo cages in
which Zakia's father kept his partridges—used in the Afghan version of cockfighting—when he could afford them. A small brook
had been diverted to enter a hole at the base of the garden wall, ex-
iting through the opposite wall. Ali's 2:00 or 3:00 A.M. visits to the
garden became regular occurrences, even on the coldest of nights,
but at first she would not come down to join him.

"It was dangerous for both of us, and it was so hard," he said. "I
would wait outside her house sometimes under a rainy sky, sometimes snowing, sometimes so cold she was concerned about me in
the bad weather."

"I was always so frightened we would be caught and so worried
for him," she said. On one particularly cold night, Ali stood in the
garden, dripping wet from a frigid rain that had turned to icy snow,
and recited famous lines from a poem by the twentieth-century
Iranian poet Malek o'Shoara Bahar, which have made their way
into Afghan pop music:

Love is a nightingale pouring out his heart in song for a rose,
Bearing patiently the stinging lacerations of her thorns.[11]

"I don't read and write, which is why I don't know any real poems by heart," said Ali, "but I love hearing love poems from others and listening to them read by singers." He knew that there was a world out there in which poetry existed independently of music, and he even knew a few verses from famous poems. Songs, however, he knew word for word. Memorizing the words from music was easy, and he did not need to read anything; often he wasn't aware of the lyrics' roots in written poetry, not aware that when he recited lyrics without music, he was simply reciting poetry. They were all verses to him, arrows in his quiver.

Zakia's favorite singer was Mir Maftoon, an Afghan from the mountainous northern province of Badakhshan, a place more remote than Bamiyan. Long before dawn one morning, early in the still-wintry spring, Ali recited one of Maftoon's verses to her as she lay prone on the flat roof of her house, her chin on her folded hands, looking down over the edge:

Your two dark eyes are those of an Afghan,
But the mercy of Islam is not in your heart.
Outside your walls I spent nights that became daylights;
What kind of sleep is this that you never wake up?[12]

Touched by the verses and by his suffering in the cold, and freezing herself, Zakia finally came down to join him in the garden. And so their love story became a love affair, as Ali delicately put it. He would have stayed there in spite of the intense cold on those mornings, but come the first call to prayer, the *subh,* which came long before any sign of dawn in these highlands, people would start stirring, going to the mosque to pray or beginning early chores in animal pens and fields. He needed to be well away from her house by then.

"If someone loves someone, she should have that bravery to do whatever has to be done," Zakia said. "For a long time, I was thinking about it and thinking about doing this, and why should I regret it now? That poem moved me, it increased my courage. Those days were so cold, and he was coming to meet me anyway, even though I told him not to come, because the weather was very cold, and he came anyway, and then he recited this poem."

It was only a matter of time before they were caught. Ali slept in the same room with his older brother Ismatullah, and his nocturnal escapades did not escape notice.

"What are you doing?" Ismatullah yelled at him. "I *know* what you are doing, and it's crazy!"

One night Ali went out at 3:00 A.M. to meet her. "Zakia-*jan* and I were in the garden, and we must have stayed too late, because her mother saw us. She didn't recognize me, because at night I would wear different clothes—I wore a hat at night, which I never did during the day." He ran for the far garden wall and scampered over it in a bound.

"Who was out there with you?" Sabza demanded of her daughter, through the window.

Zakia replied that she had woken up early to grind flour and there was a farmer in the garden who begged for bread, so she went out to give him some. It was an unlikely story, and Sabza did not believe her.

"Come back inside, you *dead father's daughter*," Sabza hissed at Zakia. The curse cut deep. Of course her father was still alive, but few things were worse in Afghan society than the suggestion that a daughter might have no father to determine the rest of her life for her.

"I get really upset if someone curses me," Zakia said. "I hate being cursed. After my mother realized I was having a secret affair with someone, she mistreated me like that. I would rather she beat me than curse me." Despite the curses, her mother was at that point being kind. If Sabza suspected that her daughter had consummated her affair, she kept that suspicion to herself—voicing it would have been Zakia's death sentence. It was a serious enough offense just to be discovered showing interest in a boy, far worse to be caught alone with him; the presumption always in such cases would be that sex had taken place. Her mother apparently preferred to present the case to the family as a matter of her suspicions about something starting to go on, or the situation would have become far more perilous for both of the lovers. Also, she had not actually seen who it was, though she knew well enough that it must have been Ali.

With both families alerted and everyone on the lookout, it was even harder for the two young people to get together. It was as if their villages had become prisons, with all their families and neighbors the guards and the two of them the only inmates.

With spring came the new Persian year, 1392, significantly the year in which Zakia would turn eighteen and become legally an adult. Her birthday was unknown, because her national identity card, like those of most Afghans, gave only the year of her birth; so legally she was eighteen the moment it became 1392—March 21, 2013. By that time her father normally would have been shopping her around, hunting for a husband whose family would pay a suitably high bride price. Zakia was considered strikingly beautiful, fair-skinned with hands somehow unroughened by farmwork. Girls in that village were frequently married off earlier than eighteen, and usually the bride price was figured in livestock; four goats or six sheep was a typical sum. Zakia would fetch much more, possibly enough to help Zaman buy some land of his own; he would later claim to have turned down 11 lakhs of afghanis—1.1 million afghanis, or twenty thousand dollars—for her hand. (A lakh is 100,000.) That would be a small herd of sheep or half a *jreeb* of land.

Whom she married was up to her father, and that is not just the case in backward rural areas. It is the predominant practice in all of Afghanistan that fathers rule every aspect of their daughters' lives, even when they are adults. Their fathers decide whether they can go to school, get a job, leave the house, see a doctor, wear a burqa or just a head scarf. Once women are married, their husbands assume that power over them. No one questions male authority over women in Afghanistan. If for some reason the father is absent or the husband dies young, a brother will assume ownership of the woman. Zakia could consider herself lucky that she hadn't been married off at the age of sixteen—the minimum legal age according to both Afghan law and sharia law in Afghanistan—or even at the age of fourteen, a practice that remains widespread although it is forbidden by the constitution and subject to strong penalties under the Elimination of Violence Against Women (EVAW) law.[13] The age at which many girls are married in Afghanistan would be considered criminal sexual abuse in most countries.[14]

Once they had resolved to marry, Ali and Zakia's first instinct was to try to operate within their society's cultural framework. Ali managed to persuade his father to make a bid for Zakia on his behalf. There are exceptions to the practice of fathers choosing their daughters' husbands, but they are shrouded in secrecy, with the goal of maintaining the appearance that the husband was the father's choice. Such exceptions, not talked about openly, do take into account how people really feel and behave. In the traditional model, the wife will never see her husband until their wedding night. In cities and among elites and more progressive families, the families of the prospective bride and groom may arrange for the couple, once the fathers have chosen them, to meet and get to know each other, closely chaperoned; in some cases they will tie the *neka* in advance, so that they're formally married in the eyes of Islam but will not have the wedding party and the wedding night until later. That enables them to court and have intimacy at some level, without committing a legal or religious crime in the eyes of the community. But for the girl or boy to come up with the idea of marrying and then present it to their families openly would be considered shameful. The prospective groom might, however, conspire with his own father to initiate the idea by making overtures to the bride's father, which is what Zakia and Ali tried at first to do.

They were pleasantly surprised by how agreeable Ali's father, Anwar, proved to be about the idea initially.

"By then everyone knew, though no one talked about it publicly," Anwar said. People only had to see Ali walking along the footpaths playing his flute to know that he was in love with someone, and if they also spotted Zakia singing to herself in the fields, as she often did, it wouldn't take long to put the two together. Such interventions are also done behind the scenes in cases where everyone has already begun to suspect that the girl and the boy have somehow found love on their own.

Between the two of them, Ali and Zakia had agreed that they would give it a bit of time, first for the memory to recede of the intercepted telephone conversations and the incident in the garden, and also because Zakia's own brother was about to get married, and after that expense—the groom's family pays for everything, including the bride price—perhaps her father would be more amenable to an arrangement that would help him recoup some of his financial outlays.

"We agreed we would wait two months, but after forty days I couldn't bear it any longer," Ali said. He persuaded his father to make the approach.

The first time the two old men met, late in the summer of 2013, Zaman received Anwar graciously and politely, with green tea and cakes and nuts, dried chickpeas, raisins, and hard candies set out on trays on the floor; they sat facing, cross-legged on thin floor cushions. They had known each other all their lives and been neighbors except for the few years after they had fled in different directions from the Taliban. Their respective fields shared some of the same irrigation channels and works, and they often pooled their labor.

Anwar's opening to Zaman was formulaic, words passed down through generations and known as the *khwast-gari,* the demanding.[15] "Please accept my son as a slave to your family," Anwar said.

Zaman had expected as much and had his answer ready. "I don't want to be harsh, but I tell you that such matches did not take place between two ethnic groups in the past and are not possible now," Zaman replied. "Please, now, do not come again about this."

Anwar hopefully viewed that as a negotiating position, so over the next month he went back twice more, finally offering a portion of his fields—Ali's inheritance—as well as money and gold as the bride price. "You don't have any fields of your own. I can give you fields and money if you want, maybe enough to build a house for one of your sons," Anwar told Zaman.

"I don't care about these things. My relatives and my villagers will get upset with me if I marry her outside her ethnicity and her religion."

Having asked three times, Anwar considered the matter closed. The romance would have to end, and he told his son as much. Their families had been on opposite sides in Afghanistan's bitter civil war, although both had been tormented by the Taliban rule that followed it. But while peace had reigned between Tajiks and Hazaras for more than a decade, memories were long and prejudices died hard. Anwar had no inclination to stir up a war, and he accepted Zaman's right to decide Zakia's fate.

Examples of what was likely to happen if the father's will was defied were abundant. A similar Hazara-Tajik affair had just played out in Bamiyan around the same time Zakia and Ali's courtship had begun, and it was widely publicized. An eighteen-year-old girl named Khadija from Qarawna Village, in Saighan District, had taken refuge in the Bamiyan shelter rather than be married to a man chosen for her by her father. Khadija, a Tajik like Zakia, also had eloped with a Hazara, Mohammad Hadi, but police arrested her after hundreds of other Tajik villagers protested—even though she was of age and had formally married Mr. Hadi. After spending months in the shelter, Khadija got homesick and asked to see her family; with the supervision of Bamiyan's Tajik judges, they assembled elders from their village with the girl's relatives, including her father and her brothers, who all put their thumbprints on a document promising never to harm her. Fatima Kazimi, the head of the women's-affairs ministry in Bamiyan at the time, convened a committee of social workers, shelter officials, and police to discuss the case. The committee opposed Khadija's return to her family but the decision was overruled by the court. Khadija has never been seen since. A few weeks later, when the women's ministry asked to see the girl to make sure she was unharmed, the family calmly announced that she had run away again, Fatima said. This time, though, they showed no interest in pursuing her. In the highlands of Bamiyan, there is really no place a girl alone could run; police would have arrested her on sight. "I'm sure they killed her and hid the body where no one has found it," Fatima said.[16]

Anwar was aware of the stakes, and so was everyone involved. Zakia's family made sure she was more cloistered than ever, and Ali fruitlessly paced the pathways of her village, crossed and recrossed their fields, hoping for a glimpse of her, and tried repeatedly to call her, all to no avail. She was leaving her phone off for fear of being caught with it again. It was so very wrong, Ali felt. "Why should parents choose who we marry? It is not the mother and father who have to spend a life with the woman, it is me. No one can live with his or her mother or father forever. It's the husbands and wives you spend the rest of your life with." He vowed that if he ever had a daughter, he would make sure she could choose her own husband. "I have felt what that was like, and I would never let that happen to anyone."

Zakia drop-called him, and when he called her back, he was nearly in tears. He wanted to tell her the story of Layla and Majnoon. "Ali-*jan,* I know the story," she said. "But tell it to me again."

Layla and Majnoon grow up together, but from different stations in life, and when their childhood love blossoms, Majnoon approaches her father and is rebuffed.[17] He goes mad and wanders the streets of their town, composing and reciting love poetry in her honor until finally Layla is married off by her father, whereupon Majnoon flees into exile and the life of a hermit. She refuses all the advances of her husband, however, and remains chaste throughout their marriage. Layla and Majnoon meet, but they do not consummate their love, and she remains loyal to her nonetheless chaste relationship with her husband. Her husband finally dies, and Layla puts on a bridal gown and plans to join Majnoon at last. By this point Majnoon has wandered off into the desert, mad with grief, and no one can find him. Believing their love to be doomed, Layla dies. Majnoon hears what has happened and rushes to her grave, where he dies as well. They are united in death, and their grave site becomes a place of pilgrimage.

Like the story of Yousef and Zuleikha and another popular tale, that of Princess Shirin and the stonecutter Farhad, the Layla-and-Majnoon story is wildly popular in a society where romantic love is all but outlawed—probably precisely *because* it is outlawed. Yousef and Zuleikha is retold in a thirty-part serial that is played on Afghan television every year during the holy month of Ramadan—in part because, unlike some of the other great Persian tales, it is also a sacred story, enshrined in the Koran, so the mullahs cannot object to it even though it is a story replete with the themes of adultery, romantic love, and the coveting of other men's wives. Afghan popular music, both Westernized pop as well as folkloric versions, and poetry are rooted in traditional romantic tales, particularly these three and their many variants. In a society where the majority of women are in arranged marriages to which they did not consent freely,[18] these songs and poems summon the emotional life they will never have the chance to experience themselves.

Every once in a while, even in Afghanistan, a true love story comes along that echoes those of the past and arouses the whole country. The famous tale of Munira and Farhad in 1991 came at the end of the Communist regime and the beginning of the civil-war period. Kabul was in civil turmoil as the mujahideen battled one another. Rival factions used truck containers as roadblocks and as protection from shelling and gunfire, so the containers were a ubiquitous feature of the cityscape. Munira and Farhad were young people who had fallen in love, but as Sunni and Shia their own union was forbidden. Due to be married to other people on the same Thursday, they arranged to meet secretly one last time the night before, but the only place they could find to be alone was in one of the shipping containers. While they were inside, the owner of the container came along and latched the door from outside. They were too frightened to cry out and be discovered, and by the time the owner opened it again, the oxygen in the container had been depleted, and he found them both dead in each other's arms. Their bereft families, united like the Montagues and Capulets over their shared tragedy, dressed them both for burial in the wedding clothes that had been intended for the arranged marriages that would never take place.

The story fired the imagination of the country and infuriated the mullahs. None of the clerics would agree to preside over their double burial, and instead elders of both families stepped in and performed the funeral rites—under Islam any knowledgeable person can do so.

Neither Zakia nor Ali could have imagined this yet, but their own misadventure would soon be on its way to a similar sort of fame. Munira and Farhad belonged to their parents' generation. A younger generation of Afghans would find in Zakia and Ali's story justification for expressing love openly and proudly, and older Afghans who had loved secretly and guiltily could find vindication, knowing they were not alone.

3

ZAKIA MAKES HER MOVE

When Mohammad Anwar trudged home after a long day tending the fields in the late summer of 2013 and opened his door, Zakia was sitting there on floor cushions and drinking tea with his daughter-in-law.

Anwar's house was a dwelling that shouted poverty but was scrupulously clean—earthen floors swept, carpets shaken and beaten, latrine isolated and limed. The home was made up of four separate rooms, each a little building opposite the courtyard wall. Afghans love walls around their compounds; it is how they keep their women safe from the view of outsiders. Anwar had run out of money for mud bricks, and the wall was only three-quarters complete, with a jagged gap where he hoped one day to install a gate. There was no running water—the nearest water came from a well a few hundred yards away, beside the main road—nor any electricity, save for a tiny lightbulb and wire in one room that could be connected to a nine-volt battery, when they could afford one. The family's two-inch-thick Afghan mattresses were quarter-folded and stacked along the rooms' interior walls during the daytime; bamboo mats or the cheaper plastic mats were used where they could not afford carpets. There was no furniture; thin cushions were scattered around for seating. At mealtimes a plastic sheet was unrolled on the floor to make a dining area, and meals were taken communally, everyone eating from a common plate with their fingers, according to Afghan custom. Like the rest of the dwellings in Surkh Dar village, the homestead was nestled into a narrow valley that rose from the road into the northern mountains; they had used the steep hillside to create the back wall in some of the four rooms. After only a ten-minute climb up the slopes nearby, one could glance back and Anwar's house and the rest of the village would seem to disappear into the landscape, its walls and roofs made of the same earth as the bare slopes all around. Anwar's house was also old, built by his grandfather, and decades of wind and storms had softened all the edges so that it seemed not so much erected as grown in place.

Anwar sat down to tea with Zakia, dazed with surprise. Zakia sat twisting her wrist with the opposite hand, as she often did when nervous, but was otherwise composed. There was already a lot on Anwar's mind those days; harvest time for potatoes, their most important cash crop, was not far away. Prices were good that year, and harvests were likely to be bountiful, although labor-intensive. He might even begin paying down the debts he had incurred with the marriage of his eldest son, Bismillah, several years before, and his next-oldest son, Ismatullah, the year after that. Sons are highly prized in Afghanistan; they are the measure of a man's worth. Though daughters can bring a substantial bride price to their fathers, they are disdained. A man with many sons is considered a rich man no matter how poor it makes him. Anwar had five sons but only three daughters, so he was proud but perennially broke.

Many Afghan men do not even know how many daughters they have; if you ask them how many children in their family, they're likely to reply "five" if they have five sons and five daughters, for instance, since daughters don't count. Press them for the number of daughters and often they will have to consult with a child or a wife to be sure. Anwar, however, is not one of those men.

As if it were the most natural thing in the world, Zakia calmly poured Anwar some tea.

"Why are we here?" he said. "What is this, daughter?" He used the term as an older man addressing a young woman, nothing more.

Things had been coming to a head for months now; it was nearly a year since Ali's return from the army and months since their secret engagement. Zakia was on her third phone, keeping this one hidden in her underclothes after first her brother and then her father found the earlier ones. Although Sabza had not been able to identify Ali that dawn when she caught her daughter with him in the garden, and Ali managed just in time to climb the wall and run off, by then everyone had a pretty good idea with whom Zakia was involved, even if they couldn't prove it. Once Anwar had formally asked for Zakia's hand, it was no longer a secret in either of their villages. "Everyone knew about it. I just made up my mind: I'm not free here at home, so I have to go to him, and I just went," Zakia said. "I just thought about Ali, and I thought, 'I have to go to him.' I was hopeful he would keep me or accept me, but I didn't know. I just had to do it, even if I wasn't planning."

What she didn't say, and could not say, is that she and Ali had become lovers and she had no other choice; there could never be another Afghan husband for her.

She told Anwar that she wanted to see Ali, and that they needed to discuss something with him. Unfortunately, Ali was away working on a day-laborer job some distance from the village and would not be back until Friday.

"I am sorry, daughter. You cannot see him," Anwar said. He pretended not to know what was in the offing, but it was all too clear. Just her presence in the home of another man, even chaperoned by his daughter-in-law, was an outrage to public morality. He walked Zakia halfway home, to the highway that is the boundary between their two villages.

When he came back, he saw neighbors gathered in the lanes, whispering among themselves, and it was clear that word was out and Zakia had been spotted on the wrong side of the highway.

One of Anwar's neighbors came over to talk to him about it, so he decided to preempt the inevitable gossip and telephone Zaman, Zakia's father. One of his sons dialed for him, since he did not know how.

"Your daughter came over to my house, and she may now want to run away with my son," Anwar told him. "It's better that you agree, because if that happens, it will be too late."

"If that happens, I will demand five hundred thousand afghanis, and I know you are in debt already. You're standing looking down the edge of a cliff, and this will put you over it," Zaman replied.

That was an impossible sum, more than nine thousand dollars.

"My debts are not your problem, but if they run away, there will be nothing for you."

Zaman still refused.

Over the next month, Ali and Zakia were rarely able to speak to each other, because Zakia's family watched her so closely. When they did manage to get a few words together, she told him she would come again and that if his family would not take her, they would run away. She said she was now legally an adult and no one could stop her. "We agreed that if Ali's family did not accept this, then we will go somewhere secretly that no one knows—just somewhere, we didn't have any idea where. After the first time I went to their home, I said that they could send me ten times back and still I would come again. It's because I really loved him. I was very determined. I really loved Ali, and my decision was final. It was a strong decision."

The next time she saw an opportunity, she made her move, heading to Ali's uncle's house rather than to his own, thinking to evade pursuers that way. His uncle called Anwar, while Ismatullah restrained Ali from leaving to join her. Ali fought back against his older and much bigger brother, and finally Ismatullah, infuriated, smashed him in the face with a rock to subdue him, leaving a bruise that would take many months to heal. (It was still prominent when I first met Ali the following February.)

Anwar reached his brother's house and confronted Zakia. "You cannot do this," he said. "What are you thinking? Daughter, why are you doing this?"

She pleaded with him openly to take her in to his family so she could marry his son. "We love each other, and we want to marry, and no one should stop us." She was dry-eyed and determined not to cry.

"That is not your decision. It can never be," Anwar said. He took her by the arm and forcibly walked her back to her own home, with two of his sons helping and Ismatullah still holding Ali back from intervening. It was nearly midnight, and the Zaman household was already aroused, aware that Zakia had bolted. Gula Khan was on the rooftop with another brother.

"Let's go before they attack us," Anwar told his sons as they left Zakia in front of her house. "You can see how angry they are."

When he got back home, Anwar, too, beat his son, shouting at him that he was bringing disgrace and humiliation to both his own family and Zakia's. "We didn't want their family to be disgraced," Ali said. Months later part of him agreed with the punishment he received and part of him was still angry about it.

"That night was very bad," Zakia said. The following day was the first day of the main potato harvest, and everyone would have to be in the fields, but the entire family stayed up late screaming at her. "That night my father and my mother both beat me," Zakia said. "It was the first time they had ever done that to me." Gula Khan and her other brothers had always been the enforcers of her virtue. In the course of that parental beating, she finally realized how dire her situation was. "While they were beating me, they were saying, 'We will kill you if you don't listen to us. We have to do this. We have to kill you.'"

The next day both families were in their fields, side by side, both Zakia and Ali bruised. Harvesting potatoes by hand is back-breaking work, and no one spoke across the low mud walls and sometimes just footpaths that separated their two domains. Zakia dared not look at Ali, nor he at her.

No one expected that she would try to bolt again that same

night, but that is what she did. When her family was asleep, exhausted from the day's exertions, she crept out at about 11:00 P.M. and went again to Anwar's home. This time Ali was half expecting her and was still up when she arrived.

"My whole family wanted to send her back," said Ali. "They wouldn't agree. I saw there was no place to go, so I brought her to the women's ministry." It was late at night, but the guards at the ministry building summoned a woman who headed the provincial human-rights office, Aziza Ahmadi, who came down and arranged for Zakia to be admitted to the Bamiyan Women's Shelter, a short distance away.

"I was happy to be in the shelter at first, because I knew that my life was at risk now, and I wanted to see my case handled legally," Zakia said.

She had no idea then, in October 2013, that she would still be there nearly six months later.

At first Zakia cried inconsolably. "She would cry for one or two hours straight, even during late nights," said the shelter director, Najeeba Ahmadi (no relation to Aziza Ahmadi). Other than a small plastic bag of clothing she had brought along to Anwar's house, Zakia's lone possession was the tattered photograph of Ali that she kept beside her thin mattress on the floor. Ali's mother gave it to her when she visited the shelter herself, partly because Chaman wanted to make sure the shelter authorities knew that Ali's family was behind her and partly to reassure and comfort Zakia. Later the police would confiscate the photo from the shelter and make copies of it to distribute to checkpoints in the manhunt for the lovers.

The shelter workers sat with her in those first days, trying to calm her down. "You are a brave girl, stop crying," they would say. "You are the one who had the nerve to fight for your rights."

"I feel pity for my parents," Zakia replied. "I miss them, but I am worried about what they will do."

Najeeba had seen this many times before. "In Afghan society families disown their children and do not forgive them," she said. "Thinking about such things would disturb her and make her cry."

"I love him, and I'm not going to give him up," she declared in one breath and then, in the next, "I don't know what to do. On the one hand, there is my lover and on the other hand my family."

She appealed to Najeeba for guidance, but all the other woman could do was tell the girl to look in her own heart. "We would not tell her which side to take," Najeeba said. "It is her decision. But we always said, 'Think carefully before you make any decision.'"

Zakia always came back to the same thing. "I want to marry the boy."

"If that is what you really want, then do it," Najeeba said.

"Don't you think it is wrong?"

"Whatever your heart believes cannot be wrong," Najeeba said. "Now that you have fallen in love, you should fight for it till the end, until you achieve what you have wished for. Once you are married, you can still try to reconcile with your family. It might take a few years, four or five or even eight years. It might happen soon, or it might take a while."

The easiest way to calm her crying fits was to get her talking about Ali.

"Tell us what his good qualities are. What qualities made you want to marry him?" Najeeba would say.

"He is supportive, and when you have the support of someone, that's everything you can expect in your life. You always seek someone who will stand by your side and support you all the time, and he has all these good qualities. He is very kind, active, and he belongs to a very gentle family," she would reply. "I have so much love for him, and I feel that he loves me as much as I love him. He is hardworking, and he is ready to sacrifice everything for me," Zakia said.

"Besides," she would add with a smile, "he is handsome."

When she was calmer, she mixed well with the other girls and young women, many of them about her age. She had a keen sense of her rights as a person and lectured the other girls on that. By all accounts the prettiest of Zaman's seven daughters, Zakia grew up adored by her father and either admired or envied by her siblings, which gave her a self-possession unusual in a young Afghan woman, a self-possession that had turned to anger and resentment when her brothers tried to control her once she came of age. "Although she was uneducated, she kept everyone busy. She used to make jokes, tell stories, recite poetry," Najeeba said. "She had a very funny and charming personality, and once Zakia was in the shelter, all of the girls were actively involved with her. She was a good, active, brave, amusing girl."

As weeks turned to months, though, she grew disenchanted. "At first I was happy at the shelter," Zakia said. "Later on I realized they couldn't resolve my case." She began to ask for permission to leave the shelter so she could be with Ali. Technically, women's shelters are not jails, but in practice they function that way by agreement between the courts and the police, women's groups, and the women themselves. Shelter officials repeatedly convened a committee of representatives from these groups to discuss whether Zakia could be safely discharged, as she requested.

"The committee members said, 'If we allow her to leave, where would she go?'" Najeeba said. One or another of Zakia's family members were always waiting outside the shelter or, if they went to court, outside that building. The committee repeatedly turned down her request.

Such groups are one of the laudable outcomes of Afghanistan's landmark Elimination of Violence Against Women (EVAW) law—but as Zakia found, they are also examples of its limitations. When the EVAW law was enacted in 2009, it was hailed as a model of legislation on behalf of oppressed women in many underdeveloped countries. At first glance the Afghan constitution adopted after the fall of the Taliban had already admirably enshrined the rights of women.[1] Written with expert help from American and European scholars, it declared that women should have equal rights with men, that a girl became a legal adult with full civil rights at age eighteen, that no girl could be married before the age of sixteen and would have to consent to any marriage, and so forth. The problem was, there were no penalties decreed for violating those declarations of equality and no enabling legislation was enacted to, for instance, penalize a father who married his daughter off at age fourteen or beat his wife because she glanced at another man. Under the Afghan penal code, even rape was not a crime—unmentioned in civil and criminal law, it was treated as a family matter, under the purview of shariah law religious courts. Similarly, shariah law was all that applied if a husband beat his wife, even if he beat her to death; more often than not, the shariah court would approve of his crime if it was based on his belief that some transgression of his patriarchal rights had taken place.

The EVAW law changed that. Rape, wife beating, and forced and child marriage were given criminal penalties. Many customary practices were outlawed; one of those was what the EVAW law called "denial of relationship," the practice of families controlling a person's choice of spouse. Prior to EVAW, Zakia in effect had no legal right to choose to marry Ali; that choice belonged to her father alone, no matter her age. Prior to EVAW, the lovers would have been jailed and prosecuted for attempted adultery at the least, and adultery if there was a suspicion of sexual relations. Adultery was subject to penalties ranging from flogging to ten years in jail, or even to death by stoning.[2] Without EVAW women's shelters would not have the role they've come to have, in protecting women from violence that had not even been a crime prior to the passing of the law, and without shelters like the one in Bamiyan, Zakia would have long since perished. If there is one thing more than any other that made the story of Zakia and Ali possible, it was the EVAW law. In a way they had the Taliban to thank for it. The suppression of women during their six years in power had outraged most of the world, and after their fall the promotion of decent treatment for Afghan women was a cornerstone of international policy toward Afghanistan. EVAW was a direct outcome of Western intervention and a response to the excesses of the Taliban regime that preceded it.

Nonetheless, Zakia and Ali were lucky to have survived for as long as they had. EVAW is also an imperfect law, particularly when it comes to implementation in a fiercely patriarchal society and in backward, rural places where most judges have no law degree or any other legal qualification; many still believe that the world is flat and that it is nonsense or blasphemy to suggest otherwise.

In another Hazara community a year and a half before, in Ghazni Province, a sixteen-year-old girl named Sabira was lashed a hundred and one times after being accused of adultery—although she later was proven to still be a virgin. Her only crime was to have been alone in a shop with a man she said had raped her. She was apparently too inexperienced to understand what constituted rape.[3] EVAW law meant nothing in her defense, local judges refused to apply it, and the mullahs and former jihadi commanders who ordered the lashing were never punished, even after a nationwide outcry.

As long as there were no judges in Bamiyan willing to sanction Zakia's family for staking out the Bamiyan shelter and the courts, implicitly but clearly threatening violence against her if she got out, the limitation of EVAW law there was just as clear. Only the intervention of people like Fatima Kazimi, the head of the women's ministry in Bamiyan, and shelter officials protected her from her family's retribution.

Despite the threat they posed to her, Zakia's own family members had visiting privileges, and her mother and father came frequently, as did her sisters. "They would urge me to come home and would say, 'This is not good, this is not fair that you are here,'" Zakia said. "They would not curse me, just try to make me understand. They would tell me, 'Don't be afraid of us. We're not going to do anything to you.' But I knew they couldn't force me to come home with them, so this was the way to get me to come home, and I knew what they would do to me. One hundred percent, they would kill me even before they got me home. Before coming to the shelter, just for having an affair they were threatening and beating me. Now that I had done this big thing by running away, I knew they would do something terrible to me," she said.

Zakia's case went to court several times, where the judges, who were all Tajiks like Zakia's family, would insist that she could marry Ali only with her father's consent. Ali's family claimed that Zaman and his sons had bribed the judges to side with them, and

Zaman claimed that Anwar and his sons had bribed the women's ministry, the police, and the governor's office to support Zakia. Possibly all of them were right; corruption is pervasive in Afghanistan, particularly in Bamiyan. Still, both sides would have been taking bribes to act in line with their ethnic allegiances.

Like most Afghan judges, the chief judge of the Bamiyan Province Primary Court, Judge Attaullah Tamkeen, was not a law-school graduate.[4] His only legal experience was the study of shariah law at Balkh University, according to one of his legal colleagues on the panel that heard Zakia's case, Judge Saif Rahman, who also had no law degree. Some Afghan judges are even less educated, being only graduates of madrassas, religious schools where the students spend most of their time learning to recite the entire Koran from memory. In a society that reveres its male elders, most judges are old, and whatever legal knowledge they have predates Afghanistan's current constitution and any legislation of the last decade that gave women some rights, in particular the EVAW law. If the judges had a passing acquaintance with Afghanistan's constitution, they would know that Zakia was legally an adult and entitled to choose her own spouse. EVAW law makes her rights more explicit and criminalizes her family's acts, although "denial of relationship" is probably the least prosecuted of all crimes in Afghanistan.

"In any society it's not just the law that shapes everything," said Rubina Hamdard, a lawyer with the Afghan Women's Network who followed this case closely. "It's the behavior of the judges and how they implement the law. Here in Afghanistan and in this case especially, it's true, judges are the limitation of the law. Judges resolve runaway cases by sentencing the girls to one year in jail even though they're over eighteen and although there isn't a law against running away—but there is a law against penalizing running away."

Backed up by the Bamiyan court, her family's persistence finally wore Zakia down, and on February 2, 2014, she was taken out of the shelter to meet her mother, her father, and three of the judges, along with half a dozen elders from their village. Their version is that she had petitioned to be released to them; her version is that she had petitioned to be released on her own because she was eighteen. At the hearing, Judge Tamkeen had called in her family members and worked out an agreement. They pledged not to kill or otherwise harm her for having run away from home, and they would drop any charges against her (this court was still treating running away as if it were a crime). Her father, her uncle, and several elders all put their thumbprints on a document approved by Judge Tamkeen, confirming the agreement to take her home from the shelter and not to harm her, and her consent to that. Called before Judge Tamkeen, surrounded by her obviously angry relatives, Zakia agreed.

Pledges like the one signed by Zakia's family have dubious value. For all the talk about Afghan honor, the concept of honor as it is applied in Afghanistan has nothing to do with keeping one's word, especially when it comes to promising not to kill a woman.

Gul Meena was an eighteen-year-old who had been married off as a prepubescent child to an abusive husband. She ran away with a neighbor, who became her lover, a man named Qari Zakir, fleeing their village in Kunar Province, in 2012; they managed to marry on the grounds that her previous marriage was illegal. Somehow her brother and father found her a year later and visited on the pretense of reconciling with her.[5] When they left, Mr. Zakir lay dead in his bed, his head nearly severed from his neck with a knife. Ms. Meena lay grievously wounded in the next bed, her head mangled by fifteen blows from an ax; police were seeking the brother for personally carrying out the attack. Such ultraviolence is often a distinguishing characteristic of honor killings[6] in Afghanistan. They are rarely "clean" kills, and instead reveal the depth of hatred and passion aroused by the woman's transgression. By some miracle and thanks to the work of the doctors at the hospital in Jalalabad, Gul Meena managed to survive; sympathetic journalists and aid workers donated money to help finance her care and pay for medication and food,[7] since she had no family left that would do so.

It is common for families to resort to subterfuge to get runaway women back. In a village in Dashte Archi District in Kunduz, in 2010, a twenty-five-year-old man named Khayyam and a nineteen-year-old woman named Siddiqa wanted to marry, but the woman's family had already promised her to someone else. The couple fled to Kunar Province, but emissaries from both families came to them to persuade them that all was forgiven and they could return to their village to be married properly. Instead, when they got there, the entire male population of the village turned out to watch the local Taliban commander pronounce them guilty of adultery and sentence them to death by stoning. They were both put in separate large holes while their neighbors and family members began chucking stones at them. Interviewed later, Nadir Khan, one of the villagers, did not object to the stoning, though he said that he did not himself throw stones. As it began, "They said, 'We love each other no matter what happens,'" he related.[8] The stoning was enthusiastic, and some of the villagers picked up rocks so heavy they were hard to lift, pummeling the couple from close range. The evidence of the crowd's enthusiasm for the executions was clear from video recordings made on several villagers' cell phones, copies of which began circulating nationally on social-media sites.[9] Siddiqa was seen sinking slowly to her knees and then, after being hit on the head by one especially large stone, collapsing to the bottom of the pit they had put her in, apparently unconscious; her agony was obscured from view by the blue burqa she wore. When she recovered and tried to crawl out of the pit, one of the men shot her three times in the head with his AK-47. Her lover, Khayyam, could not be seen in the video, as so many of his neighbors were crowded so closely around him; he was stoned to death in minutes.[10] Although the stonings were carried out by the Taliban, after the village later fell into government hands, the Afghan police were reluctant to prosecute most of the perpetrators, despite abundant video evidence of their apparently willing involvement in the crime.[11]

Like any young woman in Afghan society, Zakia well knew what awaited her if she went astray, but it was also hard for her to believe that those closest to her could become her killers, and she said that she vacillated from wanting desperately to believe their assurances to knowing she was lost if she did. "They pressured me to make me say that I wanted to go with my parents. I had to say that. I had no way to say no," Zakia said.

Judge Tamkeen took her aside and gave her a lecture about ethnic loyalty. "Do not marry that boy, or you will dishonor me and our entire ethnic group," Judge Tamkeen said, according to Zakia's account. Like most of the judges in Bamiyan, he was Tajik and a Sunni Muslim. Ali as well as Fatima Kazimi, the head of the women's ministry in Bamiyan, and most of the other officials in Bamiyan including police were all Hazaras and Shia Muslims.

None of the representatives from the women's shelter were present during that hearing—Najeeba Ahmadi, the shelter head, had gone to Kabul on personal business and returned only toward the end of the day, and Fatima Kazimi had not been informed of it. Late in the day, after hours of pressure by the crowd of officials and family, Zakia agreed to put her thumbprint on the document consenting to her return to her family. Najeeba had arrived by then and was told of the agreement; she stalled for time, saying it was too late in the day, there was paperwork to do before she could legally release Zakia, and they should all come back in the morning. She spent the night working the phones, alerting other women's leaders and sympathetic officials to what was about to happen.

The next morning, February 3, Najeeba brought Zakia from the shelter to the court, where her family had assembled again; this time the group was larger, including her brother Gula Khan, two male cousins, her parents, Sabza and Zaman, the six village elders, plus the panel of three judges, headed by Judge Tamkeen. Fatima Kazimi was also there, backed up by the deputy governor, Asif Mubaligh, and the deputy police chief, Ali Lagzi.

Fatima Kazimi is a presence; big and slightly rotund, usually dressed in a purple silk head scarf and a dark modesty trench coat, she exudes self-assurance and authority. Fatima and the deputy governor took Zakia aside, over the strenuous objections of her family. "Do you understand," Fatima asked her, "that you have signed an agreement to return home with your family?"

"Yes," Zakia said in a small voice.

"You don't have to do it," Fatima said. "You can always change your mind, and we will protect you if you do. You just have to say in court, in front of the judges, that you don't want to go."

When they returned to the courtroom, Zakia stood up and said she wanted to stay in the shelter. Judge Tamkeen leaped to his feet and ordered policemen to take her out by force and return her to the family. Zakia screamed, "I don't want to go home!"

The judge threatened to send them all to jail.

"This is a violence against her and a violence against women," Fatima retorted. "You can't do this." She asked the deputy police chief to intervene, and he ordered the policemen to bring Zakia back to the shelter; in the end the policemen obeyed their superiors, who were fellow Hazaras, and not the judges, who were Tajiks.

Zakia's family then dropped all pretenses of not wishing her harm. Her father and brother tried to drag her physically away from Fatima and the police, but her mother was the worst of them.

"You whore!" Sabza screamed at her, about the worst thing any Afghan mother—or any mother—could say to her daughter.

One of the men yelled, "You will not live in peace! We will kill you!"

"My mother was shouting and cursing me, my brothers and my aunt's son tried to beat me, my father and mother were tearing at my clothes and even pulling my clothes off," Zakia said. "I felt that if they got me out of there, I wouldn't have gotten home. They would have killed me on the way."

"They were ferocious," Fatima said. "There was no question in our mind—of course she would be killed if they ever got their hands on her."

The girl's scarf was ripped from her head, and Sabza pulled her jacket off as the family struggled with police to get her back.

"This girl must be hanged!" shouted Zaman.

"That was their plan. That was their decision," Zakia said. "At least then the police also found out that they would kill me, so they assured me they would not hand me over."

Zaman and his son were handcuffed and arrested and held until they calmed down, while the police pushed Sabza out of the courtroom, still screaming and cursing.

The deputy governor and the deputy police chief, as well as Najeeba Ahmadi, Fatima Kazimi, and the head of the human-rights office, Aziza Ahmadi, all witnessed the outburst and her family's passionate vows to kill Zakia. These could have been dismissed as being said in the heat of the moment, the sort of harsh words uttered in a family conflict that go far beyond any settled intention, except that their anger did not dissipate. Weeks and months later, Najeeba was still receiving telephoned death threats from Zakia's family, and they would eventually give up their farm, their livelihood, and their home in the single-minded pursuit of vengeance against Zakia and Ali.

After the Bamiyan courtroom melee, a furious Judge Tamkeen issued an order suspending Fatima Kazimi and Aziza Ahmadi from their jobs. He even ordered Fatima's arrest for questioning by the attorney general's office. "The attorney general asked us to bring her in for interrogation," said Bamiyan provincial police chief General Khudayar Qudsi. "But there is no basis for such action, so we will not recognize such requests." The governor simply told police to ignore the order, and Fatima continued to go to work.[12]

Zakia was safe back in the shelter, but her problem was no closer to being solved. Fatima acceded to Ali's request to be allowed to visit Zakia at the shelter, something normally *not* allowed, and Fatima claimed later she knew he would smuggle in a telephone but looked the other way when he did. By then Zakia and Ali were both experts in clandestine calling, and they began plotting her escape.

There was no longer any reason to stay in the shelter; as far as the lovers could see, it offered no solutions, only a temporary safety that could end anytime without warning. The judges and Zakia's family had the weight of Afghan social custom and practice on their side and the potential authority of the central government behind them. Even many of Ali's fellow Hazaras disapproved of the couple's actions.

They were also well aware of the many examples of the fate

awaiting an Afghan woman who goes astray and is returned to an angry family. "One hundred percent, they would kill me," Zakia had said—and who could know her own family better than one of its daughters? Had Fatima not intervened to prevent Zakia from going back home with her family, she might have ended up like Amina, a teenage girl from northern Baghlan Province, who was either fifteen or eighteen years old.[13] The daughter of a man named Khuda Bakhsh, Amina fled from her family's home when her father proposed to marry her to a much older man in their village in Tala Wa Barfak District.[14] Police found her wandering in the bazaar in the provincial capital of Pul-e-Kumri, asking people how to find the women's-ministry offices. She was arrested, essentially, for being a woman alone.

The police bypassed the jail and took her directly to the provincial women's ministry, on March 20, 2014—the day before Zakia escaped her shelter, in fact—and handed her over to Uranus Atifi, head of the legal department; she was put in a shelter in Pul-e-Kumri and stayed there for the following month. Then a member of the provincial council, Samay Faisal, called Ms. Atifi and said that Amina's brother and uncle had come to Pul-e-Kumri and wanted to take the girl home. Mr. Faisal offered to vouch for them, she said, so she brought the family in, and they all signed guarantee papers promising not to harm the girl if she came home and not to force her to marry the fiancé she had rejected.

"Before handing her over to her family, we talked to Amina in private and asked her if she wanted to go back to her home," Ms. Atifi said. "She said that she did want to go back, because she didn't want her case to get bigger and create more problems." Ms. Atifi took the precaution of videoing the family's pledges not to hurt the girl and the girl's consent to return. Still, Ms. Atifi was worried, and she got the brother's phone number and called him to speak to Amina while they were driving back.

"That same night I called her at eight P.M., and I talked to her and asked her if she was all right. She told me she was and that they were still driving. At ten P.M. I called them again, but this time I couldn't get through," Ms. Atifi said.

The next morning Ms. Atifi called the brother, and he coolly related to her that a group of nine armed men wearing masks had stopped their car and dragged Amina out and shot her to death but harmed no one else. The family had not bothered to report the crime to the police. The brother seemed to her suspiciously calm about his sister's murder.

No one believed the family's story that the masked men must have been relatives of the jilted fiancé. If that were the case, skeptics asked, why wouldn't the outraged fiancé's relatives have killed the brother, uncle, and cousin who were there, too, and who were supposedly returning the girl to her home and canceling her engagement?

"You know, if a husband sees his wife in bed with a stranger and kills her, he gets one year in prison at most," said Shahla Farid, a female professor of law who is on the board of the Afghan Women's Network. "If she kills her husband for the same thing, she can be executed. That's right there in the Afghan penal code."[15] More likely the husband would not be prosecuted in such a case or, if prosecuted, get anything more than a toke punishment.[16]

"I believe the two families reached an agreement, but I'm not sure," said Khadija Yaqeen, the director of women's affairs in Baghlan Province. "We don't care what deal or interfamily agreement is made or will be made. Someone was killed, and there has to be an investigation so that justice is done in Amina's case." As in so many similar ones, that apparently never happened.[17]

In Bamiyan nearly two months went by after the court hearing. In the end Zakia's father forced matters to a head by formally requesting that the court in Bamiyan transfer Zakia's case to Kabul. There, he thought, he would get a better reception, since police and government officials in the capital would not be Hazaras but Tajiks or Pashtuns, and if a judge ordered her returned to the family, the police would obey. "We talked with the girl and got her consent to transfer her case to Kabul," said Zaman. Zakia of course said she gave no such consent and that the impending transfer precipitated her decision to escape, which she did the night before it was scheduled.

Coming so soon before the transfer, the elopement, Zaman felt, had to have been staged by women's-ministry officials. "We were not even allowed to meet her in person, so we talked to her on the phone and got her consent," Zaman said. "She agreed to come home. She is not guilty at all. It is the women's director, who thought she might be in trouble due to her involvement in the case, who decided to help them escape. Otherwise how can a girl from a shelter which is guarded by police[18] escape? It must be direct involvement of that woman and others who arranged her escape." Fatima Kazimi and Najeeba Ahmadi denied Zaman's claims, as did Ali and Zakia later on.

Unknown to them all, however, Zaman's appeals to move the case to Kabul had nothing to do with the impending transfer. Shukria Khaliqi, who was then a lawyer with the group Women for Afghan Women (WAW), had heard about the case and formally requested that it be moved to the capital, with the approval of women's-ministry officials in Kabul and women's advocates in the attorney general's office. In Kabul they thought they could find a court with judges who were lawyers and who had a passing acquaintance with the law. Shukria was convinced she could win the case for the couple. Then, although they would still be at risk of attack from Zakia's family, there would be no legal impediment to their marriage and no justification for keeping Zakia in a shelter.

Before WAW could reach Zakia to tell her all this, however, the couple was already on the run. Zakia's father pressed kidnapping charges against Ali, so they were fugitives not only from her family's retribution but from the law as well. They were together, but as far as the Afghan police were concerned—and that included the police in Bamiyan—they were wanted criminals who needed to be hunted down. Fellow feeling among Hazaras goes only so far; a woman on the run would always be in the wrong in the view of Afghan authority of whatever ethnic background.

Once Zakia and Ali had escaped, however, they also became heroes to many Afghans, especially to women and young people.

Najeeba Ahmadi of the Bamiyan shelter, while insisting she had no role in Zakia's escape, nonetheless applauded her at the time it happened. "Her action shows that everyone has the right to marry according to their own will. She has tried to achieve her own wishes. Her resistance and bravery are a good example for all those women and girls who want to protect their rights. When women resist for their rights, they have the ability to achieve their goals. I don't believe Zakia has done anything wrong. Her actions are admirable, and wherever she is, I wish her the best of luck and success in her life."

Zakia and Ali themselves had modest goals. They knew that most couples who eloped were usually caught, with terrible consequences. They never expected to get very far but were determined to have some real time together while they could, even if it meant death for both of them.

4

A RABBI AMONG THE MULLAHS

The e-mail from Rabbi Shmuley Boteach on March 25, 2014, was enigmatic and urgent. "I just heard very important info about the case. Can we speak please?" Shmuley was among hundreds of readers who had gotten in touch with me after I wrote about the plight of Zakia and Ali in the *New York Times*. At the time of that first article,[1] Zakia was on month four or five of her stay at the Bamiyan Women's Shelter, her disastrous court hearing was behind her, and Ali was mooning around the valley, trying to figure out an escape plan.

Many of those readers wanted to help the couple; Rabbi Shmuley was just a bit more pushy than most, and he now had the personal e-mail address and phone number I had given him, so he was not about to let up. Somewhat wearily I called him back, because I knew he wouldn't rest until I had. Part of me had given up on Zakia and Ali after I wrote that first story; I just didn't see how their story could end well, unless the then-president, Hamid Karzai, decided to step in and resolve it for them by decree. He was quite capable of doing this had he been interested, but in this case any interest he had was bound to be negative. The earnest and well-meaning efforts of a rabbi from New Jersey were not going to sway the president of the Islamic Republic of Afghanistan, a country where most other faiths are forbidden, the only consecrated Christian church is a small chapel inside the Italian embassy, and the lone synagogue has but one surviving congregant. Plus, at that time in his administration President Karzai was scarcely on speaking terms with American officials, despite his country's dependence on American aid.[2] So, not expecting much, I called Shmuley's number in North Jersey from our bureau in Kabul.

Shmuley's assistant put me straight through, and the rabbi got right to the point, addressing me, as he always had in our many previous calls, as if we were old friends. "Rod, she escaped."

"Who?"

"Zina, Zophia, what was her name?"

"Zakia?"

"Yes, she escaped, a couple nights ago. I just heard about it."

"Who from?"

"Fatima told me."

"Really?"

I didn't know that Fatima Kazimi, the women's director from Bamiyan, was in touch with Rabbi Shmuley; he was full of surprises and, as I would see, quite determined. Fatima was the reason I knew about Zakia and Ali—and by many accounts, in particular her own, the only reason Zakia was not already dead.

The whole affair of Zakia and Ali had come to my attention only a couple of months earlier, when, on February 9, Fatima Kazimi had e-mailed every journalist working in Afghanistan for major American publications. She dictated the e-mail through her English-speaking son and sent it to me by clicking on my byline on NYTimes.com:

Dear Mr. Nordland:[3]

    I'm Fatima Kazimi, Bamyan Director of Department of Women's Affairs (DoWA), the provincial branch of Ministry of Women's Affairs (MoWA.) We are the lead protector/ defender of women's rights in Bamyan province, Afghanistan.

    I just go straightly to the point which is the case of a girl

(Tajik ethnicity) and a boy (Hazara ethnicity) that fled from their houses and came to Bamyan Department of Women's Rights (DoWA) and Bamyan Independent Human Rights Commission for the sake of safety, protection and to finally make their dream a reality, marriage. We follow up this case from its inception about three months ago, and videotaped the confession and speeches of the lovers.

As the marriage of different ethnicity in Afghanistan and especially in Bamyan is counted as a taboo, the girl's family insisting in their daughter's return as well as so many other hands that get involved in this case.

As the girl doesn't want to return to her family, and the fact that it is involved a high risk of girl's murder if she gets back (as we saw in previous cases), the DoWA and other women's rights protector including the Governor Office, Independent Human Rights Commission and Civil Society Forum continues their advocacy for this lovers.

However, instead of supporting and protecting women's rights in Bamyan, the Provincial Court has ordered my suspension and two others from our job and prosecution just because we are following this case so closely and the FACT THAT MOST OF THE JUDGES in provincial court are from Tajik ethnicity.

You can contact Bamyan Governor Office, and the Independent Human Rights Commission to verify this information and plenty of other information that we have. I was wondering if you broadcast this news as you will protect the life of this couple and the fact that we are being threatened to death.

I'm looking forward to hearing from you,
Best regards.
Fatima Kazimi

I called her right away and asked a few exploratory questions— chiefly, would the couple talk and could we take pictures? Fatima said yes and maybe. That was good enough for me. We were on the next flight to Bamiyan, aboard East Horizon Airlines, which flies to Bamiyan, sometimes twice weekly, sometimes not for months on end. I took with me photojournalist Mauricio Lima and our Afghan colleague Jawad Sukhanyar. A year or two earlier, we could have driven the six to eight hours over one of the two passes through the Hindu Kush into Bamiyan, but both have now been effectively cut off, at least for foreigners, by intermittent Taliban ambushes.

I was already primed to jump on such a story and had long been looking for this sort of opportunity. Honor killings are more often than not one of Afghanistan's dirty little secrets; instances where they come into the open are rare, and it is even more rare to have a chance to write about stopping a threatened honor killing, especially when the parties were willing to talk and perhaps even be photographed. We were en route before Fatima had a chance to change her mind; I didn't even call her again, for fear she would reconsider, and the next time she heard from us, we were knocking on her office door in the Bamiyan government office building not far from the airstrip.

Fatima received us from behind an expansive glass-topped desk, framed by windows and the glare from sunlit snow, in a room with walls lined with chairs for supplicants. After summarizing what had happened to Zakia and Ali, Fatima went to fetch Zakia from the women's shelter, bringing her back to the office under a heavy guard, two green Ford Ranger pickup trucks full of policemen. Zakia had her shawl on but was dressed in loud, bright colors, as I would come to learn she usually was, a pink head scarf and an orange sweater. She caused a stir among the policemen and the government officials who lined the hallways as she was brought in; Afghans find her beautiful, with startlingly large, amber eyes.

She was tongue-tied at first. It was not only the first time she'd ever seen a journalist, it was the first time she'd ever seen a foreigner and the first time in her life that she'd ever talked to a male stranger—moreover, the first time she'd ever talked to a man other than Ali, and Anwar, and her brothers and father. "I knew, because of my case, I had to have that courage to speak. I realized that," she said much later, recalling how terrified she'd been that day.

Expressing herself seemed painful, but with Fatima gently nudging her along, her story poured out through Jawad, who translated. "My whole family is against my marriage," she said. "I want to go ahead anyway. I request of you, I don't want to stay in Bamiyan. I can live anywhere but in Bamiyan. All I want is my love.

"The judges told me, 'We are Tajik and it's dishonoring us if you decide to marry a Hazara.' The judges, my mother, and father were all saying this to me, but I told them whatever he might be, he's still a Muslim. I'm very worried about him and his safety. My father and relations threatened him, and I'm afraid they might do something. I get death threats from my family. They say if I go marry him, they will not let us live, and if I go home, my mother and father will not let me live."

Even her sister turned against her, she said. During a visit with her at the shelter, "she started screaming at me, using abusive words. You could hear her all over the building."

Zakia continued, "I love him, and now even if I don't get to marry him, I couldn't live here, I can't go back and stay here, I have to leave forever. I have confidence in him. I know his attitudes and his good moral character. I want to live with him."

In the court proceeding, Zaman could not argue that his daughter had run away or chosen an improper mate, since neither of those acts is a crime. But breaking an engagement *is* a matter for the Afghan courts, and so her father began his suit by claiming that she had been formally engaged to her nephew, which Zakia said was the first she had heard of it.

"They kept getting it mixed up, though," Fatima said with a laugh. "One minute they claimed she was engaged to her father's sister's son, the next it was her mother's sister's son. They should make up their minds before lying like that."

Zakia's account came out fitfully and slowly at first, with long, awkward silences and monosyllabic replies. The most extraordinary thing about her was the way her rare smile could suddenly illuminate her face, enlivening everything—eyes, lips, nose. It would flicker on like sunlight from a gap in a fast-moving cloud and be just as quickly gone. Her smile would transform her so thoroughly and so engagingly that you wanted to find some way to summon it back again.

I explained to her the probable consequences of an article quoting her openly. People in Bamiyan would see it through local Internet connections, however rickety. All news is global, especially if it appears in the *New York Times*. Local news organizations might well pick it up, too. Everything she said to us would likely be heard or read by everyone she knows; if her relatives could not read, someone who *could* read would relate it to them.

Zakia's only response was that she had already been in the shelter in Bamiyan for nearly five months. She had a point. In all that time, the closest she came to resolving her status had been the abortive February 3 court hearing.

At Fatima's suggestion we talked a bit about the shelter and the other girls and young women who were there. Some had been there for years already, unable to get legal resolution such as protection from an abusive spouse and unable to leave for fear of the vengeance of their menfolk—often on both sides of their families. The worst case at the shelter at the time was that of the fourteen-year-old girl Safoora, the Hazara girl who would later help Zakia escape from the shelter. Waylaid in the shabby Bamiyan courthouse while her family disputed details of their daughter's arranged marriage, Safoora was taken into a supply room and gang-raped by four Tajik courthouse employees. The police, Hazaras, arrested the culprits; the Tajik judges vacated the cases against all but one of them—and then charged him with adultery, a criminal offense in Afghanistan, rather than rape. Then the judges lodged a similar charge of adultery against Safoora. It was absurd, because even in Afghanistan a child can never give legal consent, even if the sex had been on some physical level "consensual"—however implausible that would be in a courthouse gang rape. While the women's advocates tried to get the criminal charges against her dismissed, Safoora was kept in the shelter—primarily to ensure that her family did not honor-kill her to erase their shame.

Fatima returned to Zakia's predicament, her point clear. "What do you think I should do?" Zakia asked her.

"You have to decide that for yourself." Fatima seemed the concerned, kindly auntie.

"Will it help us reach each other?" Zakia asked me.

"Possibly," I said, not convinced. "Possibly someone like your president would read about what happened and intervene, but honestly, probably not. On the other hand, what alternatives do you have now?"

This was a girl who had never been to school, who could neither read nor write, and whose knowledge of alphanumeric characters extended to just ten digits, 1 through 0 on the telephone keypad. Only one of the eleven children in Zakia's family, nine-year-old Razak, had ever been to school. Zakia sat with her back straight against the wall, her nose still bruised from the courtroom tussle. Her colorful layers of artificial silks, tunics, and pantaloons, in the brilliance of the glare, seemed cheap and tawdry when looked at individually, little holes and rips and tears showing here and there, but their overall effect was to enhance her attractiveness. She stared at the floor for most of our conversation, and I felt that she must be wondering, "Why are these foreigners interested in me?"

She thought about it for a spell. Then she raised her head and for the first time looked me right in the eye and said, "I don't mind," and smiled briefly.

Mauricio, the photographer, had been dozing, as photographers often do during interviews when there's nothing to shoot; now it was his turn to ask for permission to photograph her. This was even touchier than the interview. Photography of Afghan women is widely forbidden, notwithstanding some famous images—the iconic green-eyed refugee girl, Sharbat Gula, photographed by Steve McCurry for *National Geographic*,[4] for instance. Because Sharbat was a child, just twelve years old at the time, it was allowed, as it would have been for older women, usually widowed and desperate and therefore excused from the strictures that normally apply. Otherwise even shooting a woman in a head-to-toe burqa can provoke men in the vicinity, whether they're related to the woman or not, to attack a photographer. Asked for permission to be photographed, most young women in Afghanistan will understandably say no.[5]

This time, however, Zakia did not think about it long at all. "I don't mind," she said, and Mauricio got right to work. The mysteries of the camera's unblinking eye; I had fully expected that Mauricio would be returning to Kabul disappointed. Every interaction between photographer and subject is a kind of seduction, in one direction or the other, and that was true even between Zakia and Mauricio, a talented photographer who looks more like a nightclub bouncer and who firmly believes in the dictum that the best picture is taken up close. In this case he got six inches or so from her face, in an effort to compensate for the bright sunlight; he is a master of the awkward portrait. Zakia accepted it with equanimity; after a while she even seemed in some odd way empowered by the attention. She was a beautiful woman who it is safe to say had never been properly, if ever, photographed.[6] Here she was being shot by a pro, and she seemed to like it.

It was true that she had little to lose. Earlier she had talked about how large and close the members of her extended family were; in addition to her four brothers, there were many cousins, who in Afghanistan are often as close as siblings. In all, her family's tribe had thirty-five homes in the area. They would all be after Ali now, since they could not get to her in the shelter. "I would wait until I reach my love, no matter how long. But I'm very worried that my family is trying to harm his family, and I'm very worried about that. If he should die, I should also die."

"Are you sure about that?" Fatima cut in and asked her, a little startled by her declaration.

Zakia looked straight at her. "Of course."

Fatima frowned. She might have approved of romantic love, or at least the legal right to pursue it, but she had a low opinion of men, honed no doubt during two years of advocating in cases of violence against women brought under the EVAW law, and she didn't think any of them were worth dying for. She reminded Mauricio to take her own picture as well, which he dutifully did.

"This is my story, too," she said. "Don't forget that you have to write about me." She looked at me sternly; I made no comment.

Later Mauricio took Zakia and Fatima outside. As Fatima and

Zakia crossed the street, Mauricio crouching and shooting, their police escort went wild and began screaming and cursing at him. One policeman unshouldered his automatic rifle and aimed it at him. They did not think it right to photograph women, whether the women had agreed to it or not. After all, how can a woman possibly give consent without a man to speak for her?

To the policemen and many others in Afghan society, this encounter would likely encapsulate the disconnect between Afghan and Western culture. It meant something else altogether to Zakia.

"It gave me hope," she said. "I was happy, because now I knew there were people who wanted to help us and cared about us." The outside world might have been mysterious to both Zakia and Ali, but they felt it was something important, and its interest in them was somehow validating. As they well knew, in the eyes of their own society, in the rules and strictures of their culture, they were now outcasts. That these apparently important foreigners were accepting them on their own terms and seemed to feel that what the lovers wanted was not in the slightest unreasonable—and was even praiseworthy—seemed powerfully enabling to this pair of isolated young people.

We had already reached Ali on his cell phone, but he felt safest meeting us at the women's ministry. Fatima felt it would be best if that meeting did not take place on the same day as Zakia's visit, so her family's spies in the government couldn't claim that Fatima was arranging assignations between them.

Ali came the next day, and it was not surprising that he was a handsome young man and a tad vain about his looks. His lush black hair was swept up and back in a pompadour, his beard close-shaven, his trousers tight, and his artificial saddle-leather shoes both pointy and holey. Like Zakia, he was poor, but he had style. His eyes were an arresting shade of golden amber, and what was most striking—I had to check the pictures of Zakia to be sure—nearly the same rare color as hers. On his cheek was a prominent, deep-set bruise, and I asked about it.

"Since this love story began, I have had two bad accidents," he said.

Since this love story began. I would soon learn that Ali often referred to Zakia and himself as the participants in a love story, as if some higher power had written it for them and they were mere mortals acting out their roles.

The first accident that he referred to was when the Humvee he was in while on military duty rolled, three years earlier, and ruined his leg. The second "accident" was the bruise his brother Ismatullah gave him when Ali tried to get to Zakia as she pleaded for his father to take her in.

Unlike Zakia, Ali was never surprised that people were interested in their story and what had befallen them. It seemed to him natural and inevitable. "Our story is the same as Shirin and Farhad," he said. "We are stuck in such a story."

It is an old Persian story, immensely popular in Afghanistan and retold in many forms in popular culture, but particularly in folk and pop songs. Shirin, the beautiful princess, tells the stonecutter Farhad that she is promised to the prince but that if he could move a mountain for her with his pickax, she would marry him instead. So he sets about carving the face off a nearby mountain, and when the prince sees he has nearly finished what had seemed an impossible task, he sends a witch to whisper to Farhad that Shirin has already married the prince. Despondent, he kills himself, and when she finds that out, she, too, kills herself.

How is this their story? I asked Ali. "If in this temporary world, they don't reach each other, then God knows they might be able to do so in the next world," he explained. Every great love must be doomed to experience its happy endings in some afterlife, it seems, whether Romeo and Juliet or Shirin and Farhad? He didn't know the story of Romeo and Juliet, so we summarized it for him; he especially liked the ending. "My ambition is also the same. Even if I were killed with my fiancée, I would have reached my ambition. If they separated us, I would commit suicide."

A pattern was beginning to emerge in the passions of this shabby, earnest young man with the shining amber eyes that seemed to light up when he started telling stories, whether his and her more recent ones or those ancient tales. When we called him the day

before to arrange meeting him, his ringtone had been a love verse
from a song retelling the story of Yousef and Zuleikha. Today's was
some lines from an Indian musical about Layla and Majnoon. The
Persian poet Nezami's epic retelling of the old Arabian story has
circulated in one version or another throughout the subcontinent
as well, and it traditionally includes these Arabic verses:

> I pass through the lands of Layla,
> Kissing now this wall, now that wall:
> It is not these lands that I love,
> But the one who dwells within.[7]

Ali has of course never read poetry, but his illiteracy has not
robbed him of literature, to be sure. It was all there, set to music.

That is how their courtship progressed, in those long, numerous telephone conversations that began when she was still just past
childhood and he not yet quite an adult. Over and over they re-
played for each other the moment they fell in love, the moment
they knew, how they knew. For Ali, what those many months in
the army were like and his fear of being rejected because of his
deformity (as he imagined it to be). For Zakia, the months during
which she wished she had said to him something different from
what she had, when he proposed across the wall. When they ran
out of gossip about the people they knew, or talk of farm life, or
antics of children and animals, he would tell her a story, often one
he had told before. Her favorite was Yousef and Zuleikha, the Islamic version of the biblical story of the Prophet Joseph (he of the
Amazing Technicolor Dreamcoat). In the Islamic telling, Yousef is sold
as a slave to Potiphar and falls in love with Potiphar's wife, Zuleikha (who is named only in the Islamic versions, not in the biblical story), but is banished. He finds his love thirty years later, when
he has gained freedom, prestige, and power and she has become an
old woman but still loves him. One kiss and she is a young beauty
again. It is not only a popular story among Afghans and in many
Muslim societies, it is also a sacred story, recounted in the Koran
approvingly—despite the themes of romantic love triumphing over

married rectitude, which are explained theologically as love of a higher sort than the carnal, romantic kind.

"I asked her how she liked it," Ali said. "Her reply to me was that I am ready to wait for you for fifty years."

The first article that I did in the *New York Times* after that trip up to Bamiyan had already generated tremendous interest. But I really began to be deluged with reader mail after I wrote on March 31[8] about Zakia's escape from the shelter and the couple's elopement, with police pursuing them as criminals and Zakia's family after them as well—a story I might have missed if Shmuley hadn't alerted me. Many of those readers demanded that something had to be done to help Zakia and Ali. Not a few readers upbraided me, too: "You've drawn attention to them, now do something about it," one wrote. Little did I appreciate at the time how prophetic those words would become. "Can't the *New York Times* just send a plane in and get them out?" If only it were so simple. None of them were quite as insistent as the rabbi from New Jersey, though, and unlike many of the others, he had a plan, or at least part of a plan. He had a wealthy benefactress, he said, who was determined to spend whatever was required to save the couple's lives, which of course meant getting them to safety somewhere outside Afghanistan. A very wealthy benefactress. Shmuley was not just any rabbi but "America's rabbi," as his own website and some news accounts[9] described him; he was the late singer Michael Jackson's rabbi, he was a television personality, a columnist, a passionate defender of Israel, a self-promoter, a Republican politician, and a friend of Sean Penn and Oprah Winfrey. He runs an organization called the World Values Network,[10] which seeks to promote Jewish values among the wider community, and he has prominent political friends on both sides of the ideological divide in America. He is a consummate networker, a talent he developed during years as Cambridge University's resident rabbi,[11] when he actively invited the interesting and the powerful to speaking and debating engagements and made many lasting friends. He is also an author; his best-known book is *Kosher Sex* and his most recent is *Kosher Lust*.[12] Both are more serious than their titles might suggest and, among other things, promote Shmuley's vision that Jews should make more children—he himself has nine.

Rabbi Shmuley had managed to find Fatima Kazimi's contacts through some social-networking site after he saw her name in the paper, and he'd gotten in touch with her independently. After that first article on Zakia and Ali ran, Fatima was disappointed that the story hadn't focused on her and on her efforts to save the couple, and for a while she'd stopped talking to us. But she was talking to Shmuley, actively. The rabbi had become my back channel to a women's activist in the Hindu Kush, which was only a couple of mountain ranges away from my bureau in Kabul.

The outpouring of interest and offers of help made me feel guilty about the various forces I had unleashed. Would all this publicity really help Zakia and Ali? "You're responsible for them now, I hope you know that," one reader wrote. He had a point. In ways that are hard to fathom, all the publicity had emboldened the couple to make the move they did. Later, when I had occasion to ask Zakia what had given them the courage to flee together, she looked at me with surprise. "Because we knew there were people who cared about us. We knew you would help us." That was an awful leap of faith, but to them it was as if they were no longer alone; if we were interested, so many others would be, and some-how—in ways they had really not thought through very fully—that would solve everything. They were no longer just Zakia and Ali; they were the *story* of Zakia and Ali, which was bigger than they were and as full of promise as it was fraught with danger.

It would not have been the first time that the glare of publicity saved an Afghan woman from an unhappy fate. In 2012 a young woman named Lal Bibi was abducted by a member of an Afghan Local Police (ALP) unit in Kunduz. The ALP are irregular militias that are trained by American Special Forces troops to act as community self-protection. At best they are a well-armed neighborhood watch; at worse they can be a criminal scourge on the communities they're meant to protect. One of the ALP militiamen, who was named Khudaidad, claimed he was entitled to take Lal Bibi in marriage because of an old *baad* contract, an agreement made when she was very young as the result of a dispute between their families. *Baad* is a common practice, in which young girls are exchanged to compensate for a marital infidelity, a murder or other transgression, or just to settle a debt. Lal Bibi and her family claimed there had been no such agreement, and they pressed charges against Khudaidad for raping her and accused three members of his unit, including its commander, of aiding him in her abduction and rape. He calmly defended himself against the charge by claiming he had married her shortly before the rape, and, he told the *New York Times*,[13] "Once the marriage contract is done, any sexual intercourse is not considered rape."

Lal Bibi may have objected to her marriage, but that was forcible marriage, a lesser crime, rather than rape, he said. The policeman produced a mullah who confirmed he had performed the marriage rite before any intercourse took place. The unusual thing about Lal Bibi's case was not so much what had happened to her but that her family members decided to go public about it. After a national outcry, President Hamid Karzai intervened and ordered the ALP unit disbanded. It was but was then quickly replaced with another ALP unit headed by the brother of the commander of the first unit. (Once again a unit allegedly trained and mentored by American special-operations troops). Defying threats and intimidation from the *arbakai* and their friends, Lal Bibi's family traveled to Kabul, where prosecutors eventually sentenced all four police officials involved to sixteen years in prison. During his trial Khudaidad dropped his insistence on the marriage defense and came up with a more novel one. He asked that Lal Bibi's veil be removed during the trial so that, he said, the court could see that she was far too ugly for anyone to have wanted to rape her.[14]

Women's advocates lobbied hard in support of Lal Bibi and her family in that case, and it was a rare win for a female victim of violence.

If Lal Bibi's impoverished and disenfranchised family could prevail against American-backed militiamen, normally accustomed to impunity for their actions, perhaps Zakia and Ali's case was not entirely hopeless. Now that they were free, everything had changed. The sort of money and support that people were offering them could well prove decisive in finding a solution for them, either by paying her family a large enough bride price to go away peaceably or by making it financially plausible for the couple to escape the country. Their story did not have to end there, in some rotting Afghan lockup or at the business end of someone's vengeful bludgeon. Unfortunately, Zakia and Ali seemed to be well and truly gone. For the moment at least, they had decided that disappearing was a safer bet than waiting around for help, even though it meant that no one could find them to offer that help.

5

A BEAUTIFUL PLACE TO HIDE

In plain sight is a good hiding place until it becomes the one place searchers realize they have neglected to look. Zakia and Ali were keenly aware that their time hiding in the house of the village's most prominent citizen was running out. By the end of March, the whole country seemed aroused by the search for the escaped lovers. The Bamiyan police might have been sympathetic to their plight and naturally tended to side with Hazaras, but once Zakia had fled the shelter, she was that most despised of Afghan women, a runaway. The Ministry of Interior in Kabul was leaning on the Bamiyan police to pursue the matter. It was all over Afghan television and radio, on the country's airwaves and news websites— many of which showed no hesitation about lifting and republishing Mauricio Lima's portraits of the lovers from NYTimes.com. The police questioned the Bamiyan shelter's staff and arrested two of its guards, holding them for investigation, although they were ultimately released, since they were guilty of nothing more than falling asleep or not paying enough attention. Fatima Kazimi, the women's-ministry official in Bamiyan, was besieged in her office by Zakia's father and a dozen of his male relatives, who accused her of engineering the escape. Ali's brother Bismillah was arrested and held for four days, his cousin Sattar jailed for two days, and his other brother Ismatullah, himself a police officer, was pressured by his bosses to come clean on his fugitive brother's whereabouts.

Najeeba Ahmadi, the director of the shelter in Bamiyan, felt more than official heat. "I believe that her family would do anything possible against Zakia," Najeeba said. "They even keep calling me using different numbers and threatening me that if they don't get Zakia, they will run me out of Bamiyan or they will kill me to take revenge for Zakia. They don't care how peacefully I try to communicate."

A male voice would come on the line of her personal cell phone. "You've taken our daughter and hidden her somewhere. You know where she is, but you are not telling us. So, for us, you and the girl are the same, and you will both face the consequences."

While all that was going on up in Bamiyan, down in Kabul I was spending an hour every morning wading through reader e-mail, mainly from concerned Americans who assumed I somehow must know how to find the couple and deliver aid to them. Rabbi Shmuley was reenergized to pursue the case. He asked me if I could act as a go-between with the couple, to let them know he had someone standing by ready to rescue them.

"We would like to communicate to them, that we want to help them get out of the country and establish a new life elsewhere where they are not in danger," Shmuley wrote in an e-mail. "But now we have no way of contacting them. If you can assist us with that, I would be very grateful. Please indeed ask them permission, as to whether or not we can be in touch with them."

I was uncomfortable acting as anyone's go-between, but I didn't feel I should just rebuff Shmuley's enthusiastic and heartfelt concern for the couple. My editor in New York, Doug Schorzman, took the matter up with Phil Corbett, the paper's standards editor, and Phil agreed I could introduce Shmuley to an Afghan fixer and translator, so he could have someone who could reach out to Zakia and Ali independently of us. It was also felt that we could share the phone numbers of principals, so long as we had permission from them to do so. Through our Afghan staff, we found a freelance fixer well respected for his integrity, Aimal Yaqubi, who had previously worked for National Public Radio.

That all proved academic, though. Ali was not answering his phone, which was continually giving an "out of coverage area" message, so we couldn't get his permission to give the number to anyone. His father and brothers claimed to have no idea where the two lovers were, other than somewhere in the mountains, and said they too could not reach Ali by telephone. It turned out later that the family had been constrained from saying anything about the couple's whereabouts because Zakia and Ali did not want them to do so.

Zakia's father was on their trail, too. When we interviewed him, it was clear that he had already developed an intimate knowledge about the couple's movements in the days after Zakia's flight from the shelter. He related to us where they had stayed on the first and second nights on the run, the name of the mullah who had attended and tied the *neka* for them, the next place they had stopped farther up the Foladi Valley toward Shah Foladi, and how the police had lost them on the road near the village of Azhdar.

What he didn't suspect, at least not yet, was that they weren't in the mountains any longer but had circled back to Ali's village and were hiding a mere three hundred yards from where Zaman was talking to us at that moment.

"I will not let it go," he said, sitting cross-legged on the floor of his house, his smallest children clustered on either side of him; from oldest to youngest, his brood spanned nearly three decades, with one wife. "I swear to God that even if it costs me everything, I will try to bring my daughter back home. She is a part of my body like one of my limbs—how can I let her go with that boy? Besides that, she was already married, and it is unthinkable to remarry someone else's wife who is already married to someone. It is against every law and shariah. There is no way that I should let her marry that boy."

This accusation of bigamy was a bombshell. Previously Zaman had claimed in court that he had engaged Zakia to his nephew—

and he famously kept changing which aunt had the nephew in question. Now that his daughter had married Ali, he was raising the stakes and claiming that a previous marriage had occurred, that a *neka* had already been tied between Zakia and her first cousin. It is plausible, and even commonplace, for a father to tie a *neka* without his daughter's presence—that is, to marry her to someone formally. All he has to do is swear before a mullah and other witnesses that she has given her consent. Her consent is required, officially, but in practice there is no requirement that such consent needs to be proved, other than by the father's oath. So now to support the bigamy charge, all Zaman would have to do is find a friendly mullah and some like-minded witnesses, then backdate a *neka* document. Even within this new account, he kept muddling his story: At one moment Zakia had run away with the boy; minutes later the boy had kidnapped her. She had escaped from the shelter; Ali had forcibly removed her from it. And so on.

Zaman at first glance did not seem formidable enough to do much of anything. He looked much older than his approximately sixty years, with skin as wrinkled as dried fruit; he was slight and stooped. Five of his eleven children were younger than Zakia, some much younger; the smallest appeared to be not four years old. He was obviously poor, but he also had sons, and cousins, and sons-in-law, and they all crowded into the living room to back him up. "I do not give up easily," he said. "If someone loses his chicken, he will search for it to bring it home. How can I not search for my daughter, who was part of my own liver? I can do everything to get her back. I will try to approach the president, and if that doesn't work, I will decide myself to do something. We are not weak in that sense."

He denied he was threatening any violence—he did not have so much as a nail file to use for a weapon, he said—but the spittle that accompanied his words, the harsh tone, all suggested otherwise, as did the death threats he and his sons had uttered in front of many witnesses in the Bamiyan courthouse. Zaman seemed like nothing so much as a dead daughter's father.

There was no pretense of impotence from Zakia's brother Gula

Khan, who was about twenty or twenty-one. When I reached him by telephone around this time, he screamed at me over the line. His tone told more than his words, which were themselves so blunt and profane they shocked and embarrassed my Afghan colleague Jawad. It was only after I insisted several times that Jawad not hold back that he fully translated Gula Khan's responses to my questions.

"If we were men, we would have done something by now," he said. "If we had cocks, we would take our revenge. How is it possible they steal someone's wife and do not even pay any attention to how we are suffering?

"She really dishonored our family, and the man she was promised to is asking for repayment. He has told us, either find his wife for him and return her or give him ten lakhs of rupees."[1]

"Their whole world was turned upside down when their daughter ran away with a man," said Women for Afghan Women's executive director, Manizha Naderi. Her organization runs seven women's shelters, although not the one in Bamiyan,[2] and Manizha is easily the most effective women's advocate in Afghanistan. "This really shattered their sense of honor within their family and their community. They have no credibility to hold their heads up in front of anyone because of Zakia. And to get their honor back, they think that they have to kill both Ali and especially Zakia. That way they can tell their relatives, 'We are men of honor. We killed her. Our honor is more important than our daughter who has shamed us.' It's really tragic, but most families think this way in Afghanistan. They would rather kill their female family members if they are thought to have committed wrongdoing than lose face in their community."

"Honor," as Afghans use the word, doesn't have the same meanings we would give it, behavior characterized by decency and honesty that brings public esteem and respect to a person. They don't even use it in the connotation of purity or chastity when applied to women (which is definition 7 in the 2015 *Merriam-Webster Dictionary*). "Honor," to Afghan men, is much more of a synonym for "women," particularly women of reproductive age seen as the property of their men. The further sense of treating a woman honorably—that is, not deceiving her sexually or romantically—is missing, which comes as a bit of a surprise considering how often honor is invoked in the treatment of women in Afghanistan.

The Dari word for "honor," *namoos*,[3] in the connotations we would give it, does not exist in the venerable Persian dictionary, the *Dekhoda*. Instead the only use of the word that has come down to Afghans as "honor," from that dictionary, means esteem and respect given for upholding and defending religious faith. Afghans do conflate honor with both religion and women, since they use religion as justification for their treatment of women (often on dubious theological grounds), but that layer of meaning is often lost as Afghans use "honor" today. Consider the notorious Article 398 of the Afghan Penal Code, which limits the punishment of *men* for murder to only two years' imprisonment for crimes of passion against women in their families. (There is no similar limitation of punishment for women who commit crimes of passion.) Article 398 says, as Kabul University law professor and women's activist Shahla Farid pointed out, that the punishment of men for murder is limited in cases where actions of the victims affect the man's honor, and it implicitly defines "their honor" as "including wives, sisters, daughters, nieces, aunts, mothers and other female relatives." In other words, as Dr. Farid translates it in Article 398, "honor" is legally defined as the women in a man's life over whom he has ownership or control. And that is how Afghans do use the term.[4]

When Afghan men say, as they often do, "We are a poor people, and all we have is our honor," what they are really saying is, "We are a poor people, and all we have is our women." Hence purdah and the Afghans' fanatical obsession with keeping their womenfolk out of public view. Hence the attitude that rape is not a crime, since women should never be in a position to be raped. If rape does happen, there has to have been some behavioral breakdown in the family of the victim; either the family did not keep her safe or she evaded their security.

I heard similar words from Zakia's father, Zaman, repeatedly. "I am a poor man. All I have is my honor." It was why it seemed logical to him to equate the loss of his daughter with the theft of one of his chickens; she was just a far more valuable piece of property.

Shortly after we met with Zaman, we went over to the village of Surkh Dar nearby and talked to Anwar, Ali's father, as well. We told Anwar about Zaman's intimate knowledge of the first days of their flight. Later Anwar related this information to Zakia and Ali, which persuaded them to set off on the run again. It seemed clear to them that Zakia's father knew someone who had seen them along the way, so it might not take him long to figure out that turning north at Azhdar village and heading back into the valley would have been much easier for an ill-equipped pair of fugitives than tackling the forbidding, snow-covered heights of sixteen-thousand-foot Shah Foladi.

Anwar was adamant that no previous marriage had ever taken place, that it was a ploy invented by a bitter father after the fact, but he was worried about the implications. Bigamy was both a crime and a terrible sin (for a woman, not a man, who can traditionally have four wives in Afghanistan), and Ali could be charged as well with kidnapping, a capital offense. In theory they could be stoned to death, because bigamy was also adultery.

Anwar tugged at his white beard nervously and asked if we could help Zakia and Ali.

Perhaps, if we could find them.

Jawad was convinced that the old man knew where they were and probably had Ali's current phone number as well but that he'd stopped trusting us when he realized we had also been talking to Zakia's family. He had come a long way from the angry father defending the cultural status quo, who beat his son for trying to bring dishonor on the community; just what had led to this transformation would take us a while to work out, but he had definitely taken Ali and Zakia's side.

The cris de coeur from *New York Times* readers had convinced me that we needed to bring the story up to date and raise its profile beyond just a print effort. Editors agreed and felt that now that the lovers were together, getting pictures of them with each other would be key to keeping interest high. People needed to see them together for them to become real; it was a love story as well as a look into the dark heart of a deeply disturbed society and the social and cultural obstacles that had prevented much meaningful progress on women's rights in Afghanistan. Without pictures the lovers' story would remain essentially abstract, lacking the power to move people—perhaps even someone who could do something to help. All we had was Mauricio Lima's portraits of the two of them, taken separately, so the paper assigned another photographer, in case we found them again, and a videographer to do a story on their romance and escape.[5]

That was all theoretical, since there could be no visuals un-less we did find them, and no one was talking about where they might be. They had left their home village of Surkh Dar in secrecy shortly after our interviews with the fathers. First Zakia, at night in a full-length shawl, accompanied by Ali's mother, had taken a taxi to the town of Nayak Bazaar, the administrative center of the mountainous district of Yakawlang. A relative had agreed to put Zakia and Chaman up for one night, but not the couple together, who would be too easily spotted. The next night Ali and his father similarly took a taxi up to Nayak Bazaar, and Anwar left the couple together there. They had thought they would easily find a place to stay but realized that people had begun looking at them suspi-ciously. Separately they could evade detection, but together they were Zakia and Ali, and people could readily add it up. In these remote mountain places, every stranger sticks out.

The road they took up to Nayak Bazaar was a spanking-new, Japanese-built highway for the first forty miles or so, quite possibly the best road in the country for as long as it lasted. There had been an unusually large amount of snow late that winter, and in their flight they passed the newly groomed ski slopes on the flanks of the Koh-i-Baba range, which at the time were still being patronized by a smattering of late-season Western skiers.[6] The road between Bamiyan and Band-e-Amir is so good that there's even a Western-funded NGO[7] devoted to promoting women's cycling that uses it for bike touring, a sport previously unknown to Afghan women and rather awkward for someone in a burqa.

The paved road ended after Nayak Bazaar. With Zakia clutching two plastic bags of clothing and Ali a small backpack, they walked up a dirt road out of the town and then left it for a trail up into the mountains. That first night they ended up sleeping outdoors, with a fire beside the path, and then the next day they walked all day until they came to the village of Kham-e Bazargan, where they knew there was a home with distant relatives who had long ago been neighbors in Surkh Dar village. They had not realized how spread out Kham-e Bazargan was; it extended along the highway through the spectacular Yakawlang Gorge for miles, and the little market area was far from the homestead they sought. Ali had been there once, but many years before, and by car, not by foot. That night, rather than enter the market and run into the wrong person, they took refuge in a cave in an area so barren they could not find enough sticks for a fire. These mountains were not as high as the Koh-i-Baba, but they still rose up to fourteen thousand feet and in those first weeks of April were still partly snow-covered. The days were as sunny and mild as the nights were harsh and cold. After a second night in the cave, they finally found the home of Zahra and Haji Abdul Hamid, which sat on its own promontory above the Yakawlang River, in a steep gorge with towering mountains on either side.

It was a typical rural Afghan home, a compound surrounded by a wall of mud wattle that enclosed gardens and yards, with several interconnected mud-brick buildings that gave private areas for the wives of the sons and communal areas for the men. There were three other homes nearby in the tiny hamlet on that knoll, but they all belonged to close relatives. The hamlet could be seen from the main well-graded dirt road, but it was a mile's hike away, down into the bottomland, across the river on a shaky log bridge, and then back up the steep knoll on which the homestead stood.

Not for the first time, Zakia and Ali approached the home with no guarantee of what reception awaited them. They were former neighbors, distantly related like nearly everyone in their village, but still they had no way to know for sure how these people would react. Fortunately, when the couple related to Haji and Zahra what had happened to them the past couple weeks, the older couple readily agreed to give them refuge.

"At any home, when we were running, we would knock on the door and say, 'We are running because we're in love,' and usually they would take us in and help us," Ali said. "It was not because we were Hazaras and they were Hazaras. It's because everyone has at least once experienced love in their early lives, and they knew what it meant to be in love, even if they didn't have their love with them still. Even the governor, when Zakia-*jan* was in the shelter, she said, 'It's not because you're Hazara that I'm helping you but because she loves you and she shouldn't be without you.'"[8]

The house of Zahra and Haji was the first place where Zakia and Ali had felt safe since their flight from Bamiyan town. It, too, was a mud-brick dwelling, but the window frames were all of hand-planed lumber, painted a cheerful sky blue; the compound was freshly swept and as clean as a place with packed earthen floors could be. The roof was supported with battens of crooked birch trunks. In the bottomland wheat and potato seedlings were already sprouting, the green making a startling contrast with the dull brown and pale golden colors of the dirt slopes above. Higher on the mountainside, another green smudge had started to appear, a dusting of grass sprouts, watered by the still-melting snow. "It was good to begin a new life with greenery and spring," Ali later said. They took walks in the steep grazing lands, reminiscent of the slopes where they spent their childhoods together herding sheep. It was as close to a honeymoon as they were likely to have. "They seemed so happy together," Zahra said. "For the whole week they were here, they were never fighting or angry."

Then one day Zahra's children came home from school and said other kids had asked them who they were hiding. An old woman, another distant relative from Surkh Dar, heard what the schoolkids were saying. She stopped into Zahra's house on her way home and spotted the couple.

Haji told them they would have to leave soon; it was only a matter of time before word got from the old lady back to Surkh Dar and then to either Zakia's family in Kham-e-Kalak or to the authorities in Bamiyan town. That evening Ali climbed to the top of the mountain, where he was able to get a cell-phone signal, and called his father. He and Zakia were down to their last thousand afghanis, about twenty dollars, and out of places to go. Anwar was also nearly broke and could not afford the cost of a taxi to reach them. "Call the journalists," Ali said. "Maybe they can bring you to us." His father said he would try, but he wasn't at all sure he could trust us; he said he would also try to raise some money from relatives.

My colleague Jawad had been doggedly calling Anwar every day looking for news, and he reached him shortly after he spoke to his son. Anwar said he did not know for sure where his son was, but he was running out of money and he wanted to try to find him. He agreed to help us reach him in the hopes that our involvement in the case could get the couple out of the country. We were on the next morning's flight to Bamiyan. At the airstrip there we were met by our two most experienced *Times* office drivers, Fareed and Kabir, who had crossed the Hindu Kush from Kabul by car overnight; the risk of Taliban checkpoints was too great for any but the most foolhardy foreigners to travel by land. Fareed and Kabir took the precaution of stripping their cars, their persons, and the contents of their phones clean of association with foreigners; there have been occasions when the Taliban have murdered travelers in the Ghorband Valley route to the Shibar Pass simply for having dollars in their wallets rather than afghanis.

We set out early in the morning, picking up Anwar and his son Bismillah a mile outside of Surkh Dar, lest Zaman's family spot us, and began driving up into the heart of the central highlands. We were in two cars, with eight people including the drivers. Also with Jawad and me were Ben C. Solomon, a *Times* videographer[9] and Diego Ibarra Sánchez, a still photographer who was on assignment for us then. Anwar was cautious about telling us where we were going, and Jawad said it was clear that he still wasn't sure if he could trust us and was trying to decide whether he should. We shifted passengers around so Jawad and I could sit with the old man and Bismillah, and for the next couple of hours we set about trying to win Anwar's trust and confidence. We assured him we would never give away Zakia and Ali's location nor divulge his role or that of his sons in helping to hide them.

Stopping in Nayak Bazaar, we all had a breakfast of freshly baked loaves of round flatbread and oily eggs in a long, low room with plastic sheeting stretched in front of the windows to keep the sun's heat in, greenhouse style. Our presence in the bazaar, which was just a half-mile-long strip of shops along the muddy road, caused a commotion. Two carloads of foreigners were hardly low-profile; we might as well have been a traveling circus. We worked out with Anwar a plan to keep the photographers away from the couple's hiding place, once we found it, until we could discern if it was safe or not for the couple to join us—and whether they were willing and able to cooperate.

I had deep misgivings and a growing sense of guilt; it seemed likely that we would expose the couple if we did find them, without any guarantee that a more visual story about them would save their lives. In fact, the opposite could happen: It might make them easier for their pursuers to find. I thought about aborting it all but then thought that if the old man wanted us to come, it might be the right thing to do. This could not be great country to be a fugitive in for long; there just weren't enough places to hide unless you really were staying in caves, and for how long could they possibly do that? The remotest corners of Afghanistan were populated, if thinly, and they would have to go out to get water and food.

It was especially difficult for a woman to hide anywhere in this society. Amina, the teenager who was killed after fleeing her family's arranged marriage in Balkh Province,[10] was picked up by the police within an hour of her arrival, during daytime, at the bazaar in the provincial capital, Pul-e-Kumri. Bibi Aisha, sold as a child bride to a Taliban commander, fled when her husband was away fighting and went to the nearest market town, where police promptly picked her up and returned her to the family, even though in that area it would have been clear it was a Taliban family. She is the girl whose nose was cut off by that husband as punishment for having run away and later she was featured on the cover of *Time* magazine.[11] Even being with a man is sufficient camouflage only if the man is taken for a brother or husband, and Afghans are quick to sniff out ones who are not. When sixteen-year-old Soheila,[12] given away in marriage years before she was born to an elderly man, fled with her cousin Niaz Mohammad, the two were repeatedly stopped by police, even before her family pursued them. Policemen somehow could tell they weren't married.

How much harder it would be for the lovers to successfully flee with foreigners in their vicinity. In the course of our search for them, we were conspicuous as probably the only Westerners within a hundred miles. For several hours we wended our way up the Yakawlang Gorge, a place of spectacular but forbidding views and only this one dusty road, no side roads at all for many miles at a stretch. When we reached Kham-e Bazargan and the homestead where they were hiding, Anwar continued to insist on the fiction that he did not know where they were. Instead he said he would go and ask directions from that distant homestead on the little knoll, a mile off the highway. Worried that if they *were* hiding there, our presence would surely give them away, I told the drivers to split up our cars a little, parking a mile apart, and persuaded the photographers to keep their gear and themselves out of sight. For them this long trip without the prospect of a single frame was a bitter pill, which both Ben and Diego took with a mixture of equanimity and frustration.

Anwar and Bismillah came back at a trot. This indeed was where the pair were hiding, and Zakia was still there—but not Ali. The night before, Haji had told them they would have to leave today; Ali took off before dawn—they weren't sure where to, but probably he hitchhiked to the next village, three hours' drive away. Haji had gone in pursuit, furious that Ali had not taken Zakia with him as Haji had asked. He took the minibus he owns, which plies the mountain roads as an informal, private bus service. As bad as all that was, it was a godsend that solved our conundrum: the worry that we would inadvertently give away the couple's location and compromise their safety. We had found them just as they were in the process of eviction, and that had nothing to do with us.

Zakia refused to come out even to talk to us, however, until her husband returned—even with her father-in-law, Anwar, there. We sat down with Anwar and Zahra to wait and to discuss what had transpired. "I'm deeply concerned. They have to go now, I did it just for God's sake to help them," Zahra said. "I support what they did—they love each other—but the problem is if it comes to a dispute between families, they might kill each other, and they might kill us, too. They might kill them and cut them into pieces."

Haji returned, having been unable to find Ali, but friends had called him to say that Nayak Bazaar was full of rumors that the pair were hiding in his place; they told him he should expect the police to arrive soon to apprehend them. "The police could arrest all of us for this," he said, apologetic but adamant. "Now they're calling it a kidnapping." He wanted us to leave immediately, taking Zakia with us. But she refused to emerge from the women's quarters, Zahra was not going to force her, and none of the men would dare enter. I promised Haji we would take them with us the moment Ali returned, which then put us in the uncomfortable position of providing them with getaway cars, but there seemed to be no alternative. I justified it by saying that we would use the car journey as a means to interview and photograph them in safety, which we could no longer do at Haji's house without putting them all at risk of arrest. I was also uncomfortably aware that we were stepping over that line that separates journalists and their subjects. We were becoming part of the story, whatever we might tell ourselves; more accurately, whatever *I* might tell myself and, as the person in charge, compel the others to go along with.

While we waited, Zahra told us about her hopes for her six children, who were all in school; her eldest, an eighteen-year-old, Ahmed Zia, was first in his class in twelfth grade, wanted to go to university to become an engineer, and was proud that he'd just been able to vote in the presidential election for the first time. (When we later spoke to Ahmed Zia, he was contemptuous about Ali and Zakia. "What they did was wrong," he said. He would never tolerate one of his young sisters behaving like that, he said. But neither would he give Zakia and Ali away, out of respect for his parents.) Zahra herself could read and write but had only a few years of school; her husband was a schoolteacher as well as a landowner. None of this could have been possible in Afghanistan a decade ago; in fact, Zakia and Ali could not have been possible, Zahra said. If today they were pursued by society and its laws, it was only the fault of ignorant, uneducated people like their neighbor. "That stupid woman," Zahra kept calling her.

So much had changed since the Taliban time, Zahra mused, when she taught her daughters in secrecy in her home, since the Taliban had closed all the girls' schools.[13] Now they could study openly, and the Hazara girls in their community did so. They could watch Bollywood love stories on television and listen to romantic music on radios and mobile telephones, which also had all been forbidden. Yet they still lived in the shadow of that time. The Taliban had injected something new and malevolent into Afghanistan's intensely private culture: the concept that honor, as it applied to women, was not an issue just for the man whose honor was at stake, the man who owned those women. Instead it was something that concerned everyone; not only the state but every man had the obligation to enforce honor, as he saw it. The Taliban had gone, but the intrusive attitude of its notorious Ministry for the Promotion of Virtue and Suppression of Vice was left behind, among people like "that awful woman," as Zahra called her. Or, for that matter, among the Bamiyan police, who were then pursuing an eighteen-year-old for the supposed crime of fleeing a place where she was staying legally and voluntarily.

Anwar sat cross-legged, alternately dialing his son's cell phone and looking out the window. The photographer, Diego, was restless and had disappeared; later we discovered he'd gone into the kitchen, in the women's quarters, and found Zakia, posing her under a beam of sunlight coming through a chimney hole in the mud roof. Diego was fond of his sunbeams and was forever trying to find them in the dark dwellings of Afghanistan. He said he hadn't understood that men were not allowed in the women's quarters; it was a serious cultural breach, one that could easily get a man killed in the wrong house. Diego's English was semifluent but spotty; it was hard to be sure what he didn't understand, versus what he chose not to understand if it got in the way of a picture.

I asked Anwar how it came to pass that, having beaten his son for starting his affair with Zakia, he now was going to the ends of the earth for him. "It is true that I punished him then, but now I have changed my mind. It happened because I saw that my daughter-in-law stood behind my son and was brave enough to say she loves my son, and now it is an honor for us to stand behind her," he said.

Zahra teared up listening to him.

"Now she is a part of my family, she is my own daughter. She is a part of my family now, and I would do anything for her as well as for him. Even more for her." As an answer it was pretty unsatisfactory, little better than a handy if heartfelt slogan. It was more likely that once Zakia's family began publicly denouncing their son and threatening his life, Anwar's pride and that of his sons was challenged, and perhaps that pushed them to rally to his side. Zaman's pride wanted to see his daughter dead; Anwar's pride would see his daughter-in-law honored instead.

About midafternoon Ali finally showed up, his arrival heralded by half a dozen children from the compound who had staked out the path from the road; again he had hitchhiked. It turned out he had gone to a village farther up the highway where he thought he could contact us by cell phone; instead we had by then reached his hiding place, where *our* phones only worked from the hilltops.

His ringtone that day, which we heard sometimes when we climbed the slopes to call him, praying we would get through to him before the police arrived, was a Pashto love song by Latif Nangarhari:

> Come here, my little flower, come!
> Let me tear open my breast
> And show you my own heart, naked.[14]

It was an emotional few minutes as Zakia packed Ali's bag for him and gathered her own plastic bags into one larger sack. We explained that we would give them a ride to the nearest safe place and wanted to interview them and photograph them on the journey as we went, so long as we could do it without compromising them further. They were strangely quiet and calm, even oddly cheerful at the prospect of this next leg of the run, while everyone else was taking it hard. They understood that there was no other course of action; everyone else felt complicit in forcing it upon them.

I asked Zakia why she did not wear the all-covering burqa to disguise herself as they fled, and she laughed scornfully. "I will not put that thing on me," she said. Similarly, I was surprised that Ali had not changed his look at all; his hair was still full, brushed up in the front and slicked back, and he had not grown out his beard much, one of the easiest things to do in a society where beards are commonplace, more so than clean-shaven faces. He laughed. "She would never agree to look at me if I did that." It was too cheerful a moment; one wanted to grab these kids and say, *Hey, you won't be choosing your haircuts and dress in jail.* They did agree, however, that they would change their costumes in the next day or two, so that their colorful outfits, especially hers, would not be so easily recognized from any published pictures.

Diego had spotted another ray of light shining through a hole in the roof somewhere and wanted to delay our departure to get both of them in it, but we insisted on giving him no more than a minute and then bolting. Ben had already run ahead so he could get in front of them for footage of them heading down from the promontory, finally together and really fleeing. The lovers held hands, unbidden, as they walked, and when they came to what passed for a footbridge—three spindly, skinny birch trunks laid across the rushing river, so thin they bounced at every step—they crossed one by one, Zakia not even bothering to take off her high heels. The rest of us crossed gingerly and awkwardly in our Gore-Tex boots, worried about all those phones and cameras falling with us into the icy torrent below.

Before we piled into the cars, I slipped Ali a thousand dollars when no one else was looking. He had never asked for it, but neither did he question it, just tucked it into his shirt. I did it on impulse, although I'd been thinking of it earlier; I made sure none of my colleagues saw me. It was all money that various readers had pledged, even begged me to pass on to the couple, I reasoned, and they would follow through on those pledges in time, no doubt. And if they didn't . . . well, it seemed the least I could do. Ali's last thousand afghanis were not going to get them far, to be sure.

Much more of an issue than the money, journalistically, was abetting their escape. It was one thing to talk to them and photograph them on the run, but we were now providing the getaway cars. Once we put them in the cars with us, the die was cast; I was no longer just an observer but in a pretty important way a participant. The money could be dismissed as a humanitarian gesture, like giving money to a starving family while reporting in a miserable refugee camp—who wouldn't? This, however, was helping people flee criminal charges placed against them by their government. There was no chance to ask my bosses what they would think about this, but that was just as well, since I suspect I know what the answer would have been and I would not have been able to obey it. Zakia and Ali were here in part—I would come to realize how much a part—because of us. As the reader had said, "You're responsible for them now." What else could we do? We had the only cars available in Kham-e Bazargan; Haji's minibus was out on its rounds. So should we have waited there until the police arrived and then photographed their arrest? How cynical and exploitative that would have been. It came down to this choice: abandon your principles and stick to your humanity or stick to your principles and abandon your humanity. True, documenting their arrest would have been the better story, dramatically speaking, but who could live with that? We all felt uneasy about it, but I told Ben and Diego, "Look, if we work with them here, they won't want to cooperate, because they need to be running. If they run into the hills, we won't be able to stay with them for long. If we put them in our cars, we'll be able to work with them in some privacy and security." Which was all true, to a point, but it was still an equivocation.

Later we would learn that the police arrived at Haji and Zahra's that evening, only hours behind us. They might well have passed us on the road, lost to sight in the dust swirls our cars stirred up.

On the long drive down to Nayak Bazaar, we had time to talk with the couple about their flight so far, and I asked if it had been worth it, escaping from the women's shelter and eloping. "Yes, it's worth it because we love each other," Ali said.

"If we had only had one day together, it would have been worth it," Zakia said. "How can I be sad? We're together. I'm with my love."

One thing that became clear talking to both of them was that their time on the run had convinced them they had no long-term future in their own country; they said they had decided that their ultimate solution would be to flee abroad.

Then Jawad and I swapped cars, letting the photographers have some time with Zakia and Ali for the rest of the ride. Ben was happy to interview and video them inside the car, but Diego wanted them outside again, against the dramatic backdrop of the barren mountain landscape.

"Look, Diego, we're on the run," I said. "The cops are searching for them. Half the country is talking about them. You can't possibly shoot them outside the car."

He was insistent, and I finally gave in a little. "But only if the road is empty and then only for three minutes, no more."

Our car was in front, some distance ahead of them, and when we arrived on the outskirts of Nayak Bazaar, we realized that the second car with Zakia, Ali, Ben, and Diego inside was nowhere to be seen and was a lot more than three minutes behind us. We doubled back, only to find Diego posing them on top of a hillock, a fair walk from the road but in clear view of anyone who came along. I often wonder how differently it all would have ended if they'd been captured there and then by that carload of police on their way back from where we'd just been, because one of us had been too journalistically eager for yet another piece of the story.

I took over the lovers' car and banished Diego to the other one. We carried on into the town, dropping the couple at the top of a side street that headed off into the mountain up a jeep track. It was nearly dark. Another two hours' walk from there would take them to a safe house, one they had used once before, and after that they would set off across the mountains for Wardak, now that they had enough money to find a driver with a jeep, and then find buses to take them to southern Ghazni Province, to one of the Hazara communities in that otherwise dangerous province. Ben Solomon wanted to follow them.

"Out of the question," I said. "How could they possibly escape with a big white American tagging along?"

My story ran in the *Times* three days later, on April 22, along with the video[15] by Ben on our website, and Diego's stills,[16] which were so good that his presumptive perfidy had to be forgiven. The cumulative effect was to take a terrific story that already had generated a great deal of interest and increase that manifold.

The print story[17] had a suitably nonspecific dateline, "HINDU KUSH RANGE, AFGHANISTAN," a large area that traversed more than a third of the country. It ended:

> They hoped to be hundreds of miles away by Saturday morning, but were not sure which way they would go. The road to the north went through Taliban country. To the west, bandit country, where they risked being robbed—or worse. The road to the south went over passes still blocked by snow.
>
> There was no road east, but they could always walk.

That was a bit of protective obfuscation. Their real plan was to wait for the snows to melt to the south and then make it over the passes to Wardak Province: Taliban country but also Hazara country. Before they took their leave, I told them I didn't think they could keep hiding in these barren, unforested mountains; every stranger was a subject of suspicion. Two youthful strangers in love and on the run were a red flag.

"Give it a few weeks, then come to Kabul," I said. With five million people in the city, there had to be somewhere they could find to disappear among them. But then what right did I have to be giving Zakia and Ali advice?

6

MYSTERY BENEFACTOR

Zakia and Ali were saved again and again by the kindnesses of strangers. Villagers who sheltered them on the run. Passersby who spotted them and chose not to call the police. Journalists who wrote about them and made it harder to dispose of them—not just ourselves but also many Afghan journalists who had picked up the story. Women's advocates who lobbied on their behalf in the face of official disapproval. Then there were the strangers all over the world, but particularly in the United States, who were moved enough by their story to try to do something about it, readers who both encouraged and sometimes shamed me into keeping on their case and later became contributors whose money, mostly in modest donations, kept the couple going. When you're on the run, poverty is a potent enemy.

There were hundreds of such readers who reached out. An American named Walker Moore wondered if he couldn't pay a bride price that would make Zakia and Ali's match acceptable to both their families; Walker Moore turned out to be a *nom de pinceau* of two collaborative painters, John Walker and Roxann Moore; the Zakia-and-Ali story reminded them of their own union, which had been bitterly opposed by Roxann's conservative Southern Baptist family in Texas, Mr. Walker said. Adele Goldberg, a professor of psychology at Princeton University, offered to make a donation to help relocate the couple. Dr. Douglas Fleming, a physician and cancer researcher from Princeton, offered to donate a hundred dollars a month to them for a year to cover their expenses on the run, and his later donations proved critically helpful. E. Jean Carroll, who wrote a relationship advice column for *Elle* magazine and also runs a matchmaking service, Tawkify.com, offered them "airfare to the US, a chaperone for Zakia, and a place for them to stay"—until they were married. She, too, later sent money that helped in their escape. Beth Goodman also offered to host them in the United States. Many had vaguer but also heartfelt requests. "I'm French, I'm a woman and I live on the same planet," wrote Louisa Roque. "How can we help their parents to open their minds and hearts?"

The response went ballistic after we finally had both photographs and video of them together to accompany the words. It was gratifying that we'd touched a nerve and moved so many people. I no longer felt that this was a case that lay outside the boundaries of hope. At the same time, it was frustrating. Helping Zakia and Ali stay on the run was no more sustainable in the long term than many of the other things that well-intentioned Westerners have been doing for Afghans, whether paying them salaries ten times the Afghan norm[1] or providing their military with steeply subsidized fuel, much of it diverted to the black market.[2] There was little that anyone could do to help the couple in any permanent way unless a government stepped in and made it possible for them to leave their country. For those countries that might have been so inclined, that was politically difficult—in part because of popular backlashes against immigration in many Western countries and in part because so many of those countries needed to show skeptics back home that Afghanistan was improving on human rights and merited their continued national investment. With criminal charges hanging over the lovers, it became diplomatically awkward and contradictory for countries that had donated so much money to rule-of-law development work in Afghanistan to then turn around and say they had no confidence in the Afghan justice system, however many flat-earthers wielded its gavels. The United States alone had by 2014 spent more than $1.2 billion on rule-of-law programming[3] to do things like train judges and promote equal rights for women.

President Hamid Karzai could always choose to step in and pardon them or order the charges dropped. But this was even more of a long shot; Karzai's wife, an obstetrician before their marriage, had rarely been seen in public afterward and no longer practiced her profession.[4] Once seen as a champion of women's rights, Mr. Karzai was now widely viewed by most women's activists as having betrayed their cause.

While there was little these readers could do to help the couple directly, their money could buy some breathing room, and it soon began accumulating in the account of Women for Afghan Women[5] after I began answering reader mail with this note:

Dear Readers,

Pardon the impersonal e-mail but so many people have written me about the Afghan lovers that I can't answer everyone right away, although I aim to do so eventually.

Many of you have asked how you could help and, previously, I haven't had a satisfactory answer.

However, now a well-respected and long-established organization, Women for Afghan Women, has decided to start a fund dedicated to assisting the couple. The group's executive director, Manizha Naderi, has assured us that 100 percent of any donations to that fund will be passed directly to the couple.

. . . .

I feel sure that WAW has the means and the capacity to get donations to them personally.

With warm regards,

Some people had taken the initiative even earlier and sent money to a trusted accountant to deliver to Zakia and Ali, which,

I had quietly had assured a few of the more persistent among them, would be a safe way to do it. Before that money could clear from the bank for the accountant to deal with, however, we had rushed off to our rendezvous with Zakia and Ali up in the mountains in Yakawlang, so it had been my own money I gave them, telling myself I was just fronting it temporarily. WAW later made donations to them easy and efficient, and the group was beyond any reproach; it was undoubtedly the most effective NGO in Afghanistan fighting for women's rights on a basic, practical level and the biggest operator of women's shelters.[6] WAW's seven main shelters are in some of the country's most difficult areas. It also runs family-reconciliation and counseling centers and homes for children whose mothers are in prison. Eventually the *Times* ran a notice on its website telling people how they could donate to help the couple. The money that came in was not huge, a few thousand dollars, partly because I advised donors who asked how much to give that large sums of money were not necessary and might be distorting or cause problems in their own right. In Afghan terms the donations were adequate to keep the couple alive and help finance a safe place for them to hide. I suspect this was the first time the *New York Times* had in effect encouraged its readers to send money to criminal fugitives, which is technically and legally what Zakia and Ali were, however bogus the charges against them. Editors in New York were as moved by the story of the Afghan lovers as everyone else was.

If only we could find Zakia and Ali to let them know about all these offers of help. For quite a while, they were not aware that a fund-raising drive was under way on their behalf. Since we had left them in Nayak Bazaar in late April, there had been no word from them at all, and Ali's phone went unanswered, sounding not so much as a lovesick ringtone. His father and brothers said they had heard from him and thought he was in Ghazni Province or maybe Wardak, they weren't sure. He called them when he had a signal; they couldn't really call him, and of course nor could we. I was beginning to think that they had gone ahead and fled to Iran, and if they had, the story ended there—my story and possibly their story. Iran would be a dead end in almost every respect. While there are

950,000 legally registered Afghan refugees in Iran, according to the UN High Commissioner for Refugees[7] the real number is as much as three times that, most of them living there illegally.[8] The Iranian government has long since stopped granting refugee status to new arrivals, so all those who have arrived in recent years are undocumented illegals, without even the limited rights afforded refugees and guaranteed by international conventions and United Nations agencies. They cannot legally work, have no civil rights, cannot send their children to school—and could never be legally resettled to a third country.[9] At any moment they could be forcibly deported back to Afghanistan, and they often are. Some are killed and their bodies returned to the nearest border post with no explanation from the Iranian authorities. For Afghan refugees, just getting to Iran could be a dangerous crossing through forbidding deserts, far worse than anything Mexican and Central American immigrants face in the American Southwest. And since an American journalist could not follow refugees to Iran, there would likely be nothing more I could do for them and little more to write about them. The only thing Iran had in its favor as a destination was language; Farsi or Persian, the language spoken in Iran, and Dari, which Ali and Zakia spoke, are nearly as mutually intelligible as British and American English.

Finally, late in April, Ali called us; they could be in Kabul the next day, he said, if it was okay with us. He wanted assurances they would be safe there, and we told him that the big city could give them anonymity they would never find elsewhere, and there was donor money waiting to help them with expenses. Two days later Zakia and Ali arrived with his brother Bismillah and moved into the home of his aunt, his father's sister, who lived not far from the old city in central Kabul, in a neighborhood of squatters' buildings erected on the steep slopes of the Chindawul Hill.

Historically, Kabul had been settled on a flat plateau with several small mountains that jut up singly from the plain, but in the past decade its population had increased from less than a million to more than 5 million residents, and squatters had moved higher and higher on the steep slopes of places like Chindawul that were once viewed as uninhabitable, carving small plots out of the rock and filling the reclaimed space with slapdash cinder- and mud-block constructions.

With no services but electricity, if that, such homes were cheaper the higher up the hill they were located. The aunt's house was a one-room shack made of mud brick and concrete, reached by a fifteen-minute climb up an already steep dirt path, which soon becomes *so* steep that it's replaced by a nearly vertical stone staircase, with two hundred fifty steps to reach the aunt's house. The entire dwelling was no bigger than an American-size bedroom, with a primitive latrine and a gas burner and a bowl for a kitchen; a curtain hung across the room to give the couple some privacy. They stowed their few possessions, mostly just clothing, in the plastic bags they'd carried them in; at first they didn't even have mattresses to sleep on, just fake-bamboo mats. The nearest water was at the foot of the hill, and they hauled it in a pair of big plastic jerry cans, like those used for gasoline, slung across their shoulders at either end of a stout stick.

Although Chindawul was a safely Hazara neighborhood, Jawad and I decided not to draw attention to Zakia and Ali by meeting them there. Instead we arranged to meet Ali alone, reasoning that they were easier to recognize as a couple than singly. We would pick him up outside the Pamir Cinema, at the foot of the hill, one of the few places he knew in the city. Half an hour before the meeting, Ali called to tell us his brother Bismillah had gone ahead to the meeting place to check it out and saw one of Zakia's older brothers on the street nearby. Did we know anything about that?

Of course we didn't, but our meeting was canceled and Ali again stopped answering his phone when we called. Another week went by before we were able to make a meeting happen, and then only by calling his father and persuading him that we had no reason to expose them to risk; spotting the brother there was just bad luck—or good luck that they saw him first and not the other way around. If that brother was in Kabul, he was probably working as a day laborer, and the Pamir Cinema is a common meeting place for laborers looking for day work, so in the future it would probably be a good place for us to avoid.

The night before, E. Jean Carroll, the advice columnist, had e-mailed to let me know she had done something that had never occurred to me would work—she sent money to Ali via Western Union. She gave me the coded number of the money wire to pass along to him so he could collect it. We relayed the details via Anwar, hoping that the prospect of receiving money would reassure Ali we were on his side.

I let Rabbi Shmuley know that Ali had come to Kabul, as I did several of the other well-wishers. Shmuley activated the fixer we had found him, Aimal Yaqubi, but Aimal had no more luck getting through to Ali than we had earlier. While we were waiting to meet with Ali, though, Shmuley had come up with a plan. He was outraged at how hard this had become. He'd gone straight to Samantha Power, the United States representative to the United Nations, and tried to persuade her that she had to push the American government to save the couple. By his account she had in turn persuaded the U.S. secretary of state, John Kerry, to try to do something, but despite their efforts both finally had come to the conclusion that they could not force the American government to change its policies and issue the couple a humanitarian visa to save them from persecution. With criminal charges against them, and the United States supposedly an ally of Afghanistan, taking them directly out of the country would mean using the visa system to help Afghans escape their own, American-financed criminal-justice system. They would have to resolve their case first, legally, or they would have to get to another country and apply for a visa there, a process that Shmuley said he was told would take them six months or more even with Samantha Power behind it.

Shmuley had come up with a novel work-around. He said he'd been in touch with his good friend President Paul Kagame of Rwanda and that Mr. Kagame would issue visas to Ali and Zakia and would let them stay as his guests for as long as it would take for them to get visas to go on to America, a process that Rabbi Shmuley said Samantha Power promised to expedite—provided the couple were out of Afghanistan. This would be financed through Mr.

Shmuley's World Values Network, using money from a mystery benefactor: a very wealthy woman, as he had said.

Not only did it seem a bizarre solution, but there was a serious complication. As it stood then, only Ali had his identity card, or *tazkera,* which was required in order to get a passport; Zakia's father had possession of her *tazkera* and was not about to give it up. So she could not even apply for a passport, and Ali would have to do so at the risk of being arrested on the outstanding bigamy and kidnapping charges.

"How hard can it be to get passports?"

"Not hard at all, if you're not worried about the FCPA."

The meaning of those initials was immediately clear: the Foreign Corrupt Practices Act, which makes it a federal crime for American citizens to pay bribes in foreign countries, even where it's a standard and locally accepted practice. His mystery benefactor would want none of that, Shmuley said. The couple would have to find a way to obtain passports legally, without getting caught on the outstanding criminal charges.

That was not hopeless, since both of them had fairly common first names—Mohammad Ali was his; he had no surname, like many rural Afghans. Zakia, too, had no surname,[10] which is even more common among women. (Kept in purdah, women have even less need of a full name than men.) So if the couple went to the passport office one at a time, that might possibly work. There was a risk in it, to be sure, especially if no officials could be bribed.

Finally, after two weeks of ducking us, Ali, out of money, agreed to meet us outside a hospital in a busy part of town. We picked him up and took him to the Ché restaurant, in the Kart-e-Seh neighborhood, which passes for upscale in Kabul. The Ché is one of a type of Afghan restaurant, rarely frequented by foreigners, in which the tables are traditional raised platforms with cushions, each in a separate enclosure arranged around a central garden. Each has room for half a dozen people; with thatched roofs, thick vines, and screening around the sides, they are very private spaces. The ostensible purpose is to provide a place for families to dine in seclusion, so the women cannot be seen by others, and they do function that way. With a cooperative management, they also provide privacy for couples and mixed groups of unrelated people, and are often full of young people willing to defy social convention, courting and even, on occasion, necking. It was a perfect place for us to sit down with Ali away from prying eyes.

Ali had changed little since we'd last seen him nearly a month before; he was still beardless, his hair still in a pompadour, a style that stood out in Kabul. He was restless and nervous, and every few minutes his phone rang on silent and he looked at it with concern. I filled him in on what we knew. There was an Afghan employee at the American embassy who had been assigned to speak to him about their case, and we programmed the number into his phone so that he would recognize it when it rang and know it was okay to answer. We told him there was a wealthy American who wanted to help him and Zakia, who had enlisted an Afghan fixer to be their go-between, and we programmed Aimal Yaqubi's number into his phone as well. He had trouble understanding why we were introducing Aimal into the matter, though I explained that as a journalist I couldn't act on behalf of someone trying to find a solution for him. "But we trust you, and we only want to talk to you. We know you will help us," he said. It was hard to explain the notion of professional distance in any way that made sense to him, all the more so since it had begun to ring false to me.

While we talked, Ali was skittish and scarcely touched the food we ordered. When we told him about Shmuley's plan to get them to Rwanda, as a way station en route to America, he looked at us blankly. I realized we had to back up and start with some basic geography; he had only the vaguest idea of other countries, let alone other continents. A map to him was a meaningless piece of paper with strange lines on it. He had never seen an African or any black person; the only foreigners he'd ever seen were the European troops who helped train his army unit in Farah, and the first foreigner he'd ever seen up close was me. From time to time, I'd catch him looking at me sidewise, as if trying to figure out what manner of beast this could be or what I was up to, really. After a long explanation about Africa—how far away it was, how different the climate, culture, and language, where it was located in relation to the United States—he said he understood, but it was clear he really did not. I didn't begin to try to explain Rwanda and what that country specifically is like. "Whatever Africa is, that would be better than hiding in caves," he said.

We told him that Women for Afghan Women had been receiving donations from people in the United States who'd read about the couple's case and wanted to help them. The organization was interested in giving him a lawyer who would fight their criminal case for them, and would he want to talk to the lawyer? He refused; as far as he was concerned, WAW was an organization that ran shelters, and shelters were bad. They would try to get Zakia to go into one, and she would be a prisoner there again indefinitely. On this there was no reasoning with him; no use pointing out that Zakia would have been long dead without the Bamiyan shelter, whatever her complaints about it. He would not consent to go to WAW's office himself to pick up money from the donors, for fear they would somehow detain him; he wanted us to do it for him, but we refused. His cell phone rang again, and this time he answered it and had a fraught conversation with Zakia. She was worried about him, he said, and when he hadn't answered her earlier calls, she'd grown alarmed that something had happened. She knew that her brothers were in town, and though Kabul was a city of 5 million people, its size was beyond their imagining; it was as remote and foreign to them as Africa would be.

We asked him if he had collected the three hundred dollars that E. Jean Carroll had sent in the name of Ali, care of any Western Union office in Kabul, but he had not. We realized that Anwar was innumerate, though he'd said, out of embarrassment and politeness, that he could take down the coded number needed to collect the money. So we wrote it down for Ali and said we could take him to one of the transfer offices; there are many of them attached to Afghan banks. Ali was fine with numbers on a telephone, but written down on paper they were just so many hieroglyphics. Jawad would have to go along to help him.

We chose a Western Union office on Darulaman Road because

it was on a busy street but set back from the road. This particular bank had been the target of a Taliban suicide bomber the year before, in an attack that had killed a dozen people; many of the walls still had scooped-out patches from the shrapnel, and the windows were cardboarded over. It was ready for the next attack; unlike lightning, suicide bombers often strike the same place twice, and the office's entry was obscured by sandbagged blast walls and HESCOs, huge metal mesh containers filled with earth. It was menacing but private. The Western Union clerk confirmed they had the money, under that code number, but Ms. Carroll had sent it to first name Mohammad, last name Ali, and as far as the bank was concerned, his documents said he was first name Mohammad Ali, no last name. It's a common problem in Afghanistan, where more than half the population gets by with only one name.[11] I relayed this to Ms. Carroll, who corrected the first wire, sending a second payment immediately. By the next day, Zakia and Ali had three hundred dollars, enough money to live on, by the courtesy of an American stranger who had simply been moved by their story. From Ali and Zakia's point of view, three hundred dollars was enough to get by on for a month, and they remained adamant that WAW was off-limits, though the organization by now held several thousand dollars in donations for them.

Ali was being uncooperative journalistically as well. Our video department wanted to do a follow-up of the piece that Ben Solomon had shot in Yakawlang. Our photo desk wanted to shoot them again, too, and send a still photographer along whenever there was a new development in their case. We were constantly bombarded by requests from Afghan journalists who also wanted to follow their case; we didn't like turning our colleagues down, and this was, after all, a story about Afghan society that Afghans needed to hear. Ali was adamant, though, that they wanted no further photography, and he did not even want his wife to talk to us anymore. They also wanted no part of the Afghan press. It was too dangerous, he felt, and it was hard to argue with that.

His attitude was not going to help us keep interest in the couple high enough to force some sort of resolution. In journalism the great stories are the ones that can bring about change. This one could change the lives of two people who otherwise had no real prospects and perhaps give some real encouragement to others like them. But increasingly my subjects seemed to want nothing to do with us if they could not see the immediate practical benefit. I tried to persuade them that cases like theirs rarely end well when kept far from public view. I could not keep their story alive if a half of it, Zakia, was no longer speaking to me. Ali claimed he understood that, but then all that he would agree to, and only reluctantly, was to arrange for Zakia to speak to us on the phone from their hiding place. That's where we had to leave it for the time being.

Shmuley called me nearly nightly in those days, worried that his fixer was having trouble persuading Ali to meet with him. I said we had done as much as we could. I suggested that Aimal should go easy; we, too, had backed off, so Zakia and Ali did not feel pressured. Meanwhile Shmuley was also in touch with Fatima Kazimi, as was E. Jean Carroll, and Fatima was regaling them both with her own tale of woe.

I heard about this firsthand when Fatima arrived in Kabul late in April. She bustled into the *New York Times* compound in Wazir Akbar Khan, the diplomatic quarter of Kabul, dressed in her usual purple head scarf and the modesty trench coat favored by many Afghan women in official life. Fatima was not happy. She had just seen a translated copy of my latest article on the lovers, published April 22,[12] and was outraged that it focused on the couple and did not mention Fatima's role in the case. "I expected you to write about me," she said. "I brought them to you." In fact, the first article did mention Fatima prominently, quoted her at length, related her role in getting Zakia to the safety of the shelter—all things that were corroborated by many witnesses in Bamiyan, including several people who'd been in the court. Fatima just wasn't the central figure in that piece, nor should she have been. She had already complained to me then that she was disappointed that the first article made it a Romeo-and-Juliet love story and not a Fatima Kazimi rescue story. Then, when they had eloped, my March 31 article[13] had revisited the issue of Fatima's role, appropriately, since some were accusing her of engineering Zakia's breakout. Again Fatima was not the focus; the lovers were.

Now Fatima wanted us to set the matter straight and write another article about how terribly she had been treated in this affair. She claimed to have fled to Kabul with her entire family because she could no longer endure the many threats she was receiving in Bamiyan. She claimed to have lost her job at the women's ministry. "The entire village of the girl's father filed a complaint against me and accused me of helping Zakia escape—or helping Ali kidnap her, as they put it," she said. "I actually didn't do anything." She purportedly did help by allowing Zakia to get a telephone from Ali while she was in the shelter,[14] but Ali and Zakia both deny she had anything to do with that—although she did allow them to have a chaperoned meeting in the shelter at one point. "Whether I say I did help or did not help, everything comes back to me from the beginning," Fatima said. "I stepped in and stopped the court from doing something terrible. Yesterday her family members came to my former home in Bamiyan, looking for me, but I had moved. My life is in danger, and I am under threat. If I don't leave the country, something may happen to me or my family." She had four children, teenagers and young adults, and a husband. "You need to write that."

I was starting to have a hard time believing any of this, thinking that perhaps Fatima had gamed this whole thing from the beginning. I was shocked to discover that she had persuaded E. Jean Carroll to send money to help protect her. Fatima was earnestly depicting her case as more dire—and more important—than that of Zakia and Ali, who really *were* in danger of being killed (as Fatima herself had pointed out from the beginning). "Only the governor is on my side now, and how long can the governor defend me?" she said.

The governor of Bamiyan has executive authority over all the provincial government offices, save the courts; he controls the police force, so he can prevent arrests, order interventions, provide bodyguards, and so forth. He is a Hazara, like Fatima, and it's an overwhelmingly Hazara place; if anyone were likely to be in danger there now, it would be Zakia's Tajik family members, whose opposition to the marriage on ethnic and religious grounds would

expose them to the anger of their more numerous Hazara neighbors. Zakia and Ali were at risk of violence at their hands, no
doubt, but Fatima?

She was insistent, though, and I said we would write about the
case again and probably mention her as well; in a piece a couple of
days later,[15] I noted the role she had in alerting us to the case. Who
was I to say, really, what the truth was in the matter? Maybe she *had*
received death threats and was frightened by them and honestly felt
that the only hope was to leave Afghanistan.

It certainly was true that anyone connected with sheltering
women in Afghanistan was under intense pressure. Just the year
before, the case of Bibi Aisha had contributed to a backlash against
women's shelters after a picture showing that her nose had been
cut off appeared on *Time*'s cover. Bibi Aisha was widely criticized
in Afghanistan after that cover picture[16]—including by officials
in the office of President Hamid Karzai—for bringing shame to
her homeland, and she now lives with a foster family in Virginia,
spurned in her own land and not only by the Taliban. The subsequent crackdown against women's shelters was led by prominent
conservatives[17] who accused the shelters of undermining traditional values, promoting adulterous conduct, and even fronting
for prostitution. One television network, Noorin TV, sent its star
"investigative reporter," Nastoh Naderi, to the Women for Afghan
Women shelter.[18] Denied entry, he stood in front of the gate and
had his crew film men as they walked in. The men were guards
who were employed by the shelter, working in the compound but
not in the building that housed the women clients. On air Mr. Naderi described the guards as johns coming to patronize the prosti-
tuted women inside. The government then tried to take control of
the women's shelters, all of which were run by either private chari-
ties or the United Nations, but was forced by an international outcry to back off and instead instituted regulations controlling their
activities, under the purview of the Ministry of Women's Affairs.[19]

Fatima continued to insist she was under threat from Zakia's
family. I had talked to Zakia's relatives, met some of her brothers

and cousins and her father, and their determination to pursue vengeance made them worrisomely dangerous. But they had never expressed to me a desire to get back at Fatima, and their anger seemed much more focused on the Bamiyan shelter director, Najeeba, and of course on Zakia above all.

Shmuley called me that night, and he was ebullient. He had just attended a genocide conference in Kigali with President Kagame, and the Rwandan president was on board with Shmuley's African rescue plan. I thought he had already been on board, but now he was apparently really on board. "Our donor, she wants to educate them, give them jobs, bring them to the United States," Shmuley said. "We have the support of the State Department, we have everything ready to go, we just need passports. Samantha Power assured me she was interested in helping them, sympathized with their plight, and she would try to get their team on board. I took her assurances to heart." The American donor, a high-net-worth individual, would pay the costs of getting Zakia and Ali to Rwanda and give them a stipend for their living expenses; President Kagame would treat them as his personal guests.

Shmuley's enthusiasm was infectious, and he did have the attention of the State Department, although I'm not sure how deep their support for his plan really went. It was deep enough, though, to energize the American embassy to reach out to Ali and Zakia through an Afghan employee, Zmaryalai Farahi. After a chat on the telephone, he told them they would have to come into the embassy to discuss it further in person. When Ali tried to visit the American embassy, however, he only got as far as Massoud Circle in Wazir Akbar Khan before he saw that they would have to pass two or three cordons of Afghan police and guards just to get to the beginning of the road leading to the embassy. Suspicious that it was a setup to get them arrested, Ali turned away and stopped answering Zmaryalai's calls.

Around the same time, Aimal Yaqubi had started calling Ali aggressively, as Ali recalled it, ordering Ali to meet with him to pick up the thousand dollars he was delivering from Shmuley. The fixer's pushiness frightened the couple, and Ali just stopped pick-ing up when he called. Ali was now no longer talking to the two contacts who perhaps could help them to safety, and he was only barely speaking to Jawad and me.

Shmuley was mystified. At my suggestion he had offered Aimal a bonus if he was able to help the couple get out of the country, but the amount was much more than I expected: $5,000. Perhaps that was the problem. In a society where two hundred dollars a month is a living wage, five grand is a lot of money. Even compared to Aimal's fees as a fixer, two hundred dollars a day, five grand was just too much incentive. In a way it was a small metaphor for the entire failed American enterprise in Afghanistan: Throwing money at the problem, however well intentioned, often makes matters worse.

Examples of this phenomenon abound. Consider a $35 million "go fly a rule-of-law kite" program, dreamed up and funded by a United States Agency for International Development (USAID) contractor, a commercial firm that is now known as Tetra Tech DPK.[20] Their idea was to stage a public event at which they would hand out kites, comic books, and posters with slogans printed on them touting equal rights for women and respect for the rule of law. Hundreds of kids and some adults showed up. Because the contractor was an American company, a large contingent of police was on hand to protect the American employees. First, no one could read the slogans on the kites and posters, let alone the text-heavy comic books; most of the kids were too young, and most of the adults who came were either jobless or policemen—neither a group with a high literacy rate.[21] Then handing out the kites went badly awry when policemen systematically stole them from the kids who had come, in order to take them home to their own cil-dren, beating some of the kids at the event with sticks when they didn't cooperate. Finally, gender equality was hard to come by. The few times any girls got their hands on the free kites, their fa-thers took them away and gave them to their sons instead. Despite critical coverage[22] that made the fly-a-kite program a laughing-stock in the aid community, the contractor deemed it such a success that it was repeated later in Herat, and the contractor continued to dream up other methods of public outreach funded by U.S. taxpayers' money.

Similarly, indiscriminate American largesse dispensed by the embassy financed a rock concert in a country where rock music is little followed, infuriating the mullahs; a yoga charity with the stated goal of getting the Taliban to the peace table via the yoga mat; an Afghan adaptation of *Sesame Street*[23] for Tolo TV, featuring the American ambassador posing in Kabul with Grover, in all likelihood a war-zone first.[24] The American embassy also pumped more than $100 million into underwriting indigenous television stations, so that any minor press conference in Kabul has more television cameras[25] in attendance than most major news events in New York City or Washington, D.C. None of this was any more sustainable long-term than flying a kite; all will come crashing down once the American-financed windfall ends.

That May when we dialed Ali's number, we got love-song ringtones, a different one every few days, but he never answered. One frequent song was "Your Unkempt Hair," by the famous Afghan singer Ahmad Zahir.

Afghan women are rarely seen in public without at least a head scarf.

> *If the early morning breeze*
> *Should ruffle your unruly hair*
> *All hearts would be ensnared*
> *In that trap of love and suffering.*[26]

❦

7

HONOR HUNTERS

The lovers had no idea how many friends they had, but late that May and early June it was hard to persuade them that they had any. Everything seemed to be going wrong for them. Zakia's family was actively looking for them. They were miserable in hiding. Escape abroad seemed impossible. Money was running out. Faced as the couple was with a hopeless situation, their suspicious refusals to accept aid made it all worse.

While their hideout at Ali's aunt's house on the hill in Chindawul seemed secure, it was crowded and small and a hard place for anyone to spend much time. Remaining in hiding was getting increasingly difficult, particularly for Ali, but if either of them still wanted to flee abroad, they had a funny way of showing it. They were no longer answering the phone at all—not to Rabbi Shmuley's fixer, Aimal, not to the American embassy's human-rights officer, not even to us at the *New York Times*. They were low on prospects and almost out of hope.

Their pursuers had come to town in force, and Zakia's brothers and cousins were being spotted often. Zakia's father, Zaman, had left Bamiyan and resettled his immediate family in Kabul. This was partly because they had suffered so much contempt from their Hazara neighbors after they became the nationally notorious villains persecuting Zakia and Ali and partly because Zaman could not bear the humiliation of facing his Tajik neighbors after the loss of his honor. Mostly, though, as they told everyone who would listen, they wanted to exact revenge on the lovers, no matter what it took. Zaman and his sons had given up their tenancy on the farm in Bamiyan and looked for what work they could find as day laborers in Kabul, expecting to find the couple there.

"Honor and dishonor is like this: According to Islamic and shariah law, the girl cannot run away from home," explained Zakia's cousin Najibullah, an uneducated farm laborer. "It will be seen by the people as, 'Ha, your daughter has run away. You should no longer live in this village. If she had not run away, her father never would have quit the village. He quit it because he is so dishonored that he cannot live here anymore,'" he said. "All the people will mock him and jeer at him, like, 'If you were a man, why did your daughter run away? Why didn't you stop her?' They say these things, so we cannot let it be. He is her father, and I am her uncle's son, but it hurts our honor, too. I cannot live in Bamiyan any longer myself when they say my uncle's daughter ran away. We could not bring her back, so people will say to us, 'If you were men, had daring and courage, why couldn't you get your daughter back from the government?'"

One of Zakia's other cousins, Mirajuddin, was sitting with Najibullah; the two young men were among the relatives left in Kham-e-Kalak, although they no longer farmed the land and would soon join Zaman and his sons in Kabul to hunt the couple down. They had been in the courtroom when the melee broke out, although Zakia says they were not among those family members who attacked her physically. They were not close enough blood relatives to feel entitled to rip her clothes off and touch her, even if violently. "Your life is your honor, like your wife is your honor, and if your honor leaves you and goes to someone else, then this life is worthless," Mirajuddin said. "If someone takes your wife, your life is not worth living." Their position reflected a broader societal concern, as the cousins saw it. "If today the government doesn't do something about this, then tomorrow the wife of a farmer will elope with a schoolboy or a businessman and will say she can't live with her husband. So in this way, after the first one left, the others will follow." Zakia, in short, had challenged the entire structure of Afghan patriarchal society, and if she was not stopped, all women would abandon the husbands chosen for them. ("First one wants freedom, / Then the whole damn world wants freedom," as the late Gil Scott-Heron put it in his song "B Movie.")

In fact, there is a lot at stake for the women's-rights movement in Afghanistan, even far beyond its borders. Afghanistan, because of the involvement of the West since 2001, is the only such country where serious efforts are under way to improve the lot of its women. "Afghanistan is still the great battleground of women's rights in the twenty-first century," says Nasrine Gross, an Afghan sociologist and women's advocate. If women could win some measure of gender equality and equal treatment before the law in a country as backward and abusive as Afghanistan, that would be a provocative example to disenfranchised women in those other countries, such as Saudi Arabia and Somalia, Pakistan and Yemen, the Gulf satrapies and Iran. "There are some countries that are very powerful in certain ways, and women's rights is not something they want to discuss," Ms. Gross says. By "certain ways," she means power that comes from possessing vast oil and gas wealth. "They use the lack of women's rights as a means of controlling their own countries, and they want to keep Afghanistan at bay in terms of women's rights so Afghanistan will not become a role model for their societies. A place so poor, so illiterate, so backward, they cannot stand it if this poor Afghanistan would be a model of women's rights."[1]

Internally Afghanistan has long been a battleground for women's rights, but the battle is one that women and their advocates have always lost. Probably in no other country[2] have so many rulers been toppled over this particular issue, going back to King Habibullah, who opened the earliest girls' schools and ushered in some rights for women before he was assassinated in 1919. His son,

King Amanullah Khan, went much further, banning the veil for women, instituting girls' education in rural areas, and outlawing polygamy. King Amanullah began his reign as a popular leader, credited with defeating the British in the Third Anglo-Afghan War. When he returned from a visit to Europe with his liberal-minded queen, Soraya Tarzi, he declared at a public event that Islam did not require women to be covered, whereupon Queen Tarzi tore off her veil and the other government wives present did so as well. Under his rule women were allowed to divorce and to choose their husbands, bride prices were outlawed, women were encouraged to work and study. But in a country with no roads and little infrastructure of any kind and a weak central government and bureaucracy, Amanullah was unable to persuade his countrymen to embrace his reforms and instead provoked an uprising of mullahs and conservatives that drove him from power in 1929.[3]

This uprising was fueled in part by British agents, whose country was eager to get back at King Amanullah for its recent humiliation. They circulated pictures showing Queen Tarzi wearing a sleeveless gown at a state function and allowing her hand to be kissed during the European tour. Even today most educated women will not shake hands with men, while bare shoulders and arms in public would provoke a riot in Kabul.

Amanullah's successor, Nadir Shah, tried to institute reforms but was himself assassinated. Subsequent Afghan rulers were much more cautious about women's-rights issues. Not until the Communist era in the 1970s was any successful effort made to extend rights to women, and the sweeping progress decreed by the Communists on gender equality was the major reason for the uprising against them by mujahideen and their followers.[4] Their problem was with feminism, not with Communism. Their jihad was first of all against women's rights, and later against schools for girls, the right to divorce, and women in the workplace and public life. They did not object to Communism as an economic or political system; it was equal rights for women that bothered them.[5] When many of these mujahideen leaders later joined with the Americans to oust the Taliban, the alliance was not motivated by the Taliban's social policies; in most cases Afghan warlords were as hard-line on women's issues as the Taliban, and often even more regressive. The Taliban at least outlawed *baad,* and they officially disapproved of honor killings not based on their own judicial processes.[6]

The concept of honor and killing women to uphold that honor is not unique to Afghanistan. In ancient Rome the paterfamilias or dominant male within a household had a legal right to kill a sister or a daughter who had extramarital sex or a wife who committed adultery.[7] Othello's murder of Desdemona was an honor killing and typical of honor killings in that the woman is given no real recourse to plead her case; the victim's guilt or innocence becomes subordinate to the man's sense of the violation of his honor. This goes some way to explaining the murder of rape victims by their own families in Afghanistan.

The eminent anthropologist Thomas Barfield[8] of Boston University, who is president of the American Institute of Afghanistan Studies, says there is a sort of blood-feud belt, where honor killings of women were historically endemic, that stretches from Spain throughout the Mediterranean basin, across the Middle East, Arabia, Iran, and Afghanistan and then ends in Pakistan. East of that, north of that, south of it—in China or Mongolia, Southeast Asia or sub-Saharan Africa, Northern Europe or Russia—the concept of honor killing is pathological and rare, rather than socially acceptable and widespread.

With the notable exception of Saudi Arabia,[9] however, most modern societies, including Islamic societies, in the honor-killing belt have successfully criminalized the practice, just as nearly all societies have moved away from the concept of men's ownership of women. Even Ayatollah Ali Khamenei in fundamentalist Iran has condemned the practice of honor killing, and as with most Islamic scholars, Sunni and Shia, he insists that honor killing has no theological basis in Islam.[10]

A weak central government throughout Afghanistan's modern history, three and a half decades of war, and low levels of education and literacy[11] have helped to sustain abusive customary practices like honor killings.[12] "Dealing with the status of women has brought down more regimes in Afghanistan than anything else," Professor Barfield says. Both King Amanullah's premature reforms and the Communists' excessively ambitious efforts provoked a strong backlash, contributed to prolonging abusive customs, and made most modern leaders unwilling to confront conservatives on such controversial issues. Even today women's groups that protest honor killings typically refrain from challenging the concept underlying them, that women are the property of men, who are in absolute control of regulating their behavior.

In that ancient honor belt, Afghanistan has been a major hold-out.[13] "The state in Afghanistan has not been able to move its writ into family affairs. The Afghans feel that is not a state responsibility," Professor Barfield says. Other states throughout that belt developed strong ruling systems where the state could and did inject itself into family and social affairs. "The state in the rest of the world has moved its power all the way down to the family level, but in Afghanistan, even today, the state is very hesitant to regulate family affairs. If there's a revenge killing, because it's murder, when it's brought to their attention, they will act, but on the other hand if it doesn't come to the state's attention, they don't look for it."

Given the attitudes of Zakia's family, she and Ali were doing their best to stay hidden, but in the crowded little house on the side of the Chindawul Hill, Ali was increasingly irritable. With the aunt and her children, as many as eight people were sharing perhaps four hundred square feet and a tiny yard. Every food purchase, every bucket of water, involved an exhausting climb up the steep hill. Complicating matters for them, Zakia was not feeling well and was constantly complaining of stomach cramps and pains and nausea—dysentery is rampant in a city that long ago outgrew what primitive sewage system it had. She did not suffer as much from the inability to go out, but she sensed that Ali's aunt resented her presence there and did not approve of her marriage to Ali. The aunt tolerated them because her brother Anwar had asked her to do so. Zakia was also lonely. She still missed her mother and father and brothers and sisters, the populous household in which she had spent her entire life, however much they wanted to kill her. She especially missed Razak, her lively nine-year-old brother, the much-doted-upon youngest male of the family. "I love him so much," she told Ali. "It's hard to think I will never see him again."

Zakia and Ali began arguing with each other over little things, and Ali was confused and defensive. This was not what he had expected their life together would be like. The long days of hiding at home were uncomfortable, but when Ali went out, Zakia worried constantly that her family or the police would find him. Suddenly one day, impulsively, he decided to rejoin the army. He had one year left on his enlistment, and he could go back without any real penalty as a deserter. Zakia was against it, and they argued, but she eventually agreed.

"I couldn't stay jobless forever," he said. "I have to do something to make back that money that we borrowed from people. They will not let us keep their money forever, one day they will ask for it." He'd had two months of freedom with his wife, and now it was time to work, as he put it. But the two-hundred- to two-hundred-fifty-dollar monthly army salary was not going to make much of a dent in their debts. There was a more practical reason to reenlist: Once in the military, stationed on a base, he would be virtually immune from arrest by the police. "I was going out a lot, and it wasn't good for me—it was dangerous—and I thought, why not join the army and be safe, plus make money?" He had managed, through the uncle of one of his sisters' husbands, to be allowed to rejoin as a bodyguard to a Hazara commander in the Afghan National Army. The commander was stationed at the Kabul International Airport, so Ali would not be far away from Zakia and could visit her on weekends. Even the uniform would help him to hide, although it meant that all his long black hair would be shorn to a military close-crop. The haircut proved to be not a bad disguise. One day when he was heading home on weekend leave to see Zakia, he passed right by his father-in-law, completely unnoticed by Zaman.

During this time we had begun talking with Ali and Zakia

again, and we decided that it was time to engage with them about the Rwanda option that Shmuley had put on the table. It seemed like they were never going to deal with Aimal Yaqubi directly, and Shmuley was insistent that we offer them this opportunity. It put me in an awkward position, but I didn't feel right letting them pass it up for lack of the right messenger. We got Ali and Zakia to sit down with Anwar, Jawad, and me, to talk it through. Again we explained what they could expect in Africa, a minimum of six months of isolation in Rwanda while they waited for onward visas—and no guarantee of those, though chances would be good. It was clear they had soured on the idea, but in any case their lack of passports was a deal breaker. Zakia had a new *tazkera,* or ID card, by then, but they were unwilling to risk going to the passport office with criminal charges still lodged against them, and without passports Rwanda was a nonstarter. Rabbi Shmuley was disappointed, but not daunted. Within a few days, he called to say that he was fed up and ready to make a move, and he wanted my advice on what to do about Fatima Kazimi.

"We're friends, right?"

"Sure."

"So tell me the truth."

"Okay."

"Should we save Fatima?"

I stalled for a moment to collect my thoughts, realizing what he probably had in mind. "Save her how?"

"Get her out, save her. Rwanda."

"Okay, I see. Can I get back to you on that?"

That June we were all getting frustrated and anxious for some sort of action. Stasis served no one's interest, least of all that of Zakia and Ali, who remained elusive and unpredictable even toward Jawad and me. The fixer Aimal Yaqubi and the American embassy were having a still-harder time pinning down Ali. The embassy began calling me to try to get him to pick up calls from them, and Aimal called us to complain that he was getting nowhere. At one point Aimal accused us of using our influence with the couple to obstruct his efforts. Aimal had five hundred dollars to give them as a donation from Rabbi Shmuley's mystery benefactor, he said, and they still wouldn't cooperate (the amount had shrunk since we'd first heard about it).

Shmuley was more frustrated with this inaction than anyone. He related to me a long conversation he'd had with an embassy official, public-affairs officer Robert Hilton, about the case. "Here we have a story that encapsulates why we're there, a story that has fired the American imagination, and you guys are not even involved in helping. You left it to a bunch of laypeople like us who don't know what they're doing."

Mr. Hilton told him, as Shmuley explained, that the embassy had to consider the sensibilities of the host country, which only incensed him. "What about the sensibilities of American readers? What about the sensibilities of a hundred thousand troops there and the trillion dollars we spent, and you can't get a woman who's going to be killed out of the country? A fricking trillion dollars, I told him."

Hilton pointed out that there were criminal charges against the couple that would somehow have to be adjudicated, and the United States couldn't be seen to be circumventing Afghanistan's legal system, in which it had invested more than a billion dollars over the past decade.

"Are you telling me you're going to abide by a corrupt judge's order to send her back to her family to be killed or raped?" Shmuley in righteous mid-rant was a force to be reckoned with. "This is ridiculous. This story has crystallized for all of us why we're there. We're there to protect people like Zakia." He had her name down by now. "All we have to do is get this woman a passport."

Shmuley was livid after he recounted this conversation to me. "I don't think the embassy is going to be helpful, but one way or another we're going to get them out, and it's going to be a big story when we get them out, and the U.S. government had no role whatever," he said. "After a trillion dollars, we can't save a woman from an honor killing because we're worried about hurting someone's feelings in the government? The American government can't do it? The American government is afraid of the Afghan government? Let them be more afraid of the American public. What the hell are we doing there? What have we managed to change there? We can't have these people die and achieve zero. So now a couple of bozos in New Jersey are going to do what the U.S. government cannot do. They seem to be under strict orders: Let's tiptoe out of Afghanistan and make no waves."

This kind of accommodation is rampant in the waning days of the Western intervention in Afghanistan. The case of a girl named Gulnaz, who was forced to marry her rapist, is a good example. The European Union suppressed a film it had commissioned that featured her plight, concerned that it would embarrass the Afghan government. British-based filmmaker Clementine Malpas found Gulnaz, then only nineteen, in Kabul's female prison, Badam Bagh, where she had been held for more than a year, and featured her in the EU-financed documentary on women in Afghanistan, which she called *In-Justice*. In the film, Ms. Malpas related how Gulnaz had been given a three-year prison sentence after she was raped by a cousin, Assadullah Sher Mohammad; Gulnaz gave birth to their child while in prison. When she appealed the case, her sentence was increased to twelve years,[14] but an Afghan judge offered her freedom if she would marry her rapist.

When officials at the EU mission in Kabul saw the film, they decided to withhold it from release, threatening the filmmaker with legal action if she allowed it to be aired. Ostensibly the reason was to protect the women in the film, Gulnaz as well as two other victims, from retribution. The EU rejected the position taken by the filmmaker that Gulnaz and the others in the film had given informed consent. It was a surrender by EU diplomats to Afghan cultural sensitivities. That was confirmed when the *New York Times* reported that e-mails from the EU's attaché for rule of law and human rights, Zoe Leffler, had told the filmmaker that the EU "has to consider its relations with the justice institutions in connection with the other work that it is doing in the sector."

In the ensuing furor, President Hamid Karzai ordered the girl released from prison—but made it clear that he expected her to marry her rapist as the court had ordered, according to the *Times*[15] account by Alissa J. Rubin.

"Gulnaz said, 'My rapist has destroyed my future,'" Ms. Malpas said, recounting their conversation. "'No one will marry me after what he has done to me. So I must marry my rapist for my child's sake. I don't want people to call her a bastard and abuse my brothers. My brothers won't have honor in our society until he marries me.'"

Women's groups objected and lobbied to have Gulnaz given refuge in a shelter. Then the news moved on and everyone lost interest in the case; the documentary was never officially released—another fifty thousand euros down the EU drain, part of some 18.2 million euros the EU spends annually on gender-focus programs,[16] not counting bilateral donor money from its member nations.

By 2014 history was being rewritten in Gulnaz's case. Mary Akrami, the head of an organization called the Afghan Women Skills Development Center, who says she was the first to open a women's shelter in Afghanistan (reportedly financed by the UN Women organization, as with the shelter in Bamiyan), claims that the international press and particularly Gulnaz's lawyer, Kimberley Motley (who took on the case after the documentary controversy erupted), deliberately distorted what had happened to Gulnaz. "The court married her by her consent," Ms. Akrami said. "She was not raped, but in fact she loved the guy and had a love affair with him. She then agreed to marry him. Her family reconciled with the man's family. They live together now and are happy. They have a child and are living in Kabul."

That is not how Kim Motley sees it, and she had visited Gulnaz as recently as mid-2014. The young woman, now twenty-two or twenty-three years old, really is married to her former rapist and does not deny that is what he is. He treats her decently, she told Ms. Motley, does not beat her, and provides for her and their daughter. Kim said that after the controversy over the documentary erupted, she at one point had offers from a dozen Western countries to provide Gulnaz with asylum. At the time Gulnaz was staying in Mary Akrami's shelter. "The minister of women's affairs and the shelter were blocking me from taking her to get a passport," she said. They saw reconciling with and marrying her rapist as the only solution that was in her interest, and history just had to be rewritten to make that possible, Ms. Motley said. "She never once denied to me that her cousin was her rapist; she was fifteen when it happened. She was even tied up when she was raped. There was never any ambiguity about that. She did finally marry him, but that's because the only way she could leave that fucking shelter was if she married this guy."

The sorts of offers of asylum that Gulnaz initially got had dried up by 2014, as more Afghan women saw flight from the country as their only salvation, and Western countries began to worry that granting asylum in such cases would undermine their efforts to promote women's rights within the country.

It was that attitude that had made an embassy rescue for Zakia and Ali increasingly unlikely, and all the more difficult for a couple with a criminal case against them. The conundrum raised by the criminal charges incensed Rabbi Shmuley. "That's the biggest farce of all. You fall in love with someone and it's a criminal case? I hope you will write something about these God-only-knows-how-many dead Americans and a trillion dollars in treasure so our government can respect a barbaric government. This is called the rule of law? I don't even know how they can say that with a straight face. Shaming them in the media is the only thing that's going to work. These people have to live like rats. Let's get them out."

Still, he couldn't get Ali and Zakia out when they had no passports—nor any legal way to secure them. But he could save someone else—and his mystery benefactor was willing to finance it, the government of Rwanda was willing to make it happen, and, he said, they were ready. They would save Fatima Kazimi. Just one thing bothered him about that. So, he wanted me to tell him frankly, did Fatima Kazimi really have grounds to fear for her life? "I'm worried that maybe she's just taking advantage of the situation and is now attempting to use this to get out of Afghanistan when we're trying to focus on Zakia and Ali, who seem to be in far greater danger." Yes, that sounded like Fatima all right, but I said nothing aloud. Answering him would put me in an ethically difficult position. If I had given him my unadorned, honest opinion, I would have said, *No, I really don't think she is in danger.* If that ruined the chance Shmuley was handing her to escape Afghanistan, what if she really was in danger? What right did I have to determine her fate and probably that of her family by expressing my opinion, particularly if I was wrong? I would get back to him, was the most I could say, and that was still kind of damning.

Up in Bamiyan even Fatima's allies were dismissive of any danger to her life. "There isn't any threat against her from other people, against her or her family. We would not let that happen," said the Bamiyan police chief, General Khudayar Qudsi. When the attorney general's office tried to interrogate her, he said, the police intervened to block it. "There was no basis, so we will not recognize such an action. The provincial attorney general based their request on accusations of Zakia's family, but there was no proof of Fatima Kazimi's involvement in the shelter escape," Chief Qudsi said. As for risks to her from Zakia's family? "It's not true. She has her own personal bodyguards who will take care of her safety, police bodyguards. That is our job and our responsibility. I think it's just an excuse so she can leave the country."

It seemed clear that what Fatima Kazimi wanted, like many Afghans, was a better life, and she had despaired of ever finding one in Afghanistan. That, however, does not qualify as "a well-founded fear of persecution" or any of the other generally accepted grounds for granting asylum or refugee status.

I felt like I had no choice but to share this view with Shmuley. My reporting had made her out to be one of the heroes of the piece, and he was about to reward her for it. Before I could reach Shmuley, though, Fatima called to say she was leaving that day for India, where she would be picking up her Rwandan visa. She had just the night before tried to leave through Kabul International Airport with a visa from the Rwandan government issued online, but Afghan airline officials had never seen an e-visa before and turned her away.

Shmuley had moved quickly. I called him back later that day, and he was in a celebratory mood. "Fatima arrived in Delhi. She's out of Afghanistan, thank God, and I hope we gave them security. They're on their way to Rwanda. Thank you for everything."

I told him I had belatedly come to the conclusion she was scamming everyone. Looking back, I figured she had probably planned this from the day of that first e-mail.

"We feel a sense of satisfaction," Shmuley said. "We got her out of there, thank God. Some people may not believe they are in danger, but we did the right thing." Shmuley reminded me a bit of the photographer Diego when he'd just found a beam of light coming through the ceiling and couldn't hear anything else anyone said.

In addition to the right to settle in Rwanda—and quite possibly becoming the first Afghans there in history—Fatima and her husband and four children would be given housing by President Kagame, and Rabbi Shmuley's benefactor was going to provide them with a twenty-thousand-dollar stipend to live on for the year, more than adequate for Rwanda. "We want to avoid an unhealthy dependency," he said.

He was finally ready to tell me who the benefactor was. "She is prepared to be named, with one caveat: so long as it does not endanger the couple." It was Miriam Adelson, the wife of casino magnate and multibillionaire Sheldon Adelson.

Ms. Adelson did not want credit as a Jewish person for saving a Muslim couple from their backward society. She was just moved by their case and wanted to help them, and anyone affected by their story as well. There was no other agenda here; Miriam's motives were purely humanitarian, he said. "The real hero of the story is not me, it was Miriam Adelson, who got me interested in their case. After a while, I became personally involved. I now really cared which direction this was going."

Fatima spent a couple of days in India, which coincided with a gala that Rabbi Shmuley's World Values Network put on in New Jersey with a variety of A-list celebrities and politicians, including Sean Penn, Governor Rick Perry of Texas, Governor Chris Christie of New Jersey, and Elie Wiesel.[17] Shmuley's aides organized a video hookup to New Delhi so Fatima could thank Miriam and President Kagame for rescuing her. Miriam might have had no particular agenda, but Paul Kagame did. Once seen as a hero in the West for pulling his country through the Rwandan genocide, Mr.

Kagame was lately in need of some good press, having been accused of murdering opponents, stifling dissent, and turning Rwanda, once Africa's bright black hope, into an autocratic state run by yet another African Big Man.[18] Like Shmuley, Miriam Adelson was a staunch supporter and defender of Israel, and Israel in turn was a staunch ally of Rwanda. The two countries' backers would see the shared experience of genocide as their bond; their critics would see governments with similarly appalling human-rights records fighting against a growing status as pariah states, despite their ennobling pasts.

The next day Fatima and her family were on the long flights from Delhi to Dubai and Dubai to Kigali.

The next time we spoke to Ali, in this case by phone, we told him that Fatima had escaped to Africa, after telling the people who wanted to help him that she, too, needed to be saved. He was astonished.

"Fatima went to Africa?" He laughed for a couple of minutes, then regained his composure. It was, he said, one more reason not to consider Africa as a way out. He and Zakia didn't want to be someplace where the only other person in the country who spoke their language was Fatima Kazimi.

His vehemence surprised me, and I asked why he felt that way. "She didn't help us at all," he said. "She didn't help me, she didn't help Zakia escape, she didn't do anything for us. One day we will run into each other and talk." It was an emotional outburst.

I said it was pretty undeniable that Fatima had prevented Zakia's family from taking her out of court that day and probably killing her. "That was all she did, and I respect that, but besides that she didn't do anything for us." That was underselling Fatima quite a bit, whether or not she had used the couple's situation to her own benefit. I didn't understand his attitude and would not for some time to come.

8

THE IRRECONCILABLES

Hope is not much of a plan, but it was about the only plan they had. "This world is sprung with our hopes, the past is built on our hopes, you spend your life with hopes," Ali said in his dreamy way on one of the few times in May when we were able to reach him, "and I'm just hoping now that God will help us." When Ali did choose to answer his phone, either he would barely listen to us or he would suddenly appeal to us to make the couple's decisions for them. The worst thing was that Ali was unwilling to come down to earth and get serious about their safety. Given the number of sightings of Zakia's male relatives not far from the Chindawul area of Kabul where the couple was hiding with his aunt, it was clear that place was no longer safe. Since the aunt was Anwar's sister, it wouldn't be hard for Zakia's family to find out where she lived, at least the general area, and then stake it out until Ali or Zakia came along. That might well have been what was already happening with the near misses. Ali always agreed with us when we lectured him about this, but we could have been talking to a wall.

One day Jawad and I sat down and wrote out a list of talking points for the next time we had Ali on the telephone and he was in half a mood to listen or if we were able to meet with him when he was on leave from his army post:

- They can't just stay in hiding forever. Sooner or later they will be caught. That's what everyone who works on these family disputes says.
- If they're caught, they'll both be taken to jail. That could well mean that Zakia would be sexually abused in custody, which happens routinely. Jail for a woman is much worse than a shelter, which is at least run by other women.
- They should think about at least talking to the people who run the Women for Afghan Women shelter. They don't have to do what they say, just hear them out.
- The WAW lawyers are very good, and recently they won a case similar to Zakia and Ali's, and while the case was in court, the woman had to stay in their shelter for only a month.
- The lawyers say their case is a strong one and they're certain they can prevail legally. They cannot do that, however, unless Zakia is no longer a fugitive and is somewhere so they can produce her in court. She could come into the shelter while Ali can stay in hiding.
- The head of WAW, Manizha Naderi, is happy to talk to Ali, and although she is in the United States now, she will call him in the evening, and this is the number she will be calling from.
- The WAW shelter is nothing like the one in Bamiyan. If they decide to go to the shelter to discuss their case with the lawyers there, we can go with them and guarantee that they can leave if they want to do so.
- If they ever change their minds and decide to leave Afghanistan, they're going to need to have passports, and they're not going to be able to get them safely while there are criminal charges against them. They need to get the legal case settled. The only countries they could go to without passports are Iran, which is dangerous, and Pakistan, which is difficult.

We drilled away on these talking points every time Jawad got Ali on the phone, and with his father and brothers as well, but he would not even agree to go to the shelter and hear what the lawyers said, let alone agree to Zakia's checking into the shelter so their case could go to court. When we spoke to Zakia, she deferred to Ali.

A week or more went by with no answer, just an out-of-service message on his number, and then finally came one of the familiar ringtones, from the blind Iranian singer Moein and his song "Past":

> Have no grief about the past,
> For the past has passed.
> Grief can never remake the past.
> Think of the future, of life, of joy.
> And if thirst should find no river,
> Just drink one drop, and be satisfied.[1]

This time Jawad made some headway, and Ali agreed to meet with us that Friday; his commander had given him a three-day leave. "He was scared," Jawad said. "I told him, 'Look, we haven't done anything to you. We've been to your house, been to your father, we could have turned you in anytime. You just have to trust us.'"

"Even today I didn't tell my wife I was going to see you, because she might have said no," Ali said. "The last time you came to see us"—when Zakia's brother was spotted near the Pamir Cinema—". . . well, she's very nervous about me. She doesn't want me to go out at all. She thinks I'll be arrested, so she'll be in big trouble."

Again, we suggested, all the more reason to consider the shelter for her until their legal case was finished. Manizha Naderi of WAW had offered to make that more palatable for Ali by giving him a job as a security guard at the shelter, guarding the outside wall; he would not be allowed inside, since the shelters were female-only spaces, but he'd know Zakia was safe, and they could have chaperoned meetings from time to time. Nothing persuaded him.

"My wife said she cannot be there for even one day. She cannot be separated from me even one day," he said. I wondered if that was his wife speaking or him.

Manizha and her top lawyer at the time, Shukria Khaliqi, came up with a solution. Shukria found a way to take the couple's case to court without having Zakia stay in the shelter. "All they have to do is give us permission to take on the case," Manizha said. "Both of them would just need to meet Shukria. Shukria can go to wherever they say and take their testimonies. Then, after the case goes to the judge, Zakia would have to come to court to testify on her own behalf. I am really worried that they will somehow be caught by the police." If they were, it would be too late for Zakia to opt for placement in the shelter; women can voluntarily stay in shelters while their criminal cases are adjudicated, but only if they come in on their own. Once they're arrested, they are jailed until their court date.

Driven by a need for more money, Ali finally agreed to meet with Shukria, although without Zakia. They were broke again, and they could receive the donors' money from WAW only in person, so that WAW's accountants could verify that the right people had gotten it. In a society where corruption is the norm, people have to go to extremes to prove that their actions aren't dishonest. Ali repeatedly asked us to pick up the money for him. It just wasn't right for us to put ourselves in the middle of that, and besides, we wanted to get him in to meet WAW's capable lawyers.

Tough and articulate, Shukria is somewhat overbearing, and immediately on meeting him she dominated Ali, insisting he put his trust in her.

"I'll resolve this case in a month," she told him. "I'll work on this case until I find success. I'll get my contacts in the Ministry of Interior to put pressure on the elders up there, and I'll do it in complete confidence—I won't even register the case, so even my staff won't know about it." Ali, on the sofa near her desk, leaned away from her as she spoke, seeming to diminish physically under her peroration.

Then the accountant came in to hand over a thousand dollars to him from the donations WAW had received, following a ritual often used when an illiterate person is involved in a formal transaction. The accountant read out loud a document saying that Ali confirmed receiving the payment. Ali verbally confirmed that he understood that, put his inked thumbprint to the document, and exchanged the document for the money; during the transaction an aide videotaped every step.

Afterward Ali was buoyed. "As long as they do not ask to remove Zakia from me again, it's okay, they can take the case," he said. "Whoever defends the truth, I am ready to serve them." He was in such a good mood that he agreed to arrange for us to talk to Zakia in person and to bring her to Shukria so she could formally agree to be represented by WAW.

Ali perked up even more when he heard that Jawad had received a call from one of the elders from Kham-e-Kalak, Zakia's village, and the elder wanted to come and talk to us about their case. The elder had an idea that the *New York Times* was some sort of NGO and thought we might be able to act as intermediaries between Zakia's family and the couple. His name was Abdul Rab Rastagar, and Jawad and I arranged to meet him at the Herat Restaurant in Shar-e-Naw, downtown Kabul. It was large and always crowded and very public, with the traditional raised eating platforms scattered among trees around a garden, but without privacy screening. Diners would leave their shoes under the platforms and sit cross-legged among mats and cushions. Eating on mats on the floor is the norm in Afghan homes; this was a refinement of that practice, probably originally designed to keep livestock away from the table. A peacock in full finery roamed the aisles between the platforms, trailing a six-foot-long tail array and squawking loudly. We went early and chose seats from which we could watch the front entrance, in case Mr. Rastagar came in heavy. We knew he had been in touch with Gula Khan. The last time Gula Khan had spoken to us on the phone, he'd sounded as angry at us as at his sister; apparently someone had been reading or relating to him *Times* articles on the case.

Mr. Rastagar arrived alone and looked harmless enough. He was an older man, in his fifties probably, but quite self-possessed; the term "elders," as Afghans apply it, can mean either very old men, revered for their antiquity, or somewhat older men of position, revered for their power. Mr. Rastagar was an example of personal advancement by virtue of massive foreign aid. For the first couple years after the Taliban fell, he worked for an organization called UN-Habitat, which carried out rural-development programs in Bamiyan. Then he went to work as a supervisor for the provincial juvenile-detention center, a government-run facility also financed by international donors. His lofty title gave him the position that Zakia's family was so impressed by and in turn had made them entrust to him the important mission of contacting the NGO known as the *New York Times,* which they believed was in touch with the couple. Later we learned that Mr. Rastagar was just a glorified guard, a shift supervisor.

When Mr. Rastagar took off his shoes, there were holes in the soles of his socks. He sat down cross-legged on the platform with us, dressed in a brown *shalwar kameez* and wearing the Afghan *pakol,* the flat felt cap common throughout the country. He got right to the point.

"No one is telling you the truth about this case," he said. "Mohammad Zaman had to leave everything and come here to Kabul to work like a common laborer because of this case. The truth is that the girl was betrayed by Ali's sister. She brought her out so Mohammad Ali could come and rape her. Then the sister went to her and said, 'Zakia, now your fiancé won't marry you.'" Mr. Rastagar meant the putative fiancé that Zaman had arranged for Zakia—one of his nephews. "You see, the sister wanted to marry Zakia's fiancé, and that's why she did all this. So she said, 'I'll marry him, and you can marry Mohammad Ali. But Zakia absolutely didn't want to be with Mohammad Ali. She was raped, and that's why they took her to the shelter. They did not let her father and mother visit her because she was regretting what happened and she wanted to come home."

Mr. Rastagar paused, making eye contact with an effort, to see how that was sinking in. "There's more."

"Really?"

"Yes, two of his other sisters, they're prostitutes. We all know they're prostitutes, and I'm sure it's their fault that this happened."

How did he know this?

"I worked with them at UN–Habitat," he said. "Of course they're prostitutes. They worked there for the foreigners."

As he did?

"Yes, but they were girls. Everyone in the village knew they were prostitutes. When a stranger came to the village, we all knew whose house they were going to."

This counternarrative was delivered with smooth assurance, as if it were the most obvious explanation possible and, once apprised of it, any listener would see the rightness of Zakia's father's cause.

I suggested that Zakia would not have climbed out of the Bamiyan shelter and eloped with Ali if he were her rapist.

"The government set up that escape," he said. "She didn't want to. She's in hiding. No one knows where she is. Or if she is with him in the mountains, okay, she is with him in the mountains, but she didn't want to be there. Honestly, the father has been oppressed in this case."

Zakia's father was the real victim of the entire story, he continued. "Now he's in Kabul almost as a beggar because he's lost everything, everything," he said. "He didn't take care of his children, especially his daughters. He didn't do well by them, it's true. I don't approve of the man for this. He shouldn't have let his daughter go into the fields for this affair to take place."

But you said it was a rape?

"Or rape. It couldn't have taken place if he didn't let his daughter go into the fields unchaperoned. I wanted to beat Zaman myself, I was so angry at him."

He was particularly worked up about the shelter, letting a girl run away like that. "The shelter must have helped her escape," he said. "I have twenty-five children under my charge, and why do *they* not escape? It is just not possible." It was easy to imagine Mr. Rastagar subduing a passel of small children.

Officials in Bamiyan had made everything worse by not listening to the old man Zaman and his sons and by throwing him out of their offices when he came to complain, which by all accounts he did often. "The governor said to Zaman, 'Don't talk to me anymore, or I'll put you in jail next,'" Mr. Rastagar said.

That had led to an unstable situation, a rent in the fabric of the social order that could have far-reaching consequences. "The outcomes are going to be bad. The husband will do something, the first husband"—the one he had earlier described as the fiancé—"he is armed now, and he would kill anyone in this. I saw the father, he wants to commit suicide. The father, Zaman, he is weak, a weak person, but he is saying he will kill himself or else he will go and join the Taliban and go to Ghorband"—a notorious, Taliban-controlled district athwart the highway between Kabul and Bamiyan—"and if he finds any Hazara on the road, he will kill them."

In other words, suicide and mayhem, the random execution of strangers of the wrong ethnicity—it's the sort of thing that follows naturally when two people are foolish enough to fall in love.

"I don't like this father. He didn't raise his kids right," Mr. Rastagar said. Now he seemed eager to establish his credentials as an honest broker. "He didn't send his kids to school, so they grew up blind, and when blind persons go out, they get into trouble."

How about five thousand dollars—would that be enough to make old man Zaman happy? Just asking theoretically.

"I will work as hard as possible to resolve this case." Mr. Rastagar ignored the sum.

Seven thousand?

"The father will not return to Bamiyan. There's nothing left for him. Everyone turned on him. We have an Afghan proverb: When you are in need, your friends become strangers."

Ten thousand?

"The outcomes now are going to be bad. The first husband will do something, and it will be something that no one will be able to undo."

Mr. Rastagar said he would talk to the father. He added that he knew that already the first husband had spent twenty thousand dollars as a result of the elopement, to pay the bride price for the bride he never laid eyes upon, the wedding party that never took place. He would talk to Zaman. He was meeting him that afternoon, in fact. We told him we would find someone who would be authorized to negotiate for the couple, something we could not do. Our questions were merely exploratory.

When we parted, his last comment was peculiar. "If they do really love each other, it's okay."

The meeting was a modestly encouraging development. However mean-spirited the narrative Mr. Rastagar was peddling, it was clear that he was ready to deal and was probably acting on behalf of Zakia's father. Piling on charges of prostitution and rape was only a way of raising the stakes and improving Zaman's bargaining position. For their part, Ali and Zakia were ecstatic at the prospect of a negotiated settlement with her family. Although they realized there was every possibility her family would take any settlement money and still try to kill them, nonetheless it would mean the criminal charges against them would be withdrawn, the law would no longer be looking for them, and they would be free to get their passports. Ali scoffed when he heard the amount of twenty thousand dollars. "That is ten lakhs of rupees," he said, meaning afghanis. "In our village the usual bride price is less than three lakhs. You could marry three wives for ten lakhs."

There was no question of Jawad and I getting involved in any real negotiations, so with the couple's approval we turned to WAW and Shukria. We told her that Rastagar had floated a twenty-thousand-dollar figure, and she just laughed. She would be surprised if the family would not settle for five thousand, which made possible a settlement within the range of what donors had already sent to the couple; we told her that there were donors as well who had pledged to make up a bride price if that was not enough.

We were in Shukria's office when she called Rastagar and began to talk with him about the case. She quickly took his measure and started barking orders at him. He would get Zakia's father and he would bring him to her office to discuss the case, she told him. No, not next week, but two days later, on Saturday, she said. He promised to do so. "Don't be late, I'm a busy person," she said.

"This is fantastic," Manizha Naderi said. "Don't worry about what the elder is saying now. They always do that. That's what the people were saying about my nephew—that he raped and then kidnapped her. This is really great news, actually. We might have a chance in resolving this story."

Manizha was referring to the case of her own nephew and his wife, which was strikingly similar to that of Ali and Zakia. That couple eloped against the wishes of her family, who opposed it not because of ethnic or religious differences but because of class differences. The girl was from a family of Sayeds, people who consider themselves direct descendants of the Prophet Moham-mad, a sort of Islamic nobility, who tend to want their children to marry other Sayeds. After the couple eloped, the girl's fam-ily claimed that she had already been married to her first cousin, and they even produced a mullah and witnesses who claimed to have been present when her father (although not the girl herself) had tied the *neka* on her behalf; they produced a *neka* document as well. Manizha persuaded her nephew to bring the girl to the shelter, and she remained there while Shukria brought her case to court. She won it with a simple stratagem: She challenged the girl's family and their witnesses to produce a single image of the alleged wedding ceremony. Since nowadays nearly everyone with any means at all has a camera phone, videos and stills of wedding ceremonies are typically taken by many of those present. When none of them could produce such an image, the judge invalidated the family's *neka* and legalized the couple's own marriage. It was that case that made Shukria so confident she could win Ali and Zakia's case, since there were witnesses who could confirm that until they eloped, Zakia's father had claimed only that she had been engaged, not married—and had changed his story regarding which cousin had been her intended.

The good news about a possible reconciliation gave a welcome boost to Zakia and Ali just as the home front began to unravel. Re-lations with Ali's aunt had become tense, and not just because the apartment was overcrowded. "They feel in danger, too. Even we do," Ali said. "Until we negotiate and make a deal and come together, we feel in danger. It's even risky when you're together with your friends. Someone who is your friend can harm you worse than someone who doesn't even know you. He might not realize what he's telling someone about you. If he's close to you, he will be dangerous to you."

One day Ali called Jawad, deeply agitated. We had given him a letter, on *New York Times* letterhead in Dari and English, with a copy to both him and his wife, a "To Whom It May Concern" letter that asked whoever read it to please call our bureau in Kabul and included Jawad's and my phone numbers. My thinking was that if one or the other of the lovers fell into the hands of police, the evidence of some foreign interest in their case might possibly prevent the worst from happening to them—particularly to Zakia—and it might help alert us to their situation more quickly. Now Ali was calling from his military deployment to ask whether that letter would protect Zakia from arrest by the police if she went out alone and was stopped.

No, it wouldn't, we told him. The most we could hope for was that it might protect her from summary rape, and that was iffy—the great majority of policemen cannot read or write, so she would have to be lucky enough to encounter someone who was senior enough to be literate and savvy enough to care what foreigners might think. It was a long shot.

What was going on? we asked Ali. It turned out that he had been transferred to Bagram Air Base, the massive American military base a couple hours' drive from the capital. "My wife called me and complained about my aunt and her daughter-in-law, who are mistreating her. She was upset and asked me to send her back to Bamiyan. I thought my aunt was someone I could trust and expected she would give us refuge, but now it seems she has slapped me in the face and my wife cannot stay with her. I don't know what to do. Sometimes I think I should commit suicide."

The country was in a state of suspense over the bitterly disputed results of the April presidential election, and it was clear there would have to be a second, runoff election in June. As a result, Ali's unit had been activated in preparation for deployment somewhere in the provinces to protect polling places, hence the transfer to Bagram. There was no longer any question of leave days every weekend; now he and Zakia were reduced to talking by phone again, and his next leave would not be until after elections, many weeks away.

Matters came to a head in their hideout, and the aunt demanded that Zakia leave as soon as possible. Zakia had been feeling ill for several days and wanted Ali to take her to a hospital. Relations had soured with Ali's aunt to the point where the aunt would not take her, and Zakia could not hope to find her way there alone. Moving out would also require a man to escort her; social norms made it nearly impossible for her to find another place on her own, and anyway Ali had unwisely—but typically—taken most of their money with him.

Ali said he would try to get permission to leave the base, but the next day when we spoke to him, he was even more despondent. Turned down for a leave because of his unit's pending deployment, he had tried to get a guard on the perimeter to let him sneak off the base but had been rebuffed. He had called his father to come down from Bamiyan to take care of his wife, but Anwar would need a couple of days to travel, and Zakia was increasingly frantic about leaving.

"It's because of my bad luck that these things keep happening," Ali said, and he told Zakia on the phone that he would try to escape. In a more levelheaded moment, much later, he was more honest about himself. "You buy danger for yourself by the things you decide to do."

We pleaded with Ali not to try to escape from Bagram, saying it could only end badly. He might not have known that base well, but I did. The largest American base in the country, Bagram was heavily guarded, with patrols, high-tech monitors, trip wires, pressure sensors, video cameras, surveillance blimps, and fences within fences. The Afghan National Army billets were within the broader American perimeter. Not only would escape be nearly impossible, but Ali risked being shot if he tried it.

We offered instead to arrange to take Zakia somewhere safe

ourselves, perhaps to a guesthouse or to the home of a woman. I called an Afghan-American woman who lived outside Kabul with her Afghan family—educated, Westernized people who were sympathetic to Zakia and Ali's plight—and she agreed to put Zakia up until Ali could join her. Ali refused the offer flatly, and we argued about it; I asked him why he didn't trust us. "I trust you. I even trust your dogs," he said, which is a common expression, invoking Afghans' almost universal contempt for canines. "But Zakia would never agree to stay with someone she doesn't know." Meaning he would never agree to let her. We suggested that she go to the WAW shelter until he could join her, but he rejected that out of hand.

It was two days before we heard from him again; his phone had stopped answering, and we suspected, rightly, that he'd gone ahead with his escape plan. He and two friends had climbed the main fence, carrying a blanket to drape over the rolled concertina wire that lay on the other side of it. He was crawling over the wire when a patrol came along and caught him.

"They nearly shot me when they saw me in the wire," he said once we got him on the phone; he had been locked up in solitary confinement during those two days when we could not reach him. "I was given a hard time, accused of being a spy. They told me you haven't spent one month in the army and now you want to sneak away from the base?" Taliban infiltrators were a constant worry in the Afghan National Army.

In the coming week, he tried twice more to escape the base and was each time punished. "I told them if you stop me a hundred times, I will still try to escape."

Anwar reached Kabul several days later after a dangerous journey. Hazaras need to take great care on both of the two main highways connecting Kabul with the Bamiyan Valley, one through Wardak Province slightly to the south, and the other through Parwan to the north. Both roads have stretches that go through Taliban territory, and while the roads are normally under government control, the Taliban do occasionally manage to set up flying roadblocks, as they are called, and Hazaras often do not get through alive when that happens. Reports of roadblocks ahead forced him to turn back twice. Anwar was delayed, too, by the funeral of someone in their village; however urgent his son's and his daughter-in-law's entreaties might have been, funerals take precedence over nearly everything, and Anwar was an old man, inclined to the long view.

Once in Kabul, though, he calmed his sister down. She agreed to give them a few days to find another place to stay. I passed Anwar a little money to help with that—Ali was still in the army lockup, so he could not go to collect money from WAW—and the last thing we wanted to see was Zakia and her father-in-law wandering the streets of Kabul, inviting arrest.

Ali was calmer when he heard that his father had arrived, and he thought he would soon find a way to get off the base to join them. In the meantime he had a request. Once they moved Zakia out of his aunt's house, how about if we got WAW to give them all the money they had received, and he would buy a house in Kabul so they did not have to rent any longer? A few thousand dollars would, he thought, be enough for a smaller home.

"Ali," we said to him, "your wife is in hiding. The police are searching for you both. Zakia's family is looking to kill you. You're in jail on the base. And you want to buy a house?"

That day Jawad got a call from Anwar, who also thought fugitive homeownership was a dumb idea. Jawad had called Anwar before, usually through one of his sons, but the old man had never before called him, and he did so now with Bismillah's help. He wanted to thank us for all we had done for his son, and he wanted us to know that he thought his son was wrong and foolish to have spurned offers of help and rejoined the army. Unless they were able to make a deal with Zakia's family—and even if they did—the couple's only hope to really live in peace was to leave Afghanistan. Anwar also wanted to meet us in person; it turned out he had lugged down from Bamiyan a hand-woven felt rug, which he said was a thank-you gift for helping his son. It was probably worth a month's earnings, yet I had no choice but to accept it.

Ismatullah called as well. "Ali does not realize what he has to do," he said. "He is too young to understand what is good or bad for him. Tell him he needs to listen to you. He needs to go outside the country. His life is in danger." Jawad asked Ismatullah why he didn't tell his brother that himself. But Ali was not answering his phone to his older brother. "He is tired of listening to everyone tell him what he has to do," Ismatullah said.

Then, to our surprise, a few days later Ali was freed from the base lockup and even managed to get out of Bagram on a leave, determined to desert for good this time. When we met Ali in Kabul, Jawad and I spent most of the time trying to persuade him to find a better hiding place, one where we could visit them more safely than if they were sharing a house with an Afghan family. They needed to *not* stay with relatives; relatives provide a trail to them. In response Ali was his usual blend of nervously insecure and unreasonably cavalier. He was hopeful that the mediation that Shukria was running with Zakia's father was going to bear fruit; in addition, Ali's aunt's son, Shah Hussein, had been meeting with Zakia's brothers to talk about a deal. "Didn't it occur to you," we asked, "that her brothers might follow his aunt's son or figure out where he's living, find her, and then find the two of you?" Again he brushed that aside. We said we would be willing to get them a private house with a wall around it and a driveway, which would make it possible for us to drive off the street and not be noticed by neighbors when we made a rendezvous with them. We would pay the four hundred dollars a month it would cost. Finally Ali agreed, as he often did, just to get us off his back, but instead of moving to the sort of place we'd suggested, he moved out of the aunt's house in Chindawul and into another house a few hundred yards down the hill. It was only a hundred dollars a month, so he suggested we could give them the three-hundred-dollar-a-month savings over what we had proposed; we refused to pay any of it. We had an ally in Anwar, and Jawad set to work persuading the old man that moving again, away from Chindawul and into a secure house, would be a good option for them as well as for us. The last thing I wanted was to feel responsible for their capture.

Reconciliation was starting to look less likely, too. Shukria was having a hard time with Zaman and his sons and supporters.

Initially willing to talk, Zakia's father had become aggressive and uncooperative. He accused Shukria of hiding Zakia in the WAW shelter and demanded to be allowed to look for her there.

"That man used such bad language," she said. "It was unacceptable." Amid her shouting and his cursing, she drove him from her office and WAW's administrative compound. Something had happened to make Zakia's family less willing to negotiate a settlement, and we would soon find out what that was.

There were many times when I marveled at my growing involvement with this couple. The line between observer and actor had first been crossed when we helped them escape from the police pursuit in Yakawlang, but now, with each passing week, further compromises seemed easier to make than to refuse: helping them with their housing, giving them advice, trying to talk them out of situations that might prove disastrous, urging them toward a sensible course of action. That's the thing about stepping over the line; once you do, it's hard not to do it again. Having helped them get this far, how could I just stop? I knew that if I turned my back on this young and often foolish pair of lovers, it would only be a matter of time before the worst happened, and I would never be able to forgive myself. The more I did for them, however, the more they expected me to do; the more dependent they became, the more independent they wanted to seem; the more I did, the more I felt obliged to do. I felt like their personal Friar Laurence, in an increasingly compromised scenario.

It's not as if Zakia and Ali's case was particularly terrible. On the scale of horrendous abuses of women in Afghanistan, Zakia's situation, so far, did not rate very high. Consider Lal Bibi, the young woman who was abducted and raped by a pro-government militia commander, who then married her to escape prosecution; or Bibi Aisha, her nose and ear cut off by her Taliban husband; or Gul Meena, chopped up with an ax and left for dead—all were far worse cases.

There were some cases similar to Zakia's as well, such as that of

Amina, whose family gave the same sort of guarantees and assurances that Zakia's family promised her if she returned.[2] Then they killed her on the way home from a shelter—exactly what Zakia thought would happen to her if she left the shelter to return to her family. Similarly, Siddiqa[3] was coaxed home and then stoned to death with her intended by her neighbors and relatives. Even more similar was the story of Khadija and Mohammad Hadi, who were also from Bamiyan, also a Tajik and Hazara couple. When Khadija was taken into custody, her lover's angry neighbors drove his entire family out of Bamiyan and he lost touch with Khadija, until she disappeared and lost touch with everyone.[4]

So while there are many worse cases, they are expressions of the sort of fate that awaits Zakia and Ali if events were allowed to follow their natural course. While things had not gotten as bad as they could have, it was still possible that they would. Like it or not, their story had become mine, and I could not turn my back on it as I nearly had after that first encounter in February 2014. It had become clear that no one was going to step in and rescue them, whisking them away to safe lives in America or Sweden. I realized I would have to start thinking seriously about getting them out of Afghanistan myself. I had already stepped across the line; why not follow the story to its inevitable conclusion? If they ended up dead, I would always regret not having tried harder. In this effort I had one supporter, Rabbi Shmuley. During one of our late-night talks, he started in on me after he finished with the American government. "You're the only one who can make this happen. You have to make sure this story has a happy ending, and a happy ending is not living in a cave in Afghanistan."

9

BIRDS IN A CAGE

An Afghan woman alone is easily run to ground, and suddenly, one day in June, Zakia became that woman, her husband ripped away from her, his aunt ready to disown her, and the police actively searching the Chindawul area for her. Her family had finally caught up to the couple, capturing Ali and turning him over to the police. This all happened just days after Zakia had learned what everyone had begun to suspect: she was pregnant.

Gentle-spirited Jawad would later describe that day as the most stressful of his life. I'm not sure what was worse, being there in the middle of it, as Jawad was, or not being there at all, as I was. When the call came that Ali had been arrested, Jawad was enjoying his Friday off out of town, an hour away from Kabul, while I was in Doha, Qatar, working on a Taliban story. Jawad got the news in a call from Shah Hussein, Ali's cousin and the son of the aunt who took the couple in and then kicked them out; both Shah Hussein and Ali had been picked up by the police. It was about 1:00 P.M. when Jawad heard, and he raced back to Kabul, spending most of the next eight hours continuously on the telephone; all I could do was check in from time to time and nudge matters along. "I must have made fifty phone calls that day and gotten another fifty," Jawad said; he had phones on two of the country's cell-phone networks, and he kept them both going, along with the bureau landline. The first call he made was to Anwar, who was with Zakia at their new home when the arrest happened. Shah Hussein had already called them with the news, and both of them were in tears. "Can you solve this for us, please?" Zakia asked Jawad.

Jawad called me in Qatar, and said, "What should I tell them?" I asked him where Ali had been taken. It was to the headquarters of Police District 1, and he had been arrested not far from where Zakia, Anwar, and he were staying in Chindawul, among the squatter dwellings that every year creep farther up the side of the steep little mountain above the Pamir Cinema. Surely if the police caught him near the Pamir, it would only be a matter of time before they canvassed the hillside neighborhood and found Zakia as well. For Ali it was just an arrest and possibly some jail time; for Zakia it was quite possibly the end of life as she knew it, with disgrace and defilement waiting for her in a police cell and the real possibility that the police would then hand her over to her family, which would be the end of her life, full stop.

"There's only one thing to do. Tell them they both need to get as far away from there as possible, and they should split up and go different ways." Jawad relayed the message.

Ali had thought his cousin Shah Hussein would be his guarantee of safety, and they stayed friendly after he and Zakia moved to the new house and away from the aunt. Shah Hussein often visited them, partly out of friendship, partly as protection. He was a senior noncom in the Afghan National Army and very much the older brother to his cousin, seven years his junior, and he tried to rein him in. Ali had started going out frequently, to visit friends or just to get air, and it was driving everyone in the family crazy, most of all Zakia. Shah Hussein had taken her side and tried to lay down the law.

"Don't leave the house," Shah Hussein told Ali. "If I come back

and find you are out, I'm going to shackle you to the furniture."
He was in the military police and produced a set of handcuffs to
back up the threat.

But that day, June 6, 2014, Shah Hussein was on leave and suggested that he and Ali go together to a wedding. Zakia said she was
okay with that, that as a man he could not be cooped up indoors all
the time. She had a house to keep, food to cook, laundry to do—
the men had no work to do inside. Shah Hussein was tall and well
built, an imposing man. "He thought if he was along, then I would
be okay if we ran into her family," Ali said. They set out in civvies
and had only just walked down the hill and turned in to the road
along the Kabul River (more an open-air sewer than a river, where
heroin addicts hang out under the bridges) in front of the Pamir
Cinema. Suddenly Ali heard someone shouting at him and turned
as Zakia's little brother, Razak, the nine-year-old, flung himself
at him, grabbing his lapels and screaming, "You kidnapper! You
eloper! Now you're finding out it's not so easy!" Ali pushed the boy
away only to see a policeman come up right behind him, leveling
an AK-47 assault rifle at him.

"Don't move. If you do, I'll kill you," the policeman said, adding,
as if to establish his credentials for violence, "I'm already answering
one charge for killing someone, so another one won't matter much."

Right behind him was Gula Khan. They had all been lying
in wait, probably staking out the neighborhood. The policeman
ordered his two prisoners to a guard shack nearby, and by then six
of Ali's male in-laws were all over Shah Hussein and Ali, manhan-
dling them and demanding to know Zakia's whereabouts, until
more police arrived and restored order. They were soon transferred
to the Police District 1 station house, where there was a lockup.

"The police wanted to know where she was, and I said in
Bamiyan," Ali told me. "I didn't care how much they beat me.
I wasn't going to confess and betray her." Her hiding place, as
he well knew, was only a couple hundred yards up the steep hill
nearby. The police said his father-in-law had accused him of kidnapping and murdering Zakia, and they wanted to know where
he'd dumped her body. Believing the worst, they beat him with

the butts of their rifles, then threw him into a cell and beat him some more in an effort to make him talk.

At some point Ali managed to pass his phone to his cousin, so that he would be able to call Anwar, Zakia, and Jawad, since Shah Hussein didn't have their numbers himself. After Zakia's relatives confirmed that Shah Hussein was not involved in the case, police freed him, but when he went outside the PD1 station, a gang of Zakia's relatives jumped him, beating him with bricks until he managed to run off. He regretted not having worn his uniform—they could never have treated him in public that way if he had. Once he was sure no one was following him, Shah Hussein climbed the hill to Ali's new house, but by the time he got there, Zakia and Anwar had fled; at Ali's aunt's house, his cousin changed into his uniform and went looking for them.

No one ever found out for sure how Zakia's family tracked them down, but some theories emerged. The extended family in Afghanistan is a powerful organization in its way and is normally so large, with relationships maintained over such a distant degree, that even the poorest family will have relatives far and wide, high and low. One of their distant relatives was a taxi driver, and before this whole affair he had driven Shah Hussein from Bamiyan to a house where Ali's aunt had previously lived. Although the aunt moved later, it was not far away from her previous home. That was Ali's theory anyway. Another possibility was that Shah Hussein, who had been meeting with Gula Khan and some of Zakia's cousins in an effort at reconciliation, might have been followed home. Anwar's theory was that someone had followed him down from the mountains when he came to town the week before. He'd had that creepy feeling that someone was following him, he said, though he could never spot anyone. My own theory? The aunt gave them up. Their relationship had soured, she was tired of being responsible for them, and she did not get along with her new niece. They had fortunately moved out of her house just before the capture, but it was to a place not far away, which would explain why the family had the neighborhood staked out, but not the actual house. Whatever the real explanation, it was a lesson in how hard it is to hide in Afghanistan, even in a city of 5 million people, many of them stuffed into dense slums. With its strong family networks, Afghan society is just not anonymous enough.

Zakia and Anwar's first stop was to the aunt's house, where Zakia borrowed a full-length *hejab*,[1] something she almost never wore. As a getaway costume, it was hard to beat; all that anyone could see were her eyes and her high-heeled shoes. The blue burqa would have been even better, but as Zakia often said, she wouldn't be caught dead in that thing. Anwar told his sister to take Zakia down into the city, and the two women wended their way between the mud masonry houses parallel to the river, high up on the hill. Zakia had no idea where anything was in Kabul and could not move around alone without arousing suspicion, so the sister agreed to help guide her, but she made it clear she was not happy about it. Anwar went straight down the steep path to the river.

"It was a difficult day for all of us," Jawad later said. "They kept calling me, calling me. 'What can you do for us?' Shah Hussein called me, Zakia called me. Anwar called me, and you could feel the pain and helplessness in his voice, and then he started crying, 'What should I do, what can I do?'"

Jawad called me again in Doha. "What should I tell them?"

"There's only one solution. You have to persuade them to take her to the shelter before the police find her. Have they left the house?"

"Yes."

"Why don't you meet them in your car, get them off the street, and drive around until they can decide what to do?"

Jawad agreed, and thus began a scramble in which the three of them tried for hours to find one another. Jawad still doesn't know if that was by accident, because they had such a poor knowledge of the city, or because Zakia and Anwar feared that he would some-how force them to put her in the shelter and therefore were avoid-ing him.

Zakia and Ali's aunt soon managed to meet up with Shah Hus-sein, who did know the city, and the aunt gratefully went home, leaving Zakia with Ali's cousin. "See what you have brought to us?" the aunt said on parting. Stepping out with Shah Hussein, however, was perilous enough in itself, because he was not proper *mahram* to Zakia—not a close enough male blood relative, or husband, to be allowed to escort her, although Ali had asked him to do that for them. Should they be arrested, those would be additional charges the police could bring: attempted *zina,* that novel Afghan offense of attempted adultery, in which a non-*mahram* couple are assumed to be on their way to have sex simply on the basis of their being alone in each other's company, even on a public street.

Complicating matters, Shah Hussein was under strict instructions from Ali, who had whispered them to him as his cousin left PD1: Take her back to the mountains and under no circumstances let her go to the WAW shelter. Zakia had relayed that message to Jawad, and for much of the day her only purpose in talking to him was to implore him to somehow use our supposed powers to get Ali out of prison. She refused to let Jawad come and pick her up, again because of the impropriety of being with an unrelated man. So Jawad concentrated on finding Anwar, thinking he could talk sense to Zakia, and also so she would have an acceptable *mahram* along. "He's an idiot. My son is stupid," Anwar said angrily in one of his many phone calls to Jawad. "Why was he going to a wedding? He never listens. How can I take her now? I don't have anyplace to go."

Jawad let the folks at WAW know what had happened, and the lawyer Shukria also called Zakia, trying to persuade her that going into the shelter was her only safe option as a woman alone and that it would not be the sort of prisonlike situation she had endured in Bamiyan.

At last Anwar told Jawad he was near a bridge across the Kabul River and there was a hospital nearby—that could only be the Ibn-Seena Hospital, so Jawad went there, parked in front of an abandoned police traffic kiosk on the bridge, and told Anwar where he could find him. Several calls later the old man climbed into his car. With Anwar along there was someone present who could be Zakia's *mahram,* so Jawad was able to persuade Zakia to let him pick her up, and she would be safely off the streets. He found her not far from the Allauddin Crossroads, in a Hazara neighborhood in western Kabul, standing beside the road with Shah Hussein, who was now in his full army uniform.

Zakia still wanted no part of the shelter. She removed her veil in the car, and her face was streaked with tears, slashing paths through her ruined makeup, mascara smeared to make raccoon eyes. "Let us go into the mountains, Uncle," she said to Anwar. She had taken to calling her father-in-law "uncle" as a token of affection and respect. He called her "daughter," as he had that first night she came into his home. He said okay, and they asked Jawad if he would take them to the edge of town. There was a minibus station there where they might find a late ride past the Paghman Mountain, which hems in the Kabul plateau from the west, and then into Bamiyan. That road was risky at night; the danger of the Taliban was compounded by the danger from Zakia's family, who might be lying in wait for them, knowing it was the most likely way for her to flee. Shah Hussein could not go with them; the next morning he had to report to duty, which he, unlike his cousin, took seriously, so it would just be Zakia and the old man. They would not be able to stay in Bamiyan city or their own village with the police looking for her; the authorities were no doubt alerted in Bamiyan as well that Ali had been arrested, and they would expect Zakia to go back to the valley.

Jawad was distressed at how upset Anwar seemed. "He looked so tired and beaten down." He realized that escaping into the mountains would mean they would have to leave cars and roads and climb, and he just felt too tired to do that. Their escape on the Shah Foladi mountain had nearly killed him, he felt, and he could not face it again. Still, he held his tongue and did not object overtly to Zakia's escape plan, except to say that he was worried about his high blood pressure. And, he added to Jawad, "Zakia is pregnant. She shouldn't be running in the mountains."

Zakia got the message that Anwar couldn't handle it; perhaps she felt the same way. She turned in her seat to face Anwar and spoke to him. She seemed quite calm and determined to be strong. "Uncle, don't worry about me. I'll be safe, and I'll stand by your side, and we will get the boy out. I will go to the shelter." Jawad could see that she was doing it for Anwar more than anything else; she knew that her husband wanted her to keep running, but she couldn't do that if it meant doing it without the old man or leaving him behind somewhere along the way.

Shukria had left her office at WAW and gone home, and reached there by phone at first she was reluctant to come out, but finally, in the middle of the night, she called the shelter. They sent her a minibus, and she rendezvoused with Jawad. Everyone piled into the minibus for the ride to the WAW shelter. Speaking quietly, Zakia kept reassuring her father-in-law that it would be all right. The gates of the shelter's compound swung open, the men dismounted, and the minibus drove in with just Zakia and Shukria. Jawad got his car and dropped Anwar off in a neighborhood where Anwar thought he might know someone. "I felt sorry for him," Jawad said. "He lost everything, he had no place to stay, his son was in jail, his daughter-in-law in the shelter, and they all thought this shelter was going to be like the one in Bamiyan and that she would be there for months and months." Jawad called Shah Hussein once more, to let him know where he had dropped his uncle. That phone did not ring, so he called Ali's phone, which Shah Hussein still had.

There was a new ringtone on it now, the song "Majnoon" by the Iranian singer Moein.

> In my soul I bear
> The pain and sorrow of your love:
> Do not let me wait any longer
> Watching for you by the roadside!
> I am crazy, I am possessed,
> Wild with love, I sing:
> I am Majnoon!
> Layli, without you
> I cannot live.[2]

"Zakia is in the shelter," Jawad told Shah Hussein. "Your uncle is safe." That night, though, Anwar would sleep on the street.

At the police station, Ali had been in for a rough time. As far as the police were concerned, he was at the very least a sex criminal for running away with a woman without her family's permission, quite possibly a kidnapper, and perhaps a murderer. "They beat me with rifle butts," he said. "Over and over until I grabbed the rifle butt and said, 'Please stop, you're not allowed to hurt me, and I'm just here because I love her and she loves me.'" The beatings stopped for a while, but he was refused food or the right to use the bathroom. Sharing a cell with four other men, he was obliged to soil himself and lie in the wet.

The next day detectives from the Criminal Investigation Division came to question him again, and he persisted with his story that Zakia had stayed in the mountains somewhere in Bamiyan and he had come alone to Kabul. "They didn't believe me. They already knew so much about my case," he said. Someone had been talking. They knew what house he had lived in with his aunt, that the couple had recently moved to another house nearby and where it was. Zakia and Anwar had been able to escape only because police bureaucracy had moved too slowly to follow up on Ali's arrest.

I suggested to Jawad that he go to the police station the next day, Saturday, to try to see Ali, while I wrote an article from Jawad's reporting about what had happened to the couple; there was just enough time to make the early deadlines for the Sunday bulldog (the print edition that comes out on Saturday afternoon), and I had a head start because I'd already written a tentative lede for just such a story when we'd begun to suspect both that Zakia was pregnant and that Ali would get caught.[3]

When Jawad and Anwar got to PD1, Zakia's family was there in force, hanging around outside the station, glowering and jeering at them as they walked past. At the lockup the jailers said that only the old man could visit his son, but this gave Jawad a chance to talk with the PD1 police chief, Colonel Jamila Bayaz. She was famous as the first female police chief of an Afghan police district.[4] I had interviewed her when she was appointed earlier in the year; it was something the Ministry of Interior liked to boast about,[5] since the lack of female officers,[6] especially in key positions, was an issue that was important to the international community. I had heard that Colonel Bayaz was quite good—later in 2014 she was promoted to brigadier general, one of only four female general officers in the Ministry of Interior and its police agencies at the time. There had been a fifth one, in charge of gender issues, Brigadier General Shafiqa Quraishi, but she fled the country and sought asylum abroad.[7] During my earlier interview with Colonel Bayaz, her deputy, a man, a senior official who wouldn't be named, another man, and two or three other policemen all crowded into the room. When I asked Jamila questions, they answered for her. "As things like my promotion happen, it motivates other women to do more," she said when she managed to get a word in edgewise on her own interview. She did say something else, though, quite unbidden and, as it would later turn out, quite plaintive. "I am sure our international friends will not abandon us," she said. I later learned, from Western diplomats in Kabul, that she had applied to the Canadian government for asylum.[8]

At the time of Ali's arrest, though, Colonel Bayaz had been on the job for six months and was earning a reputation as a tough advocate for better treatment of women by the police, and she seemed very much in charge of her station. Jawad found her sympathetic to Zakia and Ali's story—although unaware of Ali's mistreatment in her lockup by the detectives (she was in direct charge of the uniformed officers only). "I know it's a love story and the boy eloped with a girl who loved him. Higher-level officials have told me, 'Please make sure he doesn't escape.'" As everyone in Afghanistan well knows, escapes from Afghan lockups and prisons are routine and not very expensive, an opportunity for guards to supplement their incomes.

No one was more aware of that than Zakia's family members, on their stakeout of the district police station. "We know you want to bribe that woman police chief to get him out, but we're not going to let you," Zaman told Anwar as he came out. "We have friends, too, you'll see."

Shukria came to the police station later that day, carrying a signed statement from Zakia that she had not been kidnapped. The bigamy charges had gone away—perhaps her family did not feel they could make that charge stick, although they were still claiming she was married to a cousin she had never met. Or perhaps the attorney general's office just didn't believe the bigamy charge, since the judges in Bamiyan had themselves attested that Zakia was engaged, not married—and breaking an engagement is a civil matter, not a criminal one. But the detectives handling the case were not interested in the fine points Shukria presented to them; they were treating it as a criminal kidnapping offense, and they deemed an exculpatory letter from Ali's wife and supposed victim insufficient.

For a second day, Ali said, he was beaten by officers and denied food and use of the toilet. Later in the day, he was moved along with some of the other detainees into a steaming-hot shipping container that served as their temporary jail cell due to overcrowding in the PD1 lockup. "We were five people in the container, and they brought a crane in to move the container to another place."

"Don't you want to take these detainees out first?" the crane engineer asked the detective in charge.

"No, these people are criminals and not to be considered human. Just move the container with them inside it."

The prisoners were just banged up a little, but for a terrifying few minutes they thought Kabul was being destroyed in an earthquake. Afterward Ali would always think of this ordeal whenever he had to move a birdcage with a quail or a canary inside. Nothing is more unsettling than a prison that moves, with the inmates having no idea where they're going.

Ali was philosophical about his rough treatment by the policemen at the PD1 lockup. "Life is not easy for any of us. I've undergone a lot of hardship, but I care about my life." Regarding his tormenter, he said, "Perhaps he is a person who doesn't care much about his life. Perhaps he just doesn't love his wife. He might have married someone he didn't love. It could be that his father or mother forced him to marry his wife. I am thankful to God that I don't have that problem."

At the time, though, Ali thought his life was over. Zakia

thought her life was over. Anwar was sure that their life together, at least, was over.

I was relieved. Now the couple had no choice but to let Women for Afghan Women take their case to court. Once they were no longer fugitives from the law, they could easily get passports. Also, Zakia was safe. Her pregnancy was no great surprise; we'd been hearing that she was sick on this or that day or off to the hospital because of nausea—the usual sort of first-trimester complaints. Like most Afghans, Zakia and Ali were not interested in family planning, unless by that one means planning a very large family. Ali had laughed when we asked him if they wanted children. "I don't mind. Yeah, why not? A person has to have children for when he dies, so someone will remember him." Under different circumstances we might not have found out so soon. Pregnancy is not something many Afghan couples are willing to divulge outside the family, especially when it doesn't show, but Anwar had accidentally confirmed it in the excitement of the night before. Now Juliet was with child and her Romeo was in jail, indirectly in the figurative clutches of the Capulets and their sympathizers. If that was not going to win the lovers some serious support, in and out of Afghanistan, perhaps nothing ever would.

10

RELUCTANT CELEBRITIES

It was a variation on the riddle of whether a falling tree makes a sound if there is no one in the forest to hear it: Could Zakia and Ali really be celebrities if they scarcely knew about their celebrity? What could modern celebrity possibly mean to someone who had never used a personal computer or gone on the Internet? Who could not read or write, had never watched television, and did not own a radio? Who in short was unplugged from electronic society (the single exception being cell phones, which they only partly knew how to use)? Many Afghans now saw the couple as celebrities; nearly every Afghan radio and television station and newspaper covered their capture, especially the Dari outlets, and young Afghans began starting Facebook pages and Twitter campaigns in their support. Jawad was besieged by Afghan journalists who were enlisted by the BBC or *60 Minutes,* or Australian, Canadian, and German television to cover the story. But locked up without cell phones, Zakia and Ali had little idea of the storm of attention building around their predicament.

At Women for Afghan Women, Shukria was working hard to

find a resolution to their case, and because she had already started working on it before Ali's arrest, she was well along. Her first legal move was to petition the attorney general's office to move the case to family court, as a dispute between families, not a criminal case. Then she worked out an arrangement for the police to come to WAW's shelter to interview Zakia. "They won't arrest her and take her to the detention center," Manizha Naderi of WAW said. "They will allow her to stay in the shelter until she's convicted in court. And we won't let that happen. Fingers crossed!"

In the meantime Zakia had plenty to say and was widely quoted; WAW was only too happy to arrange interviews, because Manizha sees public outreach and education as a vital part of her organization's mission.[1] Under the circumstances, speaking out seemed to Zakia the natural thing to do, and she was no longer afraid of the sound of her own voice, although she would have been surprised if anyone had tried to explain to her how famous she and Ali had become. "I am by his side, and at court I will say no one kidnapped me, that I came by my consent and will, and I want to be with him for the rest of my life," Zakia said. "If I see my father and brothers, I will tell them, 'Whatever has happened, has happened, and it is nothing you can change. Why is it any of your business that this has happened? This has just happened. You cannot change what's in my heart, so stop trying to do anything about it.'"

She was still worried about her family's retribution. "If I fell into my parents' hands, they will do something to me, kill me or something else even worse. There is nothing they want to do except to kill me. I haven't even seen my aunt's son—how is it possible that I would have been married to him? There was no *neka*. How is it possible? I said this to my father and asked them, 'Why do you lie?' But if it is left to my father and mother, they will not agree with me even in ten years." Mostly, though, she was worried about Ali and about her father-in-law. "He is ill and has high blood pressure, and he must be very worried. They have to let the boy go, that is all."

Zakia's father, Zaman, was stunned by the onslaught of interest about his daughter's case. Nothing could be more galling to a potential honor killer than the glare of publicity. Zaman had soon adjusted his narrative to the prevailing mood.

"My young son"—this would have been Razak—"saw him and went to the police and told the police this person has done this crime, he kidnapped my daughter. What can we do? If we *could* do something, we *would* do something. I am a poor person and don't have the power to harm anyone. What can I do? If I was a rich and powerful person, I would do something. No one is listening to me. If I would kill him, everyone would blame me for it. But you see, we handed him to the police." That was true, but it was Zakia they most wanted. They had hoped Ali would lead the authorities and hence her family to Zakia. There is not all that much honor in killing the offending man, since a man is just seen as doing what men do, whether it's seduction or even rape. It is the death of the woman that is required by this concept of honor.

"The police asked me to come and give a statement, and I went and did that," Zaman said. "I told them what that boy has done. He kidnapped my daughter. Isn't that true? We want the girl back, and we want to hand her to her husband and see what he does with her." He meant his nephew, the supposed husband by Zakia's first marriage, which she never attended. "The boy we married Zakia to has made claims against me. He spent a lot of money, and he wants it back or he wants his wife back. All I want is that the girl should be handed to her first husband. Then it is up to him whether he accepts her as his wife or not. If that doesn't work, I will leave it to God. I can't do anything myself. I lost everything and came here to Kabul with fifteen family members, and we're all working on the streets."

The police were in no hurry to interview Zakia at the shelter, so Shukria went to the Ministry of Interior on Sunday and won permission for Ali's criminal case to be dismissed if she could produce Zakia to swear that Ali had not kidnapped her and that they were married. She and three WAW staffers took Zakia to PD1, the police station, and Zakia made her declaration; they managed to get her in and out by a side entrance to avoid her family. When Shukria later went back to PD1 to tell Ali how things were going, Zakia's father and uncle saw her. They blocked her way and demanded the right to visit Zakia at the WAW shelter. Shukria agreed they could visit in a couple of days, after they had calmed down. They were so angry that it was clear to her that they would kill either the girl or Ali on sight.

"Stop shouting at me!" she told the men, shouting back at them. "You will never see her without my permission, and you will never get that permission unless you calm down and behave with respect." Never having been really yelled at by a woman, particularly one who exuded authority, Zakia's relatives were easily cowed—for the moment.

After Zakia and Shukria's visit, the police accepted that they no longer had a criminal case but instead a family dispute. Ali soon saw a difference in the way he was treated. The beatings stopped; he was given food and allowed to use the toilet facilities. "They even offered me cigarettes," he said. He had quit smoking at Zakia's request after they arrived in Kabul; this was the first time he'd broken his vow to her.

The day after their encounter with Shukria, Zakia's family began fighting back. Her father and her brother Gula Khan showed up in the WAW offices as part of the entourage of a high official from the Ministry of Interior, who introduced himself as a director general, a department head of some sort. He never produced a name, but he demanded to know why the *New York Times* had delivered Zakia to the shelter and what the paper's role in the whole matter was. "We know that the *New York Times* brought the girl here, and why did they do that? We know that the U.S. embassy and the *New York Times* helped the girl and the boy and support them." Behind him, Zaman and his sons, emboldened by having a powerful man in their midst, were screaming at Shukria and the other women present, demanding to get in to see Zakia. Shukria stood her ground, told the official she had no idea what he was talking about, and made sure that WAW's guards kept the visitors from the living quarters of the shelter itself.

Then Zaman had a lawyer petition to move the case from a civil proceeding in family court to the attorney general's office, as a criminal investigation. Zaman surprised everyone when he produced a *neka* document signed by a mullah and a host of witnesses, fifteen in all, saying that Zakia had been married to her father's nephew. The *neka* was dated a year and a half earlier, but that is not an unusual practice.

"A lot of people do the *neka* like this during the engagement, because it gives the couple more freedom to sit and talk and go places alone without people talking about them," Manizha said. "My own family does it, too. They do a preliminary *neka* during the engagement and then another one during the marriage ceremony. So it's legal." If that were true, then it would mean that under Afghan law Zakia *had* been legally married to her cousin—or at least her family had enough witnesses willing to establish that was the case.

Manizha and Shukria were worried. "After talking to Mohammad Ali, his father, and Zakia, we don't think that Mohammad Ali and Zakia did the *neka*," Manizha wrote in an e-mail. "They just ran off, and that's it. There is no *neka nama* [marriage certificate] like her father has. Or any witnesses! As you know, a *neka* isn't legal without two male witnesses! His father asked Shukria if she can just make one up. This isn't good! This will spell trouble for the couple. Zakia's father is very stubborn. He would rather see her rot in jail than just let the case go."

There was little doubt that Zakia's father had concocted her first wedding ex post facto, but proving it would be hard. Zaman wasn't arguing that it had been consummated or even that she had ever met her cousin and putative husband. In court in front of witnesses, he had only claimed an engagement; the judges in Bamiyan, otherwise so friendly to the family, had acknowledged that openly. But now he had the paperwork, and he had witnesses, including a mullah, to establish that a marriage took place.

Zakia and Ali had none of that, no document to prove that they had really tied a *neka* up in Foladi on the day after Zakia's escape. First they said they had the document at home, but none of Ali's brothers could find it. Then they said that the mullah who had signed it, Mullah Baba Khalili, had disappeared. Then they

had supposedly reached the mullah by phone but he refused to testify that he had signed the *neka*. We began to think that Manizha
and Shukria were right, and they just had not bothered. As people
who didn't read, they might not have taken the *neka* document to
be as important as was the fact that a *neka* ceremony had occurred,
presided over by a mullah, witnessed by the requisite two males;
the paperwork was a formality that meant little to them, since they
could not read it.

My journalistic position also seemed to be unraveling fast. We
went to a public seminar sponsored by the Ministry of Women's
Affairs (MoWA) for its provincial directors; there were a couple
dozen Afghan journalists there, plus Jawad and me. Husn Banu
Ghazanfar, the imperious minister of women's affairs, was presid-
ing. When she and her entourage came in, she was angered as
she noticed us in the press section. We knew she had been upset
over an interview I'd done with her a few weeks earlier. Little of
it was published, since she had said almost nothing usable.[2] The
only quote I used from the interview was her criticism of Fatima
Kazimi's claim that Fatima's life was in danger.[3]

There was more to Minister Ghazanfar's anger than that, however. Interrupting the proceedings when she saw us, she summoned
MoWA's public-relations adviser, Abdul Aziz Ibrahimi, to confer
with her. Ibrahimi, like a large proportion of women's-ministry
employees, is a man. He came and told us the minister wanted
us expelled from the public session. "She's unhappy because the
parliament and the president are complaining about MoWA helping us to make a Romeo-and-Juliet love story, and that is wrong.
President Karzai is especially unhappy that you made a Romeo-
and-Juliet story out of this." I thought about standing my ground
against being kicked out, since there were other journalists there,
but it seemed unwise. The profile of the *New York Times* in this
whole case was already getting uncomfortably high. President Karzai's hatred of the paper was well known; he had at that point not
given an interview to anyone from the paper since 2008.[4] The war
was getting ever worse. The election fiasco was deepening, and
in the course of that year Mr. Karzai's government, with what we

believed to be his encouragement, had already threatened to expel me, would soon try unsuccessfully to expel *Times* correspondent Azam Ahmed,[5] and would later that year successfully expel *Times* correspondent Matthew Rosenberg.[6] The cases against us were spurious and had nothing to do with the lovers' story, but I was keenly aware that my role in Zakia and Ali's case might embarrass the paper at a sensitive time.

On June 9 Shukria told Jawad that Ali's family was going to have to come up with a *neka* document by the scheduled court hearing the next day. "Otherwise the relations which they had in the last three months will be considered inappropriate and they'll be charged with adultery," she said. Under criminal law that could mean a penalty of ten years in jail. Under shariah law the couple could get death; technically, the courts had the option of applying either code. Jawad met with Anwar and the brothers, and they finally admitted to him that they had no *neka*. Their story then was that the mullah and witnesses all signed a blank sheet of paper, intending to fill it in later with the legal niceties and the necessary stamps. That paper was with Mullah Baba Khalili, and it was too dangerous to go to his home in the Behsood District of Wardak Province. Now that the mullah had heard that the couple had been arrested, Anwar said, "He is afraid and does not want to give the *neka* letter to us. He is denying that he tied this *neka*. I sent my son to talk to him and convince him to give us the *neka* letter. I gave him all that money to tie the *neka,* and he promised. He is such a liar. But now I am worried. If their case goes to the attorney general's office, there is need for bribe money, and I don't have any money to give them."

As far as Anwar was concerned, all such problems were addressed only one way in Afghanistan: through sufficient bribes to the right people. That was not going to work in this case, although it was hard to make him understand that the case was too high-profile for the old rule—who bribes the most wins—to apply.

Ali's arrest and Zakia's detention were huge news in Kabul, and young people were quick to lionize them; the Facebook groups and Twitter feeds devoted to them had continued to proliferate.[7]

Videos of them were ripped from the *Times* website and embedded in Afghan Web pages, posted on YouTube, dubbed into Dari and Pashto.

One of Zakia's biggest fans was Zahra Mousawi, a former anchorwoman for Tolo TV, who refuses to play by the patriarchy's rules. Breezing into the Blue Flame restaurant in the midst of the controversy over the couple's detentions, Zahra headed to a secluded corner booth at the hideaway garden restaurant with two unrelated men. She had no head scarf on—she did not even have one handy—and she was wearing a normal blouse and skirt, not the usual shapeless trench coat over a long dress that most Afghan women in public life adopt. Zahra had driven herself to the Blue Flame in her own car, alone, with no *mahram*. She not only shakes hands with men—most Afghan women, even women officials, do not—but men she knows well she will greet with a hug or a kiss on the cheek, even in public.

She is one of the few women in Afghanistan who dares to do what she does. "I drive, and I don't wear a head scarf, and I really don't have much trouble," she said. "The other women activists all say, 'But it's Afghanistan. You have to be like them.' I'm ready to pay the costs not to be, but no one else is. They're really not ready for big changes." To some extent Zahra overstates how easy it might be. She has the benefit of Swedish as well as Afghan citizenship, so she can leave anytime, and she has a highly educated, tolerant family. Zahra, too, had started a Facebook campaign to free Zakia and Ali. "The only hope is the young. The future is the young, and that's why I want to applaud Zakia. It's her life, and she has decided how to live it."

At the attorney general's office, young couples began showing up at the Elimination of Violence Against Women Unit (EVAW), which is staffed mostly by female lawyers, to file complaints of denial of relationship, something that would have been unheard of even a year earlier. "Ali and Zakia's story will have a great impact on the future generation," said Qudsia Niazi, the head of the EVAW unit. "Young people now are starting to realize that there is no restriction in religion or in the law about who you can marry.

Any Muslim can marry any other Muslim." There were even street demonstrations to protest the pair's lockup.

But while support grew, the prospects for resolution of their legal case diminished. If the mullah did have the paper, he wasn't going to provide it.

Then, just when it looked hopeless all around, on June 11 the attorney general's office issued an order out of the blue that Ali should be released without bail, all charges dropped.

21/3/1393[8]

Attorney General of the Islamic Republic of Afghanistan
Release Order

The dossier of these two people should be studied, verified and retained after a complete investigation is done. Mohammad Ali who had a *neka* with Zakia should be released from detention and she should be handed to him. The Ministry of Women's Affairs should assist them in forming a family life and finding a place to stay.

Duly noted, Office of Governmental Relations

Dossier should be referred to Legal Office for further legal formalities.

Ali was free, but Zakia was still stuck in the shelter until he could produce the *neka;* the attorney general's office had to see it before they would approve her release. Possibly his brother would find the mullah and get it—if it existed, though none of us any longer believed that was the case. Then suddenly word came that Ali and Anwar and three witnesses could go to the attorney general's office with Zakia and formally tie a new *neka.*

Just how this came about was mysterious, but somehow it was no longer necessary for them to produce the original *neka* that the mullah did or did not do for them in Foladi on the second day of their elopement. The resolution didn't come about from a bribe; it is clear that Anwar had no money—he was asking us for even a small amount to survive on, and we were trying to arrange for him to get some from the donations on account at WAW. The couple's attorney, Shukria, just shrugged it off without explanation, and her tone suggested we not ask her too many questions about it. So Anwar's other sons came down from Bamiyan with a fresh *neka* signed by a friendly mullah and witnessed by a couple of men from their village. They delivered it to WAW to produce for the attorney general.

Ali was ecstatic. "Before being arrested I was a hundred percent happy. Now that I am freed from the government's claws and when my wife is released, I will be a thousand percent happy. We are so happy that we cannot fit into our clothes anymore."

Zakia was still in the shelter, but now that a *neka* had been produced, she would be out soon. We spoke to her the night before they were due to go to the attorney general's office and get the new *neka* registered and approved.

"I feel I am born once again to this world," she told us. "I missed him so much I cannot count how much. I'm so happy that I won't be able to go to sleep tonight. I wish after I get released that we could have a happy life again and go and live in a place that is safe for us. We cannot stay in Bamiyan or Kabul anymore. I love him so much I cannot possibly explain it to you."

Qudsia Niazi, from the attorney general's EVAW law unit, told Zakia that if she wanted to press charges against her parents, for unlawfully trying to force her to marry against her will and trying to prevent her from marrying Ali, those were crimes under EVAW law and she could do so. Zakia demurred. "About my father my feeling is that it would be better if he would agree to this, but now that he doesn't agree, I cannot say anything about the matter to him. But I don't want to bring charges against them, because they are my father and mother and I couldn't bear to do anything to them. I can't see anything happen to them or happen to my brothers from such a thing. Once I get out of here, my father and mother will not even want to see me, I know that, but I don't want trouble for them."

Later we asked her how she had found the WAW shelter compared to the Bamiyan one. She was glad that her stay in the Kabul shelter was so short, but she didn't like it as much as the one in Bamiyan. "They were so strict here."

Ali laughed. "Women are only happy when they are free to wear makeup," he said. Having weathered a couple of crises in Kabul in which archconservatives accused WAW's shelter in Kabul of being a bordello and the people who ran it of being pimps, Women for Afghan Women was sensitive to anything that might give conservatives ammunition against them. Makeup was one of those things, so it was banned inside their shelters.

At the time the details of how their case had been settled, and so quickly, were a complete mystery. In addition, Zaman and his sons and nephews disappeared from the picture overnight, as if someone had come along and swept them away with a broom. When Ali stepped out of PD1, there was no longer an in-law stake-out in evidence, and when he was reunited with Zakia at the shelter and she stepped outside the walls that surrounded it and onto the street, they looked around themselves apprehensively, but Zakia's family was not there either. Some speculated that President Karzai must have intervened behind the scenes, but that seemed hard to believe after the antipathy of his women's minister only a few days earlier—which her aides blamed on anger from the presidential palace over the high profile of the case and the embarrassment it was causing the country.

All the public attention made Zakia and Ali nervous, too. They were confused and didn't know what to make of it. Neither of them knew what Facebook was, or an online news agency, or even the Internet, except that they were something mysterious, like the *New York Times,* for that matter, that could have a big im-pact on their lives. They did not much enjoy their celebrity. People would stop them on the street and ask to take selfies with them, and Zakia would pull a veil across her face and she and Ali would reluctantly oblige.

The lovers soon decided they would return to Bamiyan. Ali explained it this way: "In Kabul I know it is a big city, but I don't know it and I don't know who all the people are. If I look at them,

I don't know which one knows me now." Their faces were easily recognizable due to the heavy local press coverage, and I felt somewhat guilty about their predicament. "If they know me, I still don't know them and don't know if I need to be worried about them. In Bamiyan you know your enemy, in Kabul you don't." That wasn't the only reason, though. Ali kept it to himself, but he was steaming that we had encouraged Zakia to go into a shelter.

For the time being, they had decided against going abroad, he said. Africa they had already ruled out. In America there would be pockets of other Afghans, but they would still be lost souls. "In America we wouldn't know where is the food store. Where can you borrow food on credit and pay them back later? We wouldn't know where to go for that," Ali said. I didn't bother to tell him stores in America don't usually give food on credit.

Zmaryalai Farahi from the American embassy called him around that time; the publicity, plus pressure from the home front thanks to Rabbi Shmuley Boteach and his friends in high places, had aroused their interest again. Now that the couple no longer had criminal charges hanging over them, there was no political-diplomatic reason they could not get visas. This time Zmaryalai offered to come and meet them at a place of their choice, rather than asking them to run the police gauntlet and come into the embassy.

Ali said he would rather talk on the phone and asked Zmaryalai whether, if they got visas to America, they could bring along his father, mother, brothers, sisters, and their children, eighteen persons in all. When Zmaryalai said he greatly doubted it, Ali flatly told him they had changed their minds, that they were staying in Afghanistan and no longer wanted to flee abroad, and with that, for the near future at least, he pretty much dashed what little chance they had of going to America themselves. If they were not pushing, no amount of pushing from others on their behalf was going to carry the day. I asked Ali why he hadn't just left his options open and kept his doubts to himself while talking to the American embassy. He offered an odd aphorism for someone from rural, pasta-less Afghanistan: "This is the dish, and this is the spaghetti.

Whatever is there, is there. Maybe later we will think about it."
With a death threat still looming, "later" seemed like a faraway
place.

For American officials this was a relief. The American embassy
reported back to Samantha Power's staff that Ali, criminal case
now dismissed, had decided to stay in Afghanistan and was no
longer looking for asylum abroad. Problem solved.

"I've never worked harder on a case since the Wikileaks thing,"
Shmuley quoted one of Power's aides as telling him. "I am so frustrated by our embassy's unwillingness to help." Now there was
nothing more they needed to do.

Even if Ali and Zakia had decided to try to leave the country, the American embassy had little to offer them. While there
had been criminal charges against them, the embassy's reluctance
was understandable; now that the legal charges against them were
resolved, however, all the embassy was willing to offer them was
advice: flee to another country, apply for refugee status there.
The United Nations High Commissioner for Refugees would
then consider their request for resettlement, and the United States
would inform the UNHCR that it was following their case. All of
this *might* help push things along faster, *might* lead to resettlement
in the United States, but there would be no guarantees. I spoke
to UNHCR officials in Kabul, and they agreed that the process
would be a protracted one, even with the United States following
the couple's case, even with well-heeled sponsors willing to help
them and guarantee them jobs, language training, education.[9]

The two were looking at six or seven months as refugees before they could get resettled to the United States, maybe twice as
long—and that was only if U.S. officials did follow up on their
case, which they had only sort of promised to do—always adding
"No guarantees." There is another method that American officials
could have used, but they ruled it out, I suspect, for fear that it
would open the floodgates for other potential honor-killing victims. This was humanitarian parole,[10] and it can be used to take
people straight from their own country, without the need of their

first becoming refugees. It is used in cases of extreme emergency, such as for people who need specialized medical care in the United States that is unavailable in their own country. Or in cases where someone's life is in imminent danger. The lovers seemingly qualified there. In the American embassy's interpretation of humanitarian parole, however, Ali and Zakia did not satisfy the condition that their lives were in imminent danger.

Even if the United States had chosen to offer humanitarian parole—and the embassy nixed suggestions from Washington that they do so—it is no longer the magic bullet it once was for extreme cases. It was used, for instance, in the case of Bibi Aisha, disfigured by her Taliban husband. The Grossman Burn Center[11] in Los Angeles offered to reconstruct her face, cutting-edge medicine no one in Afghanistan was qualified to do, and Women for Afghan Women, with the embassy's enthusiastic support in such a high-profile case, applied for humanitarian parole for her. Using immigration lawyers in the United States, WAW did manage to get humanitarian parole for Bibi Aisha—after eight months of waiting, most of that time due to delays by the Department of Homeland Security, undertaking its exhaustive security checks to confirm to its satisfaction that this seventeen-year-old victim of the Taliban was not a terrorist trying to sneak into the United States under medical cover.

It was little wonder that the couple stopped speaking to everyone and gave up on leaving. They could have been more patient, though; as long as the embassy was interested enough to continue talking to them, there was always the possibility of an option being worked out. With Shmuley's Africa option also off the table, their lives were a crapshoot, dependent on the chance that Zaman and sons did not find a way to take their revenge.

"When your story came to light, I was fortunate that I do have friends in positions in the American government who could help," Shmuley said when I talked to him about the lovers' present dead end. "Senator Cory Booker, I discussed the case with him, for instance, and especially Samantha Power, who was uniquely positioned to assist because of her international portfolio—she has always cared, instantly and immensely—gave me a lot of time, to her immense credit and at a time when it's been pretty darn busy in the world. She could easily have said, 'It's a terrible story, just one among millions that require our attention,' but she didn't do that. And with all of that, there still has been the snail-like pace of the American government. The strictures are not just ones of immigration. Those are understandable after 9/11, I understand that. The disappointing part to me is how the American government couldn't go officially on the record to condemn the violence against this woman, or the intended violence. There wasn't a single American reading these stories about this couple who were going, 'Oh, I sympathize with her family.' They can't even publicly condemn it, because we don't want to be seen dictating to the Muslims about their culture. Neither do I believe that we can lose thousands of soldiers to liberate Afghanistan from the monstrous barbarity of the Taliban and then not have the right to speak out against that barbarity. We can't be dictating to the Afghan people how they should be living? Give me a break. This isn't a domestic issue, brutality against women. We're not talking here about a woman who wants to put on a miniskirt and dance at a disco—she wants to marry the man she loves and live an Islamic, religious life. If we can't condemn her treatment, our mission has no meaning. Notwithstanding how much the U.S. government did not want to offend the Afghan government's sensibilities, what about offending the American public's sensibilities? The officials I spoke with were all very well-meaning, but they spoke about how they were handcuffed, about not playing into this narrative of the U.S. controlling Afghanistan. It's our taxpayers' money that is being spent there—we have the right to demand the most minimal impact on the country. If we can't even say something like that, help people in that kind of situation, what was the purpose of the entire American mission? You have to redeem the lives of our soldiers with some moral progress."

❦

11

BACK TO THE HINDU KUSH

The problem with helping people too much is that they don't learn how to help themselves. Governments know that, but it doesn't stop them from giving money to increasingly dependent societies. *We* knew this, but it didn't stop us from helping Zakia and Ali. They weren't going to do it on their own, it seemed. They were just making one bad move after another.

The day after Zakia's release from the shelter, they disappeared, and even Ali's brothers couldn't find them. It was rumored that they had fled to Iran. Finally Ismatullah, Ali's older brother, got a call from them asking him to approach us and get money from WAW on their behalf so they could fly to Herat, a city in western Afghanistan. We told Ismatullah that all they needed to do was get in touch with the shelter and ask for some of the donors' money, but they had to do that themselves—they couldn't expect someone else to do it for them. The shelter needed to verify that they personally received the money.

It turned out that Ali was keeping his distance from us because he was angry that Zakia had been kept in the shelter. He felt she never should have gone there and instead should have fled with his father and his cousin. It was an unreasonable attitude, but then he had waited for her for more than six months outside another shelter, and his attitude was as understandable as it was foolish. He didn't seem to appreciate that in the less than a week they both spent in custody they'd had all their legal problems resolved.

Herat in some ways seemed like a good place to hide; the western city was much more relaxed than many places in Afghanistan, big enough to get lost in easily, ethnically diverse. But Herat was close to Iran, and the jumping-off point for many Afghans fleeing there, and we all worried that the couple now intended to go that route. When we refused to act for him, Ali called WAW's Manizha Naderi himself and persuaded her to give him another thousand-dollar installment from the donors' money. He wanted more, but out of concern that he might use it to go to Iran, Manizha decided to limit the amount the organization would give him at any one time. The result was the couple did not have enough to afford air tickets to Herat.

Three days later, June 22, we got another call from Ismatullah. "Ali and his wife are now in Bamiyan, hiding. They came back because they couldn't go to Herat by ground," he said. The roads were too unsafe; it is a telling fact that fourteen years after the American intervention in Afghanistan began, many of the country's major cities and provincial capitals are connected by roads that are not safe to travel, even for Afghans. The brother said he would try to persuade Ali to call and talk to us. "I want you to help them leave the country," he said. "We really need your help. They can't stay here long. Already Zakia's relatives held a meeting because it seems they knew they came to Bamiyan. They'll do something for sure."

The next day Ali called and missed us, but Jawad called him back. His ringtone was a song by Jamshid Parwani, an Afghan crooner, called "Gonjeshkak Telayee":

> *Little goldfinch, who lives at my girl's,*
> *I am waiting for you.*
> *Tell me, when will you come?*

Come to me, come from my ravishing girl,
Come sing to me how she is,
And go tell her how am I,
My naive little messenger.[1]

Ali asked us, as he'd asked the American embassy, whether, if they were able to get to a third country, the whole family could go along. We told him that was doubtful. There are Afghans who have gotten entire families out like that, on grounds of family reunification, but it takes many years, sometimes decades. They might be allowed to take close relatives, like father, mother, and of course their own children, but that was all. That was the last we heard from him for nearly a month.

When they resurfaced, we learned that the couple had gone back with Anwar to the family home in Surkh Dar late that June, when Zakia's father and brothers were still away. Having given up their fields and moved to Kabul to hunt for the couple, it was too late for Zakia's family to resume farming that season, and they continued to stay in Kabul as day laborers, street vendors, and the like. More distant relatives—cousins and in-laws—and some of Zakia's younger siblings were living in Zaman's house, but they had less of a personal stake in hunting the couple down. The fields were rich and green, on their way to a bumper potato crop, and the young lovers were happy to be in the midst of Ali's family again, living an almost-normal life. At night Ali and his brothers took turns standing guard outside their house, but they were not very worried.

Ali and Zakia were, relatively speaking, flush with cash; the thousand dollars from Women for Afghan Women was more than they needed for necessities, so Ali and Anwar decided to spend much of it on gold jewelry, bracelets, and chains for Zakia. That is, in some ways, a method of storing money, by putting it into gold—although the gold dealers sell dear and buy cheap—and stashing it in the relative safety of adorning a woman's untouchable person. It is also a way of showing how much they valued her. "We bought gold for her even though we were in debt and couldn't afford it," Anwar later said. "Because we are happy with her and wanted to show it to her, that we love her and we know she abandoned her family for our family, so we bought her gold and would be willing to buy her more if we could."

Zakia had given up a lot to be married to Ali, and that point was driven home when he encountered her little brother, Razak, while walking toward the bazaar in the town. Razak blocked Ali's way, brandishing a penknife. "I'm going to stab you, and then you'll see whether it's so easy to elope with girls," he said. Ali laughed him off and brushed him aside, but it was a reminder of the way the anger had hung on and spread throughout her entire family.

Zakia was heartbroken about her little brother's stubborn hatred. "I love him so much, more than anyone in my family," she said. "He was so upset by this. He had more anger than my older brothers, even. It's very sad. I really love him." Mightn't there one day be a chance of reconciliation with him, a chance to explain what had happened once he was old enough to understand? "He wouldn't listen, he wouldn't accept it, even if I explained it to him. Maybe when he grows up, he'll change, he'll understand. Maybe if he falls in love with someone, then he might understand. I hope so."

Despite the bad tidings of the encounter with Razak, those first few days home were happy ones. The couple threw a party for close family and a few of the Surkh Dar village elders, who after all the publicity had become far more supportive of the couple—at least on the Hazara side of the road. While Ali's family and friends do not boast of this, support among the Hazaras, who are more numerous in Bamiyan than Tajiks, was a factor, in addition to their shame and embarrassment, in driving Zakia's male family members away. The Hazara elders wanted Anwar's family to throw a wedding party for the entire village—insisted on it, in fact—so they would have to do that soon, before the beginning of Ramadan, the month of fasting, which would begin in July 2014.

Ali's mother was thrilled to see her son back; he had been

close to her, he said, and he knew that she was unhappy that he and Zakia had gone away and were thinking of trying to leave the country. Now he was under the same roof with the two women in his life.

Chaman had once said to Ali, "You are the son of a poor person, so try to do good things and try to make your life better."

"I never forgot that," Ali said. Chaman hated when she saw him smoking, for example, and told him to stop. "And I did stop," he said, and laughed. "For a day." But he took care not to let her see him smoking after that.

During his long courtship of Zakia, Ali had made friends with a young Tajik man about his age who lived in her village. He had become Ali's confidant—a fellow conspirator who also believed in love. They'd been in the army together, and after the love affair became infamous, he called Ali to rekindle their friendship—secretly, for fear of being seen as a traitor by other Tajiks. It proved to be a fortunate alliance. One day in early July, Ali was working in the fields, watering vegetables by hand after a dry spell, when his Tajik friend called him. "Gula Khan is back," the man told him. "They're planning to catch you in the fields, and they're on their way now. He has a pistol and a knife." Running atop the berms between irrigation ditches, Ali made his way across the fields and, by a roundabout route, back to Surkh Dar and the family's home. He could see Gula Khan running after him, but he'd had enough of a head start to reach safety. After a hurried family council, Zakia and Ali decided to return to hiding in the mountains. Their wedding party would have to wait until after Ramadan.

They headed back to Yakawlang again but this time found a lukewarm reception at the home of Zahra and Haji Abdul Hamid in Kham-e Bazargan. "We offered to pay them for our food and everything, but they said they couldn't afford to keep us, and we only stayed there for four days," Ali said. Notoriety, it seems, had made Zakia and Ali toxic, despite the older couple's earlier sympathies. Or perhaps Haji was still angry at Ali's disappearing trick the last time, leaving Zakia with them against his wishes.

From there they went farther into the mountains, almost to the province of Ghor, staying as paying guests with families in areas so remote they hadn't heard the story of Zakia and Ali. "We went on up to Dara-i-Chasht, where we had no relatives to stay with," Ali recalled later. "We did not know anyone there. It was a hard time for us. We had a little money to spend, we ate little, and tried to survive. The weather was still cold at night, and we didn't have enough clothes and other necessities. There was no electricity, and we just had an oil lantern. No one from my family could come to visit us. It was a long way and very difficult to get there, and there was no telephone coverage. There wasn't even a road for vehicles to go on, and you had to walk for three hours to get there. It was so hard for us."

They spent Ramadan in that remote place, through most of July 2014, and felt the absence of family all the more keenly. The shared hardships of the daily Ramadan fast, with no food or drink between dawn and sunset, and the nightly breaking of that fast with the Iftar meal, are an intensely communal experience, and it was the first time they had experienced it alone, in the company of strangers or just each other.

Through it all, Zakia was pregnant. Without older women around, she had no way to gauge whether her morning sickness and other pregnancy complaints were cause for alarm. The nearest medical care was in Nayak Bazaar, a three-hour hike followed by a long wait and then a three-hour ride in a bus—an entire, exhausting day's travel round-trip. They made the trip twice, for checkups, but the clinic had only maternal-care nurses, not doctors or midwives. Should anything go wrong, it would be a still-longer trip to find real medical care. "Everything was difficult up there. There was only shelter for us," Zakia said. "It was worth it that we were together, but we wanted to have a life, and after a while it was hard to bear."

One day Ali's brother Bismillah made the trek up to their hiding place and begged them to come back to Bamiyan. The Bamiyan police chief had vouched for their safety if they did, and the local elders still wanted their wedding party to take place. "I just wished that my father-in-law and my brothers-in-law would give up and leave us in peace," Ali said. "Whatever happened has happened. They should forget it and pardon us."

So they went home. The wedding party was held in Anwar's house, and it was a relatively large affair, with two hundred fifty guests; Anwar spent fifty-one thousand afghanis on food and preparations—putting him another thousand dollars or so deeper in debt. Ultimately it was a gloomy occasion for the family, with everyone aware of a threat no one thought would go away; at such a big event, there was safety in numbers, but when the guests had all gone, the threat remained.

While Ali and Zakia had been in the mountains, Ali's family had come to a joint decision, and now they wanted to make him accept it: There would be no peace for either of their families if the couple stayed in Afghanistan. They had decided he and Zakia should leave the country as the pair had earlier planned. It was time to get serious, return to Kabul, and obtain passports. They had to reestablish contact with the journalists, the embassy, and even the people from Africa. Taking the entire family, there was no hope of that, but Anwar would go along. That way Ali could find work and Zakia would still have a *mahram* with her.

The family had already told us this was what they wanted to see happen, and they wanted our help to persuade the couple it was their only solution. Anwar said he would make sure his son began answering his telephone.

When we called Ali, his phone's ringtone was by Ahmad Zahir, the martyred Afghan pop singer, verses from his famous song "I Don't Say It." Ahmad Zahir was the Elvis Presley of Afghanistan, a crooner who is still popular today but in the 1970s had really electrified audiences—especially young women and girls, much to the anger of the conservative establishment. The son of a former prime minister, Zahir was so popular that the Communists feared him as well, and many of his songs were loaded with politically critical double entendres. During the early Communist regime of President Hafizullah Amin, Mr. Amin put Zahir in jail.

Then came the wedding of President Amin's daughter. The Communists took power, vowing to outlaw arranged marriages and abusive customary practices like *baad,* in which girls are sold at young ages to settle a debt or a blood feud, and *baadal,* in which families swap brothers and sisters in marriage, a deal that usually guarantees at least one or two unhappy spouses. President Amin flouted the socialist ideology and arranged a *baadal* wedding for his daughter, Ghul Ghutai, and his son, Abdur Rahman, to their first cousins, the son and daughter of the president's brother. Ghul Ghutai was furious, and she fought bitterly against the marriage but eventually agreed. At the last minute, however, she refused to show up for her wedding unless Ahmad Zahir could sing at it, so the president ordered him released and the charges against him dropped if he agreed to sing at the wedding. The first song he chose was "I Don't Say It":

> *I don't ask you to set me free*
> *from the prison of the body:*
> *Rather, take me bodily to paradise,*
> *and there in that garden*
> *Fill my heart with joy.*
> *Remember, O Death the Hunter,*
> *remember this soul, like a bird in its cage,*
> *Sit in a garden and remember me.*[2]

At the wedding, where both sexes mixed together, they say the bride fell in love with the singer. While Ahmad Zahir was singing, Ghul Ghutai "burst into tears, and people noticed it and didn't like it," according to Abdul Jalil Sadid, a violinist and composer who was a contemporary of Mr. Zahir. Rumors of the subsequent love affair between the singer and the president's daughter were rife and infuriated the president and people around him, Mr. Sadid said. Soon after the wedding, Zahir was killed in a car crash along the dangerous Salang Pass, but few thought it was an accident.[3] "I believe the pro-Communist regime at that time was behind his murder," Mr. Sadid said. No one ever found out for sure, because a short while later, in early 1979, pro-Soviet troops rushed the presidential palace, killing President Amin and much of his family in a coup d'état that ushered in the Soviet occupation of Afghanistan. That wedding story is a distant memory in the Afghanistan of today, some of its details inconceivable in their liberalism.

When Ali finally answered our phone calls, he said he had made up his mind to do as his family asked. "All we want in life is that we should get to a place where it is safe for us to live together, where we can spend life in a happy and peaceful environment," Ali said. "We are now happy and ready to leave the country for someplace safe and friendly. Can you help us? You're the only ones we trust."

First they would need passports. Now that their marriage was legalized, that process was straightforward. They could get passports at the passport office in Bamiyan, but news of their application would be all over town between the day they applied and the day, a week later, when they returned to pick them up. They thought this seemed dangerous—it would be too easy for Zaman's relatives to lie in wait for them on their return. The national passport office in Kabul was crowded and busy and could do passports for any province. For that and many other reasons, going to Kabul was their best move. They'd been caught there once, but they'd been careless.

This time, we told them, if they wanted our help, they were going to have to listen to our advice. Stay somewhere far from the center of town, in a Hazara neighborhood where the in-laws were unlikely to go. Once there, stay indoors and off the streets. Either together or singly, they risked being recognized wherever they went. We would pick them up in our car and accompany them to their appointments, which would keep them off the streets and out of public buses and give them a measure of reassurance.

They finally flew down to Kabul on August 12, after Women for Afghan Women sent them air tickets paid for with the donors' money. Jawad took off from work to meet them at Kabul International Airport. Anwar was with them, looking rumpled and small in his farmer's clothes and beat-up old turban; Zakia and Ali were in their finest, she in white leather high heels and a powder-blue dress laced and buttoned up the front from feet to neck, he in pointy white leather shoes, a *shalwar kameez,* and an elaborate gray jacket with blue piping around the pockets, both of them shabbily splendid. Just starting to show, Zakia was hiding her pregnancy well. It was the first flight of any sort that Anwar and she had ever taken and the first time Ali had been in a civilian aircraft. "We could see people down below," Zakia marveled, "and they looked so small."

12

MULLAH MOHAMMAD JAN

The lovers returned to Kabul to find they had become yesterday's story. The celebrity they never knew they had was proving transitory. The news beast, its attention span challenged, had lumbered on past them. Since nothing much new had happened, the *Times* had understandably lost interest and my editors told me to stand down on the Romeo-and-Juliet story. The couple would have had to get killed to make our news pages in those days. A few local publications did articles on them, and the BBC ran a video journal off an interview with them that August,[1] just before they left Bamiyan, but their lack of accessibility had cooled the interest of the local press. Zakia's family's interest, however, remained high. We called her kin from time to time, just to check in and take their temperature, and it was still on the boil. Otherwise, though, without all the intense press attention, they were just Zakia and Ali, a couple of farm kids from the middle of nowhere in a country with a war that America was both losing and losing interest in, rather than the story of Zakia and Ali. Even Rabbi Shmuley had stopped calling me so often, as Gaza blew up and Hamas lobbed rockets into Israel and Europe took the Palestinians' part, fueling

perhaps Israel's worst public-relations crisis—at least since the previous one—and provoking an ugly manifestation of anti-Semitic
attacks throughout Europe that summer. Shmuley had asked me
to bring him up to date on the couple's situation, which I did later
that August, but I could tell he was distracted and no longer quite
as stirred up by their case. "So basically what's special about their
case is your interest in them, but you're not doing any more stories
on them?" Sheepishly I conceded that was the case—barring either
some great success in their lives, which did not seem imminent, or
some disaster, such as an attack on them by her brothers, which remained a real possibility. I was no longer so sure that further stories
about their situation would help them much just then. For me they
were an unquieted guilty conscience. It was bad enough to break
all the rules to help them, but to have broken them without helping
enough—that would just not do.

The American embassy did arrange for its refugee officer to
meet with Zakia and Ali, along with Anwar, after they came back
to Kabul that August. Now that they were no longer fugitives,
it was no problem for them to come in and meet with American officials as well as Afghan staff and translators. As I explained
to the American officials before the meeting, Zakia and Ali had
hoped that they could find a solution that would allow them to
stay in Afghanistan and with Ali's family, but as time went on, it
became clear to them that Zakia's family would never relent and
they would always be hunted in their own country. Enduring exile
in the mountains as her pregnancy became more advanced focused
their minds (and, importantly, those of Ali's family) on their future
and what that held for them and their child. They just had to go
through that period of cutting off all possibility of escape in order
to confront what life would be like without escape. Now they
had, and after narrowly escaping from Gula Khan, they were much
more determined to leave. The embassy officers again outlined to
them what U.S. policy would be in their case: Get to a third country, either Pakistan, India, or Tajikistan, and apply to UNHCR for
refugee status, and then the American government could possibly
take an interest in their case. They came away from the meet-

ing encouraged by the attentive concern, although they had been promised little of substance.

After the embassy visit, we met with all three of them at the New Design Café in Kabul's Wazir Akbar Khan neighborhood. Quite possibly the most pleasant restaurant space in Afghanistan, the café was designed by Afghan architect Rahim Nomad, with walls of mud plaster and handcrafted brick, with soaring interior domes and a quiet central courtyard, with heavy Nuristani-style wooden furniture and native fabric cushions. The place has a charmingly authentic Afghan character, which has made it popular in Kabul's expat community. More to the point at the time, though, it had become all but deserted as the worsening security situation in Kabul had made restaurant life off-limits for most foreigners. Around the corner from the New Design Café, Taliban insurgents had burst into the Taverna du Liban in January 2014 and gunned down every patron they could find, most of them foreigners, diplomats, and aid workers, killing twenty-one in all.[2] The New Design Café is on the same street as the Norwegian embassy, however, and benefits from its security. With virtually no other customers during the daytime, it made for a discreet but safe rendezvous.

I asked them if they had thought about where, given the embassy's guidance, they might go. Their reply was a question: Where did *I* think they should go? I protested that it was not up to me, that we could not be in the position of telling them what to do with their lives. I didn't bother to try to explain, yet again, that it was beyond what any journalist should ever consider doing for them. Jawad and I explained in more detail what the embassy's advice meant to them in practical terms, though by now they had heard it many times. Iran was a dead end, and while they said they realized that, they did not want to rule it out—they knew people who had gone to Iran and had found jobs and a life there and had come back, although they'd been told of others who had gone and never been heard from again. Much more reasonably, they could go to Pakistan and would not need passports to do so. The border is porous, well traveled, and a minor bribe on the order of ten or twenty dollars suffices to cross it. Once in Pakistan they could go directly to the UNHCR office in Islamabad and apply for status as refugees and asylum seekers. The big problem with Pakistan was that although it was home to 2 million Afghan refugees, most of them were Pashtun refugees, and Dari would not be the common tongue. The couple had also heard nothing but bad things about how difficult life was in Pakistan, and the preponderance of Pashtuns there worried them. The Taliban, after all, were Pashtun in Afghanistan and in Pakistan, and Pashtuns hated Hazaras.

If they waited until they had passports, there were two other options. They could go to India, where there was a small Afghan refugee population, but, again, relatively few people would speak Dari. Finally there was Tajikistan. The former Soviet republic was, after all, populated by Tajiks, and while many Tajiks spoke Russian, most people spoke the Tajik dialect of Farsi, which was nearly the same as Dari. However, there were relatively few Afghan refugees in Tajikistan, the poorest of the former Soviet republics, and getting there would require not only a passport but also a visa—and visas were not easy to get for Afghans. Still, it was possible, and Tajikistan, they agreed, seemed like their best bet.

We began to describe what they would have to do to apply for passports, and it quickly became clear that even such a simple process was going to prove daunting for them, and not until Jawad offered to go along did they agree to do it. "You have to help us," Zakia said. "Without you we are three blind people."

They were fortunate, because the passport office in Kabul had recently undergone a reorganization in order to stamp out corruption. Previously, unless huge bribes were paid, it had taken weeks and months to get an Afghan passport. Now anyone could go and, if the applicant's documents were in order, be assured of a passport in days with the payment of the government's modest fees. It was a huge and rare success for the country's anticorruption efforts.

The next day Jawad took the three of them down to the passport office, in a ramshackle compound full of government offices of various sorts, all with lines of supplicants outside and knots of people gathered around scribes, squatting on their haunches before low boxes used for writing or copying out documents by hand. Photocopy machines sat outside in the courtyards, easy enough to manage in a place where for three hundred days a year it never rains.

The moment Zakia and Ali walked in, they caused a sensation. "I was really worried about them," Jawad said. People photographed them with their phones, some approached them, others wanted to be photographed with them. Overall the response was positive and admiring, particularly among younger people. There were mullahs there as well, and many people who made phone calls to share the news that they had spotted the Afghan lovers. Jawad was all too aware that one of those people might be a distant relative getting in contact with Zaman and the clan, or just a social conservative or a Tajik nationalist. "It's a big chance we were taking, going there," Jawad said. "Anything could have happened." Fortunately, Jawad was permitted to take their receipts so he could return and pick up their completed passports for them, without Zakia and Ali risking a second visit in person.

The passports would be issued on the basis of their *tazkeras*, national identity cards that all Afghans are supposed to have. These list only the year of birth, the person's name, and the father's name, not much more. To conform to international passport standards, Zakia and Ali both had to choose a surname, and each picked the name of the father's family, Ahmadi in Zakia's case and Sarwari in Ali's. They also had to choose a birthday. Most Afghans do not know their dates of birth; many have only an approximate idea how old they are, since birthdays normally are not celebrated. Co-incidently they both picked the twenty-third of August. Ali and Zakia's twin birthdays, the first ones in their lives, were just six days away; they would turn twenty-two and nineteen.

When I saw the identical birth dates on their passports, I asked them about it, and they burst into amused laughter at the realization that, officially, they'd both been born on the same day.

Around this time I managed to bring their case to the attention of the Canadian authorities. The comparative numbers of Afghans in Canada and the United States offer a revealing contrast. Canada, which pulled its last combat troops out of Afghanistan in 2011, had 62,815 Afghan refugees and migrants;[3] the United States, ten times as populous as Canada and with a much larger military and civilian presence in Afghanistan, had only 70,000, according to the International Organization for Migration. Canada was much more sympathetic to Afghan asylum requests, so much so that Afghans who do manage to sneak into the United States usually head north of the border before applying for asylum. Another advantage— potentially an important one in the case of Zakia and Ali—was that the Canadian immigration process provided for something called a ministerial exception, in which Canada's minister of citizenship and immigration can exempt applicants from the usual procedures and admit them outside normal asylum requirements. Whereas the analogous American procedure, humanitarian parole, often takes many months, Canada's system can take a matter of weeks. The Canadians have been enthusiastic supporters of women's causes in Afghanistan, and their diplomats' initial reaction to the case, although voiced only in private, was one of sympathy and concern. It seemed worthwhile for the couple to hide out for a few weeks and see where the Canadian inquiry went. In addition, I had gone to a back channel in the American government to see if there might still be some hope there. Again it was likely to be weeks before there was any word.

Life in Kabul settled into a tedious waiting game for the couple and Anwar, and this time Zakia managed to have her way, insisting, usually successfully, that Ali stay at home and off the streets. It wasn't easy for them, we knew, especially for the two men. Zakia said staying in seemed natural to her, and she did not mind it. She was busy growing a baby. The only time they all went out together was in Jawad's company, when he picked them up in a car to bring them to the New Design Café, which Anwar particularly loved. We tried to get them there as often as we could, if only to give them some respite from the dreary monotony of hiding out in the two rooms they rented from an Afghan family. A sparsely furnished place with masonry walls and half a dozen bedrooms, that house had been divided up to accommodate three or four other small families; more than twenty people shared the home and its tiny dirt yard behind a high wall made of cheap, crumbling brick.

The men did have to go out occasionally, to do the shopping, and they alternated such forays for safety's sake. "When it is my turn, I go out and walk down to the road," Anwar related. "I try to find someone to talk to, some stranger who wants to have a conversation. If I can't, then I sit and watch the traffic and the people go by and get relief that way."

The first glimpse I had of Ali at the New Design Café was startling—I had not seen him in person for weeks. The flashy, cheap new clothes were no surprise, but unlike the last time he came to Kabul, now he had taken some pains to change his appearance. The beard he once hated was growing in, still short but full. His long locks had been shorn to the skull, a military buzz cut—shorter than what he'd worn while in the military. He seemed nervous, too, glancing around a lot, fidgeting in his chair until I asked him what was wrong.

"I quit smoking," he said.

Zakia's insistence?

"Yes. She doesn't like the way it smells."

I repeated the old line that kissing a smoker was like licking the inside of an ashtray, which he found hilarious.

I asked Ali what his ringtone was that day, and he laughed. Though he did not know the name, he played it for us, and it proved to be another famous poem set to music, a verse by the thirteenth-century Persian poet Saadi Shirazi, who like many Persian poets was fascinated by nightingales and roses and often imagined a particular relationship between the two, one that was more literary than literal.

> Love is what the nightingale does for the sake of the flower,
> Enduring the hundreds of cruelties that come from its thorns.[4]

Where on earth did he get so many ringtones? I wondered. He thought it was odd that I didn't know.[5]

During those weeks in the late summer of 2014, our long talks grew increasingly interesting as all three of them loosened up. Ali had always spoken easily, but I learned more about him every time we talked. Anwar started to open up as well, and finally even Zakia surmounted the male-female divide—enforced in part by her husband—to confide some of her thoughts and to emerge, finally, as much more fully realized a person than she had previously seemed. We still could never speak to Zakia alone in person, but we were able to do so on the phone—although with her watchful husband's knowledge and permission, which had been a long time coming. For a man to allow even that much access to his wife by another man was convention-breaking in Afghanistan. Zakia acquiesced in her husband's control over her. She was still the girl who had scolded an older boy for riding on her donkey, but now she was careful to cloak that in the role of the self-effacing and even subservient wife. How did she like her husband's new haircut? "I have to like it—he's my husband." (She clearly did not like it.) How did she feel when he rejoined the army? "That wasn't a good thing to do." (She was furious.) Was he staying home enough? "He is trying." (Not well enough.)

When Ali enumerated her virtues, obedience was first on his list, followed by faithfulness and supportiveness. "I want my wife to accept what I tell her, when it is in her interest," he would say. "She should be honest and straight, too, and I want her to be faithful. She should be a friend to her friends and an enemy to her enemies. She should know how to deal with everyone." An idealized woman, in other words, but first of all an obedient one.

Zakia does not retire from the field; subservience seemed to be more of an obliging pose than an abject surrender. "I don't like ordering her to do things. I would never order her to do work for me," Ali said. "I request that she do things. I cooperate with her in the chores, I help her in cleaning the home, fetching water. I don't like being tough with women at all. They are innocent and weak. It is unfair to be tough with women in any way."

She takes that all in stride, sometimes with a light-up-the-room flash of smile but usually with no comment. When he starts joking around about taking a second wife, though, she speaks right up.

Dead Father's Daughter: Zakia's family came from Kham-e-Kalak village, Bamiyan Province, adjoining Surkh Dar, where donkeys were their only form of transport. (*Quilty*)

Under the Gaze of the Buddhas: The Bamiyan Valley from the vantage point of the Great Buddha Solsal, photographed from inside the niche where the Buddha's head had been. The shelter in Bamiyan from which Zakia escaped is on the upper plateau at the foot of the brown foothills in the center. (*Sánchez*)

Honor Hunters: Zakia's father, Zaman, with three of his younger children at his home in Kham-e-Kalak, before he moved to Kabul to hunt down his daughter. (*Lima*)

"If you love me, I also love you": Ali's father, Mohammad Anwar. (*Sánchez*)

Mystery Benefactor: Fatima Kazimi, then the head of the ministry of women's affairs in Bamiyan Province, who rescued Zakia from her family and later fled Afghanistan, successfully winning asylum in the United States for helping the lovers. (*Lima*)

Dead Father's Daughter: The first *New York Times* portrait of Zakia, February 2014, while she was still held in the Bamiyan shelter. (*Lima*)

A Beautiful Place to Hide: The home of Zahra and Haji Abdul Hamid in Kham-e Bazargan, where Zakia and Ali twice hid while fleeing. (*Sánchez*)

Zakia Makes Her Move: This picture of Zakia and Ali on the run, first published in the *New York Times*, has become iconic, with many Afghan artists painting versions of it. (*Sánchez*)

Where did they ever get this idea? Holding hands is not something often done in Afghanistan, even among married couples and especially not in public. (*Sánchez*)

The Irreconcilables: The Chindawul neighborhood in Kabul, where the couple hid until Ali's arrest. In this view, the Pamir Cinema building is the pale yellow building in the foreground; Ali was captured nearby. (*Quilty*)

Mullah Mohammad Jan: Anwar and Ali prepare for their flight to Tajikistan, buying suitcases at a marketplace in Kabul. (*Sukhanyar*)

BELOW **Honor Hunters:** Ali's father, Anwar, near the Kabul River the day after his son was arrested. He had no idea where to go, and no place to stay. (*Quilty*)

A Dog with No Name: The compound of Anwar's house in Surkh Dar, with the new guard dog chained outside. (*Quilty*)

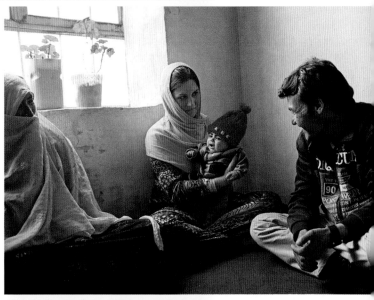

ABOVE **"We have our proof":** Ali's mother, Chaman; Zakia with Ruqia, age two months; and Ali, February 2015. (*Quilty*)

LEFT **"She can smell her family in the air":** Ali, in the family home in Surkh Dar, still in hiding well into 2015. (*Quilty*)

"He is still nervous when he holds her": Ali with his daughter, Ruqia, at his father's house in the village of Surkh Dar, in September 2015. (*Hayeri*)

"Whatever happens, we had this time together": Zakia and Ruqia, at home in Ali's father's house in Surkh Dar village, Bamiyan, in September 2015, eighteen months after the lovers eloped. (*Hayeri*)

"Now they will all go to school": Ali's parents, Anwar and Chaman, at home with their newest grandchild, Ruqia, in September 2015. (*Hayeri*)

Birds in a Cage: Ali trapping quail in the family fields; he keeps birdsongs on his cell phone. (*Quilty*)

"Enmity like this they will never give up": Ali working the fields, armed and ready, in February 2015. (*Quilty*).

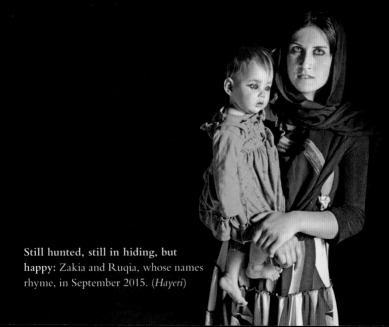

Still hunted, still in hiding, but happy: Zakia and Ruqia, whose names rhyme, in September 2015. (*Hayeri*)

"Just go and do it," she retorts. "I'm in charge of this family, and I'll throw you out."

"My liver," he replies, chastised, "as long as I'm alive, I would never do that." Calling a mate "my liver," *jegar-a-mah* in Dari,[6] is a much more intimate term of endearment in Afghan culture than "my heart" or "my darling," and by this time it had become the way Ali usually addressed Zakia. Talking about her to others, she was Zakia-*jan,* but between the two of them they were each other's *jegar.* He only ever addressed her by name these days when, for whatever reason she might have, she decided not to answer him—like when she was angry at him for going out and risking this thing they had.

That happened less and less during this second sojourn in Kabul. "Married life is a good life," Ali said. "When you're a bachelor, you only have half a life. With a wife you become complete." In what way? "When I was single, I was never home at night. Now I am always at home." It is more than that, though, he concedes: a feeling of pain he says he had ever since childhood, that led him to seek out the flute, the pain of loneliness, the pain that drove him to music and poetry. "Music is a solace to the pain. To people who are in love, it is a balm," he said. Lately he had even stopped playing the flute. "I don't need to anymore, because I have reached my love."

During these long conversations, Anwar sat quietly, but he was interested and attentive. At times, though, I felt he was brimming over with something to say, so one day I asked him, "Mohammad Anwar, we've heard their stories. Now what about your story? Did you marry Chaman for love?" It wasn't an unreasonable guess, since I knew he and his wife had married quite late—he was in his mid-thirties by then, and while that might have been partly because of the disruptions of the civil-war years, it was still unusual.

"If you spend forty years with someone, how is it possible that you would not love them?" he said. "She is a good wife, respected me, obeyed me, provided me with children, made me tea, always looking after me, always thinking of me." He seemed to be reaching for more nice things to say about her. "Always making me tea." Afghans drink a lot of tea, usually green tea without sugar, and always without milk.

Was it always love between them? Anwar said it was. Zakia and Ali listened raptly to his father's story of courting his mother, hearing it for the first time. Anwar was seated at the table, but his son and daughter-in-law were kneeling at his feet; they weren't fond of chairs.

"In those days there were not so many love stories as there are today," Anwar said.

"She was my maternal uncle's daughter, and we used to go to each other's home when we were children, and we liked each other. In my son's story, I remembered what had happened to us and saw similarities in their story, and this is why in the end I could not oppose him."

As her close relative, Anwar had plenty of opportunities to visit his cousin Chaman, and since the families were poor, their houses were one room shared by everyone. Once she was no longer a little girl, Chaman would be veiled during such visits, but there were many opportunities for furtive conversations, which they both looked forward to. One day he went to his uncle's house knowing that the uncle was out, pretending to want to meet him, and instead found himself briefly alone with Chaman. "I said, 'I love you, there it is.'" When she didn't answer, he went on: "If you love me, I also love you."

As they listened, Ali was wide-eyed and Zakia's mouth was frozen into an open O.

Chaman made no reply to Anwar's overture that day, but he soon came again. "She was shy. After a couple of days, I said to her, 'What's your response?' and she said, 'Okay, it's fine.'" She didn't say much, Anwar recalled, but it was plenty. Over the ensuing months, they would find ways to meet and talk secretly. "I would do it so no one would see me, but she could hear me," he said. Finally he asked his paternal uncle (his father had long since died) and his mother to approach Chaman's father and ask for her hand. No one else ever knew of the secret courtship, other than Anwar's mother.

"I didn't even touch her before we were married," Anwar added. The couple burst into a peal of laughter, rocking back on their haunches, and Anwar blushed right through his deeply tanned face, the furrowed, leathery skin turning a deep purple. Despite his embarrassment he seemed to get real pleasure from telling the story.

"Afterward I never thought of taking a second wife, even when harvests were good," he said. "Second wives are an evil caused by arranged, loveless marriages. When a man cannot be happy with his wife, he seeks a second one to make him happy."

It must be hard for him, then, away from Chaman these many weeks and facing the prospect of going abroad for months or years without her? "The loneliness is worth it, to gain happiness later," he said. Meantime, thanks to his sons, Anwar had gotten comfortable with his cell phone. When we first met him, he had never made a call himself and received one only when one of his sons handed the telephone to him. Later he learned how to return a received call. Now he had four numbers stored that he could use: those of Jawad, Zakia, Ali, and Chaman. He called his wife every day, he said.

I asked him about his married sons and daughters—hadn't their unions been arranged for them traditionally? Yes, he said, but he and Chaman had managed to make sure they were love matches nonetheless, by working behind the scenes. Ismatullah, his second-oldest son, he caught looking at a girl in a yearning way, confronted him, and then engineered the match with her father, with neither his son nor the father ever the wiser. Bismillah, the eldest son, and one of his sisters were married in a *baadal* arrangement with a sister and brother from another family. In this case, however, Anwar said, Bismillah had asked about the girl, and then Anwar made sure first that his daughter wanted the young man she would end up with, before proposing the *baadal*. She did not know him, but they connived to clandestinely check him out before she agreed.

"I suppose I am not that different from my father after all," Ali said. "Like the saying, 'Children are good students of their parents' bad habits.' But in that time it's surprising. In those days these things were not so common and very hard. It's really surprising. People weren't educated then like they are now." It was interesting that Ali often referred to Zakia and himself as educated people, by which he perhaps might better have said "enlightened." In this sense, though, in their willingness to defy social and cultural norms, in their insistence that they had rights of their own, Zakia and Ali were more enlightened than many of their more formally schooled countrymen.

Zakia smiled and looked at Anwar with admiration. Her amber eyes shone. It was a happy moment all around. "There's a saying we have," Ali said. "'When you're looking for it in the sky, you will find it at your feet.'"

They were starting to look forward to leaving Afghanistan. They each had their specific plans, quite modest. Zakia's plan was to have "all the necessities that are needed for a home, like TV, computer, washing machine." More long-term, she wanted to learn to read and write and then, someday, "If I had a chance to study, I would study law." She had been impressed to learn during her time at Women for Afghan Women that there was such a thing as a woman lawyer and even, in the Kabul courts, a few women judges. Anwar wanted to be able to go out openly again and see his daughter-in-law's child born and the two young people safe. He knew that his son would never have left without him along to help with his wife and to make life that much less lonely. Ali's ambitions were specific. "First I want to work to save up the money to pay off my father's debts. It will be better to work than to study, because we owe so much money and those debts have to be paid back, first. Second, I just want to have a life with my wife."

In the relaxed mood at the New Design Café that day, Anwar began talking about those debts in detail that he had avoided before. His total indebtedness was seventeen lakhs and twenty-six thousand afghanis, or about thirty-one thousand dollars, he said. Some of that debt had been accumulated by family disasters—his son Ismatullah had crashed his police vehicle and then fled the scene, resulting in huge fines that Anwar had to pay for him. Family weddings and bride prices caused more debt. "We're a big family of eighteen, and most of the time we were short of money and had to borrow," Anwar said. Worst of all were the bribes associated with Zakia and Ali's case, which totaled eleven lakhs of afghanis, about twenty thousand dollars in all. To raise those funds, Anwar had in effect mortgaged six of his ten *jreebs* of land, giving the land over to creditors who farmed it until he could repay his debt.[7]

I was aware that the family had paid bribes to support Ali and Zakia, but this was a huge amount for a poor family; where could it all have gone? Anwar detailed it, and while I have no way to prove what he said is true, he seemed so guileless and credible that it was hard to disbelieve him. There were bribes to the governor and the police chief not to pursue criminal charges against the couple, bribes to the Ministry of Women's Affairs to take up their case, bribes to people connected with the shelter, on a weekly basis, to keep Zakia there rather than hand her over to her family. Having bribed the police chief, they had to bribe his subordinates as well.

"Do you mean to say," I asked, "that you paid bribes to Fatima Kazimi," the Bamiyan women's-ministry head who saved Zakia from her family? Anwar and his son insisted that was so. (Fatima would later deny it vehemently when I told her about his charges. "He is a simple-minded man," she said of Anwar. "I only wanted to help them.") It explained why Ali and Zakia had been ungrateful to Fatima and also to the shelter head in Bamiyan, Najeeba Ahmadi, while acknowledging that their actions had probably saved Zakia's life. I had no way to know for sure if they were telling the truth, but neither could I see any reason for them to lie about all this. Anwar said he had never paid Najeeba herself anything, but he claimed that others associated with the shelter had demanded money from him.[8]

The summer in Kabul is prolonged by a good couple of months, and it was well into September by then. The days stay warm, even as they grow shorter and the nights become chilly. Flocks of green parrots remain in the urban treetops, perfectly camouflaged except for their loud song. It is an odd time, an Indian summer without any frost preceding it and with Kabul's tall, hardy Persian roses still in full bloom. On one of those days, Zakia surprised me by addressing Jawad and me directly, outside the earshot of her husband or father-in-law, something she had done only once before.

"I have a request," she said. "We have to go soon. I cannot keep him in much longer. It is okay for me, I am a woman. But he is a man, and he has to go out. He cannot stay in all the time like this. I know he will go out and get caught. Please take us away from here soon, in the next weeks or even sooner."

Ali and Anwar returned, and I asked them if they really wanted to flee now, rather than wait in the hopes that something could be worked out for them in Afghanistan, perhaps through the Canadian embassy or by persuading the Americans to let them go directly from Kabul. They had made up their minds to leave, they said, and were not about to change them. "Do you know," I asked, "how hard it will be for you in another country, another culture, for many months, possibly years before you could see your other family members again?"

Ali had a ready answer and began reciting these lines in Dari:

> *Traveling away from home*
> *Is so depressing and hard,*
> *Even if you are a prince,*
> *It is demeaning and harsh.*

Then, surprisingly, Anwar joined him, smiling his elfin smile, and they continued to recite in unison:

> *Even if you are a prince,*
> *It is a hardship to bear.*
> *However many carpets may*
> *Lie beneath your tender feet,*
> *Yet they will feel like a bed of thorns.*[9]

Neither of them was sure of the name of the poem, or the author, but they well knew where it came from: the story of Mullah Mohammad Jan and his beloved Aisha. Those verses are part of a longer folk poem that tells their story, set in nineteenth-century Herat. Mohammad Jan was a young teacher from a countryside village who took his class to an annual festival in Herat where poets and scholars held recitations on the grounds of the palace. The sultan noticed him and remarked jokingly on his long beard and his erudition, and asked his name. When he said Mohammad Jan, the sultan corrected him and said, "Henceforth, it shall be Mullah Mohammad Jan."

Flush with the sultan's recognition, he set off for home and on the way saw an unveiled young girl running toward him, as if someone were chasing her. She stopped nearly face-to-face with him. He was smitten, and as her brothers called her to rejoin them in the orchard where they had been playing nearby, he asked her name.

"Aisha," she said.

"I am Mullah Mohammad Jan," he replied as she ran off.

He began frequenting the orchard in the hope of seeing her again. He soon did, and they began meeting secretly, talking for hours. They remained chaste but agreed to marry. Mullah Mohammad Jan asked his father to approach her father, Issaq, who was a general in the sultan's army. Issaq rejected the suit, confined his daughter to home so the pair could not meet again, and then arranged for her marriage to one of the officers under his command.

Aisha was inconsolable, writing verses for her beloved by night and weeping by day. Mullah Mohammad Jan stopped going to his classes and similarly spent his time writing poetry about Aisha.

In an effort to console Aisha, her mother arranged a picnic among the girls of the village, where they could sing and dance. At first Aisha refused to take part, until the other girls and her mother gathered around her and demanded that she sing as well. Taking up a drum, she began to sing one of the verses she had written, a poem called "Where Are You Going, Mullah Mohammad Jan?" She sang in a high, clear voice that carried through the forest:

> Let us go to Mazar, Mullah Mohammad Jan,
> And see the fields of tulips, O my Beloved.

> Go tell my beloved that his lover has come,
> His narcissus flower has come,
> His flower has come to take him.

On the high mountains I wailed
And called upon Ali, the lion of God,
Ali, Lion of God, cure my pain,
Tell the lord of my prayers.

Let us go to Mazar, Mullah Mohammad Jan,
And see the fields of tulips, O my Beloved.[10]

The sultan's grand vizier happened upon the wood and, hearing her singing, pulled up on his horse as the girls hurried to put on their veils. "Who is this Mullah Mohammad Jan?" he asked Aisha, and she told the grand vizier her love story. He relayed it to the sultan, who summoned the scholar before him and heard his story as well. The sultan gathered his guard, and they marched on General Issaq's compound, where the sultan ordered Aisha's father to sanction the marriage.

Mazar-i-Sharif is a northern Afghan city famous not only for its spring fields of tulips but also for its shrine to the Prophet's son-in-law Ali, and annually the newlyweds of the previous year make a pilgrimage to Mazar's great Blue Mosque in Ali's honor, a custom still followed today. That year Aisha and Mullah Mohammad Jan went, accompanied by court musicians reciting Aisha's song, "Where Are You Going, Mullah Mohammad Jan?"

I had been hoping that someone like the sultan would arrive and give Zakia and Ali the happy ending their love affair deserved, and so I had not said much when they appealed to me personally to save them, to find their solution for them, to tell them what to do and how and even when to do it. It was true, though, as Zakia had said, that every day that passed, the risk of their being found increased. Ali called to say they had run out of money, so we agreed to ferry Anwar and him to the Women for Afghan Women offices. We met him on the rutted little backstreet in the Saray Ghazni neighborhood, at a street corner that had become our standard meeting place. It was close to where they were hiding, but not too close;

they could walk there without crossing main roads and risking detection. We did not want to take any chances that one of our drivers might see exactly where they lived and, intentionally or otherwise, spread the word. As we drove past the Zarnegar Park, near the city's central Abdul Rahman Mosque, Ali squeezed himself behind the car's door post, to hide. He said he thought he had just spotted Gula Khan, Zakia's brother, on the roadside, selling small bottles of water. I looked that way, and it was Gula Khan all right. He did not look like a happy man.

It was around that time we found out how Ali and Zakia's case had really been resolved. I'd bumped into Hussain Hasrat, a women's-rights activist and a former official of the Afghanistan Independent Human Rights Commission (AIHRC), who was one of those who had started Facebook pages to campaign for the couple. Mr. Hasrat was discouraged about the outcome, much as he was relieved to see them released, because, he said, it was not any sort of legal victory. Due process, such as it was, had been circumvented, and on a secret order from President Karzai the attorney general had issued the decree resolving the entire matter. Sima Samar, the chairperson of the AIHRC, had personally visited Mr. Karzai and asked him to order Ali's release from prison and allow the couple's marriage to be confirmed. "Three hours later they were freed."

I went to Ms. Samar, and she confirmed that account.

"Yes, I did take this case to President Karzai, and he immediately took action. He asked his staff to call [Minister of Interior Mohammad Umer] Daudzai and have [Ali] released. I told him it's just a Tajik girl and a Hazara boy. The only so-called crime was their different ethnic grouping, and also it's illegal [to try to prevent their marriage]—they're an officially married couple."

Her human-rights commission, so outspoken on other matters, remained silent on the case in public, perhaps out of concern over the ethnic issue. Ms. Samar is Hazara herself, and enemies of the commission have sometimes derided it as a Hazara institution, although other ethnic groups are well represented there. Similarly, Mr. Karzai never publicly acknowledged his role in their release, so it was hardly any sort of legal precedent, which is no doubt just the way Mr. Karzai wanted it. At the pleasure of the sultan.

As the long Afghan summer approached its end, I began to realize there was not going to be any deus ex machina resolution, not anytime soon anyway—no rescue by any embassy or grand vizier. Nor was the couple going to wait much longer, hanging around in Kabul until someone in Zakia's family ran them down. Either they would give up and flee to Iran or, since they refused to consider Pakistan, we would have to get them visas to Tajikistan.

Jawad and I did a quick reconnaissance of the Tajik embassy, on Street 15 in the Wazir Akbar Khan neighborhood. The stench of corruption there was notable, even in a country like Afghanistan that consistently ranks among the most corrupt countries in the world.[11] At the Tajik embassy, just getting past the guard at the gate required a bribe, as did getting past the guard at the door to the consulate. All just to go inside and get a visa-application form. This turned out to be money wasted, because Afghans with visa-application forms stood waiting for days outside the gates for the opportunity to submit those forms.

"You will never get a visa unless you pay," one of the supplicants outside told us. He was a burly Afghan Border Police patrol commander, in charge of a remote outpost in northern Badakhshan Province, an area where the only road passed through a patch of Tajikistan. This overlap required him to apply for a visa, which even he was having trouble obtaining. He had letters from the border police command, the Ministry of Interior, the Ministry of Foreign Affairs, and he had already been waiting for a week. Every day they told him to go and fetch yet another letter. "All they want is money," he said. "It's the only thing they care about in that country." We waited a few hours, nervously aware that a few hundred yards away on Street 15, earlier that year, a Swedish radio journalist named Nils Horner[12] had been standing outside on this street, interviewing Afghans about the attack on the Taverna du Liban, when two men ran up and shot him in the head with a handgun. It is a street full of news organizations, aid groups, and embassies and thus replete with police and guards, but the killers were never

caught. At the end of the day, the Tajik consular office closed without our having had the chance to speak to any visa officer. As we
were unwilling to bribe them, we had been rendered nonexistent.
Waiting outside on that street for so long had been pointlessly risky,
and we were not going to do it twice.

The Consultant was a young man in his late twenties, soft-spoken
and cautious, self-possessed and swaggeringly unctuous, a man
used to doing things for other people that desperately needed to be
done. He was heavyset, clean-shaven, hair-creamed, dressed in a
freshly starched white *shalwar kameez* and a long black herringbone
waistcoat—the picture of Kabuli prosperity.

Getting visas for four people to Tajikistan? No problem at all,
he said. He understood how much trouble it was, going through
normal channels, how difficult it is to spend all day waiting in the sun,
sometimes days and days, and after all, it's a simple thing. Afghans
were welcome in Tajikistan, as Tajiks were welcome in Afghanistan.
He would not only take care of it, he would do it possibly the same
day, no more than a day or two, in extraordinary circumstances
possibly three days. He did not want anything for himself, not at
all. He merely wanted to make sure everything went smoothly. He
would ask only the fees that he himself had to pay; there would be
no profit in it for him at all. He was being charitable. He would not
take one afghani more than the matter required.

Jawad handed over the passports the next morning, but three
days later they were still waiting. There had been unexpected problems, issues, the Consultant said; a national holiday connected with
the presidential inauguration, and then unspecified complications.
Finally, a week later, Jawad went to the man's office, a shabby little
storefront right on the sidewalk, a single room with a desk facing
the plate-glass window, the lower two-thirds painted over for privacy, a smelly latrine out the back door, accumulated dust on every
surface. The filth of the place was in sharp contrast to the Consultant's exquisite grooming.

"Our passports?" Jawad asked in his carefully polite way, never confrontational, even though they were by then ten days overdue.

The Consultant shrugged toward the unkempt pile on his desk, hundreds of passports, most of them the maroon-covered Afghan ones, with a smattering of other nationalities. "Come back tomorrow."

The next day the Consultant picked Jawad up in what he called his mobile office, a bright red, brand-new Toyota Corolla, decked out with flashing blue-white LED lights below the front and rear fenders and along the running boards—pimp lights, people called them. They drove around for a while until the Consultant indicated the center console box. Jawad lifted the lid, where there was a pile of forty or fifty Afghan passports. The Consultant had no idea where their specific passports were but invited Jawad to root through the pile until he found them, which he soon did.

A couple of weeks later, Jawad brought the couple and Anwar to see the Consultant. He'd been suspicious when Jawad had called him and asked him to meet with what Jawad referred to as "my friends," just to give them some advice about going to Tajikistan. It was not normally part of his services, he said, and he was about to hang up when Jawad mentioned he was willing to pay a fifty-dollar fee. The Consultant insisted he did not need to be paid, that it was not about money, but he was busy and would have to skip other work, so he agreed to take the fifty dollars anyway. He set a meeting place for them in front of the bakery on Lane 6, off Street 15, and when Jawad and the three of them arrived, the Consultant gripped the old man, Anwar, by the arm and led them all off to the shade of a big tree on the corner; he had no intention of taking them to his place.

Under the tree he rather rudely looked them all up and down. True, that was part of his assignment, but no one ever looks at women like that in Afghanistan, not openly anyway. Zakia was in her electric blue long dress, its numerous little bone clasps up the front cinched tight almost to popping with her pregnancy, which was still not evident except to those who knew her well; on her head was a stylish matching blue scarf. The white leather high heels—those would have to go, he said right away. Something plain. As for her dress, that was no problem; she would have to wear a full black *hejab* and keep her face veiled, so the dress would not show anyway. Ali had on a T-shirt and nondescript trousers—they would do, but his pointy white leather shoes would have to go. Then there was Anwar, who in his attempt to look less conspicuous had changed his old silk turban for a white skullcap, but the rest of his clean but well-worn clothes said "farmer," and where they were going, that meant "refugee." With Anwar, he said, it all had to go, everything new. "Look at Jawad," he told them. Jawad was wearing Western clothes and nothing flashy. "That is how you should all dress."

"Listen, Uncle," the Consultant said—focusing on Anwar as the weak link—"you speak the language, so you won't have any problem. Be brave, don't be shy. If you're shy, they will suspect you and there will be problems for you. Tell them you're just coming to see Tajikistan and you might come again and do some business. Say you have a business in Afghanistan—whatever comes in your mind as a business, tell them that. But be sure to change your clothes. And don't be afraid of them. If they ask you for a bribe at the airport, just leave some small notes in your passport and let them take them. They're very greedy. That's their nature, this is how they are. The police especially are very greedy, but don't worry, it won't be a problem."

The next flight to Dushanbe was on Wednesday, three days away; they aimed to be on it, the three of them and Jawad. As an American I didn't need a visa but had decided against going along, because it would only draw more attention to them, even if I pretended to be traveling separately. Few foreigners fly from Afghanistan to Tajikistan.

There was some good news before they left. Zakia had had another bout of morning sickness, and her doting men rushed her down to the hospital, a well-worn routine now; usually the doctors sent them to the pharmacy with a prescription, and since they could not read, they had no idea it was merely vitamins, just a placebo. This time, though, the doctor at the hospital was concerned enough to order an ultrasound. Fortunately, the baby was okay, the doctor said, but, he regretted to tell them, it was a girl.

How did Ali feel about that? "A girl? Why not? We are happy to have a baby girl. When I heard it, I was happy. We want the child to be a good child, is all. Obviously, men as fathers prefer to have sons, and women as mothers prefer girls, because daughters will help their mothers when they grow up, and sons will help the father. But I was very happy." He sounded a little as if he were trying to convince himself. "At least she will choose her own husband, because she will be the one who has to live with him, not us." He had no intention of reproducing the large families of his father's generation, he said. "The most I would prefer is one daughter and one son. More is so difficult to provide for economically. In the past, people did not have much awareness and they were not educated, they did not know much, so that's why they would have so many. Of course it's God who will care for and protect the children, but it's better to be careful yourself, too." The couple agreed that it would be Zakia who chose their daughter's name, but what that might be, she refused to say.

Zakia was more introspective, contemplating a daughter. "Of course we don't mind whether it's a boy or a girl—it's all God's property, boy or girl—but what is important, I don't want her to be like us. Now we're going to Tajikistan, and we can't even read and write. I've never been anywhere but Bamiyan and Kabul and the mountains. I don't even know where Tajikistan is. I want her to be educated, to be good, and someday, after all this bad experience we have had, these bad times, I want her to do what she wants to do."

It was one thing to be illiterate down on the farm; the need to read was never all that pressing there. Their months on the run, though, especially hiding in a big city, had made them keenly feel their handicap. "If you can't read and write, it's just as if you're blind," she said. Street signs are mysterious. The numbers on currency, meaningless. Instructions on packets of medicine, labels in the supermarket, a sign on a shop door saying "Back in an hour," a note from the doctor—all indecipherable. Typically, half the packaged food on sale in Kabul supermarkets is long past its expiration date; they would never know. "Someday I hope we can learn to read and write," Zakia said, "It should be possible, since we're still very young and will have a long life—although it's never really known how long we have to live."

Her smiles still lit up rooms, and she smiled a lot those last three days in Afghanistan. "We are ready. I got a veil, I didn't need much. The men needed much more than me. In one way I'm happy, I'm excited because we will be free there, but in another way I'm worried, since we've never been there before. Will we manage to live there okay?"

Ali reacted as he usually did, with a love poem memorized from a song. As usual, he knew neither the name nor the author, just the words:[13]

> *Though I am far away and cannot see you*
> *There's no reason to think I could be unfaithful.*
> *My loyalty to you is such that your name is always on my lips.*[14]

There was still enough money on deposit with Women for Afghan Women to give them what they'd need for living expenses for a good three months in Tajikistan, possibly more, and they made a final visit to the NGO to withdraw it and to talk to the group's capable country director, Najia Nasim. Beautiful and charismatic, Najia carried the day on many of the group's regular crises by sheer force of personality, and her warmth and directness was a dose of what the couple needed on the eve of their departure. "You should be optimistic about the future. Tajikistan won't be a problem. You'll get through it. There will be a lot of bureaucracy, and it may take a long time, but you're young and you will get through it.

"You know you are both very famous now, and you must take care until you are out of Afghanistan. Separate into two groups on the plane, Zakia and Anwar together and Jawad and Ali together, and don't talk to one another on the way.

"Zakia, you are lucky. Ali cannot wear anything to cover his face—if he does, everyone will suspect him." They all laughed. "But you can wear something to cover your face. I do it myself when I go to the provinces."

Jawad checked on their preparations and realized they had planned to bundle up their possessions in cloth and tie the bundles with string, checking that as their luggage; it would not do. He helped them buy a suitcase each, just one, so they did not look as if they were moving to Tajikistan forever.

In our last meeting, Ali began laughing to himself—a habit he had when he was introducing an embarrassing subject. "What's up Ali?"

"You're not going to leave us there, are you? Just once we get to Tajikistan, leave us on our own and we'll end up begging in the streets?"

"No, Ali, we're not going to abandon you there, don't worry. Once you're refugees, we'll come and visit you, and there are Western Union offices all over the country. People will be able to send money to help you."

On Wednesday morning Jawad picked them all up at the usual place. They were late, though, so when Jawad saw that Anwar was still dressed like a peasant from Bamiyan, ancient silk turban and all, it was too late to do anything about it. He figured the old man would be forgiven his retro look by virtue of his age; could Tajikistan really be all that different from Afghanistan's predominantly Tajik north, after all? Traditional dress was common there.

Everything went smoothly at Kabul International Airport; no one recognized Zakia with her veils on or Ali with his close-cropped head. The passport authorities seemed indifferent, and the group was soon aboard the hour-and-a-half-long Kam Air flight to Dushanbe.

❧

13

IN THE LAND OF THE BOTTOM-FEEDERS

Tajikistan's two biggest exports are aluminum from the state-controlled monopoly—the proceeds of which are believed to be funneled into offshore companies belonging to the dictatorial president, Emomali Rahmon—and prostitutes. Women from Tajikistan fill brothels throughout South Asia, including in Afghanistan, where indigenous prostitution is rare, despite the poverty. As the American ambassador to Tajikistan described it in a report to the State Department, "From the president down to the policeman on the street, government is characterized by cronyism and corruption."[1] The country is so broke with such a trade deficit that its only hope is foreign investment, but the few investors who dare to come rarely stay long. One prominent Afghan businessman told me he had closed his factory in Dushanbe, putting dozens out of work, because the annual bribes demanded by the tax office exceeded his annual gross profits.[2] Mahmadsaid Ubaidulloev, the chairman of the upper house of the Tajik parliament, a rubber-stamp body like all of the country's democratic institutions, was not just corrupt but, as described in another leaked State Department cable, deeply delusional. Discussing the Afghan War with the American ambassador, Richard E.

Hoagland, Mr. Ubaidulloev, who was also the mayor of the capital city, Dushanbe, warned the ambassador about extraterrestrial wars to come. "We know there is life on other planets, but we must make peace here first," Mr. Hoagland quoted him as saying. Worried about the rampant drug smuggling across the shared Afghan-Tajik frontier, the State Department's Bureau of International Narcotics and Law Enforcement (INL) contracted with a Tajik firm to make winter uniforms for the country's border force, only to discover they were being made of lightweight summer material by female Tajik workers who went unpaid for their labor. Another INL project provided the border patrol with bomb- and drug-sniffing dogs, highly trained animals that can sell for more than a hundred thousand dollars each. An INL inspection discovered that the dogs were being used as watchdogs in freezing conditions and had been put out to stud to breed other dogs for sale. The INL recommended that any future dogs sent there be neutered first to prevent that from happening again. In addition, many of the sniffer dogs could not be accounted for at all.[3] As the border guards were poorly paid and underfed, there was speculation that some of America's dogs had been eaten.

In retrospect, I should have known better than to help the lovers flee to Tajikistan. We just did not appreciate how brazen the corruption was there. After all, we thought, they were Muslims and Tajiks, like Afghanistan's second-largest ethnic group and like Zakia's family—how different could they be, even in a former Soviet republic? And anyway, what would corrupt Tajik officials care about three poor Afghans?

"Dushanbe Airport," reads a publicity blurb on its website in English, "is indeed a delight for the passengers as it caters varied services in a truly graceful way. It is categorized as a 'civil airport' as both the common masses as well as the officials belonging to the armed forces like the Military." Predictably, decades of Communist rule have left their mark; the terminal is ugly, squat, functional, and small.

The plan for them all to travel separately unraveled as soon as they reached immigration, because of one unexpected detail: the landing cards. An immigration officer pointed to the pile on a counter, and Zakia and Anwar looked at it blankly; Jawad, coming up behind, realized the problem and joined them to help them fill out the cards. It drew attention to the whole group, all the more so because Anwar was the only man in the terminal wearing traditional garb. The Tajik immigration officers knew a moneymaking opportunity when they saw it and grilled all four of them; the officials scoffed at the few small bills the group had offered in their passports and demanded a hundred dollars each to let them into the country, even though they had valid visas. They settled for fifty somonis apiece—about ten dollars. Bad as that was, it seemed more annoying than threatening. Tajik airport officials were crooked, it seemed, but cheap.

The four of them found a hotel in a neighborhood close to downtown Dushanbe that had been recommended by the Consultant as relatively inexpensive, in an area frequented by Afghans. A sprawling, Soviet-era place, the Hotel Istiqlol ("Freedom") had two separate wings. Anwar and the lovers stayed in one side, and Jawad in the other. He paid for them and the desk clerk refused to give him a receipt. When the shift changed the next morning, the new desk clerk asked for payment again or, absent that, since they had no receipts, a little bribe to start the day.

Because their visas were valid for up to a six-month-long stay, their plan was to find an inexpensive apartment and settle in there, waiting to see if there was any progress on visas from the Canadians or the Americans, before claiming asylum as refugees. If there was progress, they could return to Kabul within those six months. Once they were refugees, the Tajik authorities would cancel their visas, forbid them residence in cities like Dushanbe, and force them to relocate to remote parts of the country. Covered by the rugged Pamir Mountains, more than 50 percent of Tajikistan is over ninety-eight hundred feet in elevation, with many peaks above twenty thousand feet, and 93 percent of the land area mountainous. It is a place of breathtaking beauty, however ruthless and unscrupulous its apparatchiks might be; tourism is unsurprisingly rare.

On their second day in Dushanbe, Ali and Anwar went out house-hunting around midday. They were separated from Jawad by a few hundred feet when four men came and surrounded him. They wore cheap suits with no ties.

"They showed me their badges and said they were secret police. They said, 'What are you doing here?' and 'We are going to deport you.' I said, 'What have I done?' They said, 'You came here yesterday, and you're walking around like this in the city?'" The suggestion was that merely doing so was an offense.

A car pulled up, a ratty old Lada, with two more policemen inside. Two of them shoved Jawad into the backseat between them while two others got in the front. "Let me call my friend," Jawad said, and took out his phone—thinking to warn Ali to get out of the area—but they snatched it from him and told him to shut up. Then they came right to the point, as they dangled handcuffs in front of his face. "Give us your money." He took out a pocketful of somonis, but they scoffed at that and began methodically searching him. "They touched me everywhere, all my pockets, everything, until they found my money," he said. Because Jawad did not trust the hotel, he and the others had taken their cash with them when they went out. Jawad was stripped of all the money he had, nearly a thousand dollars, and turned out of the car. The policemen told him to return to his hotel, and when Jawad protested that he now did not have taxi fare, they gave him 20 somonis. The first taxi that stopped demanded thirty but finally settled for twenty when Jawad said he had just been robbed.

"You've met our police, have you?" the driver said. "Welcome to Tajikistan. We have no crime here. We just have police."

The Tajiks also claim to have the world's biggest flag, a banner nearly a hundred feet high by two hundred feet wide, flying on a hill in the center of town and visible from nearly everywhere in the capital. This is the country's only serious claim to any respectable sort of fame, but it's not true.[4]

As an Afghan, Jawad was no stranger to corruption, but the blatancy of it in Dushanbe astonished him. "It's always money, money there. It's worse than Afghanistan," he said. "They are like fishes—their mouths are always open, and they're saying, 'How much money do you have?' They openly ask you for money. No one in Afghanistan would do that." Jawad also was an ethnic Tajik, but these were not people he recognized or felt any kinship with at all, even though they spoke the same tongue. These were post-Soviet creatures, inhabiting a regime that was thoroughly rotten. "We expected a greedy, corrupt country, but not like this," he said.

The plan had to change. We discussed it and decided that it would be best if Ali and his family immediately applied for refugee status instead of waiting; it was only a matter of time until the police turned their attention on them as well. Once registered, they would have some measure of international legal protection. It was dumb luck that they weren't together with Jawad when he was picked up; as it was, finding their way blind back to the hotel was difficult. They did not know its name—the sort of thing that happens when you can't read signs—but they managed to explain to a taxi driver where they were staying, well enough for him to understand and take them there (overcharging them by a factor of five).

They all went to the UNHCR office early the next morning and were there when it opened, but the door staff simply told them to go away, without any explanation. They stayed and insisted on speaking to someone, standing in the street and worrying that the police would come at any moment. Finally, after many phone calls between the American embassy in Kabul and UNHCR, an official came out, a thin woman in some sort of uniform, with a miniskirt so short that it shocked the Afghans. When they explained that UNHCR in Kabul had sent word about their case, the official called them liars and sent them away again. They had the impression that unless they paid someone, no one was going to help them. Advised by UNHCR in Kabul to keep waiting, they persisted, and after a few hours a female staffer came out and wordlessly handed them a slip of paper on which was written the name of an organization, Rights and Prosperity, and its address. That simple act had taken nearly six hours, with no one else in line ahead of them. Fortunately, Jawad was there to read it for them.

The staffers at Rights and Prosperity were sullen but cooperative and explained what would happen next. The trio would have to establish a residence, then go to the police station in the neighborhood and register with the police, leaving their passports there for a few days. When they got the passports back, they could then return to Rights and Prosperity and begin the formal process of applying for refugee status. Jawad helped them find an apartment, looking over his shoulder the whole time, but the secret police did not show up again.

Once Ali and family knew where to go—the location of the police registration office and the Rights and Prosperity NGO—it seemed risky for Jawad to remain with them and likely that his presence might draw unwelcome attention to them from the police. At three o'clock the next morning, Jawad went to the airport for the five-o'clock flight to Dubai. He borrowed three hundred dollars from Ali for his travel expenses, but this time he hid the cash better, deep in the lining of his laptop bag. At the airport the immigration police had the same openmouthed, bottom-feeding approach as they closed in on him. "How much money do you have?" and "Give us all your money," and "Tell me the truth, do you have dollars?" were their conversational openers. He insisted that he had none, and although they pulled his possessions apart and body-searched him thoroughly, they never found it.

Zakia and Ali and Anwar were now on their own, at the beginning of what they thought would be a long road toward resettlement in a third country. When they appeared for registration at the police station in Dushanbe, they were extorted to pay bribes; the standard ten-dollar fee for registration became fifty dollars each, and then, before they were allowed to leave, the police demanded another hundred; so they paid a total of two hundred fifty dollars, when the official fee would have been closer to thirty for all of them. Then they had just two simple steps left: picking up their passports after registration and returning to the Rights and Prosperity office to lodge their claims for refugee status.[5]

It was clear by now that Tajikistan would only be a transitional place at best, even though they spoke the language; there was little or nothing for them there. Everywhere they looked, they saw evidence of the corruption and degradation that came out of decades of being part of the Soviet Union. Even the country's mosques were subjugated, with the authorities giving mullahs a selection of sermons they were allowed to read and jail terms if they did not. A taxi driver offered to find Anwar a second wife for the night. Another pointed out that "in that building are eighty girls who give massages" and told him how little it would cost. Prostitutes plied the street corners at night; uniformed policemen were their pimps. Drug dealers were everywhere. Tajikistan is an important staging area on the drug route between Afghanistan's poppy fields and the proliferating heroin cribs of Russia and the former Soviet republics. Anwar was horrified. "I have nothing but contempt for this country," he said later. Hopefully it would be different in rural areas, where once registered as refugees they would be obliged to stay until their cases were processed.

By October 6, Zakia and Ali and Anwar had their passports back from the Tajik police's registration office in Dushanbe, where again they'd been extorted for another hundred dollars. Jawad had arranged a taxi that could take them directly from the police station to the Rights and Prosperity office to lodge their applications for refugee status. Oddly, they did not go immediately. The next day, when Jawad called, Ali told him he was going to wait yet another day to complete the process because it was raining heavily that day. Then they let another whole day—this one of dry weather—go by before going to the office. Asked later why they had delayed so long, Ali shrugged and said, "We were negligent. I don't know why." Finally, on Thursday morning, October 9, three days after they retrieved their passports from the police registration office, they got into a taxi and went to complete their applications as refugees. A few blocks from the Rights and Prosperity office on Hofiz Sherozi Avenue, two plainclothesmen standing on the street flagged the taxi to a stop and ordered the three passengers out of the car. The three-day delay might not have mattered, although perhaps it gave the secret police time to decide what to do with them.

It was the middle of the morning, and the street was full of passersby; none showed any sign of concern as the secret police-men systematically searched the two men and then demanded that Zakia give them her purse. Ali tried to stand in front of her, but they shoved him out of the way and threatened to handcuff him if he tried anything else. They made Zakia take off her gold brace-lets and hand them over; they found the five thousand dollars the couple carried—their entire savings and the remainder of all the donor money from WAW.

When Zakia did not give up her bag, a policeman tore it from her hands—something that in Afghanistan would have been tanta-mount to touching another man's wife. Ali snapped and lifted a fist ready to strike the policeman. On his fist was his antique turquoise ring, which they noticed as they grabbed his arms. The ring was his proudest possession, given to him by his mother, who had it from her mother, who had it from hers, the oldest and most valu-able thing he owned. "Please don't take this ring, please! Think of God, think of Mohammad!" Ali pleaded with them. He grabbed one of the policemen by the lapels, but that only infuriated them, and they began beating and kicking him. Still, people passing by did not bother to look—or did not dare.

"It is better to die than to live in a country like that," Ali said. "No one has ever touched my wife's bag, but those cowards did. I tried to hit them, and they saw my ring and grabbed my hand and took the ring, and they started punching me, hitting me."

Satisfied they had stripped Zakia, Ali, and Anwar of anything of value—including their cheap cell phones—the policemen hailed a taxi, put them in it, and paid the taxi driver the fare to the border with Afghanistan, telling him to take them there and nowhere else. "Leave this country," they said. They were forced to abandon in the new apartment their suitcases, full of what meager possessions they had brought along; the taxi driver said he had not been paid for any side trips. "I guess it was our destiny," Ali said.

Their deportation did seem to be more than a random act of corruption, as was probably true of Jawad's earlier robbery. Ta-jikistan is a Soviet-style police state where nothing happens by ac-cident. The reasons for the robbery and expulsion remain murky.

Perhaps, in a country characterized by pimping policemen and roving drug dealers, a happy ending for some unknown Afghans' love story had aroused official contempt in an anonymous apparat-chik's office, somewhere up there on that hill in the center of Du-shanbe under the world's not-biggest flag. Or perhaps some Afghan employee at the American embassy in Kabul or in the UNHCR office there, who disapproved of Zakia and Ali's love affair, had informed on them deliberately. Besides the American embassy and UNHCR, Jawad and myself, no one else knew that they were going to Tajikistan and exactly when. We had even been careful to misinform the Consultant, advising him that their travel date was weeks away, not days.

Too frightened to defy the policemen, and with no funds left, Anwar and the lovers had no choice but to do as they'd been told. The road from Dushanbe to the Tajik border town of Panj-e-Payon took them to within two miles of the border, but the taxi driver refused to go the rest of the way unless they paid him more money. They'd been left broke by the police, however, so they got out and walked. Once they were at the border on the Tajik side, the Tajik border guards demanded another bribe to let them cross. Since they could not pay, they were made to wait for several hours, sitting in the sun by the roadside. When they protested that Tajik policemen had robbed all their money, the border guards threat-ened to arrest them for slandering government officials. Finally, at 2:00 P.M., the border crossing closed for the day and they were told to come back in the morning. They slept by the road that night, and the next day they managed to convince the border policemen that they really were out of money and got across, but then they had to walk three miles before they could find a taxi. Fortunately, they had a distant relative in the city of Kunduz, about forty miles to the south, and they persuaded the taxi driver to take them there to be paid. The relative also loaned them bus fare for the all-day journey back to Kabul, and by the following day they had returned to the capital, hungry, dirty, exhausted, and discouraged, with no money and none of their most valued few possessions.

Why had they waited so long to put in their applications as

refugees? we asked Ali. It seemed like they wanted their asylum bid to fail. Then to raise his hands to policemen? Ali laughed his nervous laugh and looked at the floor. "I don't know the reason. We just got negligent. Of course humans do not see their future, what's good for them or what's bad. Maybe that was our destiny. We really can't say."

Jawad and I tried to persuade them to flee to Pakistan instead, where there would be no government go-betweens or police registration, less danger of such rapacious treatment from the police, and, most important, the opportunity to apply directly to the UNHCR rather than through a corrupt, government-controlled apparatus.[6] Jawad would go with them and make sure everything went okay. They listened politely and said they would think about it. They agreed to go to the UNHCR office in Kabul the next day to discuss their options. We made an appointment for them at nine the next morning, but when we went to find them, they were gone. At the crack of dawn, they had gotten into a minibus headed back to Bamiyan.

Zakia and Ali did not say this, but I am sure they felt it: We had all let them down. This was their story now, and for better or worse it was going to end in Bamiyan, perhaps after a long and happy life or perhaps abruptly and violently today or tomorrow or the next day. At least in Bamiyan, as Ali had said previously, they would know what their enemy looked like and what to expect when they met him.

Much later, one afternoon in the depths of the winter to come, Zakia was alone and saw Anwar's cell phone unattended. She picked it up and made a dropped call to Jawad, as she had often done before with Ali. Jawad called back expecting the old man and was surprised to hear Zakia answer on the first ring. She just wanted to talk and seemed wistful, perhaps lonely, looking back over her life with Ali so far. Jawad immediately put her on the speakerphone so no one could accuse him of impropriety, and we talked to her together. "I wish I could have succeeded to marry

Ali with the consent of my parents, so we could live in Bamiyan without risk and have relations with my family, so we would go to see them and they would come to see us, and we would have a better and happier life," she said. "What we have done now is not a good thing. It is a bad thing, because we cannot live freely. We are always in danger. I wish we could have achieved a reconciliation between our families. That would be better than leaving our country."

That did not mean she was unhappy, she hastened to add. "I'm thankful, I'm glad for what we did, but they were against it and will always be against it. I am happy because I am together with him, and I am where I should be and should have been, with him. Whatever happens to us, we had this time together."

A DOG WITH NO NAME

In Afghanistan vengeance is a dish that never grows cold. None-theless Ali's family struggled to persuade him that Zakia and he remained at risk and they really should find a way to leave. After the Tajik debacle, the family opposed the couple's decision to come back to Bamiyan and pressured them to return to Kabul to wait a little longer and explore other options. So they dutifully went back to Kabul in early November 2014, but it was clear that Ali was not happy about it. Anwar and the rest of the family thought they should try again, this time through Pakistan or India, or at least spend some time in Kabul to see if anything else would develop from the Canadians or the Americans. Anwar came along again to Kabul as well. But Ali lacked the patience of the old man; it was apparent that he was just accommodating the family pressure and they would not stay long.

Manizha Naderi from WAW met with them to discuss their options. She had always been convinced that Zakia's family would eventually kill the couple unless they fled, and probably no one in Afghanistan has more experience at rescuing women threatened with honor killings than Manizha does. Accepting that they were so opposed to Pakistan, Manizha suggested India, where she could introduce them to an Afghan-refugee organization in Delhi that would help them. Jawad could go with them there, even I could go with them there, and it was a civilized place, where Afghan refugees were decently treated by the authorities. Living there would be tedious, with few people around who spoke their language and months of waiting ahead of them, but safe. We would find a way to help them surmount the language barrier. What was seven months or even a year of waiting, compared to the spans of their entire lives? This is not an argument persuasive to young people; to them a month was an eternity. They said they would think about it, which was as close to a no as anyone ever got out of them.

We made another round of visits to the Western embassies and diplomats, but the Canadians seemed to have lost interest, and the Swedes and Germans became the latest among several European countries to say they agreed with the Americans that they could consider the couple only as refugees in a third country. Holland and Norway ignored the couple's overtures, and of course, when it came to the Americans, they had foiled their only chance. They did not have the sort of money, twenty thousand dollars or more apiece, that human traffickers demand to smuggle people to Europe, where they could easily claim asylum. We were not going to encourage that route even if the money could be found, conscious of the risk that they would drown in a flimsy boat or suffocate in some truck container en route. Bereft of options that they were willing to consider, they were much more inclined to take their chances and face the future among family and friends—Zakia by then considered her in-laws to be her only family.

Then, in late November, as Zakia's pregnancy approached its ninth month, none of them could see fleeing as refugees until after the baby was born. Zakia felt she needed the stability of being in a place they knew. She felt more urgently the need of having womenfolk around—her mother-in-law and her new sisters-in-law. They announced that they would return to Bamiyan to overwinter there, perhaps reconsidering refugee options come springtime. Anwar was persuaded by the pregnancy as well. I offered to buy them air tickets from Kabul to Bamiyan so they could be spared the rigors and risks of the mountain roads and the Taliban checkpoints, and they got ready to fly home, this time for good, or at least for the winter.

Before they left, Ali called and asked if we would give him the money for the air tickets and he would take care of buying them himself. Then, a few minutes later, Zakia called from Anwar's phone and warned us that he planned to keep the money and have them all travel by land; both she and Anwar thought that was a mad plan.

It turned into their first fight. We told Ali we would give them only nonrefundable air tickets, not cash so he could go instead by road, and he realized that his wife or father had warned us of his intentions. He turned on his father, and they quarreled bitterly.

"You cannot take your wife by road!" Anwar yelled at his son. "She is pregnant—you must be crazy! You don't listen to anyone!"

"She is my wife, and I will decide what to do." He turned to Zakia. "We are going by road. If you are my wife, then come with me."

"I am your wife, but I am also the mother of our child. I will not go by road," Zakia said. "Uncle is also not well enough for that trip."

Ali stormed out of the house and headed off to Bamiyan on his own, taking a minibus with what little money he had left. The robbery in Tajikistan had wiped out everything, and the donor well was dry at WAW. I don't know where he even got the five hundred afghanis for the minibus fare.

Ali's brother Bismillah called from Bamiyan and asked Jawad if he could call Ali and try to calm him down, get him to return to Kabul and take the flight with his wife and Anwar. "You're like a brother to him," Bismillah said to Jawad. "Warn him he has to behave properly to his wife and respect his father." As he always did when upset, Ali had switched off his phone, and we couldn't reach him. Now, on top of everything else, Jawad was being asked to be Zakia and Ali's marriage counselor.

We got the air tickets for Zakia and Anwar, and they would fly up to Bamiyan on the next flight, three days later; after all the last-minute wrangling, the only seats available were in business class, so I splurged for them. The next day Jawad's phone rang, and it was Ali calling him back, from the Shibar Pass in the minibus, halfway to Bamiyan. He had calmed down and was already revising his account of the fight. "I *had* to leave like that," he said, "Otherwise I would get angrier with my father, and that isn't good. The only way to avoid disputing with my father was to leave him behind and come to Bamiyan on my own." On the way he planned to stop to see a friend who wanted to give the couple a wedding present—the friend lived in a remote corner of the province, which is why Ali had wanted to go by road, since it passed that way. That, and the money from the air tickets. Jawad talked to him for a long time, and Ali promised to meet Zakia and Anwar at the Bamiyan airfield.

A couple of days later, Anwar and Zakia went to Kabul International Airport for their flight. They boarded early in business class, so they were already seated as the planeload of passengers filed past them. Some of them recognized Zakia and smiled broadly, chuckled; a few of the older ones scowled, and she avoided eye contact with men in turbans. She was glad when the privacy curtain between classes was pulled, and she said nothing and looked uneasy when a flight attendant asked her for an autograph.

There's a saying that marriage only really begins after a couple has survived their first fight. Ali was at the airport in Bamiyan to meet their plane. He hugged and kissed cheeks with his father and took Zakia's hand in his. Ali's own version of that particular saying went like this: "Until you roll a car, you can't be a good driver." Fortunately, he's never driven a car, but neither had he ever been a husband.

Bitter cold set in the month after they arrived back in Bamiyan, but they viewed it as a friend; the fields were frozen, there was no work, and it would be difficult for the men in Zakia's family to return home. If they did, they would be noticed; there is hardly any good reason to go to Bamiyan in the winter. Few cars come over the two main passes from Kabul when the snows are deep there; the Hajigak Pass is often closed for most of the winter, and Shibar Pass is not much better. The couple settled into Anwar's mud house and talked about building an extra room on it come springtime. One of the rooms had underfloor heat, a traditional Afghan setup where brush is burned in a crawl space beneath a suspended earthen floor, keeping the room above efficiently warm for many hours. The small children and the old couple shared that room at night; the others piled on blankets and made do with *bukharis* when there was enough fuel to go around. In all there were eighteen of them sharing no more than four small rooms, ten adults and eight young children, the grandchildren of Anwar and Chaman.

Semitranslucent plastic sheeting was tacked over the small windows of the mud buildings in the compound, which would remain closed up for the long winter. It would be dark inside, with smoke stains on the timber-and-wattle ceilings. Neatly stacked in the courtyard next to the still-unfinished compound wall was the winter's supply of fuel, scores of firewood bundles. These mostly consisted of brush and twigs, and a few bigger sticks, collected on long expeditions into the mountains by a group of the men taking the family's two donkeys, their only form of transport. No one in the family had so much as a bicycle. There was a newcomer to their compound then, a dog chained to a stake—a rare sight, because most Afghans despise dogs and rarely keep them at their homes.

That December, Zakia went often to the hospital with labor scares and asked to be taken there whenever she felt faint or nauseous. At last it really was labor, and just after midnight on December 27, nine months and eleven days after eloping, Zakia gave birth to a baby girl. No one recorded the weight, but the new parents worried that she was too small, too weak, and she coughed too much. Zakia came through it badly anemic, had a blood transfusion, and was kept in the hospital for four days.

At home Zakia and the baby shared the room that had underfloor heating with Chaman and the small children. The cold was so severe that it was an emergency, and the newborn and its mother came before everything else, so they were given the warmest room and the thickest blankets. At first Chaman changed and cleaned the baby, picked her up when she cried, walked and rocked her to sleep, and did everything but feed her. Zakia took her when it was time for the breast. "I'm happy to have another baby in the house," Chaman said. "But I still want them to go abroad, somewhere safe. I love the child and I love my daughter-in-law, but they have to leave."

Zakia could not decide what to name her daughter, so a couple of weeks after the birth she asked her brother-in-law Bismillah to choose the name for them. "He is the eldest son in the family, so all should accept that," Zakia said. "I didn't have a good name of my own to give her." Bismillah spent a day thinking about it, then came to Zakia and said, "What about Ruqia?" He liked it, he said, because it rhymed with Zakia. Both were originally Arabic names, with multiple meanings, but one of those meanings was the same for both: "ascendant" or "higher." So Ruqia it was.

The love story of Zakia and Ali and the travail that attended it is both exceptional and ordinary. Exceptional because it has not ended in violence, at least not yet, and because it got told at all. Ordinary because no matter how hard the mullahs and the patriarchs of the country try to stamp it out, love happens, and it happens a lot. No one really knows how often, since it all transpires out of sight behind the walls that surround nearly every Afghan home. The *Night of the Lovers* radio program is a rare window into the romantic lives of Afghans, and after more than a year on the air it was still receiving hundreds of submissions from lovesick Afghan young people every week. Information is even harder to find on how many love affairs are cut short by honor killings. In so many cases, lovers are thwarted before they get very far, or if they do go far, they are tracked down and killed. Usually no one hears about these killings—except in the communities where they take place. The male elders approve of the honor killings and conspire to keep them secret from the authorities. "Just five or ten percent of these cases of violence against women are ever publicly known about," says the women's-rights activist Hussain Hasrat.

Nobody heard about the story of Layla and Waheed, for instance, until it was too late. Both employees of tailors on the same street in Kabul, they met through work. Like Zakia and Ali, they were different ethnicities—Layla was Pashtun, Waheed was Tajik. They were similar in age, too, Layla eighteen and Waheed twenty-two. They also knew each other from early childhood, growing up in the same neighborhood. Once Layla reached marriageable age, Waheed sent emissaries to her father but was rebuffed, seven times in all. Finally they eloped together; accounts vary as to whether they got married or just planned to do so. They were able to stay hidden for some months by the dangerous stratagem of going to one of the country's worst districts, Imam Sahib, a Taliban-infested area in Kunduz Province, and staying there in the home of a distant relative. Word reached them, however, that their families had discovered their hiding place and had alerted the police, who were on their way, as had happened in the case of Zakia and Ali.

On February 20, 2015, Layla and Waheed fled the relative's home in a taxi, sitting in the backseat together. They had already made a pact to kill themselves if anything happened to the other or if they were caught and forcibly separated or imprisoned. Now Layla told Waheed she had bought what are branded in Afghanistan as Pakistani Gas Tablets, a rat poison in tablet form that when ingested or moistened releases deadly phosphine gas (a pesticide so powerful it is banned for that use in most countries). The lovers agreed to take the tablets if the police caught them. Approaching the edge of Kunduz city, they came to a police checkpoint. Convinced they would be discovered, Layla began washing a handful of tablets down with a bottle of water. Waheed tried to intervene, and they wrestled in the backseat, but he wasn't able to prevent her. Seeing it was too late, Waheed despaired and took some of the tablets himself. As it happened, the driver just slowed down at the checkpoint and the police waved them through. Soon both young people were convulsing, and the terrified taxi driver rushed them to the hospital. Layla was dead on arrival; Waheed survived after his stomach was pumped. Dr. Hassina Sarwari, who runs the women's shelter in Kunduz, went to the morgue to view the girl's body. "How difficult it is to live in a country where you die if love comes along," she said. No one heard about their case when they were still on the run. It was too late by the time anyone did.

The public attention to Zakia and Ali's story has given them some degree of protection. It helped to pressure Afghanistan's president into resolving their criminal case, so they no longer needed to worry about being hunted by the police—though they were still hunted by her family. Along the way they became heroes to people in their own generation and to all Afghans who believe in love. They may yet become martyrs of love as well. They each continue to insist that if one of them were killed, the other would commit suicide. In that case Anwar and Chaman would bring up Ruqia, and Zakia and Ali will have been just another typical Afghan love story after all.

Underlying the refusal of the United States or the international community to do anything more for these lovers is a presumption that taking them out of Afghanistan to safety would be yet another marker of failure, an admission that their own society and its laws cannot protect them. By leaving them in Afghanistan, we are saying that our massive investment in the country's rule of law and its treatment of women did have some success, that the couple is proof of that. They are free, and they are alive.

They would not be alive if it were not for groups like Women for Afghan Women, which would not exist without foreign financial support. Without foreign intervention there would be no shelters in Afghanistan, no EVAW law, no prosecutions (however limited) for stoning women to death or forcing little girls to marry old men. Zakia and Ali's legal case was not resolved through the legal system, not really; it was resolved by an exceptional and secret decree of the president of Afghanistan, one that established no principle in law, that was his to give and a future successor's to take away. Even though the EVAW law was cited to resolve the case, it was not the real engine of the final decision to release Ali and let the couple formalize their marriage. In the face of a public outcry on their behalf, it was merely expedient to do so. In addition, Zakia and Ali's survival was financed and subsidized by concerned donors, without which they would not have lasted much more than that first month on the run. And they were abetted by my using the considerable resources at my disposal as a foreign journalist.

Committed to the narrative that the rule of law and the pursuit of women's rights are success stories in Afghanistan, no Western embassy wanted to admit failure in such a high-profile case as this. None has even commented on the situation publicly. If Zakia and Ali are killed, those who turned them down for asylum will know who they are. When such blame is passed around, there will be plenty to reserve for myself—both for failing to succeed in helping them escape and for shining what ultimately was an unhelpful light of publicity upon them, making them too famous to hide but not important or famous enough to be saved.

Perhaps we all should have pushed them harder to go to Rwanda, as Shmuley Boteach had urged early on. Bizarre as that solution may have sounded, it actually worked. Fatima Kazimi, her four children, and her husband were all successfully processed by the UNHCR in Kigali, as refugees fleeing danger and persecution in their country of origin, and the United States accepted their request for asylum. That claim was based entirely on Fatima's role in saving Zakia's life and protecting her from her family. Just over a year after their arrival in Rwanda, Fatima and her whole family were in Baltimore, safe from whatever danger—real or imagined— they had faced in Afghanistan. When Ali heard the news, he had no bitterness over the irony of it. "Okay, they exploited our case, but we don't have any problem with that. We wish them well." He did not think that route would have worked for Zakia and him. "The difference between us and them is that they weren't illiterate," he said. "They were literate so they could find out what to do. It would have been much harder for us."

A combination of poor weather in Bamiyan, grounded flights, and bad news elsewhere kept us from visiting the couple for much of the winter, but Jawad and I managed to get there late in February 2015. By then Ruqia was gaining weight and the weather had eased and was just normally cold; the snows came in light dustings that were more decorative than cumulative. Ali's brothers and Anwar were worried about the continuing drought and its effect on the next season's crops. When we spoke with Zakia about the couple's plans, she insisted to us that she wanted to try again to flee Afghanistan, perhaps in the spring, but first she would have to convince her husband that it was the right thing to do; he was reluctant to try again, she said.

"With Ali it's only God who has any power over him. No one else can force him to do anything." She said that at least Ali was no longer going out unless accompanied by his brothers. He was awkward around their daughter, though, Zakia said, which amused her. "He likes to take her and hold her, but when he does, he becomes shy and doesn't want the others to see him holding her," she said. "But he loves her, I know that."

From her own family, Zakia had no news at all, which was perhaps just as well, she said. "I don't know what they're doing and whether they know about the baby. I don't think they do."

"Yes, I'm reluctant to leave," Ali said when we asked him about this issue. "Your homeland is that place you will always love, and even though there are threats to our lives, every pass in this country is precious to me." But he insisted he knows that leaving would be best and is ready and willing to do it as soon as possible. Zakia is the problem. "I have a life partner, she has equal rights to me. If she's not satisfied with going abroad, we can't do it," he said. "Life partner" was a term I had never before heard him use. It was not part of the lexicon even of educated Afghan society, and it sounded false from him.

When we talked to Zakia in front of her husband and family about leaving Afghanistan, she was diplomatic to the point of opacity. "Whether I go or I stay, it doesn't matter, as long as we're happy, and we are," she said. She flashed her transformative smile and hardly seemed worried about any threat to their happiness. When I voiced that observation, she immediately contradicted me. "No one knows what is going on in someone's heart," she said. "No one can ever know that."

When we talked to Ali alone, he was not surprised to hear

that Zakia had said he was the one who opposed leaving. "When anyone else asks her, she says she wants to go, it's true," he said. "When she talks to me, she says she wants to stay here." Why would she want that, with a new baby to worry about? Ali smiled knowingly, the way he often did when he prepared to make a profound observation or deliver one of his many aphorisms. "Because when she's here, she can smell her parents in the air," he said. "The smell of her parents, her mother and father and brothers and sisters, is here. She can still smell them. That's what she tells me that she won't ever tell you." I knew what he meant, that smell of one's childhood, so deeply rooted in a place, the one we never forget no matter how old we get.

Sometimes the argument in Anwar's house about leaving Afghanistan became bitter and contentious. Ali's brothers and father are all adamant that the couple needs to go abroad, that they cannot remain like this indefinitely. "Enmity like this, they will never give it up," said Bismillah. Zakia's father and brothers abandoned everything because of Zakia's love story; as they would see it, honor killing is all they have left to redeem their tattered lives. Zakia and Ali owed it to themselves, their baby, and their family to go once winter was over, the family kept saying. Early in February the argument blew up, and harsh words were exchanged between Anwar and Ali; it was sparked when someone asked Ali where the *neka* document was, to be sure he could get it quickly if they had to run again.

"We're done with running away," Ali said. "There is the proof of our *neka*." He indicated Ruqia, who was then less than two months old. "This is our big proof that we are married, and now neither the Afghan people nor the nation can do anything to us. We have our proof." The child was swaddled tightly, as Afghan infants usually are, with a red knit cap on her head, bearing the letters ABC, and her face carefully made up. Her eyes were framed in black, with charcoal eye shadow on her eyelids top and bottom, and deep black mascara on her eyelashes; she looked a little like a baby raccoon. (The eye shadow is called *surma,* made from a ground black stone, and many rural Afghans believe that making up babies' eyes like that, for both boys and girls, helps their sight develop better.)

Ali's brothers took Anwar's side, criticizing Ali for again letting romance run wild over common sense. They insisted that Ali and Zakia had to make serious plans to flee the country; once abroad, they could find work and send money back to help resolve the family's debts, so it would help everyone. As long as they stayed in Afghanistan, they were a burden to the family with a death sentence hanging over them, and once dead they would be no help to anyone.

They all had heard of Afghans who'd escaped abroad and were later able to bring other relatives along or who with even simple jobs were able to send fantastic sums home; Zakia and Ali could be their vanguard, a hedge against an uncertain future. Ali angrily replied that they wanted him to ruin his life by leaving his country so he could pay off their debts. They retorted that much of that debt was due to him.

What's more, Ali's oldest brother, Bismillah, scolded him, what future did any of them have in Afghanistan? "Look around you. One day the Taliban will be back. Security gets worse every month. No one wants to fight for this government—look at you. Did you? The foreigners are all leaving, most of them are gone already. Where will you and Zakia be when the *takfiris*[1] come back? They'll be a hundred times worse than Zaman and Gula Khan."

Remarkably, this tension had no apparent effect on the relationship between the family and Zakia, who arguably might be considered the original source of their troubles. In Anwar's house she was treated like a princess by everyone—even, the brothers insisted, by their wives. Three of Anwar's five sons were now married and living under his roof. The brothers said that they treasured Zakia even more than they would have otherwise because of her decision to sacrifice everything in her life for Ali and their family. Having once opposed the couple's love affair bitterly, they had come to embrace it wholeheartedly. "In this house Zakia does no laundry, no cleaning, no cooking," said Ismatullah, the one who had smashed Ali in the face with a rock when he tried to join

Zakia at their uncle's house. "We won't let her work as long as she's here," said Bismillah. Asked how her sisters-in-law felt about that arrangement, the brothers were bemused by the question; naturally they would be happy about it, because they had been told to be happy about it and women must obey their husbands. Also, it was a venerable tradition in Afghan homes to revere and coddle the newlywed bride, who always gives up her own family to move in with her husband's, and that special treatment intensifies once she becomes a mother. That may well be one of the reasons Afghanistan's birthrate is the tenth-highest in the world.[2] Zakia told us that the sentiment was genuine, even from her sisters-in-law. "It's really true. My sisters and everyone are always telling me not to do any work," she said.

"We have a saying," Anwar said. " 'When a flower is too precious to leave outside, you put it in a vase on the table.' Zakia is like that flower to us."

There was something else to thank Zakia for, a kind of epiphany provoked by what the lovers had been through. Her love affair with Ali had a galvanizing effect on his family's attitudes toward education. In a sense Ali's frequent references to Zakia and himself as educated people acknowledged their understanding that the world had changed and it was time for Afghanistan to become part of it. In this new world, Anwar was saying, women had rights, too, and love was not wrong. Educated people were those who knew and accepted that; uneducated people were all the others. Anwar's family was now educated, Zaman's family was not.

More concretely, the trip to Tajikistan and the months in hiding in Kabul had convinced them all, and importantly Anwar as the head of the family, that illiteracy was not just a condition, a fact of their lives; it was an affliction that cursed and limited them. Handicapped like that, they could not cope in the world outside their farm and village, but they could no longer ignore that outside world.

So one of the unexpected consequences of the love story of Zakia and Ali was that in the 2015 school year, which in mountainous parts of Afghanistan begins after winter ends, all seven of the school-age grandchildren in Anwar's household were going to school, five of them for the first time. (Two others had started the year before.) Five of those seven are girls. Of Anwar's eight sons and daughters, now all adults, only two of them could read and write, and neither very well; Anwar now wants each of his grandchildren to at least stay in school long enough to become literate.

"Those travels taught us that we couldn't tell the difference between a house and a public toilet. We were helpless because we couldn't read," Anwar said. "It made us think how important this education is."

The impact of the couple's love story went beyond their family as well. "The younger generation in Afghanistan saw this as a successful love story and discussed and debated it in their circles, especially in cyberspace," said Zahra Sepehr, head of a Kabul-based advocacy group called Development and Support of Women and Children.[3] "It had a tremendous positive effect in the society and gave young people the encouragement that religious and ethnic differences are no hindrance to a successful marriage based on love." Ms. Sepehr said that the couple's own example ended up saving a woman in Kabul from an honor killing. The woman named Soheila, was twenty-one, and a Shia Hazara, and the young man involved, Jawed, was twenty-five, a Sunni Tajik—like Zakia and Ali with the sexes reversed. Both of their families opposed the union. "The couple approached my office. We did a mediation between the two families, gave them the example of Mohammad Ali and Zakia, and told them marriage is the right of every person. Everyone has the right to choose the person he or she wants." Ms. Sepehr said the mediation did not succeed in persuading all their relatives; the boy's father and uncles, and some of the girl's uncles remained opposed. But it encouraged the couple, Ms. Sepehr said, and it did reach Soheila's father, who knew that his daughter's love was so strong that she would run away if they prevented the marriage. His solution was a practical one, and very Afghan. He put his daughter into hiding and spread the word among their families that he had killed her, then quietly arranged for Soheila and Jawed to elope to Pakistan, where they now live in safety—and secrecy, with her father's honor publicly intact. It's what passes for a happy ending to an Afghan love story. "This happened because of the example of Zakia and Mohammad Ali," Ms. Sepehr said. "Now when I talk to any couple like this, I tell them their story."

On January 11, 2015, Zakia's brother Gula Khan returned to the valley. At first no one knew where he was staying, but he'd been spotted on the road and then in the bazaar, and family friends told the couple about the sighting. Later they learned he was staying in the house of his father-in-law in Kham-e-Kalak. Anwar and his sons were wary; the brothers took turns standing guard at night. The Bamiyan police were informed and promised to keep an eye out, but even Ismatullah, himself a policeman, thought that was an empty promise. (Like most Afghan policemen, Ismatullah was not allowed to bring his service weapon home when off duty.) Anwar no longer had his old shotgun, which he had sold when the family ran out of money. So after Gula Khan's return, Ali's older brothers brought home the dog and staked it outside. He was a mongrel with plenty of bark, and they put him in the gap in their compound wall as an early-warning system. They fed the animal well, but it would remain a dog with no name. In communities where people get only one name, animals get none.

Zakia forbade Ali to go out alone (actually, as she put it more diplomatically, Ali agreed to accept that restriction after they discussed it). "It's difficult to protect yourself from your enemy, because you don't know when they will act against you," Ali said. Then some money arrived, sent via Western Union by an anonymous donor, who wanted them to have a thousand dollars to help with baby expenses.[4] Half of it they spent on fuel and food for the winter, and with the rest Ali bought a gun. When he went to the fields with his brothers, he would tuck the nine-millimeter Russian-made Makarov pistol into his belt (he didn't see any point in paying extra for a holster) and pull his shirt out to cover it, but only partly. Even so, he had trouble concentrating on field work, constantly looking up when anyone appeared on the horizon. Ali said he thought the gun qualified as a baby expense.

"I'm fine with that," the donor said when he heard about it. "Of course he has to protect himself and his family. That's his first responsibility."

There had been no indication so far that the determination and anger of Zakia's family toward the couple had cooled at all, and there are many such cases where families have waited years before exacting vengeance. The family of a girl named Soheila, from Nuristan, pursued her for eight years after she broke off an arranged child marriage, attacking her, the employees of the shelter where she stayed, and the man she wanted to marry, and prompting authorities to jail her.[5]

Soheila was a victim of the abusive traditional practice of *baad,* but even by the standards of *baad* her case was shocking. Nine years before Soheila was born, her father's grown son, Aminullah, eloped with the intended wife of his father's cousin, setting off years of violent feuding between two sides of their family. When Soheila was born, her mother died in childbirth. Aminullah was her half brother, by a second wife of her father's. Her father, Rahimullah, decided to resolve the family feud by giving Soheila in *baad* to the cousin who'd been wronged by his son. So Soheila was being sold, at birth, by her father on behalf of her half brother to resolve a dispute that began long before she was born. When Soheila turned five, the two families tied a *neka* with the approval of a mullah, arranging for the celebration and consummation of her marriage to the cousin when Soheila reached the legal age of sixteen.[6]

No one told the girl about her betrothal until she turned thirteen, and once she knew, it did not take her long to figure out that her white-bearded husband would be sixty-seven when they wed—and she would become the fourth wife of what would be considered a very old man in Afghanistan, where the average healthy male life expectancy is closer to fifty years.[7]

On the eve of her wedding day, Soheila ran, going to the only place she could think of—to her maternal uncle's house in a neighboring village. Her uncle said he would have to return her to her family the next day, and out of desperation she asked her male cousin, Niaz Mohammad, if he would help her run away. She later said she acted not out of love but simply because she had no other options, yet just the act of being alone together made Soheila and Niaz adulterers in the eyes of Afghan society and law, and they soon decided to get married. Later love came as well, and then pregnancy.

For eight years Soheila's father and her half brother, with the help of other men in their family, pursued her and Niaz from the remote mountains of Nuristan to Kabul's slums. They first tracked them down when Soheila was pregnant with the couple's child, and her father persuaded the police to arrest them both on adultery charges; their baby was born in prison. Later, Women for Afghan Women managed to get Soheila and her child out of prison and took her into one of its shelters. Soheila's family fought bitterly against the divorce case the organization brought to vacate her child marriage to the elderly cousin. They showed up in court with a dozen witnesses claiming that Soheila's *neka* was not tied until she was sixteen years old. When the court ruled in her favor, the family pretended to be willing to take her back in while her husband's court case continued and then attacked her and WAW representatives when they showed up at their home, the women in her household setting upon her and beating her and the men taking out guns to shoot at the social workers. Soheila escaped with help from neighbors, but afterward her family members threatened to kill her lawyer and called Soheila with so many death threats that she began recording them to show police. Finally, in May 2014, Soheila's divorce from the old man was final, after a mandatory waiting period under Afghan law, clearing the way for charges against her real husband to be dropped. He had spent most of four years in prison; she had spent most of those four years in the shelter.

Eight years after she fled the arranged marriage, there was no sign that her family members had lost their determination to either bring Soheila back to marry the old man or to kill her. An Iranian filmmaker, Zohreh Soleimani, made a documentary on her case[8] and actually persuaded Soheila's father and half brother to discuss her on camera. They were unabashedly frank about what they would do to her if they could.

"If the court grants her divorce, he would say, 'What is the court?'" the half brother, Aminullah, said of their father in the interview. "If she runs away, unh," he said, gesturing as if pulling a trigger. "We are not afraid of dying, we are not afraid of killing. For us it is like killing a sparrow. If she is not coming back to us and goes with that donkey of a man, she will be killed." His unapologetic vitriol was all the more extraordinary considering that it was Aminullah's own elopement thirty-three years earlier that had caused Soheila to be sold in *baad* in the first place. Even more ironic, he told Ms. Soleimani in the interview, in an effort to justify the idea of child marriage, was the fact that he had engaged his own daughter to an older man when she was only three days old. More ironic still, that daughter had recently eloped herself, rather than fulfill the bargain with the old man. Despite their failures, Mr. Aminullah and his father both stick to the view that the women in their family are their property and that their rights over them are absolute.

It is a commonplace view in Afghanistan, but rare to hear it enunciated with such frankly murderous intent. Soheila's father, Rahimullah, was if anything even worse than her half brother. "My child belongs with me," her father said. "Me or someone from my tribe, we will find her. Even if she goes to America, we will find her. Wherever she is found, she will be killed. With all the strength that God has given me I will ask God, before they take another step, 'God, kill both of them.' She will be lost to both worlds."

Soheila and her intended, Niaz Mohammad, were finally married in September 2014, formally, but it was a sad ceremony. Niaz Mohammad had contracted hepatitis in prison, and complications from that condition led to diabetes; he is too ill to work. Only a few of his own family members attended the wedding, and during it Soheila's phone rang. It was her brother again, she said, promising to kill her, one way or another, one day or another.[9]

Memories are long in Afghanistan when it comes to matters of honor or perceived honor. Zakia and Ali take a somewhat fatalistic view about the whole situation, one common in their society: this is just their destiny. They are largely indifferent to the role that they and their story have played in Afghan society. They are confused when anyone suggests that they have become symbols for Afghanistan's youth and harbingers of a change that remains elusive and distant. For all their defiance of their society's norms, their ardor was romantic rather than revolutionary. Zakia will probably never be a feminist as anyone in the West would understand that concept. Strength of character, determination, independence of spirit—these are intrinsic character traits rather than political postures. Zakia still believes in obeying her husband, as long as he is sensible. Her husband believes in telling her what to do, so long as she agrees. They both believe in love, but it never occurred to them that this might in some way threaten the established order.

Still, Zakia will not be ruled the way so many other Afghan women are ruled. If she and Ali ever do manage to escape the country, she may well decide to learn to read and write one day, as she has said she wants to do, and Ali says he would join her if she did. Or she might decide to go to work or to school, and that would be a negotiation as it is for families anywhere, depending on how many children they have, how much money they can earn. On the other hand, if they do not manage to leave Afghanistan or decide against doing so, the backbreaking work of life on a subsistence farm may well prove too hard for such luxuries as education and literacy, at least for themselves.

Whether they leave or stay, their children, whether boys or girls, will be educated. They will choose their own mates, they will make their own lives, and ultimately it is they who will be the ones who will realize Zakia's human potential. It is probably not a potential that she could ever really fulfill by staying in Afghanistan. "Whatever happened has happened," as both Zakia and Ali often said, and repeated when they went back to Bamiyan to face whatever fate awaited them and their daughter. "What will be, will be."

After a fresh fall of snow in February 2015, a year after I first met the couple, Ali went out trapping birds with his brothers up in the mountains above his village. He was much more relaxed there than when he was working in the fields and the bottomland by the river; the Tajiks never climbed the mountains on that side of the north-trending gorge, and he even left his pistol at home. Ali is still a big bird lover, and the quails and snow finches he usually hunts are prized for their song as well as their meat; even the little snow finches, not much bigger than sparrows, are tasty, though they are eaten only as famine food, since their song is so pretty. Instead they are kept in handmade cages of twigs and thin branches woven together. Ali has birdsongs recorded on his phone and often holds the phone behind his back and plays them, to prompt the real birds to sing.

Snow finches are best trapped after a fresh snowfall, because charms of them forage for food on their feet but dislike snow. So the trappers scrape the snow from an area twenty or thirty yards in diameter and then lay out fish line that is so fine the birds cannot see it and sprinkle a little grain around. Every few inches there is a loop in the fish line with a slipknot, and when the birds step into it and get tangled up, the knot inevitably cinches closed until soon a slew of the birds are hopping about not aware at first that they have been made prisoners. Ali and his brothers scooped up eighteen snow finches that day and trudged home extremely pleased with themselves. "We're such good friends, my brothers and I," said Ali, "that people don't even think we're brothers." Zakia stood near the guard dog in the unfinished gateway of their home and rewarded their return with her remarkable smile. Soon the mud house of Mohammad Anwar was filled with the chatter of the young men amid the cheery-sounding songs of their captives. Even indoors everyone's breath exhaled frosty clouds into the thin mountain air. More than a month of winter still lay ahead.

EPILOGUE

Spring of the Persian year 1394 was kind to Bamiyan, thanks to a blessing of late-winter snows and early rains after a season of drought and then perfectly clear blue skies, warm with cool mountain breezes, silver birches in full leaf up and down the lanes, patchwork fields painted in the many shades of verdancy.[1] There was even a dusting of downy green on the barren golden hillsides, good forage for sheep. It was the kind of spring weather that makes lovers fall in love again or reminds them of when they first did. In Surkh Dar the nights no longer needed heating, so Zakia slept with Ali rather than in the warm room with the other women and children. During their "pillow time," as Ali referred to those minutes before sleep, they reminisced about earlier days, when their love hadn't yet learned how to walk and talk. What happened to them then was a mystery, and nothing is quite so thrilling to young love as jointly unraveling the clues to their creation story.

"What was it for you?" he asked on one of those nights.

"You were so friendly, and I loved how you behaved to me," she said.

He didn't know what to say for his part, but a couple of nights later he remembered the donkey. "For me it was that time on the donkey," he said.

"The donkey?" She hit him playfully. "Donkey?" But she remembered it, too.

He was still unsatisfied with *her* answer, though; it seemed too vague. A few nights later, he asked her if it was the birds, that time she was watching him playing with his quails when he should have been working in the fields.

"No, it wasn't the birds," she said. "It was just your good behavior to me. You were kind, and you had good character. You didn't take hash or sniff glue or smoke cigarettes like a lot of the other boys."

"I smoke cigarettes now."

"You didn't then, and you should stop." She was always trying to get him to stop.

The next night he brought it up again; it was on his mind. "So it wasn't the birds?"

"I never liked the birds," she said. "Why do you keep them in cages? They have wings—they should fly. Why don't you let them go?"

He was a bit shocked by this. "Because I love them," he said.

AFTERWORD

One day early in the spring of 2016, Ali called us, frantic. He could no longer control his wife, he said. She wouldn't listen to him, just went and did what she wanted to do. Somehow Zakia had found a cell phone of her own, and she was making calls on it without his permission. She was even using the "drop-calling" technique of their earlier courtship. The couple had had arguments before, but they were minor by comparison to these new ones. At one earlier point, she had even walked out on him when he flatly refused to buy a gas canister on which to cook meals. Ali saw nothing wrong with doing it the way his family always had, cooking on a pile of twigs and branches. Zakia felt that was too smoky and too primitive, and besides, firewood was really no cheaper than gas. She stormed out of their house, and of course there was no place she could really go, since returning to her own family was out of the question, so at length she went to the home of Ali's uncle, in the next village. Ali came over later the same day and agreed to buy her the canister, and she came back. However minor that spat might have been, it did teach Zakia a distressing lesson: Cut off from her own family because of their determination to kill her, she really had nowhere to go, no one to turn to if things went wrong between her and Ali.

The cooking-gas argument was trivial compared to this newest round of disputes. These were so much worse than those earlier marital spats, Ali told Jawad in one of his calls that spring. This could be the end of everything. Zakia's demands were unreasonable and irreconcilable. She was being crazy and even, he said, ungrateful.

I had always felt uncomfortable with Ali's easy adoption of his dominant role in a patriarchal society, and uncomfortable, too, with his view, often expressed, that his wife's obedience to him was her best character trait. It was a position that completely overlooked her rejection of such obedience when the man in control of her life had been her father, who wanted to stop her from marrying Ali in the first place. How could Ali expect complete obedience to himself when he had insisted that Zakia reject obedience to her father so that the couple could be together? Therefore when Ali started ranting about her disobedience and the unreasonableness of her demands, I was disposed to side with Zakia—that is, until Ali finally got around to sharing what had set off their fight in the first place.

Zakia wanted to return to her family for a private visit. Not only that, she wanted to invoke her right as a young wife of nearly two years to make a long visit back to her own family—a common practice among many Afghan families. She was talking about a month, or maybe even three months, he said. Ali was both angry and distraught. On the phone she'd gotten, she had been talking to her sisters and then later even her brothers. They had assured her that all was forgiven and she could come back without fear of danger or harm from her family, despite all that had been said, despite the public humiliation that their now-famous elopement had brought on the family. All was forgiven. As Ali well knew, and so did we, this was a timeworn strategy by families who fail in their initial attempts to carry out an honor killing of a woman they feel has betrayed them by her behavior, and marrying against the wishes of her father was just such behavior. "They can see that being openly hostile with us didn't work, so now they're planning to change their approach so they can get close enough to achieve their goals," he said. "But it doesn't matter what I think—it's what my wife thinks. Before today she was standing by my side and taking my side, but now I don't think I can persuade her any longer. She thinks her family really has forgiven her. I have no way of stopping her, except by violence, and I can't use violence against a woman and against my wife." Manizha Naderi, the executive director of Women for Afghan Women, put it succinctly: "She is just trying to commit suicide."

So far Ali had managed to stop Zakia from leaving the home and actually meeting her family members. In the conservative climate of their village of Surkh Dar, where they were still living, it's a difficult thing for a woman to leave the house alone, without her husband or a close male relative along. In Zakia's case everyone was aware of the threat to her and the fact that she and Ali had been living under what amounted to house arrest, which would make it even harder for her to go out alone. But she had done it before and might well do it again, Ali worried. "In the past she would ask my permission even to make a telephone call. Now her mind is completely changed—I think they must have used some magic amulets or charms of some sort to change her mind, but it's completely changed, and she won't even ask my permission."

Unbeknownst to Ali, Zakia had already, without her husband's permission, called my colleague Jawad Sukhanyar—again using the drop calling she'd learned during Ali's courtship of her. This was through 2015 and into 2016, as she grew increasingly lonely and began to miss her own family more and more. She would find someone's untended phone, drop-call Jawad with it, and he would call back—always very nervous about it, so much so that he often made sure to put the call on speakerphone with me or another witness around, so no one could suspect him of any funny business. It wasn't that at all; she had just come to trust Jawad, like an older brother, and he was someone safe to confide in, to discuss her loneliness and the growing difficulty of living with Ali's large family, who were no longer always so thrilled with her presence as they once had been. Nineteen people in four small rooms made of mud, tensions were inevitable. She was the only one who hadn't lived with them all since birth and so, ultimately, was the outsider.

Now, Ali said, Zakia was likely to make a terrible mistake and go back to her family, and he was worried she would be killed. "I will try my best not to allow her to do this, but we are humans," he said, dusting off another in his endless stock of aphorisms, "so sometimes we drink raw milk even though we should know better."

This would turn out to be a crisis that finally made a solution to the couple's dilemma possible. In recent months Ali had really turned against the idea of trying to flee Afghanistan. He had grown complacent and felt safe in his family home; most of Zakia's relatives had relocated to Kabul, so it was much harder for them to get at Zakia. With the reestablishment of contact between Zakia and her family, Ali tentatively began to reconsider the idea of fleeing, and even to agree to take steps to do something about it. Zakia, on the other hand, really did want to leave the country, even as she pined for her family while still in it. She was a young mother, and her child's welfare was more important to her than anything else.

In the meantime, with Ali's support, we persuaded Zakia that she should allow WAW to host a meeting with her family at their Family Guidance Center in Kabul. The group had a lot of experience in such cases, and their counselors would bring her parents and her together in the safe, neutral territory of their center. If it went well and they felt that the family was serious about reconciliation, they would counsel Zakia that it was okay to return to them—and then, as a safeguard, monitor what happened next. What often happened in such cases, though, was that the family's anger would boil over during the meeting and the girl would then see that returning would be futile or even deadly.

Zakia did not even get that far. When Benafsha Amiri of WAW called Zakia's brother Gula Khan to try to set up the meeting, he rejected the idea furiously, cursing her and WAW and denouncing his sister. "She is the one who has done wrong to us, not the other way around. She dishonored us by running away with a stranger. *She* should come to *us*." Benafsha concluded that there was little hope of reconciliation and related to Zakia what had happened. "She eventually agreed to stand back, at least for now, about meeting them," Benafsha said.

Manizha Naderi at WAW had the idea of inviting the couple as guest speakers to the group's annual fund-raising gala in New York City in May of 2016. With that formal invitation, they could apply for normal, nonimmigrant visit visas to the States and, once there, just declare for asylum. Of course, the visa authorities at the American embassy might well turn down their visa applications, but there was no harm in trying. Ali had at first rejected the idea, but now that Zakia's family was back on the scene, he agreed.

They came down to Kabul that April and met with Jawad and me the evening before their visa interview. We advised them that the important thing was never to lie to a consular officer during their interview, even if it was something embarrassing or awkward. For instance, the officer would surely ask if either of them had been arrested—and of course the answer was yes, Ali had been arrested on the charge of kidnapping, however bogus it might have been, since the supposed victim was his willing wife. The next day they put on their nicest clothes and walked over to the American embassy. They took our advice to heart, and when the consular officer interviewing them asked if they intended to stay in America and not return after the WAW gala, Zakia said yes, they did want to stay. Ali objected and said no, he would hope to return to Afghanistan, but his wife might not want to. I imagine the visa officer had a good chuckle over their naïve honesty, yet he also had no choice but to reject their application for a visa.

They left disheartened, particularly Ali. Having been against leaving in the first place, at least in recent months, and having come around only grudgingly to the idea of leaving, once he was denied the right to leave, it seemed to him a cruel blow. They headed back to their mountain hideout.

Then something completely unexpected happened. A source I'm unable to name contacted me and said there was good reason to believe that the American government, although obliged to reject the couple's application for a nonimmigrant visit visa, might be likely now to take a completely different position were they to apply to enter the United States under what is known as humanitarian parole. Furthermore, they might well get that humanitarian parole, even though it was understood that they would then apply for asylum in an effort to stay in America permanently.

This was an entirely mysterious and surprising development, which would before very long have an equally mysterious and surprising outcome. Humanitarian parole is a legal means for the government to allow someone into the country who would otherwise not qualify for a visa, and it's meant for people whose lives are clearly in danger. Usually the parole is granted to someone in urgent need of medical care of a sophisticated nature that can be found only in the United States; it had never been used before to protect a potential Afghan honor-killing victim. When I raised humanitarian parole with American officials more than a year earlier, they literally laughed in my face at what they saw as the absurdity of the notion.

I was understandably skeptical, but my source was insistent. Not only might they get humanitarian parole, they might well get it in time for the WAW gala in New York City, then just over a month away, on May 25. Just find them a good immigration lawyer, because the legal procedures involved were complex, he said, insisting that humanitarian parole by May 25 was actually possible. The last case in which WAW had secured humanitarian parole for a client was that of Bibi Aisha, the child bride whose Taliban husband had cut off her nose to punish her for trying to run away, but in that case it took seven months to process her application. Manizha Naderi shared my skepticism, but both of us began putting lines out to find a good immigration lawyer willing to handle the case pro bono. Within a day we had three or four who were willing to take it, even though all of them were doubtful of the outcome. We settled on Poonam Gupta, head of the immigration-law department at White & Case, a huge international law firm that was also a contributor to WAW; one of their lawyers was even on the WAW board. Not only was Ms. Gupta willing to handle it pro bono, but her firm was willing to pick up the costs and filing fees, which were considerable.

I cannot at this point report much about the procedures that ensued, due to promises of confidentiality. Suffice it to say that they were complex and involved and extremely labor-intensive, not for just the lawyers but also for Jawad and me in Kabul. We spent a lot of time chasing down and translating documents like a formal statement from the attorney general that the kidnapping charge had been completely dismissed or a copy of their much-disputed *neka,* or marriage document. WAW pulled out all the stops to expedite a passport for the couple's baby daughter, Ruqia, then a year old, getting it issued in only a couple of weeks, whereupon we discovered that the passport authorities had decided to transliterate Ruqia's name as Roqia. So all of Ruqia's vast reams of paperwork (including formal declarations that she had never worked as a prostitute, nor fought for the Taliban, nor committed human trafficking) would have to be redone.

That was a further delay, and it was already the middle of May. We were crestfallen when the United States Citizenship and Immigration Service notified the couple on May 14 that their applications had been accepted but they would not be able to check on their status for at least another seven to ten days—the first of a series of further steps. That meant the couple would miss the WAW gala, which someone behind the scenes in the United States government did seem to care about, but it wouldn't be the end of the world if their humanitarian parole came in a week or two later. Suddenly, though, there was a concern much more urgent than the gala.

Zakia had gone to meet her family in person. We heard the details afterward, from both Zakia and from Ali separately. After a series of telephone calls with her family, Zakia said her mother and sister were going to come alone to meet her out in the open in the fields adjoining her sister's house in the Bamiyan Valley. At the insistence of Ali and his father, Anwar, the Bamiyan police would watch from the edge of the field, as would other family members. Only women would be involved in the meeting. Zakia said Ali could come as well, but Ali demurred and watched with the other men from the margins.

Not only did the meeting take place, but it turned out to be neither fully in public nor only involving women. Overcome with emotion, Zakia and her mother embraced and cried, and Zakia then went with her mother into her sister's home. There Gula Khan, the harshest and most hard-line of her brothers, was waiting, with his wife, his mother-in-law, and another brother and his wife. Zakia's sisters-in-law were the angriest people present, brazenly urging their husbands to attack Zakia right there in order to punish her for what she had done.

Instead Gula Khan embraced her and said, "See, if we wanted to harm you, we could do so now. I even reject what my wife has asked me to do."

Zakia was in tears when she called Jawad a couple of days later to tell him what had happened. "I am in a mountain of pain," she said. She wanted to leave Afghanistan, but at the same time she wanted to reconcile with her family. Gula Khan, she said, "he's completely changed. I used to be so afraid of him. I was never afraid of anyone else the way I was of him. When I saw him, he hugged me, and I burst into tears, and he said, 'See, we are not going to harm you. Whatever happened was not your fault. We have all suffered a lot.' I swear to God, I did not believe them before, but after this meeting I'm going to believe them."

We talked on the phone with Zakia that day for more than three hours, about her family and their sincerity or lack of it, but also at length about Ali and her. From day to day, he was changing his mind on whether they would actually leave Afghanistan, and it was driving her crazy. "He's not like me, if I decide to do something or I say something, I mean it, I will always stick to it. With him you never know," she said. "I feel he doesn't respect me. I love him, but he has to respect me. I know how much risk I took to run to him, more risk than he took, but he really doesn't seem to care about all of that. He doesn't understand."

She wanted our help. The night after the meeting with her family, Ali had seized her telephone and destroyed the SIM card. She wanted us to lean on Ali to give her back a phone. She also asked if the next time a donor sent any money for them, could that money be sent to her instead of Ali? Previously Ali had always been the one to go to Western Union to receive cash transfers like that—a woman doing so would arouse too much attention, not to mention that going into the town would expose Zakia to risk—but that also meant he controlled how all the money was spent. She wanted her own money, she said, because it meant independence. And it meant she could spend it on what she wanted, something her husband would never agree to.

Which was? Gula Khan was sick, she said. He was having terrible difficulties sleeping at night and needed money to go to the mullah. Some rural mullahs operate almost like witch doctors, especially when the ailments they "treat" are psychological ones. But they also have to be paid. Here was the brother who had publicly vowed to kill her, the one who had beaten her on many occasions in his role as family enforcer of female virtue. Now, after one meeting, she wanted to start sending money his way; it was heartbreaking.

Ali's take on that meeting, of course, was just the opposite of his wife's. Gula Khan and the rest of her family knew they couldn't kill her right there with the police and everyone watching, so they were just playing a longer game: get her alone, perhaps wait until everyone has forgotten, and then finish her off. Ali was convinced of it and adamant about not giving his wife a phone.

The lack of a phone was not going to stop Zakia for long. The gala was just a week away, and the humanitarian parole seemed like their last, best hope, however faint. We sent word through the lawyer in New York and directly to all the State Department officials we knew who might be following the couple's case, telling them that she was close to being killed. That was on Thursday. The next two days were the weekend, when the consular section was closed. Nonetheless, word came on Friday that the couple would have an interview for their humanitarian parole on Sunday and might even get the parole entered in their passports the same day.

We called Ali immediately that Friday, but he had gone up into the mountains to trap birds and was out of cell-phone range. We warned Zakia and Anwar, her father-in-law, they would have to be prepared to leave for the daylong trip to Kabul by Saturday; could someone head up into the mountains to find Ali and send him down? They found him finally the next day, about 11:00 A.M. on

Saturday. They left Bamiyan within the hour, without even a bag between them, the couple and Ruqia, with Anwar as well.

Clearly someone in a position of power and authority in the American government was working behind the scenes to make all this happen so fast; speed is not normally a feature of the American government's immigration bureaucracy. Later I found out who, though I'm constrained not to reveal that. It was someone who read the first edition of this book and, he told his colleagues, was moved by the couple's story and wanted to see it resolved. It was for me an unexpected outcome. I had made sure to send copies of *The Lovers* to every senior official I could think of, but given the official disinterest and even hostility to Zakia and Ali's plight previously, I had never expected much to come of that effort. Neither immigrants nor Afghans were exactly flavors of the month in America during the toxic 2016 election year.

The couple had their humanitarian parole documents by Sunday afternoon, and Jawad took them out shopping for clothes on Monday so that they'd have something to wear in the very different climate and culture to which they were headed. We did something that I confess to being ethically troubled by, even though I'm convinced it was the right thing to do. The right thing, but carried out using methods that were underhanded. Zakia said she wanted to see her family, in private, before she left. Ali felt, and we agreed, that once she told them she was leaving, all pretense of restraint on their part would be dropped and they wouldn't let her out of their sight alive. WAW's counselors, too, thought it was best to keep Zakia in the dark until the last moment. So we lied to Zakia about the travel plans, saying we weren't sure when exactly they would leave, that it might be a few days before we could get them a flight. Anwar and Ali colluded with us in the deception. And then, at six-thirty the very next morning, Jawad showed up unannounced at the safe house where they were staying and said, "It's today. Now, let's go." She would have to call her family from America.

They went directly to the airport in Kabul, and just before midnight on Tuesday, May 24, 2016, they landed at JFK. Ruqia cried during the entire twenty-hour-long, two-flight journey, but they all three stepped off the plane in New York looking fresh and rested, as perhaps only those so young can do. Zakia looked positively glamorous; somehow she managed to make her black head scarf seem fashionable. Ali looked amazingly handsome, grinning broadly for every camera pointed his way.

Jawad accompanied them on the trip; I had gone ahead so I could be on the outside at JFK in case anything went wrong, but nothing did. The Homeland Security officers said they had been expecting them and that everything was just fine. The officer at the counter smiled at them broadly and said, "Welcome to America. Good luck and God bless." The next evening they appeared as guests of honor at WAW's annual gala, in the imposing Guastavino's restaurant under the Queensboro Bridge. They were too tongue-tied to say anything but nonetheless received a standing ovation that seemed to go on for ten minutes. The baby on her arm, Zakia stood close to Ali, discreetly holding his hand.

In some ways their travails were just beginning. We tend to think that once a refugee reaches a safe haven, everything else is easy. From Zakia and Ali's point of view, though, the hard part was just beginning. New York City dramatically hammered home just how hard it would be. Without Jawad they were completely unable to navigate the city; even walking out of their hotel and finding a halal place to eat was daunting. Their lawyer's office was on the fortieth floor of a midtown skyscraper; they had never seen a building taller than five stories. Ali was no stranger to hard work, but under the conditions of their humanitarian parole they would not be allowed to work until their application for asylum was accepted. That process could take a year, however; certainly many months. During that time not only were they forbidden to work, but they also were not entitled to any sort of government benefit, neither food stamps nor Medicaid, nor any of the usual refugee services paid for by the government. On top of everything else, Zakia was newly pregnant, and while we didn't tell the couple this, the cost for an uninsured hospital delivery could easily reach a hundred thousand dollars. Unlike her pregnancy with Ruqia, this one was difficult, and she was often severely nauseous.

They also had no money. What they did have, though, was friends, plenty of them—friends they did not even know they had. Through contacts I was put in touch with a terrific refugee agency based in New Haven, Connecticut, where there was a small community of Afghan refugees—a far less intimidating situation than New York. The group, Integrated Refugee & Immigrant Services (IRIS), often handled resettlement of refugees under contracts with the American government, and when I contacted the group's head, Chris George, he was very sympathetic but explained that his group had no funding for people like Zakia and Ali. Technically they were not refugees yet, pending action on their asylum request, so they had no entitlements. I told Chris I was pretty sure we could find the money to take care of them. Over the years of covering them and working on this book about them, I had compiled a list of the many people who'd gotten in touch to ask what they could do to help. There were a couple of hundred people on the list, and I e-mailed them all, explaining the situation that Zakia and Ali were in and suggesting that IRIS would be a great solution if the group could find a funding source for them. My e-mail went out early Saturday morning on the 2016 Memorial Day weekend, and by noon IRIS had pledges of funding sufficient to finance the couple for a year. It even arranged free medical care for them at the Yale Medical Group.

Jawad and I drove the three of them up to Connecticut that same day, and an IRIS welcoming party was waiting to make them feel at ease. One was an Afghan-American Yale professor; another a refugee who had arrived the year before, and his wife; as well as another Afghan woman and a couple of other refugees who work for IRIS. Zakia and Ali moved into temporary housing, an apartment hotel, where plates of food and baskets of fruit awaited them. For Zakia it was the first time she had another woman to talk to other than her sisters-in-law, and she huddled with the other women for hours. Afterward she served lunch for Jawad, Ali, and me, beaming with pride at being able to do something for us for a change. That evening an Afghan widow named Zalika, who had come to the United States as a refugee ten years earlier, made them an Afghan dinner and brought it over to them. Zalika would become an important friend for them, and especially for Zakia. Fleeing an abusive husband, she had come with her young daughter and won asylum. In September 2016 that daughter would begin college in the United States. Zalika told them it would be hard, but if they were patient, it would all work out.

For both of them, patience would be a new skill, one they found hard to master. IRIS found them an apartment, a bright and pleasant one-bedroom, which they moved into four days later, and they had money for food and necessities, as well as a food ration package. There were Afghan neighbors nearby who could help them get around. Despite all that, in the first week Ali announced that he wanted to return to Afghanistan. Zakia disagreed with him and said she would never leave. Finally they were safe—did he not see that? "I don't ever want go back, and when I decide to do something, I don't change," Zakia said. We all certainly had seen evidence of that. "My husband is not like that. Whether he wants to stay, it depends if you ask him on Monday, Tuesday, or Wednesday." A month later, though, Ali also had decided he liked being in America and no longer talked of returning. He was taking English classes and had mastered the few words necessary to catch a bus to the downtown of the Connecticut city where they were staying. "Downtown," he said in English, speaking on the phone to Jawad. Then he added, "My name is Mohammad Ali." His few new words had buoyed his confidence. "This isn't so bad. Now I feel we can do it." In their new apartment, Zakia marveled at an electric oven with gas burners, something she had never seen before, and the modern refrigerator, the built-in air-conditioning. It seemed comical to her, she said, that they had not long ago been quarreling over whether to cook on twigs or gas canisters.

THE JIHAD AGAINST WOMEN

Sherzai Amin was a pretty typical, midlevel mujahideen commander. He picked his rotten teeth with a hunting knife. He was big and slightly fat but could walk all day up a mountain on barely visible goat tracks, without breathing audibly or sweating visibly. The fifty or so fighters under his command adored him; half or more were related by either marriage or blood. Back home he had three wives and he wasn't sure how many children. Up here in the mountains of Kunar Province, he had an eighteen-year-old Russian prisoner of war named Sergey, whom he raped nightly in his camp tent, making crude jokes about it in the morning. Reports that another mujahideen unit had set up a firing squad for a group of Communist prisoners but replaced all the rifles with rocket-propelled grenade launchers brought tears to his eyes, he laughed so hard.

"Picture that," he said.

It was the height of the jihad against the Soviets and their Afghan Communist clients, in the late 1980s, and I had been a week with Sherzai's group, operating in the mountains east of the provincial capital of Asadabad. One evening he announced that the next day Sergey would have to guide us through what the muj thought was a minefield along our route. Sergey's unit had planted the mines, so he should know where they were, they said. The boy broke down and cried, pleading that he hadn't a clue where any mines were buried.

"Then you'll have to find them the hard way," Sherzai said, to guffaws from his men.

We sat up late that night, talking for hours, because Sherzai and I both had something the other one wanted. I wanted him not to kill the Russian boy. Sherzai wanted me to give him my Swiss Army knife. It had a built-in toothpick that he was enchanted with.

As we both danced around our real issues, we whiled away the hours talking about Communism and what it meant to the muj, what they were fighting for, what motivated them to give up everything and take to these punishing mountains.

"Divorce," Sherzai said.

"Divorce?"

"The Communists have given *women* the right to divorce *men*."

"Most countries allow women to divorce."

"No, only Communist countries. And jobs, they want to send women out to work. And schools, send girls to school, sitting next to boys. They want to turn our women and girls into prostitutes. Then, when they're prostitutes, they send them to the police or their stupid army."

One of his men piped up. The Communists had opened a home for war widows and had distributed soap to all the women there, he said.

"Soap?" General outrage greeted this news.

What was wrong with soap for widows? "Was it some sort of inferior Communist soap?"

They looked at me pityingly, just another ignorant foreigner— albeit one from a country that provided their weaponry and finances, so they couldn't be too hostile.

"Orgies," one of them said. "They're giving them soap to start orgies. Soap, then group showers, then orgies." The inevitability of that progression seemed to make sense to them.

Sherzai came back to the subject of divorce. "Are women in your country really allowed to divorce without their husbands' permission?"

"Yes, if they have a good reason, and we're not Communists. Some places have no-fault divorce, where they don't even need a reason to divorce their husbands. Also, many women have jobs. All girls have to go to school, usually with boys."

He had trouble processing all that. "Americans sound like Communists."

"No, Communism is about politics and economics, not about women's rights."

"The first thing our Communists did was take our women away. They want me to get rid of two of my wives."

"Polygamy is illegal in America, too, and in most countries, but that doesn't make them all Communists."

This discussion was unfortunately not endearing me to my hosts, who began to regard me with suspicion and concern. Either I was crazy or America was, they weren't sure which. This was not helping Sergey's cause any either. But Sherzai still wanted my Swiss Army knife. Despairing of winning him over, I decided to make a straight-up deal.

"I'll give you my knife if you don't kill the boy," I said.

"Okay, I won't kill the boy," he said, and I handed the knife over. He kept marveling at the retractable toothpick.

In those Cold War years, the mujahideen were admired throughout the free world for facing up to the might of the Soviet Union and fighting them and their Afghan proxies to a standstill and, eventually, to defeat. Their jihad was seen as an anti-Communist crusade, and indeed it was, but only nominally. A jihad against women and against rights for women is what it really was. Sherzai Amin was no outlier, and his views on women and the jihad were commonplace.

What distressed the muj about Communism was not redistribution of wealth, or the dictatorship of the proletariat, or state control of the means of production—many of those principles were already somewhat present in Afghanistan or were just beside the point in a country with a preindustrial economy. The major industries and mines, such as they were, had always been nationalized. Since the days of King Mohammad Zahir Shah, who ruled from

1933 to 1973, when he was deposed, the Afghan state had been strongly centralized,[1] however weak. The Afghan extended family practices a form of communal sharing of wealth and resources, property and responsibilities, that would rival that of any kibbutz. It wasn't even Communism's godlessness that infuriated the mujahideen, because the Afghan version of a Communist Party never challenged Islam nor advocated atheism.

What really infuriated the mujahideen about Communism and sent them on the warpath was its doctrinal and practical espousal of equal rights for women. Under Afghanistan's Communist rulers from 1978 to 1992, modern attitudes toward women were introduced to the country for the first time since the abortive attempt to do so during the reign of Amanullah Khan in the 1920s.[2] Since they were Communists and their Soviet patrons wanted to make a point, gender reform was done on a massive scale, nationwide. Schools for women were opened throughout the country; jobs were set aside for women, and they were encouraged to work. Huge numbers of women were drafted into the military and police, far more than Western encouragement and financing has managed in this past decade. The national airline, Ariana, had female flight attendants under the Communists.[3] Social laws were modified to give women rights to inherit property, to keep their children, to divorce their husbands—all things unknown in traditional Afghan culture and still not the practice today. At its heart the jihad was not a response to Communism, it was holy war against feminism. In the narrow worldview of Afghanistan's jihadis, Communism and feminism were synonyms. But they quickly learned that fighting feminism was not going to attract massive Western aid, even from womanizers like Congressman Charlie Wilson,[4] while fighting Communism qua Communism would.

The Communists brought in social and legal protections for women that were as far-reaching as those later instituted with American backing by the landmark 2009 law on the Elimination of Violence Against Women. As the EVAW law later did, the Communists outlawed abusive customary practices such as child marriage and the compulsory marriage of widows to their brothers-in-law, and they criminalized behavior like wife-beating and rape. In other words, EVAW law for the first time restored to Afghan women many of the protections that already had been granted to them by the Communists by the early 1980s and which provoked the jihad that ultimately, with massive Western aid, destroyed the Communists—and stalled any real progress on women's rights in Afghanistan for two or three decades to come.

This is a piece of history commonly overlooked in the dialogue about women's rights in Afghanistan. There tends to be an assumption now that the first time Afghan women had any rights at all was in the post-Taliban era, but in fact women were in many ways much better off during the Communist time than they are now.

Many older Afghans still speak about that period as the country's golden age. While the Communists' writ did not extend much beyond urban areas—especially once the jihad got under way—women in the cities and even in many towns were soon freer than they have ever been in Afghanistan, before or since. Dr. Ahmad Naser Sarmast, the irrepressible head of one of Afghanistan's most admired institutions, the Afghan National Institute of Music,[5] was a college student in those days, and he remembers young men and women in Kabul University greeting each other by kissing on the cheeks—something so forbidden now that even foreigners do not do it in public or around their Afghan co-workers; few Afghan women, even among professionals and officials, will shake men's hands today. By some estimates[6] over half of the urban workforce during the Communist era was female; it is a fraction of that today—even in government agencies where there are contractual set-asides and compulsory quotas from foreign donors. During Dr. Sarmast's college days, young people of both sexes visited one another's homes for lunches and dinners—equally unheard of today. Kandahar, a city so conservative now that few women are ever seen in public, and then only in burqas, was liberal and cosmopolitan even compared to Kabul. "When the Communists took over, their first activity, their first decree was to declare the freedom of women, equal opportunity for women, the compulsory education of girls until grade nine, the end of the sale of young girls for big bride prices, the end of buying and selling girls like cattle," Dr. Sarmast said. The tragedy was, as at so many other times in history, Afghanistan became a victim of the political currents and ambitions of other nations. "They were very progressive, taking society toward equality and justice especially in women's rights, but the mujahideen and all the opponents identified those progressive measures as un-Islamic. It was a war between the Soviet Union and the West, and the people of Afghanistan paid the price. And today the West is paying a much bigger price for promoting the same values and the same progressive policies toward women's rights and equality," Dr. Sarmast said.[7]

That old jihadi commander who got my Swiss Army knife, Sherzai Amin, would agree with this analysis. If Sherzai hasn't joined the Taliban by now, as most of his mujahideen brethren up in Kunar Province have, he would nonetheless abhor what the West has tried to do for Afghan women since 2001. The morning after our quasi-philosophic exchange on Communism and feminism, having raped Sergey one last time, Sherzai sent the boy out on point, a couple hundred yards ahead of the mujahideen column as it moved toward the suspected minefield. When I realized what was happening, I protested that Sherzai had given me his word; I would soon learn how little that was worth in Afghanistan.

"I said *I* wouldn't kill him." He laughed. "If he trips a Russian mine, it'll be the Communists who killed him. Anyway, he's probably lying and knows where they put the mines."

Shortly later there was a deafening explosion.

"Oh, well," Sherzai Amin said. "I guess that boy was telling the truth." He and the other muj shared a hearty laugh.[8]

Afghan men can be as hard and brutal as the rocky and treeless landscape they inhabit. "Beat your wife every day," goes a joke that is popular among them. "If *you* don't know what she did, *she* will." It is a joke that rings true. Over half of Afghan women report that they have been beaten by their husbands at some point, while 39 percent of those surveyed have been beaten at least once in the previous twelve months. Include sexual and psychological abuse and nearly nine out of ten of the country's women describe themselves as victims of their men.[9] Many Afghan men will argue that wife-beating is justified if a man's woman misbehaves. Many Afghan men do not see rapists as criminals but are much more inclined to blame and punish their victims; unsurprisingly, 11 percent of Afghan adult women say they have been victims of rape,[10] which is fifty times the rate in the West.[11] Many Afghan men approve of honor killing, or at least excuse it, hence the low level of judicial punishment in such cases.

The EVAW law was meant to change all that. Before the law's enactment in 2009, most gender-based crimes were not even considered to be crimes in Afghanistan. Since the law's enactment, there have been some notable improvements but also many dramatic failures. Still, fewer than 10 percent[12] of those accused of committing crimes against women are ever punished, and much larger numbers commit crimes that go unreported.[13]

Nothing illustrates the imperfection of the EVAW law's implementation more dramatically than the EVAW unit of the attorney general's office in Kabul and the women who work within it. When I visited in September 2014, the unit had been relocated to a recently converted storage room in an office building off Darulaman Road. Its thirteen lawyers shared the single room, big enough for perhaps four desks, even six if they were packed close together. The EVAW unit had been moved there two months earlier and still had no furniture other than one desk for the head of the unit, a small table to the side, and some armchairs and sofas along the walls for everyone else. "You could call this office itself an example of violence against women," said one of the prosecutors, Shazia Abbasi, a twenty-five-year veteran of the Afghan criminal-justice system. Small children ran around while their mothers, the clients, squatted on their haunches along one wall, some completely shrouded in burqas. A man wept openly in front of his burqa-ed wife, complaining of her gang rape by politically well-connected Afghan Local Police—militiamen who are trained by the American Special Forces—in Badakhshan. A teenage girl, a prosecutor's daughter whose school got out early that day, was doing her home-work on the available corner of the small table. The other lawyers had piles of legal papers in their laps.

Sitting on one of the tattered sofas like the other five prosecu-tors in the office on this particular day, Ms. Abbasi was deeply demoralized about the prospects for the EVAW law to really work in Afghanistan, even after a new president, Ashraf Ghani, had been installed and had sent positive signals about his commitment to women's issues.[14] As the lawyers remember, President Hamid Kar-zai had done the same in his first years; after all, he enacted the law that brought their unit into being. "This EVAW law has had some accomplishments, but they were negative, not positive, even when we succeeded," Ms. Abbasi said. "How can a law like this work in a society that is so strongly patriarchal?

"Out of ten cases," she continued, "we're lucky if two have a positive outcome, one that changes the husband or improves the situation for the woman. In the eight others, the complainants disappear, or they get killed, or they give up. It just doesn't work. How can an Afghan man accept that his wife stands next to a lawyer and speaks about him? That is in the cities. We don't even reach people in poor rural places.

"Half the time we go into court and the judge just says, 'I don't agree with the EVAW law,' and he refuses to apply it," Ms. Abbasi said.

Ms. Abbasi and her five colleagues had varying views on how effective EVAW law had been, but they were all in agreement about one thing: Given the chance, she and the others readily said, every one of them would leave Afghanistan and not come back. Ziba Sadat, in her forties and an EVAW prosecutor the last five of her twenty-three years as a lawyer, was the most adamant of them all. Her own husband, an Afghan TV journalist, expected her to stop working when he told her to do so. When she didn't, he beat her until she brought charges against him under the EVAW law. As a result his entire family disowned her and their children and launched what she described as a campaign of terror against them.

The husband was convicted and served two months in jail. Ms. Sadat has four children, a daughter and three sons, all teenagers. She showed me a recent text message on her phone, one of many from a caller who did not even bother to disguise his number: BITCH, WE WILL FIRST KILL YOU AND THEN WE WILL RAPE YOUR DAUGHTER, YOU DIRTY PROSECUTOR.

"Look here, I am a prosecutor subject to death threats, but when I complain to anyone about it, they don't help me," Ms. Sadat said.

Her misery had company. The head of the EVAW prosecutor's unit, Qudsia Niazi, is regularly beaten by her husband, as she has confided to one prominent women's activist. "She called me, and she was crying on the phone," said the activist, a prominent member of parliament who did not want to be further identified. "She told me, 'I help other women, but I cannot help myself.'"

During an interview in October 2014, I asked Ms. Niazi if any members of her staff were themselves victims of spousal abuse. She laughed ruefully. "I could say even myself," she replied. She did not want to discuss her specific case, she said, but added, "In Afghanistan the majority of those women who work have suffered violence and cannot afford to report it because of their positions. Afghanistan is a male-dominated society, and it's very difficult to change anything to do with that."

According to many women's activists in Kabul, even one of the country's first women's-affairs ministers, Massouda Jalal, a physician who served in that position from 2004 to 2006, was beaten by her husband while she was still in office. A candidate for president of Afghanistan in the country's first democratic election (she placed seventh out of a numerous field), she was the women's minister who claims to have been responsible for first drafting the EVAW law, in 2005, although it was not enacted during her tenure. "It sat in a drawer for four years," she said, "until the Americans pressured President Karzai to enact it." She said the law was drafted in her home with a committee including her husband, a law professor named Faizullah Jalal; Ms. Jalal at first dismissed as unfounded rumors the reports that Mr. Jalal beat her while she was the minister. "He has always been so much supportive and was one of the committee members for writing the law. It's just not true. He really cares about women's rights. Plus, he wasn't even in the country most of the time I was minister," she said.

A few days later, my colleague Jawad Sukhanyar went alone to see Ms. Jalal, and she confided to him that there *had* been something to the rumors after all. "You know that question your colleague asked?" she said. "Well, it's true, I *have* been a victim of violence at home. And not just me. I could tell you another woman cabinet minister who was the victim of abuse from her husband.[15] You cannot work in this society as a woman without suffering abuse." He asked her if her remarks were on the record, and she defiantly said they were. There is, she said, nothing at all unusual about her case, or that of the prosecutor Ziba Sadat, or any number of female members of parliament (MPs) and women's activists who are abused women. Yet her husband was still a good man, who supported women's rights, she said, and they are still married.

One of the saddest cases of the abuse of prominent women[16] concerned Noor Zia Atmar, one of the country's first elected female MPs. The Afghan constitution, at the insistence of the Western powers, reserved 25 percent of the seats in parliament for women, giving that body a higher percentage of female representation than the British parliament or the U.S. Congress, although many of the Afghan MPs are stand-ins for husbands, fathers, or brothers. Routinely beaten by her husband and forced to wear a burqa, Ms. Atmar divorced him and was thrown out of their home. Disowned by both his family and hers, Ms. Atmar was forced to take refuge in a women's shelter in 2013.

"The violence against women is getting worse and worse," said Ms. Jalal, the former women's minister. "Women in Afghanistan are subject to the public mentality that they should be enslaved. Even if they are working outside [the home], they have to give their income back to the male. Even after the opportunities created by these past thirteen years, they are working for the males."

Ms. Jalal blamed this state of affairs on the continued dominance of Afghan society by old warlords and jihadi commanders, and she was forced out of office by the Afghan parliament in 2006 for expressing that view. "We met in secret in my private home to draft the EVAW law because we were afraid of sabotage from extremists and warlords," she said. After the draft law was submitted to the Ministry of Justice, "I was recognized as someone who wanted to release Afghan women from fear and poverty, and by my doing this the extremists saw that I was really serious about freeing women and giving them a new life, so they removed MoWA [the Ministry of Women's Affairs] from the cabinet." The attempted downgrading of MoWA from the cabinet level aroused indignant opposition from the international community, and the hard-liners were forced to back off and allow the ministry to be restored to the cabinet; so instead the hard-liners successfully demanded that Ms. Jalal be ousted as the women's minister.[17]

Despite the EVAW law's shortcomings, its enactment and enforcement have been the international community's greatest achievement on behalf of the women of Afghanistan, with the possible (and qualified) exception of girls' schools. Yet the EVAW law only barely became law in Afghanistan and remains very much at risk today.[18] It was passed by decree by President Hamid Karzai in 2009,[19] after it became clear that it had no hope of being enacted by Afghanistan's parliament, and the Americans put heavy pressure on Mr. Karzai to use his powers to circumvent the parliament.

The EVAW law made rape a criminal offense; in the Afghan penal code, it had been lumped together with family and social issues to be handled by traditional shariah-law remedies. When rape was prosecuted criminally, it was as the crime of adultery. If the rapist had committed adultery, so had the victim, and many rape victims in Afghanistan have gone to jail for their rapists' crimes. Beating one's wife was criminalized by the EVAW law, too; previously the courts had considered such cases only when the woman suffered grievous bodily harm or was killed. Often, even in those cases, prosecutions were not pursued, or if they were, penalties were slight.[20] Under the new EVAW law, harmful or abusive traditional practices such as *baad* and *baadal* were forbidden, which both the Communists and the Taliban had previously done. Under the EVAW law, forcing a woman to marry someone against her will was deemed a crime, as was "denial of relationship," the indignity from which Zakia and Ali had fled.

Probably more important, the EVAW law decriminalized a host of actions that had been crimes and functioned to keep women in line. Accusations of running away from home, though not mentioned in the penal code, were commonly used against any female of any age who left her family without the permission of her husband, father, or brothers. The EVAW law forbade charging women or girls aged sixteen or over as runaways.

Afghanistan's women indirectly have the Taliban to thank for the EVAW law; their excesses led to the international community's determination to see Afghan women protected, and it was not lost on Western policy makers that many of those who replaced the Taliban, especially those old jihadis, were not much better when it came to women's rights. The EVAW law repeatedly acted as a brake on the worst excesses of the Taliban's successors, especially when the international community put its weight behind the law.

The Taliban era had brought the plight of Afghan women vividly to the attention of the American and European publics. They had watched in horror as the Taliban imposed their extreme interpretation of shariah law on Afghan women, banning them from education, closing all girls' schools, prohibiting them from employment, and ordering them to stay in their own homes unless dressed in a full-length burqa and accompanied by a close male relative, a *mahram,* usually meaning a brother, father, son, or husband. After twenty years of civil war, confinement of women to their homes was a harsh requirement, since in many families the menfolk had been killed or disabled during those years and their widows had become the only source of support for their children.[21] Ordering them to stay indoors was tantamount to a death sentence.

The Taliban enforcers from the Ministry for the Promotion of Virtue and Suppression of Vice prowled the streets of Kabul, beating women with sticks if they were not fully covered and properly accompanied outside the home.[22] Sometimes they beat them just for being outside the home at all. They beat men for transgressions as well, such as failing to grow a full, untrimmed beard or wearing Western clothing or listening to music on a radio in the car. But they reserved their greatest enthusiasm for punishing women. Women convicted of serious moral crimes would be taken to the National Stadium and, in front of a capacity crowd that had been rounded up and ordered to attend, stoned to death or shot in the head, always piously covered up by a robin's-egg blue burqa as they sat in the dirt waiting for the end.[23]

One of the most publicized such cases was that of a mother of seven named Zarmeena, who was convicted by a Taliban court of murdering her abusive husband and whose execution was secretly filmed by the Revolutionary Association of the Women of Afghanistan (RAWA).[24] Zarmeena's children were in the stadium, accompanied by their dead father's relatives; moved by the children's piteous pleas for their mother's life, their father's family invoked the shariah-law provision allowing them to forgive her and exempt her from the death penalty. The Taliban refused and carried out the execution anyway. On the RAWA video, her children could be heard sobbing and crying "Mama!" as the Taliban executioner fired into Zarmeena with an AK-47 assault rifle at point-blank range.

So when the American government under George Bush went into Afghanistan to avenge the attacks of September 11, 2001, there was more than just support for the goal of destroying Al-Qaeda's bases and the Taliban regime that tolerated and encouraged the extremists' presence. There was a sense of relief that a regime that had so brutalized its women could finally be brought to an end. Few would have advocated an invasion on those grounds, but this was a welcome outcome. Once both the Taliban and Al-Qaeda were driven into Pakistan, there was little appetite among the European allies and, as time went on in the United States, for a continuing involvement in Afghanistan. Support for Afghan women and redressing the gender terrorism of the Taliban's six-year-long regime was the one thing everyone could agree was a worthy cause.

After the American defeat of the Taliban, the Western nations met in Bonn, Germany in early 2002 to agree on a plan to establish an interim government that would draft a new constitution and hold elections.[25] From the beginning they made it clear to their Afghan partners that there was one redline more important than all others: gender equality.[26] When a new constitution was drafted—by American scholars and legal advisers for the most part—it enshrined both gender equality and shariah law, a difficult cohabitation but one that other Islamic countries have negotiated successfully.

From the beginning it was a hard slog, as Western egalitarian concepts confronted the realities of Afghan patriarchy. In 2003 a constitutional *loya jirga* was convened at the encouragement of the Western powers to approve the new constitution.[27] A *loya jirga* is a grand consultative assembly in which elders are invited from throughout the country to decide on major issues. It's a venerable tradition in Afghanistan, from the days when most people were nomadic or seminomadic tribals who would meet to hash out issues like grazing rights or alliances against invaders. It was in some ways a quintessentially democratic institution, but there was a major problem with it: Traditionally, only men could attend, and mostly only old men. At American insistence, though, the 2003 *loya jirga* did have women delegates, some of them extraordinarily outspoken. They were women who saw a unique, historic opportunity and summoned the courage to seize it. Few showed more grit than a feisty young woman named Malalai Joya, who had been chosen to represent the remote western province of Farah. Malalai stood up at the *loya jirga* and denounced the gathering as an assemblage of war criminals and warlords. "They are the most anti-women people in the society, who wanted to . . . who brought our country to this state, and they intend to do the same again," she said. After a stunned silence, several of the men tried to attack her physically, and only intervention by United Nations guards prevented them from getting to her. The chairman of the *jirga,* Sibghatullah Mujadeddi, derided her as a Communist, which she was not—except from the old jihadi viewpoint that equated feminism with Communism.[28]

Malalai's criticism was not overblown rhetoric. In addition to being warlords, many of those former jihadi leaders and *jirga* delegates were also, as many reports since have documented exhaustively, mass murderers, responsible for the massacres of civilians and prisoners of war during the civil-war and Taliban-war years.[29]

Malalai's courageous stance at the *jirga* instantly made her a worldwide symbol of female defiance, but within a few years she became a symbol of another Afghan phenomenon: the exodus of its best people, especially among women. The old jihadi-era warlords who dominated the *loya jirga* tent continued to call for Malalai to be killed and eventually drove her from Afghanistan permanently. Now Malalai rarely returns to her country.[30]

American and European policy makers were aware of the challenges of bringing gender equality to Afghanistan post-Taliban. They invested generously in female empowerment, gender balance, women's rights, and similar initiatives. They withheld money from ministries that did not employ enough women and would allow construction companies to bid on projects only if they promised to make as much as half of their workforce female. The United States Agency for International Development (USAID) alone spent more than half a billion dollars on women's programs in Afghanistan from 2002 through 2010, according to Nadia Shaherzad, the USAID gender-equality officer, interviewed in 2010. That did not count $4 billion spent by USAID on building girls' or mixed-sex schools.[31] The European Commission, European countries individually, and the World Bank all sank hundreds of millions more into supporting civil society, particularly female civil society. This all spawned a host of Afghan women's groups that had never existed before but now could spring to life and find generous funding overnight.

The EVAW law was the preeminent success story of those efforts, but, paradoxically, for many women the law may have made life worse. Crimes defined as violence against women nearly doubled between 2009 and 2013, in nearly every category, including honor killings, rapes, spousal abuse, and child marriages; there was another dramatic increase in 2014 over 2013.[32] Partly that has been because women are emboldened to report abuses they previously would have suffered in silence. Something else is going on as well, though, says Soraya Sobhrang, head of women's issues for the Afghanistan Independent Human Rights Commission. "It's just a male-dominated society, and now women are finding a voice and getting an awareness that they have some rights, and men feel threatened and react against that," she said. Ms. Sobhrang also blames the increased violence against women on a widespread "culture of impunity," along with insecurity and continued dominance by warlords in many rural areas. Of the six thousand EVAW cases reported in the Persian year 1392 (from March 2013 to March 2014), according to data collected by the Ministry of Women's Affairs,[33] fewer than 10 percent of them resulted in prosecutions; fewer than half of those prosecutions resulted in convictions.[34] The human-rights commission, which also tracks violence against women, logged more than four thousand such cases in the first six months of 2014, a 25-percent increase over the previous year.[35]

No one thinks that anything more than a tiny percentage of cases of gender abuse ever get reported. Even those cases that have come into public view and received heavy press coverage sometimes remain unhappily resolved, such as the case of Gulnaz, the girl whose documentary was suppressed by European Union bureaucrats and who ended up marrying her rapist after the klieg lights went off.[36] The solution for her, and her supporters in women's groups who caved in on her case, was to simply rewrite her tragic history, remove the rape from it, and then take some sort of solace in the knowledge that her rapist-husband has so far not beaten her or their child.

Another major advance embodied in the EVAW law was to decriminalize the social conduct of women, but the law's provisions for that are widely ignored. By the lowest estimates, more than half the female prisoners in the country's main prison for women, Badam Bagh, in Kabul, are held for social or moral crimes, including significant percentages for nothing more than running away or "attempted *zina*"—that is, attempted adultery.[37] Women are routinely arrested for running away, for going out alone, for being in the company of an unrelated male.

"I am fifty-seven years old, and I cannot live alone in this society," Ms. Sobhrang said. No woman can. Hardly any single women live alone; a woman is either married or living in her father's or brother's house; there is no other alternative, even in the relative anonymity of a city as big as Kabul, which now has 5 million or more residents. The only exception is widows who do not have brothers or brothers-in-law to take them in. "Only two percent of Afghan women are independent economically. Women need a place where they can stand together so they can do things for themselves. Now women have new hopes and dreams, and they need to be reassured that there's no barrier between their wishes and their achievements," Ms. Sobhrang said.

Women in Afghanistan cannot legally travel on their own but must be accompanied by a *mahram,* and in practice they neither own nor inherit property. Their husbands can divorce them with the customary Islamic declaration, "I divorce you," repeated three times, but a wife has little more than a theoretical right of divorce from her husband—one that is implemented only with great difficulty. If her husband leaves her, she has no rights to their home and he can demand the right to take the children, leaving her with neither housing nor family. If a woman's husband dies, she and her children can be taken in by the husband's family—if they agree— but in many cases the price of agreement will be that she is obliged to marry a brother of her late husband. Often that means becoming a second or third wife of that brother.

In rural areas and sometimes even in towns, a woman found alone outside her home often will be assumed to be committing or trying to commit *zina* and, if she cannot prove otherwise, jailed for attempted adultery or, if not a virgin, adultery. Unmarried women found alone by the police are commonly subjected to a forensic virginity test, at the office of the provincial medical examiner, though there is no requirement in the law for a single woman to prove her virginity on demand of the authorities. "I've seen cases where it has been done to girls as young as seven and women as old as seventy," said Wazhma Frogh, who is the executive director of the Research Institute for Women, Peace & Security.[38] "Since these cases usually come up in the middle of the night, there is hardly ever a female doctor on duty—there are so few female doctors anyway—so it is a man who does the test, and it is very intrusive."

It is a sad commentary on how bad things are for women that Rubina Hamdard, a lawyer for the well-respected Afghan Women's Network,[39] says the practice of virginity testing is in the best interests of a woman who encounters male authority. "Even if the girl who is found alone is eighteen or forty, there is no question of consent or whatever. Police would just say, 'This is not the West or America' [and force her to undergo the virginity test]. But it's a good idea, because if she's arrested, then police officials could commit adultery with her and claim the sex happened before." In other words, an invasive virginity test is justified because it might protect them from a rape at the station house, which happens so commonly that even many of Afghanistan's policewomen have been victimized sexually by their male colleagues. A recent United Nations survey, suppressed by the United Nations Assistance Mission in Afghanistan (UNAMA), showed that 70 percent of Afghan women police have reported sexual abuse on the job.[40]

Without the EVAW law, many of the other victimized Afghan women whose travails have been so well documented in recent years would have had little or no recourse, even if their cases had come to light. Lal Bibi, for instance, would have remained forcibly married to her rapist—if he even bothered with the formality of marriage, which he had really only used as a dodge to avoid a rape charge.[41] Breshna, a ten-year-old girl from Kunduz Province, raped by a mullah in her mosque, faced an honor killing by her family and even the prospect of being forced to marry the mullah who'd raped her. Women's advocates invoking the EVAW law pushed for a successful prosecution of the mullah and protected the girl (although Breshna remains at risk; her case is discussed in detail beginning on page 287). Soheila from Nuristan[42] would still be languishing in prison, as would Niaz Mohammad, her husband, for the crime of love and the temerity to run away from an arranged marriage with a pedophile—a marriage that would itself be a serious felony in most countries. It is hard to know where Bibi Aisha would have ended up if WAW had not taken her into its shelter in Kabul, but it is doubtful she would ever have had her amputated nose reconstructed. If it were not for EVAW, there probably would not have been shelters, for starters, and the women's shelters could not have taken on the advocacy role they have so often fulfilled.[43] Most of the women and girls they shelter are being rescued from EVAW-law offenses—crimes that had not been crimes before EVAW, such as child marriage—under protections that had not previously existed.

And of course there would have been no story of Zakia and Ali without the EVAW law. Shelters saved Zakia's life twice. The EVAW law was cited as the justification for getting Ali out of jail, whatever President Karzai did behind the scenes. The threat of EVAW-based prosecution, as well as the intense public scrutiny, no doubt protected Zakia and Ali from her family's retribution for as long as that attention has lasted.

Because of the EVAW law's signal importance, the international community made it one of the Tokyo Framework's benchmarks, named for agreements made in Tokyo in 2012 establishing that future development aid for Afghanistan would be contingent on progress in areas the donors felt were important. Under the Tokyo Framework,[44] the EVAW law's implementation was a benchmark to be considered a "hard deliverable" in international parlance, something concrete and quantifiable that had to be achieved if aid were to continue. The United Nations has been charged with issuing an annual report on EVAW-law enforcement and the condition of women in the country as part of that process.[45] The Ministry of Women's Affairs does the same, with an annual report,[46] although it has strived to underplay the problem; the minister from 2006 until 2014, Husn Banu Ghazanfar, was never known as a champion of her gender. Violence against women? It happens in every country, is Ms. Ghazanfar's explanation; there's nothing unusual about Afghanistan.

In fact, in few other countries is violence against women so officially, culturally, legally, and traditionally tolerated. "Afghanistan is the worst place in the world to be a woman," says Ms. Jalal,[47] the abused former women's minister. "The most dangerous place in the world to live for women." Women in Afghanistan are worse off by most measures than in all but a handful of countries in the world, and those are places like Chad, Malawi, and Djibouti, places that have little Western involvement and nothing like the massive financial aid Afghanistan has enjoyed since 2002. Even women in Saudi Arabia, by the United Nations Development Program's gender-inequality index,[48] are far better off than those in Afghanistan. Saudi women are not allowed by law to drive cars; Afghan women are, but few dare to do so.

Unlike other backward countries where women fare poorly, Afghanistan has had a huge international commitment to advancing equality of the sexes, and Afghanistan's occasional success stories have an outsize impact far beyond its borders.[49] Mr. Sarmast, the music-institute director, remembers attending a symposium in Bulgaria after his school's mixed-gender orchestra gave a concert. At the end of his talk about empowering women, a young woman from a Saudi Arabian delegation raised her hand. "She stood and, after giving me a lot of applause, said, 'What you are doing in Afghanistan? We wish even half of that could happen in our country.' Imagine how that makes the authorities in Saudi Arabia feel. How can they tolerate to see change here?"

Women's advocates were aware of the great stakes in trying to rescue Afghanistan's women from abuse,[50] and they pushed very hard in the first years of the Western involvement to see legislation such as the EVAW law enacted. Unfortunately, they were never able to succeed in getting it through the country's parliament,[51] meaning that just as President Karzai had signed EVAW into law by decree, one of his successors could erase it with the stroke of a pen.

In 2013 a female member of parliament named Fawzia Koofi forced the EVAW law onto the floor of the lower house in an unsuccessful effort to get it passed into permanent law.[52] For attempting to do that, Ms. Koofi was excoriated by her fellow women's activists, so much so that she has been shunned by much of that community. They—and their supporters at the United Nations mission and in most Western embassies as well—felt that it was a strategic disaster to bring the law to parliament, because if it came to a vote in anything like its present form, it would probably be defeated.[53] That would allow conservatives to go on and override the president's decree and have the law repealed. Ms. Koofi was accused of grandstanding to raise her personal profile on the back of the controversy; at the time she had also declared her intention to run for president of Afghanistan. "The single biggest blow to women's-rights achievements was the presentation of the EVAW law to parliament," said Ms. Sobhrang, referring to Ms. Koofi's initiative. It just was not the right time to make such a risky move, she and many other women's activists said.

"When *is* a good time?" Ms. Koofi retorted. "When will the Afghan parliament become full of intellectuals? This parliament [2010 to 2015] is weaker than the last one. We have to build momentum. Karzai could have supported this. This next president we hope will."

This is what they are up against in parliament: men like Qazi Nazir Ahmad Hanafi, an MP from Herat, a former jihadi commander who lost his right leg fighting the Soviets and is now a prominent mullah and the head of the legislative committee in parliament—the committee that is the gatekeeper for the introduction of legislation. He is clear on what he lost that leg for, not just defeating Communism but defeating the Communists' initiatives on women's rights, initiatives he is angry to see the Americans trying to bring back today. Qazi Hanafi beat back Fawzia Koofi's 2013 attempt to push the EVAW law through parliament, smothering it in amendments that no one could countenance (one allowed girls as young as nine to be married). In 2015 he said he plans to enact a substitute law regulating violence against women that would be based on what he considers to be principles of shariah law. He has made destroying the EVAW law the defining issue in his life, issuing a fifty-four-page pamphlet about the law, featuring what his critics call an incomprehensible blend of theological ravings.

Qazi[54] Hanafi is unapologetically antifeminist. Women's shelters are brothels, he insisted when I went to see him in 2014. "If it was up to me, I would declare jihad against these shelters." The women who run them "have not helped women in Afghanistan.

They have destroyed families. They have imprisoned brothers and fathers of the women whom they claim to be helping." Women's-rights activists? "Even a donkey is better than these women. At least the donkey has a tail." Shelter guards "should be over twenty-five. Before that is when a man is most horny and he cannot be trusted." Women who are abused by husbands need only go to their brothers or fathers for support; there is no point in advocacy groups to look after them or policewomen to take care of them.

"Yes, I was the person who blocked the EVAW law from being passed, but first let me ask you a question," he said. "How many die of HIV and AIDS in your country, I ask you?"

Not many any longer.

"That's not true. Thousands of people in America die of HIV. This does not happen here, and why? Because in our religion, punishment of those who commit sexual abuse is stoning, and when you stone one person who commits a crime, it establishes an example: kill one and save millions."

He has lots of problems with the EVAW law, beginning with what he claims is its authorship by the international community, not by Afghans. His biggest problem with it seems to be the prohibition on wife-beating. "Under the EVAW law, a man can get two years in prison for beating his wife. Is that just? He doesn't even have to mark her. Simply if she said he beat her, without even leaving a mark, he can go to jail. Is that just? This law is worse than those laws during the Communist time, far worse."

His version of a new EVAW law would revise or eliminate such clauses. His view is that it is okay to beat your wife, as long as you do so with moderation. "You can train her, you can punish her, but you can't mark or torture her. If you have a problem with your wife's behavior, first use advice," he said. "Second, make your bed elsewhere—this is a strong punishment and usually works. If that doesn't work, then third, beat her, but with things that don't cause damage or break bones. Like sticks, say, with a small stick or whatever—no torture. For example, if a husband breaks his wife's arm or leg, then he could and should be summoned by a judge and punished."

Having a discussion with Qazi Hanafi about gender equality is like trying to debate vegetarianism with a hyena. Like many such Afghan men, he seems obsessed with sex, and particularly with adultery. Adulterers should be killed on the spot when they're caught in the act, according to Islam according to Qazi Hanafi. (Actually, most authorities maintain that Islamic law requires four witnesses to the sexual act or a thrice-repeated confession, and a legal process, before the death penalty of stoning can be imposed for adultery.) He also seems to have a knack for catching people in the act. He cautions that you have to be sure they're adulterers and not just an innocent husband and wife. For instance, he said, he and his men during the days of jihad came across a couple copulating in the woods by a stream. Qazi and company were ready to kill them on the spot, but fortunately for the couple, "They told us they were married, so it was okay." Another time, he said, he walked into a room in the parliament building to find a female MP having sex on a desk—but it was with her husband, so he wasn't obliged to kill them either.

Qazi Hanafi is proud of his powers of persuasion, and he boasted that hardly anyone ever leaves his presence without having been converted to his way of thinking. He asked me if, having heard him out for a couple of hours, I wasn't persuaded of his rightness, and I said no, I wasn't. He had trouble believing that. The Australian ambassador had come to visit him, he said, and brought his young wife along, and after a couple hours of Qazi Hanafi, the young woman was not only ready to convert to Islam but probably would have become his second wife if she could have done so, he said. He was so proud of that imaginary conquest that he told the story twice.

Before we left, he handed a copy of his EVAW-law pamphlet to our translator. "Be sure to wash your hands and do your ablutions before you read that," Qazi warned him, quite in earnest.

Qazi Hanafi is not just some nutcase. He is widely respected by Afghan men as an Islamic scholar, however dubious some of his theological assertions, and he is powerful as a legislator. He is a man who practices what he preaches; he married off his own daughter at age fourteen, a violation of both EVAW and civil law. (He confirmed that with no apology, saying it was sufficient that she was past the age of puberty, in his interpretation of Islamic law.)

In the face of opposition in parliament from men like that, the Afghan Women's Network (AWN), the major coalition of women's groups in Afghanistan, has a simple strategy: delay bringing a permanent EVAW law to a vote for as long as possible. "We cannot take it off the agenda, but we can get it moved to the back of the agenda, and they argue over everything in parliament for so long that this parliament [2010–15] will finish before they get to it,"[55] said Hassina Safi, the AWN's executive director. "And the next parliament, we see many young people interested in running." In other words, the EVAW law's only long-term hope is a future parliament in a country that had only recently, in 2014's protracted electoral debacle, demonstrated that it was not capable of staging a fair, honest, and democratic national election and instead staggered through a half-billion-dollar exercise that was corrupted, on both sides, by warlords and former jihadis, with war criminals and unapologetic misogynists playing key roles.

Women's advocates are hoping that what will ultimately save and preserve the EVAW law will be the international community's insistence on it; changing it drastically or repealing it would lead to major cutbacks in international aid, and some donor countries might pull out of the country altogether —the Europeans in particular have been strong about that possibility. Or at least they have talked a strong game.

That, however, is betting on something that many Afghan women's leaders are beginning to disbelieve: the steadfastness of the international commitment to them. Afghanistan's women are no longer the cause célèbre that they were a few years ago, when Hillary Clinton was the American secretary of state, famously vowing in 2010 never to let the women of Afghanistan down. "We will not abandon you. We will stand with you always," Mrs. Clinton said then.[56] Now she rarely meets with Afghan women, even in her private capacity—for one thing, few of them can get visas to America any longer, for fear they will not return to their country.

Alissa J. Rubin of the *New York Times,* who has written extensively on Afghan women's issues,[57] said that Melanne Verveer, who was Hillary Clinton's ambassador for global women's issues in the first Obama administration, could not find time to discuss the issue with her in 2014. Before Hillary Clinton, Laura Bush famously became a stalwart of the U.S.-Afghan Women's Council, started by her husband, George Bush, and President Karzai to great fanfare in 2002.[58] Now the U.S.-Afghan Women's Council is all but defunct, although Georgetown University keeps a Facebook page for it alive, mostly with posts on the activities of other groups.[59] The council's presence in public life has become more virtual than real.

"I worked with the women of the West so intensely during the Taliban and up until a couple of years after the American engagement, but now I have been seeing the waning of Western women's interests in Afghan women's rights," said Nasrine Gross, the sociologist and women's activist. "I don't hear the Feminist Majority[60] shouting, I don't see the French women so much; the Scandinavian women, who used to be so present; women who are so vocal in New York, Women in Black and these people, saying, 'We want the rights of Afghan women upheld.' That is gone now. I don't get so many e-mails any longer from women abroad."

"Women are just not on anybody's agenda now," said Huma Safi, a former country director at Women for Afghan Women, who now works at Equality for Peace and Democracy, an advocacy group in Kabul.[61]

"We have come a long way if we look at the situation at the beginning of 2001," said Samira Hamidi, advocacy director of the Empowerment Center for Women.[62] "In major cities, in girls' education, higher education, the women's movement today is very strong. But will this be maintained? We need to make sure Afghanistan is not left alone. And where is the international community in terms of the Afghan government's commitments?"

In its haste for the exits toward the end of 2014, the international community proved itself ready to excuse every failure of the Afghan government, even on the so-called hard deliverables of the Tokyo Framework. One of those was a "credible and democratic" presidential election in 2014. The United States, the European Union, and the United Nations all pronounced it credible and democratic, even though the EU's own independent election monitors—the most experienced in the business—found that as many as 3 million out of the 8 million votes recorded were suspect[63] and in the end the results came after a backroom negotiation between the contenders moderated by the United States.[64] When President Karzai in 2013 replaced some members of the Afghanistan Independent Human Rights Commission with warlords, women haters, and a former Taliban official,[65] the international community tut-tutted but did not threaten any cutbacks, although the independence of that body was also a hard deliverable under the Tokyo Framework. When it came to condemning the abusive treatment of women that continued in spite of the EVAW law, there was only silence on specific cases, aside from buried and usually anonymized references in reports and briefing papers.[66]

As Shmuley Boteach was quick to point out, not once did any Western official, diplomat, or United Nations official raise a voice in public in support of Zakia and Ali, either before or after their criminal case was resolved. No one publicly condemned the rape of ten-year-old Breshna by her mullah, nor the reports of an honor killing planned against her, nor her return to the parents who had publicly vowed to kill her in 2014, nor the vocal support by other mullahs for her rapist.[67] Similarly, no diplomat or Western official ever spoke out about the intervention by mullahs of the Ulema Council in support of stoning alleged adulterers to death,[68] nor the battering of MP Atmar by her husband.[69] When WAW resolved the protracted and precedent-setting case of Soheila, sold in *baad* before she was born,[70] so she could marry the man of her choice rather than an elderly relative, no Western embassy issued a congratulatory statement, let alone any statements of support during the process. When Western officials in Afghanistan do undertake something worthwhile to help women, it is nearly always done in secret, as if they were terrified that Afghan conservatives might find out. USAID's major contractor for gender equality and rule-of-law programming in Afghanistan is the International Development Law Organization (IDLO),[71] which receives tens of millions of dollars in American government money for its Afghan programs. IDLO was assigned by the American embassy to follow the case of Zakia and Ali and report on it to the embassy; its officials refused my request to discuss their case and ones similar to it.[72] Western and United Nations public diplomacy on behalf of the women of Afghanistan has been reduced to congratulatory messages on the occasion of International Women's Day and similar concocted and uncontroversial events.

Wazhma Frogh remembers the good years, when she traveled five times to the United States, meeting with Hillary Clinton and First Lady Michelle Obama. Secretary Clinton awarded her the State Department's International Women of Courage Award in 2009.[73] Hanging on Ms. Frogh's wall at her NGO are both that medal and a framed letter from General John R. Allen, the one-time commander of the American-led International Security Assistance Force (ISAF),[74] thanking her for her help in bringing to the military's attention the depredations of an Afghan Local Police commander in Kunduz who had led his men on a rape spree in the local community. (General Allen admitted that ISAF special-operations troops had trained the offending unit, but he added that only 4 percent of such Afghan Local Police units were involved in human-rights abuses.)[75] Since then another warlord whom Wazhma Frogh tangled with, an old jihadi who worked closely with Australian and American special-forces troops in Uruzgan Province, has threatened her life repeatedly, and she no longer feels heroic. Instead she said she feels abandoned by the Americans.

"We women don't have any other ally than the West, which is not much of an ally anymore," she said. "We hardly see very strong pressure anymore. Two years ago I was a very strong voice, but now look how much I have been thwarted. I don't appear in local media. I've stopped. I have lost hope. We hardly find any hope anywhere any longer. I'm not even a voice anymore."[76]

After the warlord began threatening her, she decided to go to the United States for a few months to let the situation cool off. That March of 2014, however, she was turned down for a visa, because the consular officer felt she would never come back. He might have been right, although Ms. Frogh denies that. "They give you an award, but they don't support you when you need them," she told the Associated Press in March 2014.[77] "I always thought that if my government didn't help me, I would always be able to turn to the United States. I never thought that they would turn their back on me."

Ms. Frogh's family was forced to resort to a traditional *jirga* (all male elders in this case) to mediate with the Uruzgan *arbakai* commander; the *jirga* ordered her to give him an offering of goats and cows and publicly ask for his forgiveness. *Arbakai,* the informal militia groups aligned with the government and often used as Afghan Local Police, are notorious for their behavior toward women.

"I was forced to apologize to someone who was ruining my life and, on a daily basis, the lives of other people, including women," Ms. Frogh said. "If *I* had to apologize to someone who abuses our rights and *I* met the wife of the president of the United States, what hope does an Afghan woman in a village have?" Ms. Frogh's lament is heard often now from Afghanistan's women leaders, more than fourteen years after ousting the Taliban.

As she and other women's leaders know, so many of their accomplishments are illusory. The Ministry of Interior says it is proud, for instance, of the four female generals it now has; the Ministry of Defense boasts another two. Jamila Bayaz, promoted to brigadier general in 2015, became the first female police chief of a district, Police District 1 in Kabul (the station where Mohammad Ali was held).[78] Replaced in that job after President Ghani took office, she continued to work as a booster of the government's efforts to recruit female police and soldiers and to promote women in the ranks. It is a pretty hard sell. Both the police and the Afghan military have failed abysmally to meet their intended enlistment goals; there were only two thousand female police officers and eight hundred female soldiers by late 2014,[79] well under 1 percent of their respective forces, and every year since 2011 the government has said it plans to increase that to ten thousand, and every year it never manages to do so. Recruiting more women is important not only for the capacity of the security services to do things like search women who might be strapped up with explosive vests but also to give women abuse victims someone they can trust not to rape them when they go to the station to make a complaint—something most women will never do out of just that fear.

Like the other female generals, and most other female senior officers, Brigadier General Bayaz joined the police in the Communist era—a detail the American-led international coalition and the Afghan government leave out of their glowing pronouncements about the success of female advancement in the security services. The official announcements also leave out the other three female senior officers who have fled the country in the past few years, including the previous one in charge of female empowerment and gender equality at the Ministry of Interior, Brigadier General Shafiqa Quraishi, who fled Afghanistan in 2012, two years after Secretary of State Clinton awarded her the International Women of Courage Award.[80] Brigadier General Bayaz is careful not to mention that she herself applied to the Canadian government for asylum in 2014, according to Western diplomats in Kabul.[81]

Brigadier General Bayaz would join not only Fatima Kazimi, the Bamiyan women's ministry head who protected Zakia and later fled to Rwanda and America, but other leading Afghan women who have given up and left. Hassina Sarwari, the head of the women's shelter in Kunduz, who saved the life of Breshna, the ten-year-old raped by her mullah,[82] now wants to flee to the United States and has been talking to lawyers there about doing so. She begged me to intercede for her with the American embassy, but as we've seen, I have little influence there, and they have little interest any longer in helping at-risk women to leave. She is also applying for asylum in Germany, and officials in the embassy of that country in Kabul were actively talking to her late in 2014. Afghanistan's most famous missing person among women's-rights activists is of course Malalai Joya, the woman who electrified audiences with her fierce opposition to her country's patriarchs in 2002. She lives in Canada and visits Afghanistan in secrecy from time to time, but rarely appears in public there any longer. She is afraid to be interviewed in person or on the telephone and will take and answer questions only by e-mail for "security reasons," according to an anonymous person, reached through her website, who said he or she was the activist's secretary.[83] Ms. Joya has been quoted as saying that she is married but cannot name her husband, for his safety.[84] She is no longer a player inside her own country, where she is a forgotten figure. The battered member of parliament, Noor Zia Atmar, has fled to India, where she has so far unsuccessfully applied for asylum to a third country. There now may well be more Afghan women's activists outside the country than inside it, a trend that would be growing dramatically were it not that most Western embassies have stopped giving visas to Afghan women leaders— the visa-application rejection rate is now over 90 percent at North American and European embassies.[85] Brigadier General Bayaz said she was turned down in August 2014, for instance, for a visa to attend a Canadian government-sponsored international symposium on increasing the participation of women in the police forces of developing countries; so much for her role as poster girl for that effort in Afghanistan, but of course the Canadians were probably aware that she was planning to claim asylum and never go back. The head of communications at the American embassy in 2013, the novelist and journalist Masha Hamilton, set the tone when she argued that if we keep helping women leave Afghanistan,[86] there would be no one left behind to change things; that is an attitude that is embedded in American visa policy now, but it is not one accompanied any longer by the sort of advocacy and activism on behalf of Afghan women that the United States and its allies once practiced.

By almost any measure, the accomplishments of the international community on behalf of Afghan women have been disappointing, particularly considering the scale of the financial investment and the sweeping promises made back in 2002.

Official numbers, which are greatly exaggerated, say that some 2.5 million girls are in school who were not at the end of the Taliban era.[87] Even if it were 2.5 million, that would represent just 37 percent of students, so boys' enrollment is nearly double that of girls. Half of those girls enrolled will drop out when they reach puberty, usually about seventh grade, mostly because they are forced to do so by their families. As the result, each year after seventh grade, the numbers of girls being educated dwindles further, until by twelfth grade only 10 percent of the enrolled students are female, according to figures from USAID. I vividly remember touring a show school in Kabul, Sardar Kabuli Girls' High School, built by USAID at a cost of $27 million (in a country where an adequate, weatherproof school building for a thousand students can be built for half a million dollars), and visiting a class full of thirty or forty twelfth-grade girls. We asked the students how many of them wanted to go on to college, and nearly every hand shot up; that was unsurprising, considering what this 10 percent of Afghan girls must have endured to get as far as they had. Then we asked how many of the girls would be allowed by their families to go on to college, and all but three put their hands back down.

"All major social indicators continue to show a consistent pattern of women's disempowerment in nearly all dimensions of their lives and Afghanistan remains one of the worst countries in the world to be born female," the UN Women organization (formerly known as UNIFEM), said in 2014.[88] Women remain disproportionately illiterate; 87.4 percent of women are illiterate, compared to 56.9 percent of men. Even among women aged fifteen to twenty-four, who would have come of school age after the Taliban era, when schools were in theory available for them, illiteracy remains at 80 percent.[89] For all the official ballyhoo about girls' schools, the average number of years of education for Afghan females is seven. (This number is based on 2011 figures, the latest available; it may be better today, but not by much.) In many areas the quality of education is so poor that even seven years can leave students functionally illiterate, barely able to sign their own names.

Other indicators are still worse. On the United Nations Development Program's Gender Inequality Index, Afghanistan in 2013 ranked as the 169th-worst country in the world to be a woman, out of 187 countries studied.[90] The year before, it was 149th-worst, so by 2014 it had declined a further twenty ranks. "It is still not *the* worst country in the world to be a woman," said one Western ambassador in Kabul, the European Union's Franz-Michael Mellbin. "Yemen is." Even that is arguable, but it is still not much of an achievement considering how comparatively little international aid Yemen has received. Afghanistan has one of the world's highest birthrates among underage girls (86.8 percent) and a maternal-mortality rate of 460 per 100,000 live births,[91] a rate that has not been seen in developed parts of the world for two centuries.[92] The lives of Afghan women are not only nasty and brutish but short; life expectancy for an Afghan woman is forty-four years, compared to forty-eight years for men (according to UN Women),[93] which is a significant differential considering that there have been wars going on pretty continuously for the last thirty-five years and nearly all the combatants are male, yet still women live shorter lives on average. (Civilian casualties, including women, have been high, but never as high as casualties among combatants.) This is the state of things after fourteen years of massive international intervention, $104 billion in development aid from the United States alone by 2014, much of it earmarked to women's programs and gender equality. Counting the military investment, which also had generous gender set-asides, America[94] had spent well over a trillion dollars in Afghanistan between 2002 and 2014.[95]

When General David H. Petraeus was running the Afghan War, he was fond of saying that the American military's achievements in Afghanistan were "significant, but fragile and reversible."[96] When it comes to the achievements of Afghan women, the same could be said, although perhaps significant but disappointing, extremely fragile, and easily reversible would be a more precise description.

Many Afghan women's activists have started to come to the conclusion that they went about it all wrong by relying on the international community to save them from their own society. In their personal lives, female activists like Ms. Frogh remain prisoners of their families and the men who run them. "This was the mistake we made," she said. "There hasn't been a women's movement that has challenged what happens inside the home. We couldn't challenge the relationships and power differences inside our families, so we live in a kind of double role. Outside the home we are women's activists. Inside our homes we go to a very different place." Often a place where they are beaten and abused no matter who they are.

"Women's activists have all had a terrible time," said Ms. Koofi.[97] "Either they don't have a husband, like me"—she is a widow—"or they have a mess of a life, with lots of problems on their shoulders. We raise the awareness of women but not the standard of their lives."

For most Afghan women, leaving is not an option, improved freedom is relative, better conditions are fictional, and the elimination of violence against them is more of an aspiration than a legal reality. Zakia has so far been more fortunate than most Afghan women. Most of them have had no practical legal protection under the EVAW law,[98] and most of them lead lives unchanged by the trillion-dollar international juggernaut visited upon their country.

More typical are women like twenty-six-year-old Fatima.[99] In 2014, Kabul lawyer Sher Saeedi took on her case, referred to him by friends of friends. Fatima had borne six daughters, eleven years old and younger, and no sons. With each new daughter, her husband would beat her for failing to have a son—there are widespread Afghan folk beliefs that women can control the gender of their babies, and that men who cannot have sons are somehow defective.[100] "People say, if you don't have a boy, you're not man enough to make one," Mr. Saeedi said. Finally Fatima left her abusive husband. Mr. Saeedi got involved when the husband demanded his right to take and marry off the oldest girl, the eleven-year-old, so he could collect the girl's bride price. Mr. Saeedi told Fatima that she would lose the case if she went to court, even in Kabul city— "they always rule for the man in domestic custody disputes"—and advised her to go into hiding with her kids instead.

"There are many women in this country who the only thing they ever see is the inside of their father's house, until they are married, when the only thing they ever see is the inside of their husband's house, until they die, when the only thing they ever see is the inside of their casket," Mr. Saeedi said. "All they will ever know is the house where they are born and the house where they die and the grave in which they lie."

OTHER BATTLES IN THE AFGHAN WAR
OF THE SEXES

THE RAPE OF BRESHNA

Even by the standards of Afghan misogyny, the rape of ten-year-old Breshna by her mullah stands out, and not just for the brutality of the crime.[1] Afterward her family plotted to carry out an honor killing against the girl; the mullah pleaded innocent on the grounds that sex with the child was consensual, and then he jockeyed to marry her so he could get out of jail; she was rescued and put in a shelter but then ordered returned to her family despite the murder threat; other mullahs revised the victim's age upward to try to lessen the crime; and when this all became public, the women's advocate who protected Breshna was threatened by the office of the new Afghan president, Ashraf Ghani, and told to stop embarrassing the country over the rape of Breshna.

Breshna was rescued by Women for Afghan Women (WAW), which runs a women's shelter in the northern city of Kunduz. For most of the war, Kunduz Province had been solidly government territory, with some Taliban presence in remote districts; by mid-2014, 90 percent of the province was dominated by the insurgents, and even the city of Kunduz, its capital, became dangerous after dark, and at one point fell to the Taliban during 2015.[2] When I visited there in 2014, Dr. Hassina Sarwari, a pediatrician who ran the WAW shelter, and her colleague, Nadera Geyah, the head of the women's ministry for Kunduz Province, detailed what had happened to Breshna.[3] She was then in the shelter in Kunduz but would soon be transferred to Kabul for more advanced medical treatment.

The girl was from the village of Alti Gumbad, in an Uzbek area that by the summer of 2015 had fallen under Taliban control; the former strongmen there were Afghan Local Police (ALP), pro-government militiamen, many of whom had previously been Taliban themselves. Dr. Sarwari's take was that in Alti Gumbad they were *arbakai* by day and Taliban by night. As with so many other such units throughout Afghanistan, the *arbakai,* often branded as ALP, were trained and mentored by International Security Assistance Force (ISAF) special-operations or special-forces troops (in this area sometimes fielded by the Germans but in most parts of the country by the Americans) as an expedient solution to increasing anti-Taliban manpower.[4]

Like many of the children her age, Breshna attended Koran classes at the local mosque in the village; they were coed classes, since the children were so young (classroom segregation by sex does not begin until after puberty). After class on May 1, 2014, the mullah, Mohammad Amin, asked her to stay behind as the other children left to sweep the floor of the mosque, and when she refused and ran, he chased her, caught her, and dragged her back. Mullah Amin took her to the holiest part of the mosque, the mihrab, the Mecca-facing niche where normally the imam would stand to lead the congregation in prayers, then unrolled his white turban, a religious garment that signifies his clerical office, and tied her up with it.

"The girl said she screamed at him, 'Aren't you afraid of God? God is watching you, and if you're not afraid of God aren't you afraid of those Korans?'" Dr. Sarwari said, relating what Breshna had told her. (A copy of the police interview with Breshna, obtained later, corroborated this account.) Breshna was referring to the holy books piled in the mosque for congregants. "And he said, 'At this moment I am not afraid of anything.'" The rape was so brutal that it caused a rectovaginal fistula—a rupture in the wall between the rectum and the vagina—and the girl began bleeding heavily, by both her account and the mullah's later confession. He made her get dressed and finish sweeping the floor of the mosque, then sent her home. She was terrified to admit what had happened to her—the mullah had threatened to kill her family if she did. When Breshna began bleeding profusely at home, her mother thought she had begun menstruating unusually early and rushed her to the hospital in Kunduz. It did not take the doctors there long to figure out she had been raped; a fistula such as the one that Breshna had can be a life-threatening injury, and the girl lost so much blood that she needed a transfusion. From her hospital bed, Breshna confided to her mother and the doctors what had happened to her.

The mullah was arrested and soon confessed—sort of. His defense was the classic one, that the sex had been consensual. That the girl had asked for it and had wanted it and had even enjoyed it. That he thought she was twelve years old—an age that other mullahs would later bump up a few years in an effort to excuse what a fellow cleric had done. What follows is an excerpt from the attorney general's statement summarizing the mullah's confession:

> Mohammad Amin, deeply aware of what he was doing, has made a joke of people's trust and belief in mullahs and teachers and trampled on people's beliefs, trust and religion by committing the act of rape in a place of worship. In addition to his rape and ignominy, Mohammad Amin confessed that he kissed and hugged her so often, which cannot be forgiven, and also as he said in his statement, "that when I was penetrating her she was saying, 'Ah, ah,'" shows that this evil monster is not guilty about what he did, but he enjoyed it.

It was a story of depraved criminal conduct that could happen anywhere, in any culture. But there were plenty of "only in Afghanistan" elements that gave the case much greater significance. Dr. Sarwari went to the hospital the day after the rape and came into the girl's room to find her mother kneeling at her bedside and both of them crying. "My daughter, may dust and soil protect you now. We will make you a bed of dust and soil, we will send you to the cemetery where you will be safe." The mother told Dr. Sarwari that they had no choice, that her husband was under too much pressure from the other villagers to erase their communal shame by killing the girl.

On the same day, Nadera Geyah from the women's ministry came to the hospital and saw the crowd of angry men waiting outside, including the girl's father, two brothers, and two uncles. Inside the hospital she came across the girl's aunt. Ms. Geyah is a tough, no-nonsense woman, and she soon got the aunt to confess to what Ms. Geyah already suspected: the aunt had just been sent in by the men to bring the girl out, despite her state. "Everyone is focusing on revenge. They want to kill the girl and the mullah. They don't have the means to kill the mullah, and a lot of powerful people are behind the mullah, so they know they cannot do anything to him," Ms. Geyah said. Their plan was to kill the girl as soon as they got her away from the hospital and dump her body in the river, she said.

"The poor mother must have been under so much pressure," Dr. Sarwari said. "She cannot do anything. She is an Afghan woman. She doesn't have any say over anything."

"The girl is easy—they can get to her, she's their daughter," Ms. Geyah said. "They think they can wash their shame with her blood by killing her. It all comes down to honor. They believe she has brought shame to their family, and only by killing her can they rid that shame. She's just a child. She is sick and vulnerable, and nobody cares. Everything comes down to honor. Her own mother said, 'Let's strangle her in the hospital and say she died there.'"

When they realized what was about to happen, both Dr. Sarwari and Ms. Geyah decided that the only way to protect the girl was to have her put under the protection of the shelter once she was out of the hospital and also to go public with her story, and they did so initially with local Afghan media. The story was picked up nationally and later, when I wrote about it for the *Times*, internationally. The blowback was intense and vituperative. Dr. Sarwari said she got death threats from mullahs, many of them Taliban sympathizers—Mohammad Amin was a supporter of the insurgents, it turned out. One of his common themes when preaching was the evil of Western education, by which he meant education for girls. "They call me and curse me and threaten to kill me and my family and say they know where I live," Dr. Sarwari said. They justified this by claiming that the girl was old enough to have consented, and they began saying that she was seventeen rather than ten.

The two women's activists went on the counteroffensive and, in meetings with police and judicial officials in Kunduz, took pictures of Breshna to show around. She is a lovely young girl with striking black hair, delicate features, and she was obviously prepubescent. She had not started menstruating yet, she had no sign of any secondary sexual characteristics, and the hospital's forensic exam confirmed that ten was her approximate age. Like most Afghans, Breshna did not have a birth certificate or other documentation of her age.

Breshna was so small, though, that it was difficult to believe she was any older than ten, the age her mother agreed she was as well. Dr. Sarwari said she weighed only about forty pounds at the time and was otherwise a well-nourished, healthy, normal-size child for that age.

The mullahs started revising her age back downward, from seventeen to thirteen, but stuck to their campaign of justification. When I talked to Maulawi Faiz Mohammad, head of the Kunduz Ulema Council, a semiofficial body sanctioned by the government that nominally includes all the mullahs in the province, he said that the clerics were not trying to excuse what Mullah Amin had done. He questioned if Amin was really a mullah—police said there was no doubt—and whether it had really been a rape. "We even said that his punishment should be double what regular people get for such a heinous act," Mr. Mohammad said, once he abandoned the not-a-mullah tack. "I want to tell people that all mullahs are not lustful demons."

But, he went on, "We have been in touch with the judge who is going to lead the hearing in this case. According to him the girl is not ten but at least thirteen years old. She is more mature than what the women's-rights groups claimed her age to be. Also the judge, Mohammad Yaqub, told a meeting of the Ulema and journalists that it was not a rape case, but consensual sex was involved. He said that the girl had some kind of affairs with the imam and that this case should be dealt with not as a rape but as an adultery case. We will never try to defend a criminal, regardless of who he is, but truth should be told and allegations should be debunked and dismissed. The reason women's-rights groups claimed that she was ten and that she was raped by the imam was to defame the clerics and the Ulema."

Even in Afghanistan, legally, sex with a child cannot be considered consensual, and even if Breshna were thirteen years old, that would still be three years under the age of consent.[5] Marriages between girls that young and older men may be a commonplace practice, but they are also a criminal one, outlawed under both shariah and civil law. Also, it is hard to imagine consensual sex resulting in such serious injuries.

The police in Kunduz had no illusions about Breshna's safety and agreed to let Dr. Sarwari move the girl into the Kunduz shelter to protect her from the honor-killing threat by her family. "We will not give her back unless the family gives a hundred-percent guarantee," said Colonel Waisuddin Talash, the head of the Kunduz Police Criminal Investigation Division, who asserted that Bresha's age, ten, was not a matter of serious dispute. "The girl was a child. She doesn't even know anything," he said. "No love was involved, no temptation involved, she hasn't made a single mistake. She is just a victim." Claims to the contrary, he said, were just the product of "ignorant, backward, uneducated people" and not typical of educated Afghans. He himself had two daughters, he said. I asked him what he would do if one of them were raped. He said he would never allow them to be punished in any way. Colonel Talash seemed sincere—crisply pressed, bemedaled uniform; immaculately groomed; hero walls full of framed pictures of him with various visiting ISAF officials, German Bundeswehr officers (Kunduz was the Germans' area of operation during much of the war); and so on.

The official attorney general's report noted that Mullah Amin had proposed a solution to the entire matter: He would simply marry Breshna. "Afterward he said he would kill my family if I tell what happened," the girl was quoted by prosecutors. "He told me that when I get home, tell your mother that you want to marry the mullah."

"That will never happen," Colonel Talash said. In many rape cases in Afghanistan, that is what does happen, as an alternative to solve the honor problem for the victim's family, an abusive customary practice that is illegal, but traditional and common. The case of the girl Gulnaz, who now lives with her rapist, as described earlier in this book, is just one example.[6] It's sometimes regarded as an act of kindness toward the female victim, because it removes the family's perceived social obligation to kill her. Even in Afghanistan, though, such practices are usually imposed on older victims and stop short of marrying off ten-year-olds.

Officals could not let us see Breshna in the shelter for reasons of propriety—men are usually not allowed to enter women's shelters—and in any case she was about to be transferred to Kabul for medical care; fistulas require specialized surgery, and no one in Kunduz was qualified to perform it. I'm not sure I would have wanted to do that interview. The girl was so young—Dr. Sarwari showed me a picture, on her laptop—and had been through so much trauma.

Breshna would soon be sent to the CURE International Hospital, a facility in Kabul that specializes in female and maternal health, which had American obstetric surgeons familiar with the procedure to repair fistulas.[7] It was the only place in the country where there was specialized surgery for obstetrical and gynecological cases.

The two women's activists in Kunduz were already under a lot of pressure in their community, and word that Breshna was going to be moved to Kabul only ramped that up. Her case had inflamed not only the mullahs in Kunduz but also the Taliban who dominated her village of Alti Gumbad, which is only a short drive outside Kunduz city. Her family enlisted both Taliban insurgents and Afghan Local Police militiamen to threaten the women's groups in Kunduz. Dr. Sarwari showed us a phone full of death-threat text messages from the ALP commander in Alti Gumbad. The family assumed that moving Breshna to Kabul meant that WAW was going to send her to America. "Her brother-in-law called and said it is [our] responsibility to prevent the Americans from taking her from here to Kabul and the U.S.," said Dr. Sarwari. "People know this office as the Americans' office, and they know it's funded by Americans. They all think the shelter is an American office." There isn't a single American employee at any of WAW's shelters, although much of the group's funding does depend on grants from the American government.

"They're constantly cursing us," Dr. Sarwari said. "They say, 'Once your American husbands leave Afghanistan, we will do what we want to you.' They know where we live and how we live."[8]

A month later, in June 2014, just when we thought that Breshna's case could not possibly get any worse, the government ordered her returned to her family, to the parents and uncles who had plotted her murder. Dr. Sarwari called to give us the bad news, and she was distraught over the family's triumph. At the time the order happened, Breshna was out of the family's immediate reach. She had been taken to Kabul, but the CURE International Hospital there was unable to handle the complexity of surgery that her fistula injury required, so WAW arranged to quietly send her to India to have it done. By July she was back and staying in their shelter in Kabul to recuperate when the court ordered her returned to her family. "She's a lively, spunky girl," said Kimberley Motley,[9] an American lawyer who does legal work for the group, through her practice in Kabul. "She's very strong to even have survived this."

In the statement she made to prosecutors when they interviewed her after her rape, Breshna gave them an earful about what she thought should be done to her assailant. "Because Mullah Mohammad Amin has raped me brutally and inside the mosque, I ask the government to give him the harshest punishment, which is stoning, and if stoning is not possible, then I ask the government to do some kind of operation and make him a eunuch so he should not repeat this with someone else and so it becomes a lesson for him and others," the prosecutors quoted the girl as saying.

"The girl was in constant contact with her mother and last time her uncle," Dr. Sarwari said. "The family were complaining that she was not in Afghanistan, so I sent her uncle's number to the office in Kabul so she could talk to them. She talked to her mother and said she was happy there in the shelter but the mother cannot tell the male members of her family that she is happy there and does not want to come back. And she misses her mother. On the ride down from Kunduz to Kabul, she kept saying she wished her mother were with her.

"She has been traumatized, and we don't want to tell her. She doesn't know what is waiting for her if she goes back to Kunduz," Dr. Sarwari said. "On the way from Kunduz, she said she remembered after her father found out she had been raped, he started beating her mother a lot. He even beat her at the hospital. He was blaming her for what had happened to Breshna and to the entire family and telling her that 'I was a farmer, I was working outside. You were in charge of everything at home. How did you let her go to the mosque? Why didn't you follow her and monitor everything?'"

No one in the shelter had the heart to tell the girl her family had been plotting to kill her. She was probably too young to have realized the import of her mother's words, at her bedside the day of the rape, that she would be warm and comfortable in the grave; perhaps the girl wept along in empathy with her mother's grief; perhaps she thought she was going to die of her injuries. It might never have occurred to her that she was in mortal danger from her own family, or if it did, she had since suppressed the memory.

"That *arbakai* commander, Commander Nezam, he came with all the elders from Alti Gumbad to the governor's office and told the governor unless the shelter brings the girl back, they will attack the shelter," Dr. Sarwari said. Eager to keep the peace in a community where control seesawed between insurgents and pro-government militias, the governor supported their demand, and in turn prosecutors and police all signed off on Breshna's return to her family, and the father came to Dr. Sarwari at the Kunduz shelter and delivered a formal letter signed by the court demanding her return. "He said he would erect a tent in front of the shelter and live there and also said the villagers are after his entire family and want to kill him, his wife, and son because their family has brought shame to the village," she said.

"After he left, I got a call from Commander Nezam. He was shouting and yelling and accused me of selling the entire village's *nang* and *namoos*, dignity and honor, to the Americans. He demanded I give him the girl. I told Commander Nezam that he is not a relative and I would never give the girl to him. I told him that unless Breshna's father asks us to bring her to a court, we will not give her to anyone else. I also told him that there is no way we will give Breshna back to the family, because we found out that her uncle came specifically from Iran to kill this girl. He got so angry he told me he would destroy me. I said I'm a woman and he shouldn't display his masculinity to me. If he wanted to prove his masculinity, he should show it to a man. He texted me that if I want to live, I should not come out of my house. I left my home and am living with my parents now."

Then Dr. Sarwari had an unexpected blow. Her women's-ministry colleague, Nadera Geyah, had decided she'd had enough, not just because of the Breshna case but also because of threats she was getting from the Taliban in another case of abusive treatment of women and because the insurgents had recently taken control in her own home area, the district of Dashte Archi. "She had been under tremendous pressure a long time—the girls' madrassa in Kunduz and many other cases. She couldn't bear the pressure. She moved with her entire family to Kabul. The women's ministry helped her to get a new job in Parwan.[10]

"She is gone, and now I'm the only person between all these men and the women in our shelter. I don't know what is going to happen to these girls[11] if I leave as well," Dr. Sarwari said. "I'm so confused and so tired of all the pressure. I don't think I'll be able to bear it for very long. If I had the financial resources, I would have left the province a long time ago."

Women for Afghan Women had no choice but to return Breshna to her legal family. The law was on the family's side; they had never been convicted of doing violence against their daughter or of conspiring to do so.

When we called to speak to the head of the Criminal Investigation Division in Kunduz again, Colonel Talash, the one who had promised that Breshna would never be returned to a family who had plotted openly to kill her, he was unavailable except through a spokesman. "We handed the raped girl to her family based on her consent and will," said police spokesman Sayed Sarwar Hussaini. "The girl's father demanded from the police the return of his daughter, and with the approval of the attorney general's office we did that. We also got guarantees from the girl's family that they will not harm her." In addition, a maternal uncle of the girl as well as a fellow villager pledged their small businesses as bonds guaranteeing that the family would not harm the girl. "It is the police's job to make sure everyone is safe, and we have a responsibility to protect the girl," said Mr. Hussaini. "Unless we were sure, we would never hand her back to her family. If anything happens to her, we will find the guarantors and investigate. They wouldn't have given guarantees if they had any intention to harm her."

Dr. Sarwari did win a promise from the family to allow social workers from WAW to regularly monitor the girl's safety and be allowed to speak to her periodically. WAW asked Kim Motley[12] to get involved on Breshna's behalf. Kim managed to persuade the attorney general's office in Kabul to transfer the mullah's rape case from Kunduz to Kabul, where it would be much harder for local power brokers in Kunduz to interfere on the mullah's behalf. She was able to do that, ironically enough, because of the lack of rape as an offense in the Afghan penal code. In rural areas, Kunduz among them, local judges were ill versed in the EVAW law, or downright antagonistic toward it as un-Islamic, and unlikely to invoke it. Kim was able then to persuade the prosecutor in charge of the EVAW unit, Qudsia Niazi, to order the mullah's case transferred to Kabul so the rape could be prosecuted under EVAW law. She was not, however, able to stop the girl's return to her family.

"She cried every single day she was in the shelter, and she's ten, and she wanted her mother," Kim said. "They're trying, trying to protect, protect, protect, and you can't blame them for that—they do a great job of it. But at some point you can't keep the girl forever from her natural parents, or at some point you'd be kidnapping her yourself."

Later that summer Dr. Sarwari called to report that Breshna's father had decided not to allow the girl to travel to Kabul to testify against Mullah Amin. She looked into the matter further and talked to a lawyer from a local human-rights group who had visited the mullah in prison before he was moved out of Kunduz. The lawyer said he had worked out a deal with the family. The charges against him would be dropped, he would marry Breshna, and as compensatory payment to her family the mullah would give his thirteen-year-old niece in *baad* to one of their menfolk. In other words, an innocent thirteen-year-old as well as the victim herself would end up paying for the mullah's crime. "I asked the head of the prison if there was such a deal, and he said the mullah had told them that, too," Dr. Sarwari said. "The father said he will not allow the girl to testify. We will not let it go, though. We will push the police and the prosecutors to continue the case." Since the mullah had already confessed to his crime, the girl's testimony was not necessary for the prosecution to proceed, though it would help—particularly in convincing the court of the seriousness of the crime and the youthfulness of the victim. With her head office's permission, Dr. Sarwari offered to pay the travel expenses for the girl and her family to attend the court. The father was dubious, but as the case became nationally notorious, he eventually gave in to public pressure to agree to let her testify.

"It doesn't surprise me," said Wazhma Frogh, the women's-rights activist, reacting to that situation. "In so many cases, the women are forced to marry the rapists." Even more often the rape victim is charged with adultery, as is the rapist, as if each party had committed an offense of equal severity. "Due to the lack of a definition of rape in the penal code, rape victims are charged with *zina* and further revictimized as some of them are forced to get married to their rapists," said a report on implementation of the EVAW law by UNAMA in December 2013.[13] "This ugly crime is an everyday occurrence in all parts of the country. It is a human rights problem of profound proportions. Women and girls are at risk of rape in their homes and in their communities, in detention facilities and as a result of traditional harmful practices to resolve feuds."

"Her life is over if she's forced to marry the mullah," said Dr. Sarwari.

With WAW and Kim Motley, among others, pushing the case, it finally came to trial on October 25, 2014. Mullah Mohammad Amin was led into the judge's chambers with chains around his waist but his hands unshackled;[14] he kept his eyes skyward and under his breath recited verses from the Koran. He was a short, stocky, black-bearded man, about thirty years of age. For reasons that were never made clear, Judge Mohammad Suliman Rasuli had decided to hold the trial in his chambers rather than in one of the empty courtrooms nearby. All the seats were taken by the time they brought the mullah in, so he was forced to kneel on the floor in his shackles.

Breshna covered her face with her veil and looked away from him, and underneath the head covering her breathing was troubled and labored, and she soon broke into sobs. Purely by chance she was seated next to me. In person her extreme youth was obvious. No more than four feet tall, and perhaps fifty pounds in weight, the girl was still plainly a child in every way, including her tiny voice. She seemed so alone, although one of the women's advocates was next to her. Her father and uncle stood farther back in the room and never looked at her during the proceeding.

The mullah had two defense attorneys, whose case consisted of his testimony that he was sorry for what he had done but that the sex with the girl was consensual and he should therefore receive the shariah-law penalty for adultery of a lashing with a whip. The lawyers did not mention the number of one hundred lashes normally stipulated, since that is a devastating and often crippling punishment.

"Is it true you raped the girl?" Judge Rasuli asked the mullah.

"I need to go to the doctor. I'm not feeling well," the mullah replied.

The judge pointed out his confession, parts of which the prosecutor, from the EVAW unit of the attorney general's office, had already read into the record. "Did you make this up? Did you commit adultery with the girl? Did you rape the girl?"

"I was beaten, I was tortured, they even made me eat shit, and they forced me to give my confession. I was teaching the children, before breakfast, and it wasn't like that in the confession."

Breshna, quivering with indignation, spoke up, dropping her veil from her face for a moment. "What was it like, then?"

He shushed her with a contemptuous gesture but did not look her way. "Whatever I confessed to in Kunduz, it wasn't like that." She started to speak again, and the prosecutor shushed her as well. Then the judge shushed her. She retreated back under her veil; I could hear her chest heaving.

The prosecutor interrupted his narrative to read from the mullah's confession: " 'I took her hand and dragged her to the mosque.' "

"No," the mullah said. "She came. Breshna came and said, 'I love you.' "

Breshna again unveiled to speak up. "Hey, liar, hey, liar! God hate you! You are dirt, you are dirt! You are a vampire!"

The mullah continued, "She came and hugged me, and I told her, 'In the name of God,' she came and told me, 'Do this with me. If you don't, I'll go to my father and mother and say that you did this to me.' Satan brought this into my heart and made me indulge it. They say I did this by force, but I did it with her consent."

No one challenged his facts, such as they were, aside from Breshna, but she was never given an opportunity to address the court, and the judge kept trying to still her outbursts of outrage at the mullah's version. Neither prosecutor nor judge noted that her injuries had been so grievous that she'd needed major surgery, that she'd been tied up during the rape, that the mullah had threatened to kill her family if she told, that he had blasphemed in the holiest part of the mosque. As far as the judge was concerned, it was enough that the mullah confessed to having sex with the girl. Given her age, that was evidence enough of rape, and the hearing was soon over. "How can you commit adultery with a ten-, eleven-years-old child?" the judge said. "It's rape." He rejected the defense's argument that shariah-law punishment should be applied. By that reasoning, the judge said, the girl would have to be sentenced similarly. "She would have to get lashes then, too." He told her to approach his desk and lift her veil so he could verify her age. "She cannot commit adultery. She is a child. This is rape."

The girl continued to clamor to be heard between her bouts of sobbing. Breshna had little knowledge of courts and courtrooms and had somehow formed the idea that the judge's title was "director."

"You shamed me, liar!" she shouted at the mullah. "You brought shame to my father! Director, please hang him!"

Waiting in the corridor for the judge to rule on the punishment, Breshna's father, Najimudin, and her maternal uncle, Mohammad Rasoul, both said that the family would never assent to her marriage to the mullah and that they had never plotted to kill her. "That was totally false, wrong. She was raped and was a child," said Mr. Rasoul. "If we killed her, how could we answer to God on the day of judgment?" Her father added, "We want to see him hang for this." Ten minutes later Judge Rasuli delivered his verdict, which was the maximum under the EVAW law of twenty years in jail.

"I'm not happy with the verdict," Breshna said. "I want him to be hanged. He shamed us. He shamed my father. We want the government to give him execution." When the trial was over, the girl walked out alone, following her father and uncle but some twenty feet behind them; they still had not looked at her.

It would surprise no one if the mullah were later released on appeal, or pardoned quietly, or released early for good behavior, and if he finally ended up marrying his victim and sacrificing his thirteen-year-old niece's life in *baad* as well. In November the German embassy secretly dispatched a representative up to Kunduz to offer to send Breshna to an Afghan private school, all expenses paid. Her father turned down the offer.

Only a few weeks earlier in Kabul, five men had been convicted in the Paghman gang rapes, in which four married women returning from a wedding were set upon in front of their husbands. The accused were subjected to a rushed trial, without meaningful benefit of defense counsel, and found guilty on the basis of confessions obtained from torture and from lineups in which they were the only suspects.[15] Those men were also charged with rape under the EVAW law, but authorities imposed other charges, including armed robbery, that carried the death penalty; they could just as easily have done something like that in the mullah's case if authorities had wanted the death penalty (kidnapping, for instance, for dragging Breshna back into the mosque). The Paghman case transfixed Afghanistan for the less than two months that elapsed between the attack and the alleged rapists' executions, but, as many women's leaders pointed out, it was not really about what had happened to the women. The Paghman rapists' real sin was to have humiliated the women's husbands by attacking their wives in front of them. After the gang rape, the husbands dropped off the four women victims, who had been brutally raped, beaten, and gratuitously tortured and were badly injured, at the Rabia Balkhi Maternity Hospital in Kabul. None of them remained with their wives through that part of their ordeal, not even the husband of the pregnant victim, who was only eighteen.[16]

The following month, in November 2014, Afghanistan's new president, Ashraf Ghani, summoned Breshna's father and uncle to a meeting at the presidential palace, chaired by his legal adviser, Abdul Ali Mohammadi. The palace issued a statement afterward:[17] "Breshna, the little girl who was the victim of rape, is not at any risk from her family." Among those present were women's-ministry, foreign-affairs ministry, and human-rights officials, the statement said; conspicuously absent was anyone from Women for Afghan Women,[18] Dr. Sarwari or anyone else who had worked with Breshna, or her lawyer Kim Motley. "Breshna's father and uncle rejected the report that she is at risk and emphasized that their child was the victim of an unlawful act, so they have been trying to protect her, not to harm her anymore," the presidential statement said. Under the circumstances it is implausible that Breshna's family would have confessed to the president's staff that they intended to murder their child.

On December 8, 2014, Mr. Mohammadi summoned Dr. Hassina Sarwari from WAW for a separate session at the presidential palace. She went expecting encouragement and support for her efforts to protect the girl; she saw the earlier meeting with the family as the palace's way of scaring Breshna's relatives into not harming the girl and thought they now would be eliciting her independent view on the matter. "I told him the truth. Indeed her life *was* at risk," she said. Mohammadi showed her a pile of what he said were a hundred forty letters from human-rights groups throughout the world about the case and accused her of causing that to happen. "You're exploiting this case," he said. "I want no more stories on this. You have been exploiting this case in your own interest." Mr. Mohammadi said the president had ordered Dr. Sarwari to step down from her job at the women's shelter; the government would find her a women's-ministry position in another part of the country. Never mind that WAW, as an independent charity, was not under the control of the government. If she did not agree to take the job offered, she should just quit her work and remain at home, Mr. Mohammadi told her.

I saw Dr. Sarwari an hour after the meeting. Her eyes were red, and she broke down in tears recounting what had just happened. "I don't know what to do," she said.[19]

By the summer of 2015, Breshna's village of Alti Gumbad had been overrun by the Taliban. Her fate is unknown.

MARRIAGE BEFORE PUBERTY

By some estimates 57 percent of Afghan brides are under the legal age of sixteen.[20] Often far under. In late August 2014, a ten-year-old girl named Mina was formally married to a twelve-year-old boy named Sardar in northern Mazar-i-Sharif, the country's fourth largest city and capital of Balkh Province, considered a progressive part of the country. The union was sanctioned by a local mullah, who defended his actions on shariah-law grounds. The authorities prosecuted the girl's father, a man named Abdul Momin, who said he'd sold his daughter into the marriage for two thousand dollars because he was so poor he had no other prospects. Mina and another vulnerable daughter were removed from his home and put into the care of a shelter, after Afghan news organizations disseminated pictures of the two children at their wedding ceremony.[21] No charges were brought against the mullah who married them. The pictures showed a girl who was not much more than half the boy's height, dolled up in traditional bridal dress; he wore a starched white *shalwar kameez* with a spiffy jacket. It looked as if they were a couple of little kids playacting at something grown-up. They were both children, so the consummation of their marriage would normally wait until the girl reached puberty—although it would often happen long before she reached the legal age of sixteen. Until then the child bride would usually live in her husband's home and be put to work as a servant to her husband's family. Rape and sexual abuse of girls in such situations is a frequent occurrence; beatings and lesser forms of abuse are commonplace.

HE SOLD HIS DAUGHTER, BUT NOT HIS BIRDS

In early 2013 the *New York Times* reported that an impoverished refugee named Taj Mohammad had sold his six-year-old daughter for twenty-five hundred dollars to settle a debt with a moneylender.[22] The previous winter Mr. Mohammad, whose family lives in a camp on the outskirts of Kabul, had accumulated the debt in the course of buying firewood and paying for medical treatment for his wife and children, who fell ill during terrible winter snows that resulted in many vulnerable children freezing to death in the camps; one of those who died was Mr. Mohammad's own three-year-old son, a tragedy that I reported on at the time.[23] When the moneylender later asked Taj Mohammad for repayment, he was unable to comply, and after a *jirga* held in the camp, the camp elders decreed a *baad* arrangement in which Taj Mohammad would have to give his youngest daughter, Naghma, then six, to the money-lender's seventeen-year-old son if he was not able to repay the debt by the end of the year. Naghma was a bright girl and was attending school in the camp, but after the betrothal her prospective mother-in-law came by to demand that Mr. Mohammad's family withdraw her from school. They did not want an educated wife for their son.

In that case publicity about what had happened saved the girl—at first. Taj Mohammad's plight was already well known from reports about the freezing death of his son. After news of his daughter's sale, an anonymous foreign benefactor hired the American lawyer Kim Motley, who arranged to settle the debt and cancel the marriage. Publicly the elders and Naghma's family agreed to a settlement in which the girl would go to music school in Kabul on a scholarship and the family's debt would be repaid and the betrothal canceled.

Dr. Sarmast at the Afghan National Institute of Music offered Naghma a residential place and a scholarship. Taj Mohammad had been a musician previously, playing a lutelike Afghan instrument called a *rubab*, and Dr. Sarmast said he would try to find Mr. Mohammad a job playing that instrument somewhere, because the father insisted he did not want to be separated from his daughter. However, when Mr. Mohammad showed up with Naghma for enrollment, he also wanted to enroll two of her older brothers, who were outside the school's enrollment age. Dr. Sarmast demurred. Young enough children can always learn music, but the boys were too old to fit into a music curriculum. "Her father just wanted to do business on his little daughter," Dr. Sarmast said in May 2015.[24]

Then Naghma and Taj Mohammad disappeared from Kabul and the camps. According to women's activists who followed the case, the camp's elders had divided the foreign benefactor's money up among all the parties to the dispute, the marriage contract was confirmed, and Naghma was handed over to her purchasers, one year later as originally planned.

When I had visited Taj Mohammad the morning after his son froze to death, I noticed that despite having no money for firewood, Mr. Mohammad did own a brace of partridges, birds that are used for fighting and gambling and when trained can be quite valuable. He did not answer when asked why he had not sold them to buy fuel.

PARLIAMENTARY IMMUNITY

Shakila[25] was a sixteen-year-old girl from a remote mountain village in Bamiyan Province who was drafted by her pregnant sister, Soraya, to come stay with her on the outskirts of Bamiyan town to help her during her pregnancy. Soraya's husband was a bodyguard for a local big man in the village of Zargaran, a member of the Afghan parliament from Bamiyan, and Soraya worked as a maid for him, but her pregnancy was making it difficult for her to cope. Shakila was a shy girl who never left the home and knew no one in the local community. On January 27, 2012, Shakila's sister and brother-in-law were not home, but his AK-47 was—and so was his boss, the MP Wahidi Behishti, and a couple of his retainers—Abdul Wahab, Behishti's nephew, and Abdul Wadi—plus Mr. Behishti's wife. Shakila was alone without any of her own family members present. When her sister Soraya came home, she found Shakila in the room where she had left her, bleeding from a massive gunshot wound in the chest. The murder weapon, the AK-47 assault rifle that belonged to Soraya's husband, was nearby. Shakila was still alive but could not speak and soon died in her sister's arms.

Mr. Behishti and his retainers claimed that although they were home, they had not heard a gunshot and postulated that the girl had committed suicide. They took her body to the forensic medical examiner, who discovered that not only had Shakila allegedly shot herself in the heart with a long rifle, at an angle of sixty-five degrees from above (a much more plausible angle for someone standing above and behind her), but she had managed to lose her virginity in the process. There was still fresh semen in her vagina. Nonetheless the medical examiner declared her death a suicide, positing that she would have killed herself because she was distraught about losing her virginity.

Indignant protests by her family forced prosecutors to take a harder look at the suicide theory, and eventually Mr. Behishti and the other two men were charged with murder and his wife was arrested as an accomplice. He and his wife were released with charges dismissed, however—he had powerful friends in the Hazara community—and only his nephew, Abdul Wahab, was convicted. The Behishtis then unsuccessfully sought to overturn Mr. Wahab's conviction on appeal, but after a judge tried the difficult feat of pointing such a gun at his own heart at the same angle and pulling the trigger, he refused—although Mr. Wahab has remained free on further appeals. Shakila's arms were too short for her to have held the gun and fired it from the necessary position. Someone had stood behind and above her head as she lay on her back on the floor, having just been raped, and shot her through the heart.

Two years later no one had served jail time, and the prime suspect, Mr. Behishti himself, was never prosecuted. DNA samples taken of semen found in her body simply disappeared from the investigative file, as did fingerprint impressions taken from the weapon. The circumstantial evidence against Mr. Behishti's nephew was the same as that against the MP and rested on the absurdity of his claim not to have heard a gunshot less than fifty feet away from where he sat at the time. Yet only his nephew was prosecuted, and not very successfully.

THE VIRGIN RAPE

Sometimes the saddest cases are not the ones in which the victims die but in which they are forced to live with their shame and humiliation perpetually unresolved, their lives irredeemably ruined. So it was with the case of a girl who was beaten until she admitted having been raped, then was lashed a hundred times as an adulterer but later was tested and found to be still a virgin.

It happened in the district of Jaghori in Ghazni Province, to a girl named Sabira, who was fifteen at the time, in 2012. Jaghori is a peaceful corner of Ghazni famous for its high level of education, for both boys and girls. Largely Hazara, the community prides itself on being broad-minded and progressive, and the proliferation of girls' schools is higher than in any other part of Afghanistan, with the exception of Kabul, the capital. The community's most famous daughter is Sima Samar, the head of the Afghan human-rights commission, whose well-to-do family's philanthropies included many of Jaghori's schools. Even in Jaghori, though, Sabira ended up being publicly whipped on the orders of mullahs and elders for having been raped—despite the protests of her family, and her own claim that she was a virgin, and the insistence of the accused rapist that he'd not had sex with her. Her virginity was confirmed by a forensic exam, but it was not carried out until a couple of months after the fact. The only supposed offense anyone was able to prove against Sabira was that she had been seen alone with a tailor for five minutes in his shop in the middle of a crowded bazaar.

A report later by the Afghan Independent Human Rights Commission details her story, in an English-language version,[26] based on an interview with Sabira:

> I went to a tailor's shop where both the tailor and his assistant were present. After a while, the tailor asked his assistant to go out and bring something from the bazaar for him. When the assistant left the shop, the tailor took my hands and brought me to the closet. He asked me to have sex with him while I denied and tried to shout, but his palm was faster. He put it on my mouth and forcibly raped me. He then threatened me not to disclose the case.

Terrified by what would happen if she talked, Sabira remained silent and returned to her home.

> Days later, around four p.m., I went with my younger sister to our lands to collect some almonds, where suddenly a villager beat me with a long stick and took me to my paternal uncle's house. I saw around 50 men from my village gathered in the house. They beat me as well and asked me with whom I have had a relation. After continued beating and under the pain I felt, I finally admitted that a tailor raped me.

Later Sabira recanted her testimony and said that she had admitted to rape only to stop the beating and because it seemed less dire than to admit to consensual sex—which she had not had, but which the men beating her were convinced she had, and so they'd continued to beat her until they had her "confession." It seemed clear from the reports on the case that Sabira was simply so inexperienced that she was not really clear about what constituted either sex or rape.

When district police arrested the tailor, villagers intervened and insisted that they did not want to see a legal process and preferred to handle the case in a traditional way, through a *jirga* of clergymen and elders in their village of Nawdeh Hotqol. The government acquiesced in that and released the tailor, handing both Sabira and him over to the villagers for judgment. The villagers believed the tailor's denials and released him, but for reasons that defy logic they continued to insist that the girl had engaged in sex based on her confession to rape.

> Four clergy asked me to answer their questions, which lasted about 15 minutes. I told them that the tailor raped me, but they did not accept my answer and said that my claim was not reliable. They finally decided to lash me a hundred times, while the perpetrator was released because of his denying. I rejected their decision and said that I would appeal for an official due process. But they did not let me go.

Denied any legal process, Sabira was taken out into the desert on the edge of the village and forced to lie facedown in the dirt as crowds gathered on the roofs of homes and on nearby hillsides to watch. The lashes were administered by one of the old mujahideen, a commander from the days of the anti-Communist (and antifeminist) jihad. "One of the famous commanders [was] ordered to lash me one hundred times, but he lashed me one more, one hundred and one," Sabira said. The 101st lash was the unkindest cut of all. A hundred lashes is enough to severely injure the victim, if administered vigorously, and these lashes reportedly were. The man who whipped her was named Salaam, the junior commander to a local militia leader named Bashi Habib, another former jihadi stalwart, now working as the head of an *arbakai* unit—a sort of informal police body but really no more than a self-appointed militia.[27]

Sabira was lashed so brutally that she suffered a permanent injury to her hip. When her parents tried to stop the punishment, they were set upon by the villagers and badly beaten; her father, Iqbal Masoomi, sixty, was hospitalized for two days, and he said that his wife suffered a permanent dent in the side of her skull from the attack.

Zahra Sepehr, executive director of the Development and Support of Afghan Women and Children Organization,[28] who worked closely with Sabira and her family, said that Sabira had never been raped, nor had she engaged in sexual intercourse, as the later forensic examination done in Ghazni city showed. Said women's-rights activist Hussain Hasrat, "They felt that if we do not lash the girl, other girls will follow her and have sex, and the community will be destroyed." In other words, it didn't matter whether or not she had sex. The mere suspicion that she had was enough to warrant punishment in order to set a good example, in the eyes of these people from one of Afghanistan's better-educated communities.

Protests by women's groups over the girl's lashing forced authorities to arrest thirteen persons, who were eventually charged in the beatings of Sabira's parents. The mullahs who ordered her lashing and the two jihadi commanders who carried them out were initially charged but then released after a protest from the Ulema Council—of which one of the mullahs was a member.[29] "Many agencies or NGOs were not interested to follow the case because the Ulema Council was involved, and they didn't want to confront them," Ms. Sepehr said. The thirteen who were arrested were convicted but received minor fines of three thousand afghanis each, less than sixty dollars—for beating the girl's father and mother. No one was punished for administering the crippling lashes to Sabira.

The tailor fled Afghanistan, while Sabira spent a year in a women's shelter in Kabul. She tried to join the Afghan National Army when she reached the legal age of eighteen in 2014—her dream had been to enroll in the military academy and become an army officer. But she had stopped her education at the tenth grade when all this happened, and upon trying to enlist as a common soldier, she was rejected on medical grounds, because of the injury to her hip from the lashings. She was officially classified as permanently disabled.

As of late 2014, she was languishing in a juvenile-detention facility in Kabul, waiting until she turns nineteen. "She has just given up," said her father. "They ruined her life and took away her future." It also ruined Mr. Masoomi's future; he was fired as the village schoolteacher and did not get his job back even after his daughter's innocence was proved. Until all this happened, Mr. Masoomi's children had been doing admirably well. One is a nurse, and another is studying obstetrics at medical school in Kabul; except for Sabira, all the others are still in school.

There were eight daughters and no sons in the family, which was the heart of Mr. Masoomi's problem, said Ms. Sepehr. Not only did that mean he had no sons to defend the home when the other villagers rampaged in response to their suspicions about his daughter, but it also meant that in the eyes of his fellow Afghans he was somehow deficient as the sire of mere females.

ACKNOWLEDGMENTS

I would like to recognize the spirit and generosity of the Afghan and Iranian poets and musicians quoted in this book, who all readily extended permission to cite their work, and who are evidence that love will flourish even in the harshest of environments.

This book was conceived with the help and nurtured by the encouragement of my agent, David Patterson of the Stuart Krichevsky Literary Agency in New York City, who was instrumental in shaping it as well as placing it; they do not come any better. My editor at Ecco, Hilary Redmon, did a masterful job of guiding me through smart and insightful edits that always preserved my voice while encouraging me to make the book ever better. Copy editor Maureen Sugden's industry and intelligence were impressive, and occasionally life-saving. Thanks as well to Ecco publisher Dan Halpern, whose early and continued enthusiasm for *The Lovers* was very gratifying. The entire team at Ecco and HarperCollins, including Sonya Cheuse, Ashley Garland, Emma Janaskie, Rachel Meyers, Ben Tomek, Sara Wood, and Craig Young, welcomed this newcomer into their house with tremendous hospitality and support.

Throughout my work on this book, no one was more important than Jawad Sukhanyar, from the Kabul bureau of the *New York Times*, who was my indispensable interpreter, guide, and intermediary with the lovers and their culture. Jawad's concern and diligence saved many a day. As a reporter on women's issues, he has no equal among Afghan journalists of either gender.

My best friend, Matthew Naythons, M.D., was a constructive critic throughout every stage of both my reporting this story and writing the book. The writer Ruth Marshall was my first and most intelligent reader, whose insights and advice proved invaluable. My *New York Times* colleague Alissa Johannsen Rubin, who I am proud to say has twice been my boss, brought to bear her deep understanding and long reporting experience on Afghan women's issues, which greatly improved the context I was able to give to the lovers' travails. Thanks as well to my editors at the *Times* and especially Douglas Schorzman, whose usual enthusiasm for stories from Afghanistan gave this one a strong ride early on, making everything that followed possible.

Finally, and most of all, my heartfelt appreciation goes to my wife, Sheila Webb, and to our children, Samantha, Johanna, and Jake Webb Nordland, who all understood the importance of this book and readily accepted seeing even less of me than usual over the past year and a half.

Kabul, October, 2015

NOTES

All quotations in this book are based on my own interviews unless otherwise indicated in the notes; similarly, factual assertions not based on my own reporting are recorded here.

1: UNDER THE GAZE OF THE BUDDHAS

1. *New York Times,* Mar. 10, 2014, p. A1, www.nytimes.com/2014/03/10/world
   /asia/2-star-crossed-afghans-cling-to-love-even-at-risk-of-death.html.
   Mar. 31, 2014, p. A6, www.nytimes.com/2014/03/31/world/asia/afghan-
   couple-finally-together-but-a-storybook-ending-is-far-from-assured.html.
   Apr. 22, 2014, p. A4, www.nytimes.com/2014/04/22/world/asia/afghan
   -couple-find-idyllic-hide-out-in-mountains-but-not-for-long.html.
   May 4, 2014, p. A10, www.nytimes.com/2014/05/04/world/asia/in-
   spite-of-the-law-afghan-honor-killings-of-women-continue.html.
   May 19, 2014, p. A10, www.nytimes.com/2014/05/19/world/asia/afghan
   -lovers-plight-shaking-up-the-lives-of-those-left-in-their-wake.html.
   June 8, 2014, p. A14, www.nytimes.com/2014/06/08/world/asia/for-
   afghan-lovers-joy-is-brief-ending-in-arrest.html.
2. On the Persian calendar, the year begins on March 21, the first day of
   spring.
3. A permanent terminal building at the Bamiyan Airport was constructed
   with foreign-aid money in 2015.
4. UNESCO website, "Cultural Landscape and Archaeological Remains of
   the Bamiyan Valley," whc.unesco.org/en/list/208.
5. Barbara Crossette, *New York Times,* Mar. 19, 2011. "Taliban Explains

Buddha Demolition," www.nytimes.com/2001/03/19/world/19TALI
.html. The Taliban objected to any representation of human or animal
form, whether statues or artworks, and carried out similar depredations
on objects and paintings in the National Museum of Afghanistan.

6.

زلیخا گر بیرون آرد ز دل آه پشیمانی
زپای یوسف زندانیش زولانه میریزد

7. At least one of the girls remained in the shelter even more than a year
later, as of early 2015, according to sources in the Bamiyan provincial
government. Their names are changed for their protection.

8. تو

9. شما

10. "It's actually considered a shame if someone knows the name of your
wife," said Wazhma Frogh, an Afghan women's activist with the Research Institute for Women, Peace & Security. "No one is allowed to ask
this. We are considered the property of the father, husband, brother—
even your younger brother has the right of ownership over you. You are
not a person, you are the wife of a person, the sister of a person. We are
not considered as human beings in our own rights."

11. One popular joke goes like this: There's a knock on a mullah's door,
and he opens it to see his daughter standing there crying. "What's the
matter?" he asks. She tells him her husband has been beating her. Immediately he slaps her in the face and orders her to go home. Then he calls
her husband and berates him for beating his daughter. "I got even with
you, though," he said. "I smacked your wife. How do you like that?"

2: DEAD FATHER'S DAUGHTER

1. Hazarajat refers to the central highlands of Bamiyan and neighboring provinces, where Hazara people predominate. Some other remote
northern areas such as Badakhshan Province in the far northeast were
also free of Taliban control during that period.

2. The Hazaras were subjected to a campaign of massacres in the nineteenth
century, which they describe as a genocide, followed by their widespread
enslavement by the dominant Pashtuns. The Taliban are mostly Pashtuns.
Hazaras have long been Afghanistan's underclass, but their status has only recently begun to change. See www.hazara.net/hazara/history/slavery.html.

3. Although education was free, having children in school is costly to farm
families because of the reduced labor force.

4. Because of the dubious Afghan belief in the religious sanctity of the
burqa, it can actually be risky for foreign women to wear it, as some of
my female colleagues do in dangerous parts of the country. Wearing it
is an effective disguise only from a good distance. Afghans are quick to
spot foreigners in burqas, either from their shoes or by how they carry
themselves in such an unfamiliar garment. Similarly, male suicide bombers who have tried to dress in a burqa to get close to a target are usually

quickly spotted by Afghan guards. Afghan men often boast that they can tell if a woman is beautiful, even when she is wearing a burqa.

5.

من افراطی نی ام عاشق ترین ام
چرا با دل سیاست میکنی یار

6. The *Night of the Lovers* program's Facebook page is at www.facebook.com /arman.fm/videos.

7. The *Night of the Lovers* program had been running for sixteen months when he was interviewed in June 2015, airing close to a thousand love stories, of which only ten were happy ones—1 percent.

8. Of the 176 prisoners in Badam Bagh Prison in November 2014, according to Qazi Parveen of the Afghan Independent Human Rights Commission, 75 to 85 percent of them are convicted or charged with moral crimes. Seven of the prisoners are pregnant, three have given birth since their incarceration, and forty small children are living with their mothers in the prison. When I visited Badam Bagh on November 14, 2014, the population that day, according to inmate rolls provided by the officials on duty, included seventy-six adultery cases, twenty-two cases of runaways, seven cases of alcohol consumption, and five cases of attempted adultery, or about 65 percent moral cases. Note the runaway charges, despite the abolition, in the EVAW law of 2009, of the charge of running away from home.

9. Official figures on drug use among the Afghan security forces have shown that from 12 to 41 percent of Afghan National Police recruits test positive for illegal drugs, usually hash or opiates. Figures among army soldiers are lower but still worrisome. *New York Times,* May 16, 2010, p. A4, "Sign of Afghan Addiction May Also Be Its Remedy," www.nytimes.com /2010/05/17/world/asia/17afghan.html.

10. Desertion has been the bane of the Afghan military, which loses a third of its force annually to attrition, including casualties, failure to reenlist, and especially desertion, which is so common that the government does not dare to criminalize it. See *New York Times,* Oct. 16, 2012, p. A1, "Afghan Army's Turnover Threatens U.S. Strategy." Further data on attrition can be found in the Brookings Afghanistan Index, www.brookings.edu/~/media /Programs/foreign-policy/afghanistan-index/index20150520.pdf? la=en.

11.

عاشقی آنست که بلبل با رخ گل میکند
صدجفا از خار میبیند تحمل میکند

12.

دو چشمان سیاهی او غانی(افغانی) داری # به دل رحم مسلمانی نداری
شب ها ره روز کردم پشت قلایت یار # چطو خواب است که بیداری نداری

13. A good summary of the EVAW law's provisions is available in this report by the United Nations Assistance Mission in Afghanistan, "A Long Way to Go," Nov. 2011, www.ohchr.org/Documents/Countries/AF/ UNAMA_Nov2011.pdf.

14. UNICEF, "Monitoring the Situation of Women and Children," May 2015. By age fifteen, 15 percent of Afghan girls are married; 40 percent are married before age eighteen. The legal age of marriage under Af-

ghan law is sixteen. See http://data.unicef.org/child-protection/child-marriage.

15.   خواستگاری

16. Khadija's husband, Mohammad Hadi, now lives in Kabul, where he married again at age twenty-three, and says he is not sure whether Khadija was killed or whether she might have escaped from her family; he is reluctant to believe the worst and still loves her, he said. Unfortunately, Mohammad's family was under such threat after the controversy over their marriage that they all relocated to Kabul around the same time that Khadija disappeared.

"She had a lot of courage, she was courageous enough to escape, but we had to flee our home, and she wouldn't know where to find me," Mohammad said. He still hopes that one day Khadija will find him and says his new wife is no impediment. "If she came back, I would live with them both," he said. Marrying up to four wives is legal under shariah law, and having two wives is not uncommon in Afghanistan.

17. The Afghan version mostly tracks the great twelfth-century Persian poet Nezami's epic retelling of the original Arabian story. See "Persian Poetry: Nezami Ganjavi," on the University of Arizona's website at http://persianpoetry.arizona.edu.

18. According to Global Rights, March 2008, "Living with Violence: A National Report on Domestic Abuse in Afghanistan," 58.8 percent of Afghan women are in forced marriages, either arranged marriages to which they objected or marriages made when they were still children. See www.globalrights.org/Library/Women%27s%20rights/Living%20with%20Violence%20Afghan.pdf.

3: ZAKIA MAKES HER MOVE

1. The Afghan Constitution in English (which is the document's mother tongue) can be found at www.afghan-web.com/politics/current_constitution.html. In addition to guaranteeing women the right to education and a share of seats in parliament and provincial councils, Article 22 reads, "The citizens of Afghanistan—whether man or woman—have equal rights and duties before the law."

2. The death penalty is applied only in adultery cases where the woman was married, but Zakia's father later insisted that had been the case with her. In practice, death by stoning usually is not instituted by Afghan courts in adultery cases, although in many instances communities take it upon themselves to impose such punishment.

3. Sabira's case is discussed in more detail beginning on p. 307.

4. June 20, 2015, interview with Ahmad Zia Noori, human-rights specialist for the office of the president, who cited an as-yet-unpublished survey of Afghan lawyers in Kabul Province carried out by the Afghan Independent Human Rights Commission. Kabul would have a gener-

ally much higher level of education than the country at large. The study found that 75 percent of all attorneys and prosecutors employed in the justice system—from whose ranks judges would be appointed—had neither a law-school degree nor even a degree from a shariah-law faculty.

5. Alissa J. Rubin, *New York Times,* Dec. 2, 2012, p. A6, "With Help, Afghan Survivor of 'Honor Killing' Inches Back," www.nytimes.com/ 2012/12/02/world/asia/doctors-and-others-buck-tradition-in-afghan-honor-attack.html.

6. According to the United Nations Population Fund, five thousand girls and women are killed annually in what are deemed to be honor killings, most of them in this part of the world. See UNFPA, The State of World Population 2000, p. 5, www.unfpa.org/sites/default/files/pub-pdf/swp2000_eng.pdf.

7. Afghanistan's public hospitals typically expect patients to pay for supplementary food and for the cost of medications due to budgetary constraints and systematic corruption. In theory that should not happen, since the public-health sector is almost entirely financed by international aid, but corruption and waste prevent much of that financing from reaching beneficiaries.

8. *New York Times,* Aug. 17, 2010, p. A1, "In Bold Display, Taliban Order Stoning Deaths," www.nytimes.com/2010/08/17/world/asia/17stoning .html.

9. *New York Times,* Jan. 31, 2011, p. A4, "Afghan Stoning Video Rekindles Outcry," www.nytimes.com/2011/02/01/world/asia/01stoning.html.

10. Police acted at all only because one of the videos of the stonings was aired on national television, and then arrested only four of the leaders of the executions. "We cannot arrest the whole village," said police chief Abdul Rahman Sayedkhili. "Just a few people in the video were Taliban; the rest of them were there by force and had to obey the Taliban." Their apparent enthusiasm for the stoning suggested otherwise. The fact is, stonings still happen, both in areas under Taliban control and in those under government control. The main difference is that the government goes to great lengths to suppress news about stonings when its people carry them out and is happy to publicize them when the Taliban do so. Around the same time as the stoning case in Dashte Archi District, the council of Muslim religious leaders in Afghanistan, a government-financed body called the Supreme Ulema Council, petitioned the government to allow more shariah-law punishments for social crimes, including the stoning and lashing of adulterers (stoning to death if one party is married, lashing if both are single). See also Human Rights Watch, Afghanistan: "Reject Proposal to Restore Stoning." Nov. 25, 2013, www.hrw.org/ news/2013/11/25/afghanistanreject-proposal-restore-stoning.

11. Another notorious stoning case carried out by the Taliban was in Parwan Province not far from the capital of Kabul, on July 8, 2012, of a woman named Najiba, who it turned out was accused of having an

affair with the Taliban shadow governor of Parwan Province. He was not punished. A video of her murder was posted at www.youtube.com/ watch?v=mNsjgTv-u5o. Many of the participants can be easily identified in the video; none were ever prosecuted, although the stoning took place in an area normally under government control.

12. When I visited the Bamiyan primary court a few weeks after the attack on Zakia, Judge Tamkeen would not come out of his chambers when he heard he had a foreign visitor, but one of the younger judges, Judge Rahman, spoke in his stead. The judges, Judge Rahman said, were not trying to force an adult woman to return to a family against her will but instead were simply implementing shariah law and, under Islam, judges were encouraged to work out amicable family settlements, which is all they were doing in Zakia's case. "Islamic law permits us to find a peaceful solution," he said. He denied that the couple's differing sects and ethnic backgrounds ever figured into the judges' deliberations. "Shariah law does not prevent two people from different sects marrying each other," he said. "You can even marry a Jew or a Christian. There is no legal problem."

He also denied that Zakia's family had threatened to kill her in the February 3 melee in court, despite what numerous other witnesses said. "This is just propaganda," he said. "It never happened."

13. Different women's officials in Baghlan gave different ages for the girl. She herself might not have known and, like most Afghan women and girls, would not have had her own identity papers, so the officials were giving their estimates of what they thought her age to be.

14. *New York Times,* May 4, 2010, p. A4, "In Spite of the Law, Afghan Honor Killings of Women Continue," www.nytimes.com/2014/05/04/world/ asia/in-spite-of-the-law-afghan-honor-killings-of-women-continue .html.

15. This is a reference to Article 398 of the Afghan Penal Code; for more on this article, see p. 90.

16. Mr. Faisal, the provincial councilman who brokered the agreement to return the girl, now denies he did so. He did not even know the family, he said, and was merely making a courtesy call for a militia commander from the girl's village, who phoned and asked him for a favor, to call the women's ministry and ask them to talk to the family.

"I wouldn't do such a thing. I'm not even from that district," Mr. Faisal said. "They never should have sent the girl home with the family under such circumstances."

They never would have done so had Mr. Faisal not loaned the prestige of his name and reputation to vouch for Amina's family, Ms. Atifi said.

"I don't know about that," Mr. Faisal said. "I'm really not in the picture very much."

17. No charges had been brought against anyone for the murder of Amina as of July 2015, according to women's-ministry officials in Baghlan Prov-

ince, although an investigation was said to be still ongoing more than a year after her murder. Authorities said they were hampered due to insurgent activity in the area where Amina's family lived.

18. Guards at the Bamiyan Women's Shelter are actually civilian employees of the institution, men outside and women inside, not police officers.

4: A RABBI AMONG THE MULLAHS

1. *New York Times,* Mar. 10, 2014, p. A1, www.nytimes.com/2014/03/10/world/asia/2-star-crossed-afghans-cling-to-love-even-at-risk-of-death.html.

2. *New York Times,* Sept. 24, 2014, p. A8, "In Farewell Speech, Karzai Calls American Mission in Afghanistan a Betrayal," www.nytimes.com/2014/09/24/world/asia/hamid-karzai-afghanistan.html.

3. Fatima Kazimi's e-mailed note, which was written in English, is reproduced verbatim.

4. *National Geographic,* June 1985. A discussion of that cover's influence is in the magazine's online edition, Oct. 2013, at http://ngm.nationalgeographic.com/2013/10/power-of-photography/draper-text.

   Sharbat Gula's haunting image became iconic, and in Afghanistan it was often borrowed by artists and knockoffs of it are painted and sold in galleries.

   Steve McCurry later found Sharbat Gula in adulthood, hard-used by life in Afghanistan. Cathy Newman, *National Geographic,* Apr. 2002, "A Life Revealed," http://ngm.nationalgeographic.com/2002/04/afghan-girl/index-text?rptregcta=reg_free_np&rptregcampaign=2015012_invitation_ro_all#.

5. "In Afghanistan I could barely look at people," writes the photographer, Lynsey Addario, in her memoir. "I had to constantly remind myself not to look men in the eye." Lynsey Addario, *It's What I Do: A Photographer's Life of Love and War,* page 40. New York: Penguin Press, 2015.

6. Mauricio Lima's portrait of Zakia is in the photo insert.

7. مر على الديار ديار ليلى   أقبل ذا الجدار وذا الجدارا
   وما حب الديار شغفن قلبي   ولكن حب من سكن الديارا

8. *New York Times,* Mar. 31, 2014, p. A6, www.nytimes.com/2014/03/31/world/asia/afghan-couple-finally-together-but-a-storybook-ending-is-far-from-assured.html.

9. *Slate,* Mar. 29, 2001, "Who Is Shmuley Boteach?" www.slate.com/articles/arts/culturebox/2001/03/who_is_shmuley_boteach.html.

10. Formerly the Jewish Values Network. See the organization's website at https://worldvalues.us/about.

11. Shmuley Boteach, *Guardian,* July 5, 2011, "I Saw What Tabloid Life Did to Michael Jackson," www.theguardian.com/commentisfree/2011/jul/05/michael-jackson-rabbi-tabloid-life.

12. Shmuley Boteach, *Kosher Sex: A Recipe for Passion and Intimacy* (New

York: Three Rivers Press/Crown, 2000); and *Kosher Lust: Love Is Not the Answer* (Jerusalem/New York: Gefen Publishing House, 2013).

13. Alissa J. Rubin, *New York Times,* June 27, 2012, p. A4, "Afghan Rape Case Turns Focus on Local Police," www.nytimes.com/2012/06/28/world/asia/afghan-rape-case-turns-focus-on-local-police.html.

14. Jawad Sukhanyar and Alissa J. Rubin, *New York Times,* Nov. 27, 2012, p. A10, "4 Members of Afghan Police Are Found Guilty in Rape," www.nytimes.com/2012/11/08/world/asia/afghan-militia-members-found-guilty-in-rape.html.

5: A BEAUTIFUL PLACE TO HIDE

1. A million afghanis, about eighteen thousand dollars.

2. Women for Afghan Women's website is at www.womenforafghanwomen.org.

3.   ناموس

4. Article 398 reads, "If a person sees his wife or any of his female relatives in the state of committing adultery, or sharing a bed with another person, and in defense of his honor abruptly kills or injures one or both of them, he is exempted from the punishments of death or lashings, and will be given the punishment of imprisonment for not more than two years."

شخصیکه به اثر دفاع از ناموس زوجه ویا یکی از محارم خودرا در حالت تلبس به زنا وجود اورا با شخصی غیر در یک بستر مشاهده و فلحال هردو ویا یکی از آنها را به قتل رساند یا مجروح سازد - از جزای قتل و جرح معاف اما تعزیراً حسب احوال به حبسیکه از دوسال بیشتر نباشد محکوم میگردد.

5. Online video about the lovers by the *New York Times:* "On the Run in the Hindu Kush," http://t.co/9tJ29wsUqe; "Video Notebook," http://nyti.ms/1nbHO4q; "Searching for Zakia and Mohammad Ali," http://nyti.ms/1jIRjRx.

6. Several NGOs, including the Aga Khan Development Network (www.akdn.org/afghanistan), have been pouring money into developing skiing in Bamiyan, including programs to train Afghan women in a sport that even Afghan men have never participated in ("female empowerment" programs of almost any nature are guaranteed generous Western funding). It also requires learning how to ski or snowshoe uphill, since there are no real lifts; Afghanistan's mountains are far too craggy and often too dry, even in winter, to have ever fostered any sort of alpine or snow sports. In the winter of 2014–15, commercial flights by East Horizon Airlines into Bamiyan were canceled for aircraft repairs, though a few foolhardy Western skiers still came along a highway from Kabul that was periodically threatened by Taliban roadblocks.

7. The Mountain to Mountain organization's website is at http://mountain2mountain.com. See also Molly Hurford, *Bicycling,* Feb. 12, 2015, "Afghan Cycles, Mountain to Mountain, and Pedaling a Revolution," www

.bicycling.com/culture/afghan-cycles-mountain-mountain-and-pedaling-revolution.

8. Habiba Sarobi, governor of Bamiyan Province, was at the time the only woman governor in Afghanistan; she stepped down to run unsuccessfully for vice president in 2014.

9. That year Ben Solomon would go on to share in the paper's Pulitzer Prize for its coverage of the Ebola epidemic.

10. Amina's case is discussed in detail in chapter 3, beginning on p. 65.

11. *New York Times,* Aug. 5, 2010, p. A6, "Portrait of Pain Ignites Debate Over Afghan War," www.nytimes.com/2010/08/05/world/asia/05afghan.html. See also *Time,* Aug. 9, 2010, "What Happens If We Leave Afghanistan," http://content.time.com/time/covers/0,16641,20100809,00.html.

12. More on Soheila's case can be found in chapter 14.

13. John F. Burns, *New York Times,* Feb. 14, 1996, "Cold War Afghans Inherit a Brutal New Age," www.nytimes.com/1996/02/14/world/fiercely-faithful-special-report-cold-war-afghans-inherit-brutal-new-age.html.

14. راشه ګلی راشه
راشه ګلی راشه چه سینه درته پاره کومه
زله دخپل ځکاره کومه۔ زله دخپل ځکاره

15. "On the Run in the Hindu Kush," http://t.co/9tJ29wsUqe.

16. Diego Ibarra Sánchez's photos of Zakia and Ali are in the photo insert. His sunbeam-lit portrait of them is on the book jacket.

17. *New York Times,* Apr. 22, 2014, p. A4, http://www.nytimes.com/2014/04/22/world/asia/afghan-couple-find-idyllic-hide-out-in-mountains-but-not-for-long.html.

6: MYSTERY BENEFACTOR

1. For example: The lowest-paid employee at the *New York Times* bureau, a cleaner, makes five hundred dollars a month, the pay of a colonel in the national police. The bureau lost a two-thousand-dollar-a-month Afghan journalist to the Ministry of Interior, where salary supplements underwritten by foreign donors brought his pay as a public-relations adviser to five thousand a month—more than the usual starting salary for that profession in America, but a fortune in Afghanistan, where two hundred dollars a month is considered a livable wage.

2. Special Inspector General for Afghan Reconstruction (SIGAR), Quarterly Report to Congress, Jan. 30, 2015, www.sigar.mil/pdf/quarterlyreports/2015-01-30qr.pdf.

3. SIGAR Quarterly Report, Apr. 30, 2014, www.sigar.mil/pdf/quarterlyreports/2014-04-30qr.pdf.

4. BBC News online, Mar. 8, 2013, "Zinat Karzai, Afghanistan's 'Invisible' First Lady," www.bbc.com/news/world-asia-21699353.

5. WAW has offices in the United States and in Afghanistan, where it runs

an extensive network of shelters and other facilities dedicated to helping Afghan women. See www.womenforafghanwomen.org.

6. Alissa J. Rubin, *New York Times,* Mar. 3, 2014, p. A1, "A Thin Line of Defense against Honor Killings," www.nytimes.com/2015/03/03/world/asia/afghanistan-a-thin-line-of-defense-against-honor-killings.html.

7. United Nations High Commissioner for Refugees website, "2015 UNHCR country operations profile, Islamic Republic of Iran," at www.unhcr.org/pages/49e486f96.html.

8. Bakhtar News Agency, www.bakhtarnews.com.af/eng/politics/item/241-deadline-for-afghan-refugees-in-iran-will-remain-open.html.

9. Human Rights Watch, "Unwelcome Guests: Iran's Violation of Afghan Refugee and Migrant Rights," Nov. 2013, www.hrw.org/sites/default/files/reports/iran1113_forUpload_0.pdf.

10. Joseph Goldstein, *New York Times,* Dec. 11, 2014, p. A1, "For Afghans, Name and Birthdate Census Questions Are Not So Simple," www.nytimes.com/2014/12/11/world/asia/for-afghans-name-and-birthdate-census-questions-are-not-so-simple.html.

11. Western Union also requires a last name; the field cannot be blank. Afghan banks accept the father's tribal name in that field if it shows up on the person's *tazkera,* so in Ali's case he was first name Mohammad Ali, last name Sarwari.

12. *New York Times,* Apr. 22, 2014, p. A4, www.nytimes.com/2014/04/22/world/asia/afghan-couple-find-idyllic-hide-out-in-mountains-but-not-for-long.html.

13. *New York Times,* Mar. 31, 2014, p. A6, www.nytimes.com/2014/03/31/world/asia/afghan-couple-finally-together-but-a-storybook-ending-is-far-from-assured.html.

14. According to a source in the Bamiyan women's ministry who preferred not to be identified.

15. May 4, 2014. p. A10,www.nytimes.com/2014/05/04/world/asia/in-spite-of-the-law-afghan-honor-killings-of-women-continue.html.

16. *Time,* Aug. 9, 2010, "What Happens If We Leave Afghanistan," http://content.time.com/time/covers/0,16641,20100809,00.html.

17. UN Dispatch, 2011, "Afghan Government Cracks Down on Women's Shelters," www.undispatch.com/afghan-government-cracks-down-on-womens-shelters.

18. Maria Abi-Habib, *Wall Street Journal,* Aug. 3, 2010, "TV Host Targets Afghan Women's Shelters," www.wsj.com/articles/SB100014240527487048750045753749842918665528.

19. *New York Times,* Feb. 15, 2011, "Afghan Official Says Women's Shelters Are Corrupt," www.nytimes.com/2011/02/16/world/asia/16afghanistan.html.

20. At the time the contractor was known as DPK Consulting, but is now Tetra Tech DPK. It is one of a host of private aid contractors, most of them moneymaking entities whether or not they are officially nonprofits; none of them are considered by the United Nations and the NGO com-

munity to be independent, charitable aid organizations. They often act as the implementing agencies for government bodies, particularly for the biggest donor in Afghanistan, USAID. See www.tetratechdpk.com/en/countries/11-asia/72-afghanistan.html.

21. Literacy among recruits to the Afghan National Police is 10 percent, even lower than the Afghan population's literacy rate of 15 percent (38 percent among those over age fifteen). See *New York Times,* Feb. 2, 2010, "With Raw Recruits, Afghan Police Buildup Falters," www.nytimes.com/2010/02/03/world/asia/03afghan.html. Literacy data can be found in the *CIA World Factbook,* "Afghanistan," online at www.cia.gov/library/publications/the-world-factbook/geos/af.html.

22. *New York Times,* Sept. 25, 2010, p. A4, "Afghan Equality and Law, with Strings Attached," www.nytimes.com/2010/09/25/world/asia/25kite.html.

23. *New York Times,* May 26, 2013, p. A10, "Foreign Projects Give Afghans Fashion, Skate Park and Now 10,000 Balloons," www.nytimes.com/2013/05/26/world/asia/western-aid-finances-afghan-projects-from-silly-to-sublime.html.

24. Ibid. A trenchant correction was appended to this piece: "An earlier version of this article misidentified the 'Sesame Street' character with whom Ryan C. Crocker, the former United States ambassador, was photographed in Kabul. It was Grover, not Cookie Monster."

25. A typical press conference in Kabul, such as a presentation by the minister for counter-narcotics or the governor of Khost Province, would feature more than twenty television crews, with at most one or two of those from foreign outlets.

26.   گرزلف پریشانت در دست صبا افتد
                                                                    هرجاکه دلی باشد در دام بلا افتد
                                                                    گرزلف پریشانت در دست صبا افتد

7: HONOR HUNTERS

1. There is a further discussion of this topic in The Jihad Against Women, particularly on pp. 271–73.

2. Huma Ahmed-Ghosh, *Journal of International Women's Studies,* vol. 4, issue 3, p. 2, "A History of Women in Afghanistan: Lessons Learnt for the Future." The author blamed Afghanistan's lack of gender equality on "the patriarchal nature of gender and social relations deeply embedded in traditional communities" and "the existence of a weak central state, that has been unable to implement modernizing programs and goals in the face of tribal feudalism."

3. Ibid., p. 14.

4. Ibid., p. 7. "Thus the two so-called progressive eras of the 1920s and 1970s, while attempting to improve women's status were not only unsuccessful but also led to violent, fundamentalist backlashes by subsequent

governments. In both periods, tribal leaders who objected to the redefining of women by the state and the diminution of their general authority initiated the disruption of the modernization process."

5. See The Jihad Against Women, from p. 253, for a fuller discussion of this issue.

6. On several occasions during Afghanistan's civil war, mujahideen had also tried to destroy the Bamiyan Buddhas, blasting away at them with artillery and defiling ancient Buddhist shrines nearby.

7. Matthew A. Goldstein, *Politics and the Life Sciences,* vol. 21, issue 2 (2002): pp. 28–37, "The Biological Roots of Heat-of-passion Crimes and Honour Killings."

8. Thomas Barfield, *Afghanistan: A Cultural and Political History* (Princeton, NJ: Princeton University Press, 2010).

9. See also the 1977 British documentary *Death of a Princess,* about a Saudi princess executed for sex out of wedlock, on orders of her grandfather, discussed in a Harvard White Paper, available at http://pirp.harvard.edu/pubs_pdf/white/white-p83-9.pdf.

   In a 2009 case, asylum was granted another Saudi princess in Britain on grounds that she would be subjected to death by stoning for having committed adultery. See http://news.bbc.co.uk/2/hi/uk_news/8158576.stm.

10. Department of Justice, Canada, Monograph, Jan. 7, 2015, "Preliminary Examination of So-called 'Honour Killings' in Canada."

11. Only 38 percent of the population over the age of fifteen can read and write. *CIA World Factbook,* www.cia.gov/library/publications/the-world-factbook/geos/af.html.

12. United Nations Special Rapporteur for Afghanistan, Commission of Human Rights, 2006 report, http://daccess-dds-ny.un.org/doc/UNDOC/GEN/G06/108/09/PDF/G0610809.pdf?OpenElement. "The current trends in violence against women in Afghanistan cannot be solely reduced to culture and tradition without consideration of the conflict and post-conflict situation" and "Moreover, the limits the traditional normative framework placed on the exercise of male power over women, reigning in mere arbitrariness, have to a large extent been washed away by 23 years of boundless war, which has disintegrated the social fabric of the society. When the rule of power, be it in the hands of State or non-State actors, replaces the rule of law, the highest price is paid by those with the least power, particularly women and children. In this context, many actors deform Islam and culture from a source of justice and fairness into a justification for their tyrannical acts against women."

13. This is true in Pakistan as well, particularly in the North-West Frontier Provinces, which are populated predominantly by Pashtun tribals who closely identify with the Pashtun plurality in Afghanistan. There are also high rates of honor killings in other sectors of Pakistani society, arguably as bad as or worse than in Afghanistan.

14. It was Gulnaz's word against the man's, and he maintained it was consensual sex, not rape, even though she was fifteen at the time and had been bound hand and foot during the episode. The judge believed the man.

15. Alissa J. Rubin, *New York Times,* Dec. 2, 2011, p. A1, "For Afghan Woman, Justice Runs into Unforgiving Wall of Custom," www.nytimes .com/2011/12/02/world/asia/for-afghan-woman-justice-runs-into-the -static-wall-of-custom.html.

16. European Union External Action, "Factsheet," Mar. 8, 2015, "EU Support to Promoting Women Leaders," www.eeas.europa.eu/factsheets/ docs/150308_01_factsheet_promoting_women_leaders_en.pdf.

17. Video highlights of the 2014 World Values Network Gala are at https:// youtu.be/YnxEEeuC2RM.

18. Human Rights Watch, *World Report 2015,* Rwanda, www.hrw.org/ world-report/2015/country-chapters/rwanda.

8: THE IRRECONCILABLES

1.

مخور غم گذشته
گذشته ها گذشته
هرگز به غصه خوردن
گذشته بر نگشته
به فکر آینده باش
دلشاد و سر زنده باش
به انتظار طلعت خورشید تابنده باش

2. Amina's case is discussed in more detail in chapter 3.
3. Siddiqa's case is discussed in more detail in chapter 3.
4. Khadija's case is discussed in more detail in chapter 2.

9: BIRDS IN A CAGE

1. The word *hejab* is used in Afghanistan to refer to the full-length black robes that cover everything but a woman's face or sometimes everything but the eyes; in other places this would be called an *abaya* or a chador, while the term *hejab* or hijab normally refers to an Islamic head scarf for women.

2.

درد بلات غصه هات به جونم
نزار بیشتر از این چشم برات بمانم
درد بلات غصه هات به جونم
نزار بیشتر از این چشم ر ات بمانم
مجنون ام - مجنون ام
عاشقانه میخونم
مجنونم - مجنونم
بی تو من نمیتونم

3. "His Juliet thinks she is pregnant with her Romeo's child. So much for the good news." See *New York Times,* June 8, 2014, p. A14, www.ny times.com/2014/06/08/world/asia/for-afghan-lovers-joy-is-brief-ending-in-arrest.html.

4. An Afghan National Police district is similar to a precinct in a big American city; Kabul has sixteen of them.

5. Embassy of Afghanistan, Washington, D.C., press release, "Afghanistan Ministry Designates First Female Police Chief in the Country," www.embassyofafghanistan.org/article/afghan-ministry-of-interior-designates-first-female-police-chief-in-the-country. See also International Security Assistance Force, press release, July 7, 2014, "Afghan Police Academy graduates 51 female officers," www.isaf.nato.int/article/isaf-news/isaf-generals-attend-female-anp-academy-graduation.html.

6. Alissa J. Rubin, *New York Times,* Mar. 2, 2015, "Afghan Policewomen Struggle Against Culture," www.nytimes.com/2015/03/02/world/asia/afghan-policewomen-struggle-against-culture.html.

7. The website Good Afghan News, Mar. 10, 2010, shows Shafiqa Quraishi receiving the International Women of Courage Award from Hillary Clinton and Michelle Obama. See www.goodafghannews.com/2010/03/10/shukria-asil-and-shafiqa-quraishi-of-afghanistan-at-the-the-2010-international-women-of-courage-awards-event.

8. See p. 281 for more on Jamila Bayaz's case. She was dismissed from her post as police chief in 2015.

10: RELUCTANT CELEBRITIES

1. Most other organizations running women's shelters in Afghanistan, including the UN Women organization, shun publicity no matter how horrendous and hopeless the cases they handle.

2. Ms. Ghazanfar's main point was that violence against women in Afghanistan was a minor problem, no different from violence against women in developed countries, and that the EVAW law was doing a terrific job of improving the situation even though there had been little need for improvement, and so on in that vein.

3. *New York Times,* May 19, 2014, p. A10, "Afghan Lovers' Plight Shaking Up Lives of Those Left in Their Wake," www.nytimes.com/2014/05/19/world/asia/afghan-lovers-plight-shaking-up-the-lives-of-those-left-in-their-wake.html.

4. President Karzai did give an interview to freelancer Elizabeth Rubin for the *New York Times Magazine* in 2009 (Aug. 9, "Karzai in His Labyrinth"), but not to the newspaper itself. See www.nytimes.com/2009/08/09/magazine/09Karzai-t.html. Mr. Karzai was finally interviewed by the paper on June 16, 2015, p. A4, "Karzai, Vowing That He's Done, Discusses His Afghan Legacy," www.nytimes.com/2015/06/16/world/asia/ex-president-karzai-vows-he-is-out-of-afghanistans-politics.html.

5. As those efforts were abandoned, in my case, and overturned in Azam Ahmed's case, using the government's own legal procedures, the *Times* elected not to provoke the government by making a public issue out of

their efforts. In my case American diplomats had persuaded government officials that expelling the paper's Kabul bureau chief, which I was at the time, would be unwise. Mr. Karzai later personally approved Matthew Rosenberg's expulsion.

6. *New York Times,* Aug. 21, 2015, p. A4, "Calling Article 'Divisive,' Afghanistan Orders Expulsion of Times Correspondent," www.nytimes .com/2014/08/21/world/asia/afghanistan-orders-expulsion-of-new-york-times-correspondent.html.

7. A couple typical Facebook pages (most are in Dari): www.facebook.com/pages/Campaign-for-Supporting-Afghan-Lovers/1498540123693615 and http://on.fb.me/1BaiRht.

8. June 11, 2014.

9. Zakia and Ali, in order to qualify for asylum, would first have to apply for refugee status in a neighboring country (or any country they could manage to reach). Then they would have to demonstrate a well-founded fear of persecution, based on at least one recognized criterion: persecution because of political, racial, ethnic, or religious reasons or membership in a persecuted social group. They qualified on four of those criteria: ethnic and religious, since opposition to their wedding was based on the fact that she was Tajik and he was Hazara and she Sunni and he Shia; racial, because Hazaras are racially distinct from Tajiks; and membership in a persecuted social group, in this case, Afghans who insist on choosing their own mates. So they would probably be processed fairly quickly and granted asylum in one of those neighboring countries, which could be India, Pakistan, or Tajikistan; it could not be Iran, which prohibits new refugee-asylum applications.

Once they were in a neighboring country and registered as refugees, it would technically be up to UNHCR to decide which country was most appropriate for the couple's resettlement, and American officials had insisted that a more appropriate country would be somewhere like Sweden, which has generous language and literacy programs as well as welfare support for refugees who are illiterate. In the United States, it is sink or swim for refugees; even legal immigrants get only a couple thousand dollars and a volunteer sponsor to show them around. The couple's situation was different, though, in that they had willing sponsors in America and ones with substantial means, which few refugees normally have.

10. United States Citizenship and Immigration Services, "Humanitarian Parole," contains an outline of the law on humanitarian parole at www.uscis .gov/humanitarian/humanitarian-parole.

11. The Grossman Burn Center, press release, Aug. 31, 2010, "Mutilated Afghan girl comes to L.A. for treatment," www.grossmanburncenter .com/mutilated-afghan-girl-comes-to-la-for-treatment.php.

11: BACK TO THE HINDU KUSH

1.
گنجشکک طلایی به نزد یار مایی
گنجشکک طلایی به نزد یار مایی
من ام به انتظار ات
بگو که کی می آیی – بگو که کی می آیی
بیا از پیش دلبرم
بخوان تو به نور و برم – حوال بیار حوال ببر
قاصدک خوش باورم – قاصدک خوش باورم

2.
من نگویم که مرا از قفس آزاد کنید
آزاد کنید – آزاد کنید
قفسم برده به باغی و دلم شادکنید
دلم شادکنید – دلم شاد کنید
یاد از این مرغ گرفتار کنید ای صیاد
یاد از این مرغ گرفتار کنید ای صیاد
بنشیند به باغی و مرا یاد کنید

3. The singer's official website, www.ahmadzahir.com/sub/biography.html, includes an account of his assassination. A *New York Times* account on Mar. 20, 2003, by Amy Waldman has a differing version of Zahir's death. See www.nytimes.com/2003/03/20/world/kabul-journal-the-afghan-elvis-lives-24-years-after-his-death.html.

12: MULLAH MOHAMMAD JAN

1. BBC News, "Afghan 'Romeo and Juliet' Still Fear for Their Lives," Aug. 11, 2014, online video at www.bbc.co.uk/news/world-asia-28662822.

2. Azam Ahmed and Matthew Rosenberg, *New York Times,* Jan. 19, 2014, p. A8, "Deadly Attack at Kabul Restaurant Hints at Changing Climate for Foreigners," www.nytimes.com/2014/01/19/world/asia/afghanistan-restaurant-attack.html.

3. International Organization for Migration, World Migration chart, 2014, at www.iom.int/world-migration. See also the website of Statistics Canada, National Household Survey, 2011, www12.statcan.gc.ca/nhs-enm/2011/dp-pd/prof/details/page.cfm?Lang=E&Geo1=PR&Code1=0 1&Data=Count&SearchText=Langley&SearchType=Begins&SearchPR =01&A1=Ethnic%20origin&B1=All&Custom=&TABID=1.

4.
عاشقی آنست که با بلبل با رخ گل میکند
صدجفا از خار میبیند تحمل میکند

5. Ali had taken out a ringtone subscription with the cell-phone carrier; he paid Etisalat a fee of fifty afghanis to join their ringtone plan, to download unlimited tunes, and then five afghanis (about ten U.S. cents) to renew the plan each month. The menus were voice-guided, so he could work his way through them without needing to read.

6.
جگرمه

7. Technically this is not a mortgage, because the loan of money at interest is considered un-Islamic and most devout Afghans will not do it. Instead

the creditor gets the use of the land and any profit from it, which potentially could earn the creditor as much as or more than interest would, but that would depend on how well they worked the land and how good the harvest was, so it is considered a religiously acceptable workaround. Once the debtor repaid the principal, the land would return to him without interest charges.

8. A Western mind might shudder at the thought of such widespread corruption, but by and large the Afghans do not see things that way. Bribery is such a part of public life that most uneducated people without connections would assume that was the only way to try to influence events. For them it is more of a way of life than a criminal act.

9.

مسافری عجب دلگیر و زار است
اگر شازاده باشه خوار و زار است
مسافری عجب دلگیر و زار است
اگر شازاده باشه خوار و زار است
هزاران توشک و قالینچه باشد
به زیر پایکایش مانند خار است

10.

بیا که بریم به مزار ملامحمد جان
سیل گل لاله زار واه واه دلبرجان
سیل گل لاله زار واه واه دلبرجان
*
برو بیار بگو یار تو آمد
گل نرگس خریدار تو آمد – گل نرگس خریدار تو آمد
*
سری کوی بلند فریاد کردم
علی شیر خدا را یاد کردم
علی شیر خدا دردم دوا کن
مناجات مرا پیش خدا کن
*
برو با یار بگو چشم تو روش
همان یار وفادار تو آمد – همان یار وفادار تو آمد

11. Afghanistan ranks as 172nd-worst out of 177 countries studied in 2014, while Tajikistan was 162nd. See Transparency International infographic, Corruption Perceptions Index, www.transparency.org/cpi2014/infographic.

12. Matthew Rosenberg, *New York Times,* Mar. 17, 2014, p. A3, "Facts Elusive in Kabul Death of Swedish Reporter," www.nytimes.com/2014/03/17/world/asia/facts-elusive-in-kabul-death-of-swedish-reporter.html.

13. We were unable to determine the source of this verse.

14.

اگر دورم ز دیدارت
دلیل بی فایی نیست
وفا آنست که نامت را همیشه زیر لب دارم

13: IN THE LAND OF THE BOTTOM-FEEDERS

1. The State Department cable, unearthed by Wikileaks, was published online by the *Guardian* at www.guardian.co.uk/world/us-embassy-cables-documents/248969.

2. In addition, the businessman, who spoke in confidence because he still has relatives living in Tajikistan, was forced by the tax collector to pay his taxes into the collector's private bank account and then was later charged with tax evasion for not having paid the taxes to the government; when he complained, he was charged with extortion and defamation as well. "They are the most insanely greedy people I have ever seen," he said. "They make the Afghans look like the Swiss." He managed to bribe his way over the border, abandoning his investments. I met him a few months after his escape.

3. Eurasia.net online news report, Aug. 25, 2011, www.eurasianet.org/node/64092. The leaked State Department cable can be found at https://wikileaks.org/cable/2006/12/06DUSHANBE2191.html.

4. Piedras Negras, Mexico; Doha, Qatar; and Jeddah, Saudi Arabia, all have bigger flags than Tajikistan. See www.guinnessworldrecords.com/world-records/largest-flag-flown.

5. Under Tajikistan's laws "Refugee Status Determinations" are not made by UNHCR, as is normally done in most countries, but rather by the Tajik government, in effect, operating through the Rights and Prosperity NGO under the pretense that the organization is independent of the government, which it is not. That allows the Tajik authorities to greatly limit how many refugees are given legal status, and it also provides them with much greater opportunities for extortion and abuse of asylum seekers and refugees.

6. UNHCR officials were aware of the problem with refugee applications in Tajikistan, said Babar Baloch, a spokesman. "In some instances asylum seekers may face harassment, arbitrary detention, and deportation. We have raised these concerns with the Tajik authorities in line with UNHCR's mandate and remain actively engaged to support Tajikistan in applying asylum procedures according to the 1951 Refugee Convention and within the adopted Tajik refugee law."

14: A DOG WITH NO NAME

1. *Takfiri* is an epithet used to refer to extremist Sunnis who accuse Shias of being apostates and not true Muslims. Besides the Taliban, other *takfiris* include the Islamic State, or ISIS, and Al-Qaeda extremists.

2. Afghanistan had a birthrate of 3.88 percent in 2014. See *CIA World Factbook,* Afghanistan, available online at www.cia.gov/library/publications/the-world-factbook/geos/af.html.

3. See the website of Development and Support of Afghan Women and Children Organization at http://dsawco.org/eng.

4. *New York Times,* Mar. 9, 2015, p. A7, "Back in Afghanistan Modern Romeo and Juliet Face Grave Risks," www.nytimes.com/2015/03/08/world/back-in-afghanistan-modern-romeo-and-juliet-face-grave-risks.html.

5. *New York Times,* Oct. 20, 2014, p. A6, "Bartered Away at Age 5, Now Trying to Escape to a Life She Chooses," www.nytimes.com/2014/10/20/world/asia/times-video-presents-to-kill-a-sparrow.html. This is not the same Soheila as the girl from Kabul who eloped to Pakistan, discussed earlier in this chapter. Both use only one name.

6. Her family considered her married at age five, but consummation of the marriage would not take place until after the wedding ceremony, when she had reached legal age; in many families that would happen after puberty, although in Soheila's case it was to be at age sixteen, the country's legal age of consent. That also enabled the family to deny in court that she had been illegally married at age five. And it guaranteed the other side that she could not back out of the arrangement when she got older, because in the eyes of Islam, in their view, she was already legally married.

7. Healthy life expectancy in Afghanistan is 48.5 years for men, 46 years for women, according to the United Nations Development Program's Human Development Index for 2014 at http://hdr.undp.org/en/content/human-development-index-hdi.

8. Center for Investigative Reporting, *To Kill a Sparrow,* video at http://cironline.org/feature/kill-sparrow.

9. Nobody ever thought to show Soheila the Iranian filmmaker's video; apparently miffed by restrictions imposed on her filming, Ms. Soleimani left any actual mention of Women for Afghan Women out of it, even though the group had saved both Soheila and her husband from prison, won her legal case, sheltered her for four years during threats and attacks, and finally made it possible for them to marry officially and formally. The young woman first saw it, downloaded on an iPhone, when I interviewed her in WAW's offices. At first she was entranced and interested, though stunned to see how young she'd been when the filming started in the shelter—realizing how much of her youth she'd spent there, protected from her father and brother but not really free. She watched from behind a veil pulled mostly across her face, for modesty and in an attempt to hide her emotions. There is a very touching scene early on when her father, Rahimullah, having put her in prison, along with her young child, with his bogus accusations of bigamy and adultery, comes to visit her there. While playing with his grandson, then a toddler, he talks fulsomely about how Islam decrees that daughters should obey their fathers, who are the only ones who can choose their mates for them. As he plays with her son, it's as if she were seeing what might have been if her father had something more than misogyny in his heart, and she wept. Later her father demanded that she kill her son if she wanted to reconcile with the family. Then her half brother Aminullah appears on the screen vowing to kill her. She pushed the phone aside in disgust and refused to watch any more.

See also *New York Times,* Times Video, *To Kill a Sparrow,* www.nytimes

.com/2014/10/20/world/asia/times-video-presents-to-kill-a-sparrow
.html.

EPILOGUE

1. The Persian year 1394 began on March 21, 2015.

THE JIHAD AGAINST WOMEN

1. Every important local official in the country, from the governors of the more than three hundred districts to the police chiefs in rural provinces, was appointed in Kabul and still is.
2. Amanullah Khan's reign is discussed in more detail in chapter 7. See also Abdullah Qazi, Afghanistan Online, Apr. 24, 2011, "Plight of the Afghan Woman, Afghan Women's History," www.afghan-web.com/woman/afghanwomenhistory.html.
3. Afghan airlines now use mostly foreign women or men as flight attendants.
4. George Crile, *Charlie Wilson's War: The Extraordinary Story of the Largest Covert Operation in History* (New York: Atlantic Monthly Press, 2003). Reissued as *Charlie Wilson's War: The Extraordinary Story of How the Wildest Man in Congress and a Rogue CIA Agent Changed the History of Our Times* (New York: Grove Press, 2007).
5. See the website of Afghanistan National Institute of Music at www .afghanistannationalinstituteofmusic.org.
6. See the website of Razia's Ray of Hope Foundation, "Women and Girls in Afghanistan," at https://raziasrayofhope.org/women-and-girls-in-afghanistan.html. The World Bank's website, at http://datatopics.world bank.org/gender/country/afghanistan, says that 17.8 percent of workers in nonagricultural sectors are women, but that is based on statistics from the 1990s, and the Ministry of Women's Affairs of the Afghan government says it does not have current data for female nonagricultural employment, which seems implausible. More than three-fourths of women are agricultural laborers, nearly all of them unpaid, whereas among men half of those who work on farms receive pay for doing so, according to World Bank and UN data. My own impression from regularly seeing workers heading out of their workplaces in Kabul, where working women are more numerous than elsewhere, is that fewer than 10 percent of urban workers are female, even in the capital. See also Ministry of Women's Affairs and United Nations Development Program monograph, "Women and Men in Afghanistan, Baseline Statistics on Gender," 2008, p. 32, www.refworld.org/pdfid/4a7959272.pdf.
7. In December 2014 a suicide bomber struck a concert that Dr. Sarmast's students were staging at the French Institute in Kabul; the Taliban later announced that he had been the target. The concert had been called "Heart-

beat: Silence after the Explosion" and was intended to be a condemnation of suicide bombing. One person was killed, a German in the audience. Dr. Sarmast's hearing was damaged in the blast, but he went back to teaching and running the music institute, in between surgeries on his ears. See BBC News online, Dec. 11, 2014, "Kabul suicide bomber attacks French school during show," www.bbc.com/news/world-asia-30431830. See also Sune Engel Rasmussen, *Guardian,* May 25, 2015, "He was the saviour of Afghan music. Then a Taliban bomb took his hearing," www.the guardian.com/world/2015/may/25/he-was-the-saviour-of-afghan-music-then-a-taliban-bomb-took-his-hearing.

8. Sergey, the Russian POW, human mine detector, and mujahideen rape victim, was seriously wounded in the blast but not killed; the bomb he tripped was intended to maim. Mines that kill remove one person from the battlefield; those that maim remove three, the victim and two people to carry him out. The maimed victims are also a demoralizing advertisement to their comrades.

   To their credit, the muj did evacuate Sergey for medical treatment that saved his life. They said he deserved as much for having told them the truth, that he had not known where the mines had been put.

9. Global Rights, Mar. 2008, "Living with Violence: A National Report on Domestic Abuse in Afghanistan." This large-scale survey of Afghan women, mostly married women, the most comprehensive ever carried out, revealed that 11.2 percent of them had been raped, 17.2 percent had suffered sexual violence, 39.3 percent had been beaten by their husbands within the previous year, 58.8 percent were in forced marriages (arranged marriages to which they objected or that took place when they were underage), 73.9 percent had suffered psychological abuse from their spouse, and 87.2 percent had been subjected to either physical, sexual, or psychological abuse. See www.globalrights.org/Library/Women%27s%20rights/Living%20with%20Violence%20Afghan.pdf.

10. Ibid., p. 17.

11. U.S. Department of Justice, Bureau of Justice Statistics, "Female Victims of Sexual Violence, 1994–2010, Special Report," Mar. 2013, www.bjs.gov/content/pub/pdf/fvsv9410.pdf.

12. United Nations Assistance Mission in Afghanistan, report of the United Nations Office of the High Commissioner of Human Rights, Apr. 2015, "Justice Through the Eyes of Afghan Women," https://goo.gl/RhsrTS. See also Ministry of Women's Affairs, Afghanistan, Mar. 2014, "First Report on the Elimination of Violence Against Women (EVAW) Law in Afghanistan," http://goo.gl/DgrYPb.

13. United Nations Office of the High Commissioner for Human Rights, "Report of the Special Rapporteur on Violence Against Women, Its Causes and Consequences," May 23, 2012, pp. 73–75, www.ohchr.org/Documents/Issues/Women/A.HRC.20.16_En.pdf.

14. Office of the President, Islamic Republic of Afghanistan, Press Release,

May 30, 2015, "President Ghani: Women's Rights Shall Not Be Compromised for Peace," http://president.gov.af/en/news/47135. See also Sune Engel Rasmussen, *Guardian,* Nov. 6, 2014, "Rula Ghani, the Woman Making Waves as Afghanistan's New First Lady," www.theguardian.com/world/2014/nov/06/rula-ghani-afghan-first-lady.

15. Afghanistan during the two Karzai administrations had only three other women cabinet ministers: Husn Banu Ghazanfar, women's-affairs minister, who was unmarried; Soraya Dalil, public-health minister; and Amina Afzali, youth minister.

16. Margherita Stancati, *Wall Street Journal,* July 5, 2013, online, "Afghan Women Fear Rights Slipping Away," www.wsj.com/articles/SB10001424127887324853704578587491774651104.

17. Dr. Massouda Jalal, Asia Society, "Women's Leadership in Afghanistan's Reconstruction," Sept. 8, 2005, http://asiasociety.org/womens-leadership-afghanistans-reconstruction.

18. The Afghan EVAW law is detailed in the English-language brochure *Know Your Rights and Duties: The Law on the Elimination of Violence against Women,* Aug. 1, 2009, www.humanitarianresponse.info/system/files/documents/files/Know%20Your%20Rights%20and%20Duties%20-%20The%20Law%20on%20Elimination%20of%20Violence%20Against%20Women%20(English),%20IDLO.pdf.

19. The same year that the EVAW law was enacted, Mr. Karzai also enacted a law limiting the rights of Shia women. See Human Rights Watch, "Law Curbing Women's Rights Takes Effect," Aug. 13, 2009, www.hrw.org/news/2009/08/13/afghanistan-law-curbing-women-s-rights-takes-effect.

20. See also the discussion of Article 398 of the Afghan Penal Code in chapter 5.

21. Relief Web, Oct. 21, 2002, IRIN, "Afghanistan: Focus on the Plight of Widows," http://reliefweb.int/report/afghanistan/afghanistan-focus-plight-widows.

22. John F. Burns, *New York Times,* Oct. 4, 1996, "Walled In, Shrouded and Angry in Afghanistan," www.nytimes.com/1996/10/04/world/walled-in-shrouded-and-angry-in-afghanistan.html.

23. Jason Burke, *London Review of Books,* vol. 23, no. 6, Mar. 22, 2001, "Diary," www.lrb.co.uk/v23/n06/jason-burke/diary.

24. Video of Zarmeena's execution can be found at www.youtube.com/watch?v=G4l267pCGdA or on the RAWA website at www.rawa.org/temp/runews., with the actual execution video at http://www.rawa.org/zarmeena.htm.

25. Barbara Crossette, *New York Times,* Dec. 2, 2001, "Afghanistan's Women: Hope for the Future, Blunted by a Hard Past," www.nytimes.com/2001/12/02/weekinreview/the-world-afghanistan-s-women-hope-for-the-future-blunted-by-a-hard-past.html.

26. Oxfam, Briefing Paper, "Behind Closed Doors," Nov. 24, 2014, www

.oxfamamerica.org/static/media/files/behind-closed-doors-afghanistan
-oxfam.pdf.

27. BBC News online, Jan. 4, 2004, "Afghans endorse new constitution,"
http://news.bbc.co.uk/2/hi/south_asia/3366455.stm.

28. BBC News online, Dec. 18, 2003, "UN guarding loya jirga delegate,"
http://news.bbc.co.uk/2/hi/south_asia/3331751.stm.

29. *New York Times,* July 23, 2012, p. A1, "Key Afghans Tied to '90s Carnage,"
www.nytimes.com/2012/07/23/world/asia/key-afghans-tied-to-mass-
killings-in-90s-civil-war.html.

30. See the website of the Defense Committee for Malalai Joya at www
.malalaijoya.com. See also Malalai Joya, *A Woman Among Warlords: The
Extraordinary Story of an Afghan Who Dared to Raise Her Voice* (New York:
Scribner, 2009).

31. *New York Times,* July 21, 2013, p. A1, "Despite Education Advances, a
Host of Afghan School Woes," www.nytimes.com/2013/07/21/world/
asia/despite-education-advances-a-host-of-afghan-school-woes.html.

32. Afghanistan Independent Human Rights Commission, Report, "Violence Against Women in Afghanistan 1392 (2013–2014)," http://goo.gl/
yydQ7U.

33. Ministry of Women's Affairs, Afghanistan, "First Report on the Elimination of Violence Against Women (EVAW) Law in Afghanistan," Mar. 2014,
http://goog.gl/8EvrQk.

34. See also this UN study, which found that even in the 10 out of 110
EVAW cases that resulted in convictions, penalties were nearly all minor,
often below the minimum mandated by law. United Nations Assistance
Mission in Afghanistan, "Justice Through the Eyes of Afghan Women,"
Apr. 2015, https://goog.gl/RhsrTS.

35. AIHRC Report, "Violence Against Women." See note 32.

36. Gulnaz's case is discussed further in chapter 7.

37. Of the 176 prisoners in Badam Bagh Prison in November 2014, according to Qazi Parveen of the Afghan Independent Human Rights Commission, 75 to 85 percent of them were convicted of or charged with
moral crimes. Of the prisoners in Ms. Parveen's tally, 7 were pregnant, 3
had given birth since their incarceration, and forty children were living
with their mothers in the prison (the children are not included in the
tally of 176). When I visited Badam Bagh on November 14, 2014, the
population on that day, according to inmate rolls provided by officials on
duty, included seventy-six adultery cases, twenty-two cases of runaways,
seven cases of alcohol consumption, five cases of attempted adultery—or
about 65 percent moral cases. Note the runaway charges, despite the
abolition of the charge of running away from home in the EVAW law of
2009.

38. See the website of the Research Institute for Women, Peace & Security
at www.riwps-afghanistan.org.

39. The website of the Afghan Women's Network's is at www.awn-af.net.

40. Alissa J. Rubin, *New York Times,* Mar. 2, 2015, p. A1, "Afghan Policewomen Struggle Against Culture," www.nytimes.com/2015/03/02/world/asia/afghan-policewomen-struggle-against-culture.html.

41. Lal Bibi is discussed in detail in chapter 4.

42. Soheila's case is discussed further in chapter 14.

43. Alissa J. Rubin, *New York Times,* Mar. 3, 2014, p. A1, "A Thin Line of Defense against Honor Killings," www.nytimes.com/2015/03/03/world/asia/afghanistan-a-thin-line-of-defense-against-honor-killings.html.

44. United Nations Assistance Mission in Afghanistan, Joint Coordination and Monitoring Board, Jan. 29, 2014, "Co-Chairs' Statement, Tokyo Mutual Accountability Framework," http://unama.unmissions.org/Portals/UNAMA/Press%20Statements/JCMB-29Jan2014-joint-communique.pdf.

45. United Nations Assistance Mission in Afghanistan, Kabul, Dec. 2013, "A Way to Go: An Update on Implementation of the Law on Elimination of Violence against Women in Afghanistan," http://goo.gl/nmdz3x.

46. Ministry of Women's Affairs, Afghanistan, Mar. 2014, "First Report on the Elimination of Violence Against Women (EVAW) Law in Afghanistan," http://goo.gl/8EvrQk.

47. Owen Bowcott, *Guardian,* June 14, 2011, "Afghanistan worst place in world for women, but India in top five." The article cites a survey by Thomson Reuters Foundation's TrustLaw Woman website, about comparative conditions for women. See www.theguardian.com/world/2011/jun/15/worst-place-women-afghanistan-india.

48. United Nations Development Program, Human Development Index, online comparative tool, at http://hdr.undp.org/en/content/human-development-index-hdi.

49. For more on the international impact of Afghanistan's women's-rights efforts, see chapter 7.

50. See Nasrine Gross's remarks on this subject in chapter 7, p. 125: "Afghanistan is still the great battleground of women's rights in the twenty-first century."

51. *New York Times,* May 20, 2013, p. A8, "Effort to Strengthen an Afghan Law on Women May Backfire," www.nytimes.com/2013/05/19/world/asia/efforts-to-strengthen-afghan-law-on-women-may-backfire.html.

52. Women News Network, online news site, May 20, 2013, "Law to protect women and girls in Afghanistan stalled in parliament," http://womennewsnetwork.net/2013/05/20/law-to-protect-women-girls-afghanistan-stalled-in-parliament.

53. Ali M. Latifi, Al Jazeera English, online news site, May 30, 2013, "Afghan women in fight over rights," www.aljazeera.com/indepth/features/2013/05/201352711108360922.html.

54. *Qazi,* meaning an Islamic-law judge, is often transliterated as *Qadi* in English.

55. The term of that Afghan parliament expired June 21, 2015, but it was extended possibly indefinitely due to an impasse over electing a new one. See Mujib Mashal, *New York Times*, June 20, 2015, p. A6, "Afghan Parliament's Term is Extended," www.nytimes.com/2015/06/20/world /asia/afghan-parliaments-term-is-extended-after-squabbles-delay-elec tions.html.

56. Embassy of the United States, Kabul, State Department Press Release no. 2010/612, May 13, 2010, http://kabul.usembassy.gov/remarks_130510 _2.html.

57. Alissa J. Rubin, *New York Times*, July 31, 2010, p. A1, "Afghan Women Fear Loss of Modest Gains," www.nytimes.com/2010/07/31/world/asia/ 31women.html.

58. United States Department of State, Archive, "U.S.-Afghan Women's Council," Jan. 20, 2001, to Jan. 20, 2009. The entry on the council notes that "content in this archive site is NOT UPDATED, and external links may not function."

59. Facebook, "U.S.-Afghan Women's Council," www.facebook.com/US AfghanWC.

60. Feminist Majority Foundation, http://feministmajority.org. When checked in 2015, the foundation's website had no press releases concern- ing Afghanistan that were dated more recently than 2013, with most even older.

61. See the website of Equality for Peace and Democracy at www.epd -afg.org.

62. See the website of Empowerment Center for Women at http://ecw.org .af/empowerment-center-for-women.

63. Joseph Goldstein, *New York Times*, Dec. 17, 2014, p. A16, "E.U. Con- firms Wide Fraud in Afghan Presidential Runoff Election," www.ny times.com/2014/12/17/world/asia/afghan-voting-fraud-detailed-in-new- report.html.

64. *New York Times*, Sept. 22, 2014, p. A1, "After Rancor, Afghans Agree to Share Power," www.nytimes.com/2014/09/22/world/asia/afghan- presidential-election.html.

65. *New York Times*, July 2, 2013, p. A4, "Critics Question Karzai Choices for Human Rights Panel," www.nytimes.com/2013/07/02/world/asia/ karzai-choices-for-afghan-human-rights-panel-raise-questions.html.

66. The periodic production of such documents has been required by law by the U.S. Congress, the United Nations and some of its agencies, and by the European Union.

67. Breshna's case is discussed in detail beginning on p. 287

68. Human Rights Watch, "Afghanistan: Reject Proposal to Restore Ston- ing," Nov. 25, 2013, www.hrw.org/news/2013/11/25/afghanistanreject- proposal-restore-stoning.

69. Margherita Stancati, *Wall Street Journal*, July 5, 2013, online, "Afghan

Women Fear Rights Slipping Away," www.wsj.com/articles/SB1000142
4127887324853704578587491774651104.

70. Soheila's case is discussed in more detail in chapter 14.

71. See the website of the International Development Law Organization at
www.idlo.int/where-we-work/asia/afghanistan.

72. I refused to accept the condition that IDLO would speak to me about
Zakia and Ali only on guarantee of anonymity of the organization and
those I interviewed in it. I currently have a Freedom of Information Act
request pending to find out how much IDLO was paid by the U.S. government for work on the couples' case, what if anything it did (on only
one known instance did IDLO, through one of its Afghan employees,
interview the couple, according to Zakia and Ali), and how much it has
been paid for other EVAW-law-related projects, such as its strongly criticized program to train Afghan judges in application of that law. See also
John F. Sopko, special inspector general for Afghan reconstruction, letter
to Secretary of State John Kerry, July 22, 2013, available online at www
.sigar.mil/pdf/alerts/SIGAR-Alert-13-6%20IDLO.pdf. The letter questions IDLO's capacity to handle a $50-million rule-of-law training pro-
gram through a subcontractor and complained that the group had failed
to respond to the inspector general's concerns that it had accomplished
little of value. IDLO replied, according to a press release dated July 25,
2013 (available at www.idlo.int/news/highlights/sigars-letter-secretary-
john-kerry-incorrect) that SIGAR's criticisms were based on "incorrect
or incomplete information" and cited two cases, one an IDLO-trained
lawyer who won an acquittal of a woman charged with running away and
the other an IDLO-trained judge who sentenced a wife-beater to prison.
No names, dates, or other details were given to verify those cases.

73. See the website of the United States Department of State, "2009 International Women of Courage Award," www.state.gov/s/gwi/programs/
iwoc/2009/index.htm.

74. General Allen was replaced in Afghanistan after he became embroiled
in a scandal over the large numbers of allegedly salacious e-mails he
sent to a Florida socialite in the middle of running the American war
in Afghanistan, although the Pentagon's investigation absolved him of
wrongdoing. In 2015 he was appointed by President Obama to coordi-
nate the international coalition fighting against ISIS in Iraq and Syria.
Thom Shanker, New York Times, Jan. 23, 2013, p. A13, "Pentagon Clears
Commander Over Emails," www.nytimes.com/2013/01/23/us/pentagon
-clears-general-allen-over-e-mails-with-socialite.html.

75. The statistics on which General Allen based the assertion of a 4-percent
incidence of abusive behavior by American-trained Afghan Local Police
units have never been publicly released in any detail and are thus unveri-
fiable. Anecdotally, abusive conduct by Afghan Local Police units, most
of them trained by American Special Forces or other coalition special-
operations units, appears unchecked and endemic.

76. See also Wazhma Frogh, Towards the Light, her blog, at http://wazhma frogh.blogspot.com.

77. Associated Press, *Daily Mail,* Mar. 8, 2014, "Frustration in Afghan women's rights struggle," www.dailymail.co.uk/wires/ap/article-2576176/ Frustration-Afghan-womens-rights-struggle.html.

78. *New York Times,* Feb. 8, 2014, p. A5, "Taliban and Government Imperil Gains for Afghan Women, Advocates Say," www.nytimes.com/2014/02 /08/world/asia/womens-rights-seen-as-vulnerable-to-reversal-in-afghanistan.html.

79. Alissa J. Rubin, *New York Times,* Sept. 17, 2013, p. A4, "Afghan Policewomen Say Sexual Harassment Is Rife," www.nytimes.com/2014/02/ 08/world/asia/womens-rights-seen-as-vulnerable-to-reversal-in-afghanistan.html.

80. See the website of the United States Department of State, "2010 International Women of Courage Award," www.state.gov/s/gwi/programs/ iwoc/2010/index.htm. Brigadier General Quraishi's exile was confirmed to me in confidence by officials at the Afghan Ministry of Interior.

81. *New York Times,* Feb. 8, 2014, p. A5, "Taliban and Government Imperil Gains," http://goo.gl/eUfVij. "I'm sure our international friends will not abandon us," then-Colonel Bayaz said. The diplomats shared the information about her asylum request in confidence.

82. Breshna's case is discussed in detail beginning on p. 287.

83. As there would be no way of verifying the identity of the person writing the e-mails in response to my questions, I declined to carry out such an interview.

84. Glyn Strong, *Telegraph,* Sept. 29, 2007, "Malalai Joya: Courage Under Fire," www.telegraph.co.uk/culture/3668254/Malalai-Joya-courage-under-fire.html.

85. According to three senior European Union diplomats whom I interviewed in confidence. Many Western embassies in Kabul have actually closed their consular visa operations in Afghanistan, obliging Afghans who want visas to go to their embassies in Islamabad, Pakistan; among those are the United Kingdom and the Netherlands.

86. According to other U.S. embassy officials whom I interviewed in confidence.

87. *New York Times,* July 21, 2013, p. A1, "Despite Education Advances, a Host of Afghan School Woes," www.nytimes.com/2013/07/21/world/ asia/despite-education-advances-a-host-of-afghan-school-woes.html.

88. UN Women, Country Summaries, Afghanistan, http://asiapacific.un women.org/countries/afghanistan#_ednref2.

89. United Nations Development Program, Human Development Index, 2014, http://hdr.undp.org/en/content/human-development-index-hdi.

90. United Nations Development Program, Human Development Reports, Gender Inequality Index, 2014, http://hdr.undp.org/en/content/table-4-gender-inequality-index.

91. Central Intelligence Agency, *CIA World Factbook,* Afghanistan, 2010, www
    .cia.gov/library/publications/the-world-factbook/rankorder/2223
    rank.html.

92. Geoffrey Chamberlain, *Journal of the Royal Society of Medicine,* Nov. 2006,
    vol. 99, no. 11, pp. 559–63, "British Maternal Mortality in the 19th and Early
    20th Centuries," www.ncbi.nlm.nih.gov/pmc/articles/PMC1633559.

93. UN Women, Country Reports, Afghanistan, http://asiapacific.unwomen
    .org/countries/afghanistan#_ednref2.

94. For nearly every country in Western Europe, aside from the United
    Kingdom, this nation of only 30 million people is the biggest recipient
    of its foreign aid and would continue to be so through at least 2016. See
    Emla Fitzsimons, Daniel Rogger, and George Stoye, Institute for Fiscal
    Studies, 2012, p. 142, "UK development aid," www.ifs.org.uk/budgets/
    gb2012/12chap7.pdf.

95. Geoff Dyer and Chloe Sorvino, *Financial Times,* Dec. 15, 2014, "$1tn
    cost of longest US war hastens retreat from military intervention," www
    .cnbc.com/id/102267930.

96. For instance, his testimony to the Senate Foreign Relations Committee
    in 2011, cited in Chris Good, *Atlantic* online, Mar. 15, 2011, "Petraeus:
    Gains in Afghanistan 'Fragile and Reversible,'" www.theatlantic.com/
    politics/archive/2011/03/petraeus-gains-in-afghanistan-fragile-and-
    reversible-afghans-will-take-over-in-select-provinces/72507.

97. Fawzia Koofi with Nadene Ghouri, *The Favored Daughter: One Woman's
    Fight to Lead Afghanistan into the Future* (New York: Palgrave Macmillan
    Trade, 2012).

98. Case studies of other abused women are found beginning on p. 287.

99. Her name has been changed for her protection.

100. Sharif Kanaana, a professor of anthropology at Birzeit University in the
     Palestinian Territory, contends that honor killings in Arab culture stem
     from the Arabs' view of tribal necessities. "Women for the tribe were
     considered a factory for making men. The honor killing is not a means
     to control sexual power or behavior. What's behind it is the issue of fer-
     tility, or reproductive power." See also Department of Justice, "Prelimi-
     nary Examination of So-called 'Honour Killings' in Canada," p. 380,
     fn. 9. See also United Nations High Commissioner for Human Rights,
     "Harmful Traditional Practices and Implementation of the Law on Elimi-
     nation of Violence against Women in Afghanistan," Dec. 9, 2010, www
     .afghan-web.com/woman/harmful_traditions.pdf.

OTHER BATTLES IN THE AFGHAN WAR OF THE SEXES

1. Early news accounts about this case suppressed Breshna's name, as I
   did in stories written for the *New York Times* at the time. Subsequently,
   however, Afghan news media began regularly using her name, and even
   statements from the office of the Afghan president mentioned her by

name, in both cases in apparent disregard of an EVAW-law prohibition on the publication of the names of female victims of sexual abuse.

2. Almost the first thing the Taliban did after taking control of Kunduz was to head to the WAW shelter and hunt down the women there, but Hassina Sarwari had already fled, taking with her all the women in the shelter to the safety of a neighboring province. See Joseph Goldstein, *New York Times*, Oct. 2, 2015, p. A10, "Taking Hold in Kunduz, Afghanistan, New Taliban Echoed the Old," http://goo.gl/G0Oqq5.

3. *New York Times,* July 20, 2014, p. A4, "Struggling to Keep Afghan Girl Safe After a Mullah Is Accused of Rape," www.nytimes.com/2014/07/20/world/asia/struggling-to-keep-afghan-girl-safe-after-a-mullah-is-accused-of-rape.html.

4. International Crisis Group, Asia Report No. 268, June 4, 2015, "The Future of the Afghan Local Police," www.crisisgroup.org/en/regions/asia/south-asia/afghanistan/268-the-future-of-the-afghan-local-police.aspx.

5. Technically there is no age of consent in Afghan law, since all sex outside wedlock is considered a crime, but sixteen is the minimum legal age for marriage.

6. The case of Gulnaz is discussed in more detail in chapter 7.

7. CURE International was the same hospital where, only a month before, three American doctors had been killed by an Afghan policeman named Ainuddin who had just been assigned to guard the facility and who shot down the doctors on sight as they entered their hospital. Despite that outrage, which like so many others in Afghanistan was never explained or resolved, CURE continued to bring foreign doctors there to work on behalf of Afghan women.

8. The Women for Afghan Women shelter in Kunduz runs a separate facility, known as a Child Support Center, which cares for fifty children of all ages. It is in a sense an orphanage, but most of these children do have mothers, many of them in prison. Others have mothers who have been killed in an honor crime, and the children are there to be protected from fathers who may or may not want them. The Child Support Center is a deeply affecting place. "This one is two and a half years old," said Dr. Hassina Sarwari, who is in charge of it, pointing to a lively little girl who kept ducking behind the skirts of one of the matrons. She indicated another. "Her mother was burned alive in front of her children after the husband raped his daughter and she caught him," Dr. Sarwari said, speaking in a low voice so the kids could not hear her. She pointed to a boy in a yellow shirt, about ten. "His father tried to sell him to someone after his wife's death." She pointed out two sisters, aged nine and ten. Their father raped both of them. "Every single one of them has such a story. What if the funding stops? What if the mullahs shut us down? What will happen to them?"

9. Kim Motley is also on the board of Women for Afghan Women. See

also Kimberley Motley, TedGlobal 2014, Oct. 2014, "How I Defend the Rule of Law," www.ted.com/talks/kimberley_motley_how_i_defend_the_rule_of_law?language=en.

10. Ms. Geyah had exposed a madrassa for girls that had been indoctrinating them in extremist, pro-Taliban ideology, right under government noses and with government funding.

11. The girls Ms. Sarwari was referring to were those in Women for Afghan Women's Child Support Center, described in more detail in note 8 on p. 343.

12. Kim Motley is one of very few American lawyers practicing law in Afghanistan, and while she is not admitted to the Afghan bar, she works through Afghan colleagues who are, and she uses her high profile—and somewhat exotic background—to the utmost. A former Miss Wisconsin, the daughter of a North Korean refugee mother and an African-American father, she is a black woman in a country that has rarely seen any black Americans other than in uniform and has a hard time getting used to the idea of female lawyers of any color. Kim Motley causes a minor sensation wherever she goes and often uses that to her clients' benefit. She is one of few women in the country, even among foreigners, who drives her own car and refuses to wear a head scarf.

13. United Nations Assistance Mission in Afghanistan, "A Way to Go: An Update on Implementation of the Law on Elimination of Violence against Women in Afghanistan," Kabul, Dec. 2013, http://goo.gl/nmdz3x.

14. *New York Times,* Oct. 26, 2014, p. A12, "Afghan Mullah Who Raped Girl in His Mosque Receives 20-year Prison Sentence," www.nytimes.com/2014/10/26/world/asia/afghan-mullah-who-raped-girl-in-his-mosque-receives-20-year-prison-sentence.html.

15. During the Paghman rape-case lineup, one of the victims initially picked out a police detective and then a police cook, before choosing the actual suspect, after police detectives helpfully pointed him out to her. See also *New York Times,* Sept. 8, 2014, p. A9, "Afghan Court Wastes No Time Sentencing 7 to Death in Rape Case," www.nytimes.com/2014/09/08/world/asia/afghan-court-sentences-7-men-to-death-in-rape-case.html.

16. Ibid.

17. The full, verbatim text of the press release, as issued in English by President Ghani's press office on November 19, 2014:

> Breshna the girl who was victim of rape, is not posed to any danger by her family.

Based on the order of President Ashraf Ghani, a meeting was held at the palace this afternoon with presence of ten-year-old girl's family who was raped by a mullah in Kunduz province. In this meeting Breshna's family, representatives of ministries of foreign affairs, head of International Amnesty for Afghanistan [*sic;* apparently they meant to describe

the AIHRC, as Amnesty International was not involved] had participated. Abdul Ali Mohammadi the Legal Advisor to President Ghani
demanded explanation from Breshna the little girl's family her father
and her uncle about the threats posed to her life. Breshna's father and
uncle rejected any kind of threats posed to her from her family side, they
said the little girl who was victim of rape her self [*sic*], she is not posed
to any risk by her family. They said the rumors of any threats posed to
her was made up by some opportunists who try to exploit this case for
their personal gains in the name of advocacy. In this meeting the family
of the rape victim asked for the severest punishment to be given to the
rapist. They also assured, that "not only Breshna is safe with us but we
also protect her from the reach of any exploiters."

18. According to Manizha Naderi, the Women for Afghan Women's executive director. Manizha had the following reaction when she heard about
the statement on Breshna from the presidential palace: "I wish the palace
would look at the big picture. Rape of children is a big problem right
now. We have a three-year-old in the hospital in Kabul who was raped in
Takhar. She just came out of surgery. There was another twelve-year-old
who was gang-raped over six days in Takhar, a twelve-year-old boy was
gang-raped over a month-long period in Ghazni, a five-year-old boy was
brutally raped and died in Kandahar, another five-year-old died because
of a brutal rape in Herat. These are just a few cases that I know of. I am
sure there are many, many others. The palace needs to look at this whole
problem and make a strong statement about it."

19. Dr. Sarwari did not leave her post and, supported by her colleagues at
WAW, remained at her job through 2015, although in late September she
was obliged to flee Kunduz, along with the women and children in her
shelter, after the Taliban overran the city.

20. Farangis Najibullah, Radio Free Europe/Radio Liberty, "Afghanistan:
Marriage Practice Victimizes Young Girls, Society," Jan. 4, 2008, www
.rferl.org/content/article/1079316.html. UNICEF figures are that 15
percent of Afghan women are fifteen or younger when married; see
note 14, chapter 2.

21. Karim Amini, Tolo News, online news service, Aug. 30, 2014, "8 Year
Old Girl Married Off to 12 Year Old Boy," www.tolonews.com/en/
afghanistan/16174-8-year-old-girl-married-off-to-12-year-old-boy.
See also Sayed Arif Musavi, Tolo News, online news service, Feb. 15,
2015, "10-year-old Girl Victim of Baad in Balkh," www.tolonews.com/
en/afghanistan/18222-10-year-old-girl-victim-of-qbaadq-in-balkh, for
another case of a young girl being sold as a child bride to resolve adult
disputes.

22. Alissa J. Rubin, *New York Times,* Apr. 1, 2013, p. A1, "Painful Payment
for Afghan Debt: a Daughter, 6," www.nytimes.com/2013/04/01/world/
asia/afghan-debts-painful-payment-a-daughter-6.html.

23. *New York Times,* Dec. 30, 2012, p. A12, "Winter's Deadly Bite Returns to Refugee Camps of Kabul," www.nytimes.com/2012/12/30/world/asia/deadly-bite-of-winter-returns-to-ill-prepared-refugee-camps-of-kabul.html.

24. In an interview in May 2015.

25. Afghanistan Independent Human Rights Commission, "Violence Against Women 1390," 2012, http://goo.gl/SnuXBZ. Shakila's case is discussed on p. 29.

26. AIHRC, "Violence Against Women 1391," 2013, www.aihrc.org.af/home/research_report/1319.

27. Many *arbakai* units later go on to become ALP formations, after training by American Special Forces.

28. See the website of the Development and Support of Afghan Women and Children at http://dsawco.org/eng.

29. Zarghona Salehi, Pajhwok Afghan News, online news agency, Sept. 24, 2012, "Kabul rally condemns lashing of Ghazni girl," www.pajhwok .com/en/2012/09/24/kabul-rally-condemns-lashing-ghazni-girl, is a contemporary account of the attack on Sabira.

INDEX